American Antiquarian Society

The Colonial Clergy of the Middle Colonies
New York, New Jersey, and Pennsylvania
1628 - 1776

BY

FREDERICK LEWIS WEIS

CLEARFIELD

The Colonial Clergy of the Middle Colonies was originally published in the *Proceedings of the American Antiquarian Society* for October 1956 and reprinted by the American Antiquarian Society as a separate volume in 1957. The present work, with some minor changes, is a reprint of the 1957 publication, and is reproduced with the permission of the Society.

Genealogical Publishing Co., Inc.
Baltimore, 1978

Reprinted for
Clearfield Company, Inc. by
Genealogical Publishing Co., Inc.
Baltimore, Maryland
1991, 1995, 2003

Library of Congress Catalogue Card Number 77-93957
International Standard Book Number: 0-8063-0799-4

Reprinted from a volume
in the library of
The Maryland Historical Society
Baltimore, Maryland

Made in the United States of America

THE COLONIAL CLERGY OF AMERICA

THE history of the towns of the British Colonies in North America during the colonial period was in large measure that of their churches, and the history of these churches was largely that of their clergy. The ministers of that period were the leaders in theology, law, medicine, education, and to a considerable degree, in politics and Indian warfare. Often they were the only educated persons in a community.

The first endeavor of the founders of these colonies, which later formed the United States of America, was the continuance of the Christian institutions under which they had been born. As Francis Baylies said: "The clergy were the principal instruments in keeping alive the spirit and enterprise of the English race in the wilds of America. Nor did they confine themselves to ecclesiastical functions. Their influence was felt in the civil affairs of Government, and even in the transactions of ordinary life."

There were nearly five thousand settled ministers in colonial America, each of whom, according to his ability, education and station, was an unquestioned leader in his time and place. With the passage of many decades some of the ancient parishes which they served have ceased to exist; many are still strong and flourishing.

COLONIAL CLERGY OF THE MIDDLE COLONIES

BENJAMIN ABBOTT, b. Long Island, N.Y., 1732; member of the Philadelphia Conference of Methodists, 1773-1789; preached at Pennsneck, N. J., 1773-1789; Ord. deacon, 1790; elder, 1793; Long Island Circuit, 1791; Salem, N. J., 1792; Cecil, Md., 1793; Meth.; d. Salem, N. J., 14 Aug. 1796, a. 65.

GEORGE ACKERMAN, served in the Swamp district, Pa., 1773; Menn.

Provost ISRAEL ACRELIUS, b. Oester-aeker, Sweden, 4 Dec. 1714, son of the Rev. John and Sara (Gahm) Acrelius; ed. Upsala, 1727-1743; Ord. Sweden, 1743; domestic chaplain, 1743-1745; sett. Riala, Kulla, and Norra Ljusteroe, Sweden, 1745-1749; arriv. Pa., Nov. 1749; sett. Wilmington, Del., Old Swedes Chh., the 1st chh. in Del., now Ep., 6 Nov. 1749-9 Nov. 1756; Marcus Hook, Pa., St. Martin's Chh., 1749-1756; Chester (Del.) Pa., St. John's Chh., 1756-1756; Penn (Chester), Pa., St. John's Chh. 1751-1756; Provost of the Swedish chhs. in America, 6 Nov. 1749-9 Nov. 1756; returned to Sweden, 9 Nov. 1756; Dean of Fellingsbro, Sweden, 1758-1800; author of a *History of New Sweden*, 1759; Sw. Luth.; d. Fellingsbro, Sweden, 25 Apr. 1800.

WILLIAM ADAMS, A.M., b. New London, Conn., 7 Oct. 1710, son of the Rev. Eliphalet and Lydia (Pygan) Adams; A.B., Y.C., 1730, A.M., Tutor, 1732-1734; not ord.; preached 60 years; sett. New London, Conn., North Parish; Ledyard, Conn.; Shelter Island, L. I., N.Y., 1738-1753; Cong.; d. New London, Conn., 28 Nov. 1798, a. 88, unm.

JOHN ALDERSON, b. Yorkshire, England, 1719, son of the Rev. John Alderson (an Ep. clergyman); sett. Germantown, Pa., 1755-1755, as a Bapt.; sett. Smith and Lynville's Creek (Rockingham), Va., 6 Aug. 1756-1772; Botetourt co., Va., 1772-1781; Bapt.; d. Botetourt co., Va., 1781.

DAVID ALEXANDER, b. Ireland; attended the Log Coll. in Pa.; Ord., Salisbury (Lancaster) Pa., Pequea Chh., 18 Oct. 1738; sett. Salisbury, Pa., Nov. 1736-1749; Leacock (Lanc.) Pa., Chh. at West End, 1738-1741; member of the Donegal and New Londonderry presbyteries; Presb.; d. Salisbury, Pa., ca. 1749.

FRANCIS ALISON, D.D., b. Leck, co. Donegal, Ireland, 1705; ed. Glasgow; A.B., Y.C., 1755; A.M., Princeton, 1756; D.D., Glasgow, 1758; arriv. America, 1735; Ord. New London (Chester) Pa., 25 May 1737; sett. New London, Pa., May 1737-May 1752; Philadelphia, Pa., 1st Presb. Chh., May 1752-1779; founded an academy at New London, Pa., 1743, which became Delaware College; chaplain at Fort Cumberland, 1758; Prof. of Greek and Latin, U. of Pa., 1752-1756; Vice-Provost and Prof. of Moral Philosophy, 7 Mar. 1755-1759; Prof. of Classics and Metaphysics, 1756-1779; member, Am. Phil. Soc.; founded the Presb. Soc. for the Relief of Ministers and their Widows; Old Side Presb.; d. Philadelphia, Pa., 28 Nov. 1779, a. 73.

JOHN ALLEN, came from Eng.; sett. Woodbridge, N.J., 1680-1686; Cong.

1

TIMOTHY ALLEN, A.M., b. Lisbon, Conn., 31 Aug. 1715, son of Timothy and Rachel (Bushnell) Allen; A.B., Y.C., 1736, A.M.; Ord. West Haven, Conn., Cong. Chh., 10 Oct. 1738–27 May 1742; sett. Lawrence (Mercer) N. J., Maidenhead Chh. and Hopewell (Mercer) N. J., Pennington Chh., 12 Oct. 1748–May 1752; inst. New Providence (Union) N. J., 26 Mar. 1753; sett. New Providence, Aug. 1752–1756; Woodbridge, N. J., 1753–1756; inst. Ashford, Conn., 12 Oct. 1757–13 Jan. 1764; Granville, Mass., ca. 1782; inst. Chesterfield, Mass., 15 June 1785–1796; New Side Presb.; Cong.; d. Chesterfield, Mass., 12 Jan. 1806, a. 90.

BURGESS ALLISON, D.D., b. Bordentown, N. J., 17 Aug. 1753, son of Richard and Ruth Allison; began preaching, 1769, a. 16; A.B., Brown, 1777, A.M., 1786, D.D., 1804; Ord. Pennypack, Pa., 10 June 1781; sett. Bordentown, N. J., 1777–1796; Chaplain, U.S. House of Rep., 1816; Chaplain, U.S. Navy Yard, Washington, D. C.; member, Am. Phil. Soc.; Bapt.; d. Washington, D.C., 20 Feb. 1827, a. 73.

PATRICK ALLISON, D.D., b. Lancaster co., Pa., 1740, son of William and Catharine (Craig) Allison; A.B., U. of Pa., 1760, A.M., D.D., 1782, Tutor, 1762–1763; Prof. at Newark Academy, Newark, Del., 1761–1763; Ord. Philadelphia, Pa., 1765; sett. Baltimore, Md., 1765–1802; Chaplain of Congress, 1776; founder of Baltimore Coll. and Baltimore Library; in 1765, there were only 300 inhabitants in Baltimore; Presb.; d. Baltimore, Md., 24 Aug. 1802, a. 62 (GS).

JOHN GEORGE ALSENTZ, b. Kreutznach, Palatinate, Germany, Apr. 1734; ed. Heidelberg; Ord. Heidelberg, Germany, 1 June 1756; arriv. Philadelphia, 3 Dec. 1757; sett. Germantown, Pa., Oct. 1758–1767; Amwell, N. J., 1760, summer; visited Europe, 1762–1763; sett. Worcester (Montgomery) Pa., Wentz's or Skippack Chh., 1762–1767; Whitpain (Montgomery) Pa., Boehm's Chh., 1762–1767; Germ. Ref.; d. Worcester, Pa., 28 Oct. 1767.

JAMES ANDERSON, b. Scotland, 17 Nov. 1678; ed. there; Ord. Irvine Presbytery, Ireland, 17 Nov. 1708; arriv. America, 22 Apr. 1709; sett. Rappahannock, Va., 22 Apr. 1709–1710; New Castle, Del., 1st Chh., founded by the Sw. Luth., 1710–1716/7; N.Y., N.Y., 1st Presb. Chh., 1717–1726; inst. East Donegal (Lanc.) Pa., Aug. 1727; sett. East Donegal, Pa., 24 Sept. 1726–1740; Derry (Dauphin) Pa., 1729–1738; Swatara (Dauphin) Pa., Paxton Chh. on Fishing Creek, 1729–1732; Old Side Presb.; d. East Donegal, Pa., 16 July 1740.

JAMES ANDERSON, b. 1739, perhaps A.B., Princeton, 1759; sett. Middletown (Delaware) Pa., 1770–1793; Presb.; d. Middletown, Pa., 22 Sept. 1793, a. 54 (GS).

JOHN CONRAD ANDREAE, came from Zweibruecken, Alsace, France, to Pa., 1742; sett. Upper Salford (Montgomery) Pa., Old Goshenhoppen Chh., 1742–1751; Upper Hanover (Montgomery) Pa., New Goshenhoppen Chh., 1742–1751; Franconia (Montgomery) Pa., Indian Creek Chh., 1742–1751; Rockhill (Bucks) Pa., Indianfield Chh.,

1742-1751; Germantown, Pa., 1751-1753; Luth.; d. Germantown, Pa., 1 Jan. 1754.

JEDEDIAH ANDREWS, A.M., b. Hingham, Mass., 3 July 1674, son of Capt. Thomas and Ruth Andrews; A.B., H.C., 1695, A.M.; went to Philadelphia, 1698; Ord. Philadelphia, Pa., 1st Presb. Chh., as 1st minister, 1701; sett. Philadelphia, Pa., 1701-1747; also missionary at Hopewell, Gloucester, Burlington, and Perth Amboy, N. J., and at Staten Island, N.Y.; Presb.; d. Philadelphia, Pa., before 25 May 1747, when his will was proved.

JOHN ANDREWS, D.D., b. near Head of Elk River (Cecil) Md., 4 Apr. 1746, son of Moses and Letitia (Cooke) Andrews; A.B., U. of Pa., 1765, A.M., 1767; D.D., Washington Coll., Md., 1785; Ord. London, England, 15 Feb. 1767; K.B., Pa., 24 Feb. 1767; sett. Lewes, Broadkill, Cedar Creek Hundred, Dagsboro, and Indian River, all in Delaware, 1767-1769; Carlisle, York and Huntington, in Pa., 1769-1772; Rector, St. John's Parish (Caroline) Md., 1772-1776; York, Pa., 1776-1785; Rector, St. Thomas's Parish, Baltimore, Md., 13 Apr. 1782-1785; Vice-Provost, U. of Pa., 1789-1810; Provost, 1810-1813; memb., Am. Phil. Soc., 1786; Ep.; d. Philadelphia, Pa., 29 Mar. 1813, a. 67.

WILLIAM ANDREWS, A.B., (perhaps b. 1671, son of John Andrews of Bishops Canning's, Wilts.; matric. Lincoln Coll., Oxford, 15 July 1690, a. 24; A.B., 1695); Ord. for Va., 4 Oct. 1700; sett. St. Mary's Parish (Caroline) Va., 1702; Albany, N.Y., missionary to the Indians, 1712-1719; translator of a Primer and Prayers into the Mohawk language; Ep.

WILLIAM ANDREWS, b. Ireland (perhaps adm. sizar, Trinity Coll., Dublin, 27 May 1766); Ord. by Bsp. of London, 1770; missionary at Schenectady, N.Y., 1770-1773; sett. Nottoway Parish (Southampton) Va., 1775-1776; Ep.; Tory.

JAN ANDRIESE, was at Bensalem, Pa., 11 Sept. 1711; Dutch Ref.

ROBERT ANNAN, b. Cupar, Fifeshire, Scotland, 1742, son of Robert and —— (Landales) Annan; ed. Edinburgh; arriv. America, 1761; Ord. Marsh Creek (Adams) Pa., 8 June 1763; sett. Conewago (Adams) Pa. and Marsh Creek (Adams) Pa., 31 Aug. 1762-21 Apr. 1768; Freedom (Adams) Pa., 1763-1768; inst. Neelytown (Orange) N.Y., Wallkill Chh. and Little Britain (Orange) N.Y., 2 Oct. 1772; sett. Neelytown, Little Britain, Hamptonburg (Orange) N.Y., Graham's Chh., and Bloomingburgh (Orange) N.Y., 1768-1783; Boston, Mass., Federal Street Chh., now Arlington Street Chh., 1783-1786; Philadelphia, Pa., Old Scot's Chh., 1786-1802; Baltimore, Md., 1802-1812; Associate-Presb.; d. York co., Pa., 5 Dec. 1819.

JOHN HENRY ANTES, J.P., Esquire, b. Freinsheim, Rhine-Palatinate, 11 July 1701, son of Philip Frederick and Anna Catherine Antes; came to Pa., before 20 Feb. 1723; Ord. Bethlehem, Pa., 27 Oct. 1748; became a Moravian, 1740; sett. Nazareth (Northampton) Pa.,

29 May 1740; Oley (Berks) Pa., 1743–1744; Bethlehem, Pa., 1748–1750, as business manager; issued the call to the "Congregation of God in the Spirit," 15 Dec. 1741; millwright and miller, preacher, Justice-of-the-Peace, 17 Dec. 1745; built flour and paper mills at Frederick, Limerick, Nazareth, Bethlehem, Friedensthal and Gnadenhuetten, all in Pa., for the Moravian communities in those places; Deputy to the General Assembly of Pa. from Bethlehem; farmer at Frederick (Montgomery) Pa.; Germ. Ref.; Moravian; d. Frederick, Pa., 20 July 1755, a. 54 (GS).

VINCENTIUS ANTONIDES (alias Wickaut), b. 1670; sett. Bergen and Friesland in Holland, 1700–1705; arriv. America, 1 Jan. 1704/5; sett. Freehold (Monmouth) N. J., Holmdel (Monmouth) N. J., and Marlborough (Monmouth) N. J., all 1705–1705; Brooklyn, Bushwick, Flatbush, Flatlands, Gravesend, Jamaica, and New Utrecht, all on Long Island, N.Y., 1705–1744; Staten Island, N.Y., at Richmond and Port Richmond, 1714–1744; Dutch Ref.; d. N.Y., 18 July 1744.

JOHN ARBO, Ord. in Europe; arriv. N.Y., N.Y., 19 Oct. 1761; sett. Bethlehem (Northampton) Pa., 1761–1772; naturalized, Sept. 1768; Moravian; d. Bethlehem, Pa., 11 Dec. 1772.

ANDREW ARCHBOLD, Ord., New Castle Presbytery, 1733; suspended, 1735; Presb.

BERNARDUS ARENTIUS, inst. Willemstad, Holland, 11 Aug. 1671; sett. Willenstad, 1671–1674; came to N.Y.; sett. Albany, N.Y., 1674–1675; N.Y., N.Y., 1st Luth. or Holy Trinity Chh., 1675–1691; Luth.; d. N.Y., N.Y., 1691.

JAMES FRANCIS ARMSTRONG, A.M., A.B., Princeton, 1773, A.M., 1781; master, Nassau Hall Grammar School, 1773–1774; Chaplain, Canadian Campaign, 1776; Chaplain, 2nd Md. Brigade, Continental Army, 1778–1781, resigned, 12 Feb. 1778; original member, Soc. of the Cincinnati, 1783; Trustee, Princeton, 1790–1816; Moderator, General Assembly, 1804; Presb.; d. 1816.

JONATHAN ARNOLD, A.M., b. Haddam, Conn., 11 Jan. 1700/1, son of Jonathan and Elizabeth Arnold; A.B., Y.C., 1723, A.M.; A.M., Oxford, 1735/6; Ord. West Haven, Conn., Cong. Chh., 1725–1734; became an Ep.; Ord. England, 1735; sett. West Haven, Derby, Waterbury, Conn., 1736–1740; Staten Island, N.Y., St. Andrew's Chh., 1740–1745; Newark (Union) N. J., Trinity Chh., 1740–1745; Fredericksville Parish (Albemarle) Va., 1747–1754; Ep.; d. Fredericksville Parish, Va., 1754.

ANDREW ARNOT, minister at Midholm, Scotland; arriv. in Pa., 1753; preached in America, 1753–1754; returned to Scotland, 1754; Associate-Presb.

JOHANNES ARONDEUS, came from Overschic, Holland; Ord. Amsterdam, Holland, 9 Sept. 1741; arriv. N.Y., N.Y., 1742; sett. Brooklyn, Bushwick, Flatbush, Flatlands, Gravesend, and New Utrecht, all on Long Island, N.Y., 1742–1747; Harlingen (Somerset), Raritan

(Somerset), Readington (Hunterdon), Somerville (Somerset), Six Mile Run (Somerset) at Franklin, and Three Mile Run, all in N. J., 1747–1754; returned to Holland, 1754; Dutch Ref.

THOMAS ARTHUR, A.M., b. 1723, A.B., Y.C., 1743, A.M.; Ord. New Brunswick (Middlesex) N. J., 1746; sett. New Brunswick, 1746–1751; Trustee, Princeton, 1748–1751; Presb.; d. New Brunswick, N. J., 2 Feb. 1750/1, a. 27.

Bishop FRANCIS ASBURY, b. Hamstead Bridge, near Birmingham, England, 20/21 Aug. 1745, son of Joseph and Elizabeth (Rogers) Asbury; lic. London, England, 18 Aug. 1767; Bedfordshire circuit, 1767; Colchester circuit, 1768; Northamptonshire circuit, 1769; Hampshire circuit, 1770; arriv. Philadelphia, 27 Sept. 1771; minister at N.Y., N.Y., and vicinity, 1771–1772; Pemberton (Burlington) N. J., 1772–1772; appointed Superintendent of the missionary work in America, 10 Oct. 1772; Baltimore, Md., 14 July 1773–1778; missionary to Md., Va., and N.C., 1778–1784; Ord. Bishop, 25 Dec. 1784; Meth.; d. Spotsylvania, Va., 31 Mar. 1816, a. 74.

JAMES ASHTON, Ord. Middletown (Cape May) N. J., 1688; sett. Middletown, 1688–1712; Bapt.; d. Middletown, N. J., ca. 1712.

SAMUEL AUCHMUTY, D.D., b. Boston, Mass., 16 Jan. 1721/2, son of Judge Robert and Mary Julianna Auchmuty; A.B., H.C., 1742, A.M.; D.D., Oxford, 23 Jan. 1766; D.D., Columbia, 1767; S.P.G.; Ord. by Bsp. of London, 1747; K.B. for N.Y., 30 July 1747; sett. Staten Island, N.Y., St. Andrew's Chapel, 1747–1748; N.Y., N.Y., Trinity Chh., asst., 8 Mar. 1748–1764; inst. Rector, 1 Sept. 1764–1776; St. George's Chapel, 1 July 1752–1764; St. Paul's Chapel, 1766–1776; Tory; Ep.; d. N.Y., N.Y., 4 Mar. 1777.

JONAS AUREN, Ord. Upsala, Sweden; arriv. Philadelphia, from Wermeland, Sweden, 29 June 1697; sett. Philadelphia, Pa., Gloria Dei Chh., 1697–1706; Swedesborough (Gloucester) N. J. and Pennsneck (Salem) N. J., 1706–1713; Sw. Luth.; Sabbatarian; d. Ratkings Hook, N. J., 16 Feb. 1713.

EPHRAIM AVERY, A.M., b. Brooklyn, Conn., 13 Apr. 1741, son of the Rev. Ephraim and Deborah (Lothrop) Avery; A.B., Y.C., 1761, A.M.; A.M., Columbia, 1767; Ord. by Bsp. of London, 1765; lic. for N.Y., 2 June 1765; K.B. for N.Y., 3 June 1766; sett. Rye (Westchester) N.Y., Christ Chh., 9 Sept. 1765–1776; Bedford (Westchester) N.Y., St. Matthew's Chh., 1765–1776; Ep.; d. Rye, N.Y., 5 Nov. 1776.

ENOS AYRES, A.B., A.B., Princeton, 1748; Ord. Blooming Grove (Orange) N.Y., 1759; sett. Blooming Grove and Cornwall (Orange) N.Y., Bethlehem Chh., 1759–1762; his name stands first on the roll of the alumni of Princeton U.; Presb.; d. Blooming Grove, N.Y., 1762.

WILLIAM AYRES, Ord. 1767; K.B. for N. J., 12 Jan. 1766; lic. by Bsp. of London, 21 Dec. 1767; sett. Spotswood (Middlesex) N. J., St. Peter's Chh., and Freehold (Monmouth) N. J., St. Peter's Chh. 1767–

1776; Shrewsbury (Monmouth) N. J., Christ Chh., 1767-1776; built a chh. on West Pike Run (Washington) Pa., 1777; incapacitated by reason of insanity, 1776-1780; recovered, 1780; S.P.G.; Ep.; d. in Pennsylvania, ca. 1816.

LUKE BABCOCK, A.M., b. Westerly, R.I., 6 July 1738, son of Chief-Justice Joshua (of R. I. Supreme Ct.) and Hannah (Stanton) Babcock; A.B., Y.C., 1755, A.M.; A.M. (hon.) Columbia, 1774; post master at New Haven, Conn., 1767-1769; Ord. by Bsp. of London, 1769; lic. for N.E., 2 Feb. 1770; K.B. for N.E., 20 Feb. 1770; sett. Yonkers (Westchester) N.Y., St. John's Chh., 1771-1777; British prisoner, 1776-1777; Ep.; d. Yonkers, N.Y., 10 Feb. 1777.

JOHANNES CORNELISSEN BACKERUS, son of Cornelius Backerus; preached a number of sermons to the Classis, 1640-1641, showing proficiency as a minister, though he appears to have lacked regular clerical education; Ord. Amsterdam, Holland, 16 Oct. 1642; sett. Curacoa (off the coast of Venezuela), 1642-1647; arriv. N.Y., N.Y., 1647; sett. Niew Amsterdam, N.Y., 1st or South Dutch Chh., 1647-1649; returned to Holland, 15 Aug. 1649; went to the Dutch East Indies, Aug. 1651; Dutch Ref.

RICHARD BACKHOUSE, K.B. for Pa., 20 Aug. 1728; sett. Chester (Delaware) Pa., St. Paul's Chh. and Concord (Del.) Pa., 1728-1749; Marcus Hook (Del.) Pa., St. Martin's Chh., 1730-1738; Salisbury (Lancaster) Pa., St. John's Chh. at Compassville, and West Caln (Chester) Pa., 4 Feb. 1728/9-1741, 1742-1749; Salisbury (Lanc.) Pa., Pequea Chh., 1742-1749; Ep.; d. Chester, Pa., 19 Nov. 1749.

PAUL PETER BADER, in Pa., 1763; Moravian.

PHILIP CHRISTIAN BADER, came to America and sett. at Bethlehem, Pa., 10 Dec. 1751; house chaplain, Christiansbrunn, Bethlehem, Pa., 1753-1755; sett. Lancaster, Pa., 1755-1756, 1759-1762; South Lebanon, Pa., 1757-1758; Moravian.

HENRY BAER, Ord. in the Swamp District, Pa., 1771; Mennonite.

JOHN GEORGE BAGER, b. Niederlinzweiler, Nassau-Saarbrueck, 29 Mar. 1725, son of a Lutheran minister; ed. Halle; sett. Simmern, Palatinate, Germany; arriv. Philadelphia, 23 Oct. 1752; circuit preacher: sett. Hanover (York) Pa., St. Michael's Chh., 10 Nov. 1752-1763, 1769-1791; Conewago (Adams) Pa., 1752-1762; West Manheim (York) Pa., St. David's or Sherman's Chh., 1753-1790; Baltimore, Md., 1755-1762; N.Y., N.Y., Holy Trinity Chh., 1762-1767 and Old Swamp Chh., 1763-1767; York (York) Pa., Christ Chh., West Manchester (York) Pa., St. Paul's or Wolf's Chh., Conewago (York) Pa., Zion's Chh. and Chambersburg (Franklin) Pa., St. John's Chh., 1767-1769; Guilford (Franklin) Pa., Grindstone Hill Chh., 1767-1770; Hopewell (York) Pa., Blimyer's Chh., 1767-1791; Hellam (York) Pa., Kreutz Creek Chh. and Berwick (Adams) Pa., 1768-1791; Windsor (York) Pa., Emanuel or Frysville Chh., 1771-1776; Luth.; d. Hanover, Pa., 9 June 1791.

Bishop JOHN PETER BAKER (or Becker), b. Dilsheim, Germany, 1687; came to America, 1719; Ord. Germantown, Pa., 25 Dec. 1723; sett. Germantown, 1723-1729, 1735-1748; Coventry (Chester) Pa., 1724-1729; Cocalico (Lanc.) Pa., Conestoga Chh., 1729-1734; Lower Salford (Montgomery) Pa., Skippack Chh., 1748-1758; master weaver; Dunkard; Germ. Bapt.; d. Skippack, Pa., 19 Mar. 1758, a. 64.

HEZEKIAH BALCH, D.D., b. Deer Creek (Harford) Md., 1741; A.B., Princeton, 1766, A.M., 1774, D.D., Williams, 1806; taught school in Fauquier co., Va.; lic. 17 May 1769; Ord. Va., 8 Mar. 1770; sett. Bethel and Bethesda, S. C., 1770-1774; inst. Emmitsburg, Md., 16 Oct. 1775-1778; York, Pa., 1775-1776; Greenville, Tenn., 1785-1800; Pres. and founder of Greenville Coll., Tenn., 1794-1810; Presb.; d. Greenville, Tenn., Apr. 1810.

HENRY BALDWIN, A.B., bapt. Milford, Conn., 14 June 1702, son of Barnabas Baldwin; A.B., Y.C., 1726; sett. Bedford (Westchester) N.Y., Jan. 1727/8-1732; Presb.; d. ca. 1733.

ELIPHALET BALL, A.M., b. New Haven, Conn., 29 July 1722, son of Ensign John and Mary (Tuttle) Ball; A.B., Y.C., 1748, A.M.; Ord. Bedford (Westchester) N.Y., 2 Jan. 1753-21 Dec. 1768; sett. Ballston, N.Y., 1770-1783; Woodbridge, Conn., Dec. 1783-1790; Presb.; d. Ballston, N.Y., 6 Apr. 1797, a. 74.

JAN BANCH, a Swedish minister from Stockholm; was at Bensalem, Pa., 21 Jan. 1710, and at Six Mile Run, N. J., Aug. 1712; Sw.-Luth.

JONATHAN BARBER, A.M., b. West Springfield, Mass., 31 Jan. 1712/3, son of Thomas and Sarah (Ball) Barber; A.B., Y.C., 1730, A.M.; Ord. Orient, L. I., N.Y., 10 Nov. 1757; sett. Agawam, Mass., 1732-1735; Orient, L. I., N.Y., Oyster Ponds Chh., 1735-1740, 1748-1757; Southold, L. I., N.Y., Mattituck Chh., 1735-1740; inst. Groton, Conn., 1st Chh., 3 Nov. 1758-Dec. 1768; superintendent and chaplain, Orphan House, Bethesda, Ga., 1740-1747; Cong.-Presb.; d. Groton, Conn., 8 Oct. 1783, a. 71.

HENRY BARCLAY, D.D., b. Albany, N.Y., 1712, son of the Rev. Thomas and Dorothea (Draeyer) Barclay, A.B., Y.C., 1734, A.M., 1740; D.D., Oxford, 24 Dec. 1760; Ord. London, 30 Jan. 1737/8; K.B. for Va., 5 Dec. 1737; catechist at Fort Hunter, Albany, N.Y., 1735-1737; Rector, Albany, N.Y., St. Peter's Chh. and Queen Anne's Chapel, Fort Hunter, 1738-1746; Schenectady, N.Y., St. George's Chh., 1738-1745; N.Y., N.Y., induct. Rector, Trinity Chh., 23 Oct. 1746-1764; N.Y., N.Y., St. George's Chapel, 1752-1764; joint translator of the litany into the Mohawk tongue; Ep.; d. N.Y., N.Y., 20 Aug. 1764, a. 52.

THOMAS BARCLAY, b. N.Y., N.Y., son of John and Cornelia (Van Schaick) Barclay; K.B. for N.Y., 4 June 1707; sett. Albany, N.Y., Dutch Ref. Chh., 1709-1712; chaplain, Fort Hunter, Albany, 1708-1716; Schenectady, N.Y., St. George's Chh., 1708-Nov. 1712; Rector, Albany, N.Y., St. Peter's Chh., 1716-1728; N.Y., N.Y., Trinity Chh., 1728; Ep.; d. N.Y., N.Y.

COLONIAL CLERGY OF THE MIDDLE COLONIES

DOMINE BARCOLO, Ord. Amsterdam, Holland, 1758, for America; Dutch Ref.

Bishop MARTIN BARE, chosen Bishop, 1725; sett. East Lampeter (Lanc.) Pa., Mellinger's Chh., 1722-1758; Menn.; d. East Lampeter, Pa., Feb. 1758.

NEHEMIAH BAKER, A.M., b. Marshfield, Mass., 1720, son of John, Jr. and Bethiah (Ford) Baker; A.B., Y.C., 1742, A.M.; Ord. South Killingly, Conn., 3rd or Breakneck Hill Chh., 1746-1755; sett. Southold, L. I., N.Y., Mattituck Chh., 1756-1772; Orient, L. I., N.Y., Oyster Ponds Chh., 1756-1772; Lower Aquebogue, L. I., N.Y., Chh. at Riverhead, 1756-1764; Cong.; d. Southold, L. I., N.Y., 10 Mar. 1772, a. 52.

JOHN DOMINICUS CAROLUS BARTHOLOMAEUS, bapt. Heidelberg, Germany, 13 Dec. 1723, son of John Adam and Maria Susanna Bartholomaeus; matric. Heidelberg, 15 Jan. 1743; U. of Franecker, Holland; Ord. Amsterdam, Holland, 15 Nov. 1747; arriv. Philadelphia 13 Aug. 1748; inst. Tulpehocken (Berks) Pa., Host Chh., 16 Oct. 1748-Apr. 1751; Mill Creek (Lebanon) Pa., Tulpehocken or Trinity Chh., 1748-1751; Brecknock (Lanc.) Pa., Muddy Creek Chh., 1749-1750; ill in a hospital supported by the Coetus; Germ. Ref.; d. Philadelphia, Pa., 28 July 1768.

THOMAS BARTON, A.M., b. co. Monaghan, Ireland, 1730; Trinity Coll., Dublin; came to America, 1750; A.M. (hon.) U. of Pa., 1760; A.M. (hon.) Columbia, 1770; Ord. by the Bsp. of London, 29 Jan. 1755; K.B. for Pa., 7 Feb. 1755; arriv. Pa., 10 Apr. 1755; S.P.G. missionary at Carlisle (Cumberland) Pa., St. John's Chh., 1755-10 Apr. 1758; Huntington (Adams) Pa., Chh. at York Springs, 1755-1758; York (York) Pa., St. John's Chh., 1755-1765; Chaplain, Fr. and Indian War, 1758; Caernarvon (Lanc.) Pa., Bangor Chh., 1759-1776; Caernarvon (Berks) Pa., St. Thomas's Chh., 1765-1780; Salisbury (Lanc.) St. John's Chh. at Compassville, 1759-1776; West Caln (Chester) Pa., 1759-1776; Rector, Lancaster (Lanc.) Pa., St. James's Chh., 1760-1778; Penn (Chester) Pa., St. John's Chh., 1760-1780; Mill Creek (New Castle) Del., St. James's Chh. at Stanton, 1760-1780; Tory; escaped to N.Y., N.Y.; Ep.; d. N.Y., N.Y., 25 May 1780, a. 50.

JOHN BARTOW, A.M., b. Crediton, Devon, England, 1673, son of Thomas Bartow; adm. sizar, Christ Coll., Cambridge, 31 Jan. 1689; A.B., 1692; vicar of Pampisford, co. Cambridge, 28 May 1698; S.P.G. missionary to N.Y.; sett. East Chester (Westchester) N.Y., St. Paul's Chh., 19 Nov. 1702-1726; Westchester (Westchester) N.Y., St. Peter's Chh., 19 Nov. 1702-1726; supply, New Rochelle (Westchester) N.Y., Trinity Chh., 1722-1724; Ep.; d. 1726; will made 24 Jan. 1725/6; proved 1 Apr. 1727.

DANIEL BATWELL, A.B., b. Hampshire, England; adm. Corpus Christi Coll., Oxford, 1751; matric. 1751; A.B., 1755; distinguished preacher in London; K.B. for North America, 26 Oct. 1773; S.P.G. missionary in York, Cumberland and Adams counties; sett. York (York)

Pa., St. John's Chh., 1773–1778; Carlisle (Cumberland) Pa., St. John's Chh., 1773–1778; Huntington (Adams) Pa., Chh. at York Springs, 1773–1778; Loyalist refugee, 1778; returned to England, 1783; Ep.

MATTHIAS BAUMAN, b. Lambsheim, Frankenthal, Rhine Palatinate; came to America, 1719; sett. Oley (Berks) Pa., 1721–1727; founder of the sect of the "New Born," the "Stille im Lande" or Baumanite Chh., 1721, 1724; Baumanite, d. Oley, Pa., 1727.

ANDREW BAY, b. Ireland; Ord. by the New Castle Presbytery, 1748; sett. Highland (Adams) Pa., Lower Marsh Creek Chh., 1747–1760; Hopewell (York) Pa., Shrewsbury Chh. at Round Hill, 1747–1760; Churchville (Harford) Md., Deer Creek Chh., 1760–1768; Bethel (Harford) Md., Upper Node Forest Chh., 1764–1767, as stated supply; Albany, N.Y., 1768–1773; Newtown, L. I., N.Y., stated supply, 1773–Apr. 1775; New Side Presb.; d. 1777.

ABRAHAM BEACH, D.D., b. Cheshire, Conn., 29 Aug. 1740, son of Capt. Elnathan and Hannah (Cooke) Beach; A.B., Y.C., 1757; D.D., Columbia, 1789; Regent, U. of N.Y., 1786; Ord. by Bsp. of London, 14 June 1768; K.B. for N. J., 23 June 1767; sett. New Brunswick, N. J., Christ Chh., 17 Sept. 1767–1776, 1781–1784; Piscataway (Middlesex) N. J., St. James's Chh., 1767–1783; Woodbridge, N. J., Trinity Chh., 1769–1784; Elizabethtown, N. J., St. John's Chh., 1775–1783; N.Y., N.Y., Trinity Chh., June 1784–1 Mar. 1813; soldier, French and Indian War; tax collector, Hartford, Conn., 1785; Ep.; d. New Brunswick, N. J., 10/11 Sept. 1828, a. 88.

HENRY BEAN, b. 1730; sett. Skippack, Pa.; Menn.; d. 1 Apr. 1816.

JOHANN BEAR, sett. Elizabeth (Lancaster) Pa., Hammer Creek Chh., 1770–1778; Menn.; d. Ephrata, Pa., 15 Apr. 1778.

JOHN BEARD, A.M., b. prob. at New London (Chester) Pa., son of John and Rebecca Beard; A.B., U. of Pa., 1759, A.M., Tutor, 1759–1761; Ord. and later deposed by the New Castle Presbytery, 1772.

JOHN BEARDSLEY, A.M., A.B. (hon.) Columbia, 1761, A.M., 1768; S.P.G. missionary in Dutchess co. N.Y., 1761–1765; sett. Poughkeepsie, N.Y., Christ Chh., 1766–1782; Fishkill, Trinity Chh., 1767–1777; went to N.Y., N.Y., as a refugee, 14 Dec. 1777; sett. St. John's River, New Brunswick, Canada, 1783–1784; Parr, N.B., 1783–1784; Maugerville, N.B., 1785–1800; Ep.; d. Maugerville, N.B., 1800.

CHARLES CLINTON BEATTY, A.M., b. co. Antrim, Ireland, ca. 1715, son of John and Christiana (Clinton) Beatty; arriv. America, Oct. 1729; attended the Log Coll., Pa.; A.M. (hon.) Princeton, 1762, Trustee, 1763–1772; lic. Nottingham, Pa., 1742; Ord. Neshaminy, Warwick (Bucks) Pa., Deep Run Chh., 14 Dec. 1743–1772; missionary to Va., 1754; Chaplain, 1755; Chaplain to Pennsylvania troops at Fort Pitt, 1758; Moderator of the Synod, 1764; Presb.; d. Bridgeton, Barbadoes, West Indies, 13 Apr. 1772.

JOHN BECHLESHAMMER, sett. Amwell, N. J., after 1738; Dunkard or Germ. Bapt.

Bishop HANS GEORGE BECHTEL, minister in the Palatinate, 1727; arriv. Philadelphia, 23 Aug. 1728; sett. Washington (Berks) Pa., Hereford and Manatant Chhs., 1728–1759; Bishop; Menn.; d. Hereford, Pa., 19 Mar. 1759.

Bishop HANS JACOB BECHTEL, arriv. Pa., 1720; sett. near Pottstown, Pa., 1720; East Coventry (Chester) Pa., 1720–1739; East Vincent (Chester) Pa., 1727–1739; Washington (Berks) Pa., Hereford Chh., 1727–1739, Manatant Chh., 1725–1739; Bishop; Menn.; d. Hereford, Pa., 1739.

JOHN BECHTEL, b. on the Bergstrasse, Weinheim, Baden, Germany, 5 Oct. 1690; resided at Heidelberg, 1704–1709; Frankenthal, 1717–1726; turner apprentice, 1704, journeyman, 1709, master, 1714–1726; arriv. Philadelphia, 1726; Germantown, Pa., Germ. Ref. Chh., Feb. 1728/9–9 Feb. 1744 (lay preacher, 1728–1734; minister, 1734–1744); Ephrata, Pa., Bethany Chh., 1735–1736; Philadelphia, Pa., 1733–1744; became a Moravian and was Ord. Germantown, 18 Apr. 1742, by Bishop David Nitschmann; a Moravian, 1744–1777; sett. Bethlehem, Pa., as a Morav. brother, 13 Sept. 1746; preached at Philadelphia, Pa., 1746–1747; Germ. Ref.; Moravian; d. Bethlehem, Pa., 16 Apr. 1777, a. 86.

Bishop JOHANNES BECHTEL, son of Rev. George and Maria Bechtel; sett. Washington (Berks) Pa., Hereford and Manatant Chhs., 1759–1795; Bishop; Menn.; d. Hereford, Pa., 1795.

Bishop MARTIN BECHTEL, b. Jan. 1710, son of Bishop Hans Jacob and Elizabeth Bechtel; came to Pa. with his parents, 1720; Ord. (minister), East Vincent (Chester) Pa., 1739; sett. there, 1739–1786; Phoenixville (Chester) Pa., 1750–1786; Ord. (Bishop), 1758; Menn.; d. Pottstown, Pa., 25 Aug. 1786, a. 76.

SAMUEL BECHTEL, son of Bishop Hans Jacob and Elizabeth Bechtel; sett. Coopersburg, Upper Saucon (Lehigh), Pa., 1748–1764; sett. Hanover (Northampton) and Hellertown, Lower Saucon (Northampton) Pa., 1750–1764; Rockhill (Bucks), Bechtel's or Gehman's Chh., 1764–1802; Menn.; d. Rockhill, Pa., 15 Jan. 1802.

HENRY FERDINAND BECK, came from Pfluellingen, Wurtemberg, Germany; arriv. in Georgia, 1738; joined Whitefield's Society at Savannah; came to Bethlehem, Pa., 1745; sett. at Muddy Creek; Ord. 1754; minister at Lynn (Lehigh) Pa., Allemaengel Chh., 1750; at Philadelphia, 1760; at New York City; and several rural chhs.; Moravian; d. Bethlehem, Pa., Jan. 1783.

BECKER, see Baker.

WILLIAM BECKINGHAM, b. in England; bapt. ca. 28 Jan. 1697, as a Quaker Baptist; had been a Quaker at Cohansey; bought 150 acres of land in Upper Providence, Pa., 7 Apr. 1687, and 100 more there, 1 Oct.

1696; sett. Newtown, Upper Providence, Pa., 12 Oct. 1697-1701; sett. Nottingham, Md., 1700-1701; was living in Chichester (Chester) Pa., 14 Feb. 1701; 7th Day Bapt.; d. Chester co., Pa., 1701.

GEORGE BECKWITH, JR., A.M., b. Lyme, Conn., 1747, son of the Rev. George and Sarah (Brown) Beckwith; A.B., Y.C., 1765, A.M.; sett. Wyoming, now Wilkes-Barre (Luzerne) Pa., 1769-1770; Ord. in Conn., 22 Oct. 1772; preacher; physician; Cong.; d. Triangle, N.Y., Oct. 1824, a. 77.

JOHANN CONRAD BEISSEL, b. Eberbach, Baden, Germany, Apr. 1690; arriv. Boston, Mass., 1720; Germantown, Pa., Fall of 1720; Ord. Conestoga (Lancaster) Pa., Dec. 1724; sett. East Lampeter (Lanc.) Pa., Mill Creek Chh., at Bird-in-Hand, 1721-1733; Cocalico (Lanc.) Pa., Conestoga Chh., 1724-1729; Ephrata (Lanc.) Pa., Germ. Bapt. Chloister, 1728-1768; on becoming a Dunkard he called himself "Friedsam Gottrecht"; founder of the Society at Ephrata; hymn-writer; Tunker or 7th Day Bapt.; d. Ephrata, Pa., 6 July 1768, a. 77.

HAMILTON BELL, ed. at the Log Coll., 1738; lic. by the Philadelphia Presbytery, 30 Sept. 1740; Ord. East Donegal (Lanc.) Pa., 11 Nov. 1742; sett. East Donegal, Pa., Presb. Chh., 1742-1745; became an Ep.; Ord. London, 1747; lic. 19 Oct. 1747; K.B. for Md., 27 Oct. 1747; sett. Somerset Parish (Somerset) Md., chhs. at Princess Anne and Monie, 1748-1783; St. Mary Anne's Parish (Cecil) Md., 1767-1773; Presb.; Ep.; d. Somerset Parish, Md., 1783.

JAMES BENEDICT (prob. son of Ensign Thomas and Sarah (Hyatt) Benedict, b. Ridgefield, Conn., 1720); sett. Warwick (Orange) N.Y., ca. 1766-1776; Bapt.; d. Warwick, N.Y., after 1776.

ANDREW BENNETT, b. England; sett. Philadelphia, Pa., 1st Chh., 22 May 1758-Sept. 1758; Charleston, S. C. (Independent Chh.), 1761-1763; Barbadoes, 1763-1804; bequeathed $2,000 to the Independent Chh. of Charleston; Cong.; d. Barbadoes, 1804.

WILLIAM CHRISTOPHER BERCKENMEYER, b. Bodenteich, Duchy of Lueneburg, 1686, son of Juergen Berckenmeyer; ed. Altdorf U.; Ord. Amsterdam, Holland, 24 May 1725; arriv. N.Y., N.Y., 22 Sept. 1725; sett. East Camp, Christ Chh., Kaatsbaan, and the Dutch Ref. Chhs. at Camp, West Camp, and Saugerties, all in Ulster co., N.Y., 1725-1729; N.Y., N.Y., Holy Trinity Chh., 1725-1732; Newburgh (Orange) N.Y., Quassic Chh., 1725-1731; Schoharie (Schoharie) N.Y. and Stone Arabia (Montgomery) N.Y., 1725-1743; Athens (Greene) N.Y., Loonenburgh Chh. and Claverack (Columbia) N.Y., St. Thomas's Chh., 1725-1751; Albany, Four Mile Point, Rosendale (Ulster) and West Camp (Ulster) N.Y., 1734-1751; Rhinebeck (Dutchess) N.Y., 1734-1751; Raritan and Hackensack, N. J.; Coxsackie, N.Y., 1725-1729; and Schenectady, N.Y.; Luth.; d. Athens, N.Y., 25 Aug. 1751, a. 68.

FREDERICK JULIUS BERGER, b. Sagenroth, Switzerland, Apr. 1740, son of a Ref. Chh. minister; matric. Basel, 22 Oct. 1760; commissioned for Pa., 27 Mar. 1765; arriv. Philadelphia, before 16 Oct. 1765; sett. East Coventry (Chester) Pa., Brownback's Chh., Earl (Lanc.) Pa., Zeltenreich Chh., Brecknock (Lanc.) Pa., Muddy Creek Chh., Ephrata (Lanc.) Pa., Bethany Chh., 1765-1766; Reading (Berks) Pa., 1766-1768; suspended for drunkenness; had a chh. in the mountains, 1769; Germ. Ref.; d. after 20 May 1771.

GUILLAM BERTHOLF, bapt. Sluis, Zeeland, Holland, 20 Feb. 1656; came to America, 1683; member of the Chh. in Bergen, N. J., 6 Oct. 1684; Ord. Middleburgh, Holland, 16 Sept. 1693; sett. Tappan in Orangetown (Rockland) N.Y., 1694-1724: Hackensack (Bergen) N. J., New Barbadoes Chh., 1694-1724; Passaic (Passaic) N. J., Chh. at Acquackanonk, 1694-1724; Port Richmond, Staten Island, N.Y., 1694-1724; Tarrytown (Westchester) N.Y., Sleepy Hollow Chh., 1697-1724; Raritan (Somerset) N. J., Bridgewater Chh., now Somerville, 1699-1720; Belleville (Essex) N. J., at Second River, 1700-1724; Ponds (Bergen) N. J., Oakland Chh., 1710-1724; Pompton Plains (Morris) N. J., Pequannock Chh., 1713-1724; Richmond, Staten Island, N.Y., Richmond Chh., a union of the French, Dutch and English Ref. chhs., 1714-1724; he was the first minister of and probably the founder of 7 of these 9 chhs.; Dutch Ref.; d. ca. 1724.

WILLIAM BERTRAM, b. Edinburgh, Scotland, 2 Feb. 1674; ed. Edinburgh; Ord. by the Bangor Presbytery, Ireland; came to Pa., 1730; inst. Swatara (Dauphin) Pa., Paxtang Chh. on Fishing Creek, 15 Nov. 1732-16 Sept. 1736; inst. Derry (Dauphin) Pa., 1732-1746; Presb.; d. Derry, Pa., 2 May 1746, a. 72 (GS).

HENRICUS BEYS (or Beyse), b. Dordrecht, Holland, 1675; matric. Leyden, 13 Sept. 1694, in theology; matric. Leyden, 27 Aug. 1701, a. 27, to study medicine; Ord. Dordrecht, Holland, 4 May 1705; arriv. America, 1 Jan. 1705/6; sett. Kingston (Ulster) N.Y., Dutch Ref. Chh., 1705/6-1708; Ord. by Bsp. of London; K.B. for N.Y., 2 Feb. 1709/10; suspended by the Classis of Amsterdam; sett. Harlem and Fordham, N.Y., Ep. chhs., 1710-1713; restored to the Dutch Ref. ministry, 1713; sett. Curacoa, 1714-1717; physician; Dutch Ref.; Ep.

BININGER, see Bueninger.

JOHN JUSTUS JACOB BIRKENSTOCK, sett. Williams (Northampton) Pa., Cedarville Chh., 1733-1749; Upper Hanover (Montgomery) Pa., New Goshenhoppen Chh., 1739-1743; South Whitehall (Lehigh) Pa., Jordan Chh., 1739-1750; Easton (Northampton) Pa., St. John's Chh., 1740-1748; Upper Saucon (Lehigh) Pa., St. Paul's, Blue, or Organ Chh., 1742-1748; Luth.; returned to Germany and died there.

Bishop JOHN DAVID BISCHOFF, Steward of the First Sea Congregation; arriv. Philadelphia, 7 June 1742; Ord. Bethlehem, Pa., 1749; Indian missionary and minister of rural churches; sett. Warwick (Lanc.) Pa., St. James's Chh. at Lititz, 1756-1756; Bethabara, North

Carolina, Chh. at Wacovia, 12 Sept. 1756–1760; Bethania (Forsyth) N. C., 1760–1763; Moravian; d. Bethania, N. C., Sept. 1763.

Provost ERICK TOBIAS BJOERK, Ord. Upsala, Sweden; arriv. Philadelphia, from Westmanland, Sweden, 30 June 1697; sett. Wilmington, Del., 1st or Old Swedes Chh., 1697–29 June 1714; Crane Hook (New Castle) Del., Tran Hook Chh., Dec. 1697–1699; Chester (Delaware) Pa., Upland Chh., 1697–1714; Provost of all Swedish churches in America, 1713–1714; returned to Sweden, 29 June 1714; sett. Fahlun, Sweden, 1714–1740; Sw. Luth.; d. Fahlun, Sweden, 21 Aug. 1740.

JOHN BLACK, A.M., b. South Carolina; A.B., Princeton, 1771, A.M., 1782; Ord. Gettysburg (Adams) Pa., Upper Marsh Creek Chh., 15 Aug. 1775–10 Apr. 1794; supply, Hunterstown Dutch Ref. Chh., 1794–1802; Presb.; d. Gettysburg, Pa., 16 Aug. 1802.

SAMUEL BLACK, came from Ireland; Ord. Brandywine Manor (Chester) Pa., Forks of the Brandywine Chh., 10 Nov. 1736; sett. Brandywine Manor, Pa., 18 Nov. 1735–May 1741; inst. Mount Joy (Adams) Pa., Conewago Chh. (formerly Franklin, now Geinburg, Pa.), May 1742; sett. Mount Joy, Pa., 1741–4 Apr. 1745; Londonderry (Lebanon) Pa., 1741–1745; Peach Bottom (York) Pa., Slate Ridge Chh., 1757–1758; Rockfish (Nelson) Va., 1752–1770; Mountain Plains (Nelson) Va., 1752–1770; Old Side Presb.; d. Rockfish, Va., 9 Aug. 1770.

JOHN BLACKALL, sett. Caernarvon (Lanc.) Pa., Bangor Chh., 1733–1739; Salisbury (Lanc.) Pa., St. John's Chh. at Compassville, 1741–1742; Ep.; d. Lancaster, Pa., 12 Oct. 1743.

JOHN BLACKER, sett. Northampton (Bucks) Pa. and Southampton (Bucks) Pa., Dutch Ref. Chhs. at Richborough and Neshaminy in Churchville, 21 Jan. 1710; Dutch Ref.

JOHN BLACKWELL, sett. Vincent (Chester) Pa., 1771–1775; Bapt.

ROBERT BLACKWELL, D.D., b. Long Island, N.Y., 6 May 1748, son of Colonel Jacob Francis Blackwell; A.B., Princeton, 1768, A.M., 1782, D.D., 1788; A.B., Columbia, 1770; Trustee, U. of Pa., 1789–1822, D.D., 1788; Ord. by Bsp. of London, 11 June 1772; K.B. for Va., 15 June 1772; S.P.G. missionary at Gloucester (Camden) N. J., 1772–1777; Delaware (Camden) N. J., formerly Knowlton, St. James's Chh., 1772–1777; Clarkesboro (Cumberland) N. J., formerly Berkeley, St. Peter's Chh., Apr. 1773–1777; Colestown (Cumberland) N. J., St. Mary's Chh., 1772–1775; Greenwich in Cohansey (Cumberland) N. J., St. Stephen's Chh., 19 Nov. 1772–1777; Surgeon and Chaplain, 1st Pennsylvania Brigade, Continental Army, 1778–1781; member, Am. Phil. Soc.; Ep.; d. Philadelphia, Pa., 12 Feb. 1831.

ELIJAH BLAGUE, A.M., b. Saybrook, Conn., 26 Sept. 1730, son of Deacon Joseph Blague (Y.C., 1714); A.B., Y.C., 1750, A.M.; Chaplain to John Gardiner of Gardiner's Island, N.Y.; Cong.; d. Saybrook, Conn., 8 Apr. 1762, a. 32, s.p.

JOHN BLAIR, A.M., b. Ireland, 1720, brother of Samuel Blair; ed. at the Log Coll., Pa., A.M. (hon.) Princeton, 1760; Ord. Newville (Cumberland) Pa., Hopewell Chh. at Big Spring, 27 Dec. 1742; sett. Newville, Big Spring, 1742-28 Dec. 1748; Letterkenney (Franklin) Pa., Rocky Spring Chh., 1742-1748; Southampton (Cumberland) Pa., Middle Spring Chh., 1742-1748; these towns and churches were abandoned because of the Indian Wars; sett. New Londonderry (Chester) Pa., Fagg's Manor Chh., inst. 30 Nov. 1757-1767; Princeton, N. J., 1766-1768; Trustee, Princeton U., 1766-1767, Prof. of Theology, 1767-1769; Vice Pres. and acting Pres., Princeton, 1767-1768; sett. Montgomery (Orange) N.Y., Good Will Chh., 19 May 1769-8 Dec. 1771; Presb.; d. Wallkill, Montgomery, N.Y., 8 Dec. 1771.

SAMUEL BLAIR, b. Ulster, Ireland, 14 June 1712, son of William Blair and brother of John Blair; ed. Log Coll., Neshaminy, Pa., 1730-1735; lic. 9 Nov. 1733; Ord. Sept. 1737; sett. Middletown (Monmouth) N. J., 19 Sept. 1734-5 Sept. 1739; Shrewsbury (Monmouth) N. J., 1734-Nov. 1739; inst. New Londonderry (Chester) Pa., Fagg's Manor Chh., Apr. 1740; sett. New Londonderry, Pa., Nov. 1739-1751; Presb.; d. Fagg's Manor, Pa., 5 July 1751, a. 39 y. 21 d.

SAMUEL BLAIR, D.D., b. Fagg's Manor, Pa., 1741, son of the Rev. Samuel Blair; A.B., Princeton, 1760, A.M., Tutor, 1761-1764; A.M., H.C., 1767; D.D., U. of Pa., 1790; lic. 1766; sett. Boston, Mass., Old South Chh., Nov. 1766-10 Oct. 1769; Rev. Chaplain, Continental Army, 1775-20 June 1780; an eligible officer for membership in the Society of the Cincinnati; Chaplain of Congress, 1790-1792; member, Am. Phil. Soc.; Presb.; d. Germantown, Pa., Sept. 1818, a. 76.

CORNELIUS BLAUW, matric. Groningen, 15 Sept. 1749; came to America, 1762; sett. Pompton Plains (Morris) N.J., Pequannock Chh., 1762-1768; Fairfield (Cumberland) N. J., Horseneck Chh., 1762-1768; Montville (Morris) N. J., Parsippany or Boonton Chh., 1762-1768; Paterson (Passaic) N. J., Totowa Chh., 1762-1768; Hackensack (Bergen) N. J., 2nd Chh., 1768-1771; Schraalenburg (Bergen) N. J., 2nd or DuMont Chh., 1768-1771; Dutch Ref.

HERMANN BLOM, b. Amsterdam, 1628; matric. Utrecht, 1647; matric. Leyden, 4 June 1652; Ord. Amsterdam, Holland, before 16 Feb. 1660; came to America, 1660; sett. Kingston (Ulster) N.Y., Chh. at Esopus, 1660-28 Jan. 1667; returned to Holland; sett. Wonbrugge, Holland, 1667; Dutch Ref.

JOSHUA BLOOMER, D.D., b. Westchester, N.Y., ca. 1735; A.B., Columbia, 1758 (the first class to graduate), A.M., D.D., 1790; merchant in N.Y., N.Y.; Captain at the taking of Quebec, and a Major in the provincial service before 1762; studied theology in England; Ord. by Bsp. of London, 1769; K.B. for N.Y., 2 Mar. 1769; S.P.G. missionary on L. I., N.Y.; sett. Jamaica, L. I, N.Y., Grace Chh., 1769-1783; Newtown, L. I., N.Y., 1769-1783; Flushing, L. I., N.Y., St. George's Chh., 1769-1790; Ep.; d. Westchester, N.Y., 23 June 1790, a. 55.

ABRAHAM BLUMER, b. Grabs, Glaurus, Switzerland, 14 Dec. 1736, son of the Rev. John Jacob and Salome (Schindler) Blumer; matric. Basel, 1 Aug. 1754; Ord. 8 June 1756; chaplain of a Swiss regt., 11 July 1757–1766; vicar in Switzerland, 1766–1770; arriv. N.Y., N.Y., Jan. 1771; sett. Allentown (Lehigh) Pa., Zion Chh., 17 Feb. 1771–17 May 1801; North Whitehall (Lehigh) Pa., Schlosser's or Scrub Oak Chh., 1771–1801; South Whitehall (Lehigh) Pa., Jordan Chh., 1771–1801; Whitehall (Lehigh) Pa., Egypt Chh., 1771–1801; Northampton (Bucks) Pa., Neshimany Chh., 1771–1801; Germ. Ref.; d. Egypt in Whitehall, Pa., 23 Apr. 1822, a. 85.

RICHARD BOARDMAN, b. England, 1738; lic. 1763; arriv. at Gloucester Point, N. J., 24 Oct. 1769; sett. N.Y., N.Y., John Street Chh., 1769–1773; returned to England, 1774; itinerant Meth. preacher in England and Ireland, 1774–1782; Meth.; d. Cork, Ireland, 4 Oct. 1782, a. 44.

FRANCIS BOEHLER (brother of Bishop Peter Boehler), arriv. in America, 17 May 1752; Ord. soon after 1752; in charge of the Moravian school at Salisbury, Pa., Jan. 1755 ff.; sett. Graceham (Frederick) Md., 1762–1764; Hope (Warren) Pa., 1773–1773; Kingsbury (Dutchess) N.Y., 1773–1777; Salisbury (Lehigh) Pa., Chh. at Emaus, 1777–1779; his wife Anna served as his helper; Moravian; d. Lititz, Pa., 1806.

Bishop JOHN PETER BOEHLER (brother of Francis Boehler), b. Frankfort, Germany, 3 Dec. 1712, son of John Conrad and Antoinette Elizabeth (Hanf) Boehler; ed. Jena, 1731–1736; Ord. Herrnhut, Saxony, Dec. 1737; arriv. Savannah, Ga., 15 Oct. 1738; sett. Savannah, Ga., Oct. 1738–Jan. 1739; Purysburg, S.C., 1738–1739; Nazareth (Northampton) Pa., 1740–1741; returned to Europe, 29 Jan. 1740/1–1742; 2nd visit to America, arriv. Philadelphia, 7 June 1742; sett. Bethlehem (Northampton) Pa., 1742–1745; Philadelphia, Pa., 1743–1745; Burlington, N. J., 1743–1745; Cranbury (Middlesex) N. J., 1743–1745; Lawrence (Mercer) N. J., 1743–1745; Middletown (Cape May) N. J., 1743–1745; Princeton (Mercer) N. J., 1743–1745; Trenton (Mercer) N. J., 1743–1745; Durham (Berks) Pa., 1743–1745; Lower Salford (Montgomery) Pa., 1743–1745; Manatawny (Berks) Pa., 1743–1745; Southampton (Bucks) Pa., Neshaminy Chh., 1743–1745; Upper Providence (Montgomery) Pa., Chh. at Trappe, 1743–1745; Dover, Del., 1743–1745; Duck Creek, Del., 1743–1745; Lewes, Del., 1743–1745; returned to Europe, 8 Apr. 1745; consecrated Bishop for America at Marienborn, Germany, 10 Jan. 1748; returned to America, 13 Sept. 1753–28 Aug. 1755; sett. Bethlehem, Pa., 16 Dec. 1756–1764; final departure for Europe, 7 May 1764; next to Spangenberg, the most eminent of the Moravians in America; President of the Pennsylvania Synod; d. London, England, 27 Apr. 1775.

JOHN PHILIP BOEHM, bapt. Hochstadt, Hanau, Germany, 25 Oct. 1683, son of the Rev. Philip Ludwig and Maria Boehm; teacher at Worms, 11 Mar. 1708–1715, and at Lambsheim, 22 Nov. 1715–6 Apr.

1720; came to Pa., 1720; lic. 30 June 1729; Ord. N.Y., N.Y., 23 Nov. 1729; sett. over the following chhs., all in Pa.: New Hanover (Montgomery), Falkner's Swamp Chh., 15 Oct. 1725-1749; Worcester (Montgomery), Skippack Chh., Nov. 1725-1749; Whitemarsh (Montgomery), St. Peter's Chh., Barren Hill, 25 Dec. 1725-1747; North Annville (Lebanon), Hill or Quittopehilla Chh., 1727-1735; Mill Creek (Lebanon), Tulpehocken or Trinity Chh., 1727-1730, 1735-1748; Lower Salford (Montgomery), Reiff's or Skippack Chh., 1729-1749; Brecknock (Lanc.), Muddy Creek Chh., 1727-1730; Ephrata (Lanc.), Bethany Chh., 1730-1731; Conestoga (Lanc.), 1727-14 Oct. 1748; Philadelphia, 1729-1747; Salisbury (Lehigh), Jerusalem Chh., 1734-1736; Penn (Lanc.), White Oak Chh., 1735-1745; Lower Heidelberg (Berks), St. John's Chh., 1735-1748; Oley (Berks), 1736-6 May 1739; Whitehall (Lehigh), Egypt Chh., 1739-1741; Whitpain (Montgomery), Boehm's Chh., 1740-1749; Germantown, 1744-1749; Upper Providence (Montgomery), St. Luke's Chh. at Trappe, 1746-15 Sept. 1748; Lower Macungie (Lehigh), 1749-1749; Mr. Boehm founded at least twelve churches: Falkner's Swamp, Skippack, and Whitemarsh, 1725; Hill Chh. at Conestoga, Tulpehocken, and Philadelphia, 1737; Egypt, 1734; Cocalico, 1735; Tulpehocken near Myerstown, 1738; Providence, 1743; and Whitpain (Boehm's Chh.), 1747; he is rightly called the "Founder of the German Reformed Church in Pennsylvania"; d. Hellertown (Northampton) Pa., 29 Apr. 1749.

Bishop MARTIN BOEHM, b. Conestoga (Lancaster) Pa., 30 Nov. 1725, son of Jacob Boehm; Ord. minister at Pequea (Lanc.) Pa., New Danville Chh., 1758; Ord. Bishop at Pequea, 1761; sett. Pequea, Pa., New Danville Chh., 1758-1775; Pequea, Pa., Byerland Chh., 1758-1775; Pequea, Pa., River Corner Chh., 1775-1775; became a Moravian and later a Methodist, 1775; chosen Bishop of the United Brethren in Christ, 1800; Mennonite; Moravian; Methodist; d. Pequea, Pa., 23 Mar. 1812, a. 87 (GS).

CHARLES LEWIS BOEHME, b. Muhlbach, Palatinate, 20 Aug. 1738; matric. Heidelberg, 22 Nov. 1755; preached in Germany before coming to America at Bacharach on the Rhine and at Hedesheim near Creutznach; arriv. America, Autumn of 1770; sett. Lancaster (Lanc.) Pa., Feb. 1771-July 1775; Pequea (Lanc.) Pa., 1771-1771; Hanover (York) Pa., David's Chh., 1775-1779; Hamilton (Adams) Abbottstown Chh., 1775-1779; Germany (Adams) Pa., Littlestown Chh., 1775-1779; Latimore (Adams) Pa., Mount Olivet, Long Green, or Lower Bermudian Chh., 1775-1779; North Codorus (York) Pa., St. Peter's or Lischy's Chh., 1775-1779; Silver Run (York) Pa., 1775-1779; Hanover (York) Pa., McCallister's Chh., 1775-1781; Baltimore, Md., 1781-1783; ill with gout and epilepsy, 1782-1783; Germ. Ref.; d. Baltimore, Md., 4 July 1783.

JOHN BOEHNER, came from Krumberg, Bohemia; arriv. Savannah, Ga., 20 Feb. 1736; sett. Savannah, Ga., 1736-1740; came to Pa., 1740;

sett. Nazareth (Northampton) Pa., 1740-1742; missionary in the West Indies, 1742-1785; visited Bethlehem, Pa., 1754; carpenter and missionary; Moravian; d. St. Thomas, West Indies, 1785.

GEORGE BOEHNISCH, landed at Philadelphia, 22 Sept. 1734; sett. Lower Salford (Montgomery) Pa., Skippack Chh., 1734-1737; returned to Europe, Autumn, 1737; first Moravian missionary in America.

HENRICUS BOEL, b. Amsterdam, Holland, 1692, son of Tobias Boel; matric. Leyden, 17 Sept. 1712, in theology; came to America, 1713; sett. N.Y., N.Y., 1st or South Dutch Chh. in New Amsterdam (collegiate), 1713-1754; supply at Tarrytown (Westchester) N.Y., 1713-1754; N.Y., N.Y., Middle Dutch Ref. Chh., 1729-1754; Dutch Ref.; d. N.Y., N.Y., 27 June 1754.

HERMANUS LANCELOT BOELEN, sett. Jamaica, L. I., N.Y., 1766-1772; Newtown, L. I., N.Y., 1766-1780; Oyster Bay, L. I., N.Y., Chh. at Wolver Hollow, 1766-1780; Success, L. I., N.Y., Success Pond Chh. at North Hempstead, 1766-1772; Tory; Dutch Ref.; returned to Holland, 1780.

EVERARDUS WILHELMUS BOGARDUS, b. Woerden, Holland, 1607; matric. Leyden, 17 June 1627, a. 20; sett. Guiana, 1630-1632; Ord. Amsterdam, Holland, 14 June 1632; sent to New Netherlands, 15 July 1632; arriv. N.Y., N.Y. (then called New Amsterdam), 1633; sett. N.Y., N.Y., 1st or South Dutch Chh., 1633-1647; resigned, 22 July 1647; Dutch Ref.; sailed for Holland in the ship *Princess;* shipwrecked and died off the coast of Wales, 27 Sept. 1647.

CHRISTIAN BOMBERGER, b. prob. at Eshelbrun, Baden, Germany, 1705, son of Christian and Maria Bomberger; sett. Elizabeth (Lanc.) Pa., Hammer Creek Chh., 1733-1787; Ord. Hammer Creek, 1760; Mennonite; d. Elizabeth, Pa., 1787.

Bishop CHRISTIAN BOMBERGER, Ord. Bishop, 1772; sett. Warwick (Lanc.) Pa., White Oak Chh., 1772 ff.; Tunker Bapt.

DANIEL BONDET, A.M., b. France, 1652, of a noble French family, his mother being dau. of Philippe de Nautonnier, Sieur de Castelfranc; ed. Geneva U.; Prof. at Saumur, France; driven out of France as a Huguenot minister; Ord. 13 Apr. 1686; Ord. in England as an Ep., 1709; sett. Oxford, Mass., Huguenot Chh., 1686-1696; New Rochelle (Westchester) N.Y., Huguenot Chh., 1697-1722; New Rochelle, N.Y., Trinity Chh., Ep., 1708-1722; preached in three languages; English, French, and the Indian tongue; French Ref.; Ep.; d. New Rochelle, N.Y., Sept. 1722, a. 69.

MALAKIAH BONHAM, b. Lawrence, N. J., 1714; Ord. Baptisttown, Kingwood (Hunterdon) N. J., 1749; sett. Baptisttown, 1749-15 Feb. 1757; expelled 24 Mar. 1761; Bapt.; d. 1789, a. 76.

Father BONIFACE, sett. Fonda (Montgomery) N.Y., St. Peter's Mohawk Mission, 1673; Syracuse, N.Y., Conception Mission to the Onandagas, 1673; R.C.

Colonial Clergy of the Middle Colonies

JOHN HERMAN BONN, b. Skippack, Pa., Nov. 1719, son of Peter and Geritje Bonn; became a Moravian, 1747; Ord. deacon, 1755; sett. Bethlehem (Northampton) Pa., Jan. 1773–1779; warden; steward at Christiansspring; Moravian; d. Bethlehem, Pa., Jan. 1797.

JOHN WILLIAM BOOS, b. Otterberg, Palatinate, Germany, 8 Sept. 1740; matric. Heidelberg, 29 Sept. 1763; matric. Utrecht, 1768–1770; sett. Reading (Berks) Pa., 1771–1782; Muhlenberg (Berks) Pa., Alsace Chh., 1771–1782; Exeter (Berks) Pa., Schwartzwald Chh., 1771–1782; Heidelberg (Berks) Pa., Hain's or Cacusi Chh., 1772–1782; Oley (Berks) Pa., 1774–1782; Germ. Ref.; d. 28 Nov. 1814.

Provost ANDREW BORELL, sett. Wilmington, Del., 1st or Old Swedes Chh., 1759–1768; Chester (Del.) Pa., Upland Chh., 1759–1768; Provost of the Swedish Lutheran chhs. in America, 1759–1768; Sw. Luth.; d. Wilmington, Del., 5 Apr. 1768.

DAVID BOSTWICK, A.M., b. New Milford, Conn., 8 Jan. 1721, son of Deacon and Major John Bostwick; Y.C., 1736 (non grad.); A.M. (hon.) Princeton, 1756, overseer, 1761–1763; Ord. Jamaica, L. I., N.Y., 9 Oct. 1745; sett. Jamaica, L. I., N.Y., 1745–13 Apr. 1756; N.Y., N.Y., 1st Presb. Chh., 1756–1763; Presb.; d. N.Y., N.Y., 12 Nov. 1763, a. 43.

JOHN BOWDEN, D.D., b. Ireland, 7 Jan. 1751, son of Thomas Bowden, Esq.; A.B., Columbia, 1772, A.M., 1775, D.D., 1797; Ord. by Bsp. of London, 1774; sett. N.Y., N.Y., Trinity Chh., as asst., 1774–1775; Norwalk, Conn., St. Paul's Chh., Dec. 1784–1789; St. Croix, West Indies, 1789–1792; in charge, Ep. Academy, Cheshire, Conn., 1796–Apr. 1802; Prof. of Rhetoric, Moral Philosophy, Belles-Lettres and Logic, Columbia, Apr. 1802–1817; Ep.; d. Allston Spa, N.Y., 31 July 1817.

NATHANIEL BOWERS, son of the Rev. John and Bridget (Thompson) Bowers of Derby, Conn.; sett. Rye (Westchester) N.Y., 1688–1700; Greenwich, Conn., 1700–1708; Newark, N. J., 1708–1716; Presb.; d. Newark, N. J., 1716.

CHRISTIAN BOWMAN, b. Pequea, Pa., 1724, son of Wendel Bauman; sett. Brecknock (Lanc.) Pa., Chh. at Bowmansville, as 1st minister, before 1775–1790; Menn.; d. Adamsville, Pa., 1790, a. 66.

Bishop JOHANNES BOWMAN (perhaps son of Wendel Bowman); minister and bishop before 1725; sett. East Lampeter (Lanc.) Pa., Mellinger's Chh., 1725–1738; he was a weaver from Refton, Pa., ca. 1725; Menn.; d. East Lampeter, Pa., 1738 (possibly 1728).

ADAM BOYD, b. Ballymoney, co. Antrim, Ireland, 1692; came to New England, 1722; Ord. Sadsbury (Chester) Pa., Upper Octoraro Chh., 13 Oct. 1725–19 Oct. 1768, when he resigned; sett. Salisbury (Lanc.) Pa., Pequea Chh., 1724–1733; Brandywine Manor (Chester) Pa., Forks of the Brandywine Chh., 1725–1734, 11 Aug. 1741–1746; 1748–1758; Bart (Lanc.) Pa., Middle Octoraro Chh., 1727–1730; married

Jane, dau. of the Rev. Thomas Craighead; Old Side Presb.; d. Upper Octoraro, at Sadsbury, Pa., 23 Nov. 1768.

JAMES BOYD, A.B., A.B., Princeton, 1763; sett. Newtown (Bucks) Pa., 29 May 1769-1813 (this chh. is now extinct); Bensalem (Bucks) Pa., 1772-1813; Presb.; d. Newtown, Pa., 1813.

JOHN BOYD, b. Scotland, 1680; student, Glasgow, 11 Mar. 1701; Ord. Monmouth co., N. J., 29 Dec. 1706; sett. Tennent (Monmouth) N. J., Chh. at Freehold, 1705-1708; Presb.; d. Tennent, Freehold, N.J., 30 Aug. 1708, a. 28 (GS).

BENEDICT BRACKBILL (or Breckbuhl), b. Trachselwald, Bern, Switzerland, 1665; preacher at Bern; Ord. Switzerland, 1699; sett. Manheim, Germany; imprisoned in Switzerland, 1709-18 Mar. 1710; arriv. Philadelphia, 24 Aug. 1717; sett. Strasburg (Lanc.) Pa., 1719-1720; patented land at Strasburg, Pa., 29 Jan. 1720; Menn.; d. Strasburg, Pa., 27 Apr. 1720.

ULRICH BRACKBILL, b. Europe, 1703, son of the Rev. Benedict and Maria (Herr) Brackbill; arriv. Philadelphia, 24 Aug. 1717; sett. Strasburg, Pa., 1719-1739; Menn.; d. Strasburg (Lanc.) Pa., 19 Oct. 1739.

Hon. HUGH HENRY BREACKENRIDGE, A.M., A.B., Princeton, 1771, A.M.; master, 1771-1774; Chaplain, Continental Army, 1777-1778; member Pa. Assembly, 1786-1789; Judge, Pa. Dist. Court, 1789-1799; Judge, Pa. Supreme Court, 1799-1816; Presb.

BENONI BRADNER, A.M., b. Goshen, N.Y., 1734, son of the Rev. John Bradner; A.B., Princeton, 1755, A.M.; A.M., Y.C., 1758; sett. Jamaica, L. I., N.Y., 1760-1762; Dutchess co., N.Y., Blooming Grove (Orange) N.Y., June 1786-1804; pvt., Continental Army, N.Y., Rev. War, 1778-1779; Presb.; d. Blooming Grove, N.Y., 1804, a. 71.

JOHN BRADNER, b. Scotland; came to America, 1715; Ord. Cape May, N.J., 6 May 1715; sett. Fairfield (Cumberland) N. J., Chh. at Cohansey, 1715-1721; Cape May (Cape May) N. J., Cold Spring Chh., 1715-1721; Goshen (Orange) N.Y., 1721-1732; Presb.; d. Goshen, N.Y., 1732 (GS).

DAVID BRAINARD, b. Haddam, Conn., 20 Apr. 1718, son of the Hon. Hezekiah and Dorothy (Hobart) Brainard; Y.C., 1743 (non grad.); lic. 20 July 1742; missionary for the Society for Promoting Christian Knowledge, at Stockbridge, Mass., 1742-1744; sett. Phillipsburg (Warren) N. J., Indian Chh., 1740-1744; Ord. Newark, N. J., June 1744; Indian missionary at Allentown, N. J., Forks of the Delaware, 15 May 1743-9 Oct. 1747; Allen (Northampton) Pa., 1743-1749; Mount Bethel (Lehigh) Pa., 1742-1747; at Hunter's; Crosweeksung, near Freehold, N. J., 1745-1746; Presb.; d. Northampton, Mass., 9 Oct. 1747, a. 29.

JOHN BRAINARD, A.M., b. Haddam, Conn., 28 Feb. 1719/20, son of the Hon. Hezekiah and Dorothy (Hobart) Brainard; A.B., Yale,

1746, A.M.; A.M., Princeton; agent for the Hon. Society in Scotland for Propagating Christian Knowledge; Ord. Feb. 1748; sett. Newark, N. J., 1755-1759; Indian Chh. at Hunter's, Mount Bethel (Northampton) Pa., Apr. 1747-1759; Brotherton, N. J., Mar. 1759-1768; New Brunswick, N. J., June 1756-Sept. 1757; Egg Harbor (Atlantic) N. J., 1760-1777; Barnegat (Ocean) N. J. and Manahawkin (Ocean) N. J., 1760-1777; Berlin (Camden) N. J., 1766-1767; Mount Holly (Burlington) N. J., 1768-1777; Deerfield (Cumberland) N. J., 1777-1781; Presb.; d. Deerfield, N. J., 18 Mar. 1781, a. 61.

JOHN BRANDMILLER (Brandmueller), b. Basel, Switzerland, 24 Nov. 1704; became a Moravian, Mar. 1738/9; arriv. Philadelphia, May 1742; deacon at Bethlehem (Northampton) Pa., 1743-1745; Ord. Philadelphia, 13 May 1745; sett. Albany (Berks) Pa., Allemaengle Chh., 1745-1755; Lynn (Lehigh) Pa., Allemaengel Chh., 1745-1755; Bethel (Lebanon) Pa., 1745-1759; Mount Joy (Lanc.) Pa., Donegal Chh., 1745-1759; Friedenthal, near Nazareth, Forks of the Delaware, 1759-1767; Swatara (Lebanon) Pa., 1748-1759; Philadelphia, Pa., 1753-1754; printer and bookkeeper at Bethlehem; set up the first Moravian press in America; Germ. Ref.; Moravian; d. Bethlehem, Pa., 16 Aug. 1777.

DAVID BRANSON, b. Ernston, N. J., 1747; Ord. Pemberton (Burlington) N. J., at New Mills, 22 Dec. 1770; sett. Pemberton, N. J., 1770-27 June 1772; excommunicated, 1772; Presb.; living 1781.

JOHN BRAYMAN, sett. Warwick (Chester) Pa., French Creek Chh. at East Nantmeal, before 1769; 7th Day Bapt.

ROBERT BRECK, A.M., b. Dorchester, Mass., 7 Dec. 1682, son of Capt. John and Susanna Breck; A.B., H.C., 1700, A.M.; sett. Newtown, L. I., N.Y., 1st Chh., 1701-1704; Ord. Marlborough, Mass., 25 Oct. 1704-1731; Election Sermon, 1728; Cong.; d. Marlborough, Mass., 6 Jan. 1730/1, a. 49.

MELCHIOR BRENNEMAN, arriv. Philadelphia, 24 Aug. 1717; sett. Pequea (Lanc.) Pa., Chh. at New Danville, 1717-1728; East Hempfield (Lanc.) Pa., Chh. at Rohrerstown, 1717-1728; West Donegal (Lanc.) Pa., Good's Chh., 1728-1730; resided at Conoy, Pa.; Mennonite; d. Conoy, Pa., 1737.

MELCHIOR BRENNEMAN, Jr., b. Pequea, Pa., 1727, son of the Rev. Melchior Brenneman; sett. West Donegal (Lanc.) Pa., before 1775-1809; resided at Conoy; will made 4 Nov. 1809; proved 9 Jan. 1810; Menn.; d. Conoy, Pa., 1809, a. 83.

FRANCIS JOSEPH BRESSANI, S.J., b. Rome, Italy, 6 May 1612; admitted to the S.J., 15 Aug. 1626; student at Rome and Clermont; sent to Quebec, 1642-1644; at the Huron Mission, Apr. 1644; captured by the Iroquois and tortured; ransomed by the Dutch at Fort Orange (now Albany) from the Iroquois, and supplied with a passage to Europe; he searched but found no Catholic in N.Y., N.Y., 1644; arriv. at Rochelle,

France, 15 Nov. 1644; in Canada again, 1645-1649; returned to Italy, Nov. 1650; R. C.; d. Florence, Italy, 9 Sept. 1672.

NATHANIEL BREWSTER, Th.B., b. ca. 1620, son of Francis and Lucy Brewster; A.B., H.C., 1642; Th.B., Trinity Coll., Dublin, Ireland; sett. Ireland and England; ejected, 1662; returned to N.E., Aug. 1662; sett. Brookhaven, L. I., N.Y., Setauket Chh., 1665-1690; Cong.; d. Brookhaven, L. I., N.Y., 18 Dec. 1690.

CHRISTOPHER BRIDGE, A.M., b. Tillingham, Essex, England, 1671/2, son of the Rev. Robert Bridge; adm. St. John's Coll., Camb., 4 June 1689, a. 17; A.B., 1692/3, A.M.; inst. Boston, Mass., King's Chapel, 5 Mar. 1699-1706, as Queen's Lecturer; sett. Kingston, R. I., Narragansett Chh., Oct. 1706-1709; induct. Rye (Westchester) N.Y., Christ Chh., 17 Oct. 1710-1719; Bedford (Westchester) N.Y., St. Matthew's Chh., 1710-1719; Ep.; d. Rye, N.Y., 22 May 1719, a. 48.

THOMAS BRIDGE, A.M., b. Hackney, Middlesex, England, 1657; came to America, 1682; A.M. (hon.) H.C., 1712; merchant and preacher at Port Royal, Jamaica, 1686; moderator and Governor of New Providence, Bahamas, 1687-1688; preacher at New Providence, 1689; sett. Fairfield (Cumberland) N. J., Presb. Chh. at Cohansey, 1694-1703; came to Boston, Mass., 17 Mar. 1704; Ord. Boston, Mass., 1st Chh., 10 May 1705-1715; Artillery Election Sermon, 1705; Cong.; d. Boston, Mass., 26 Sept. 1715, a. 58.

JOHN PETER BRISAC, K.B. for N.Y., 29 Jan. 1700/1; sett. N.Y., N.Y., Chaplain in the Fort, 1701 (and poss. to 1703); Ep.

JOHN BROOKE, A.M., b. Bury, Lancashire, England, son of Peter Brooke; A.B., St. John's Coll., Cambridge, 1674/5; A.M., Oxford, 1679; curate, Woodbrick, co. York, 1703; Ardsley, near Wakefield, York, 1704; K.B. for the Jerseys, 27 Mar. 1705; sett. Hempstead, L. I., N.Y., St. George's Chh., 1705-1705; Elizabethtown (Union) N. J., St. John's Chh., 1705-1707; Perth Amboy (Middlesex) N. J., St. Peter's Chh., 1705-1707; Shrewsbury (Monmouth) N. J., Christ Chh., 1705-1707; missionary at Rahway (Union) N. J., Woodbridge (Middlesex) N. J., Cheesequake (Middlesex) N. J., Piscataway (Middlesex) N. J., Freehold (Monmouth) N. J., Rocky Hill (Somerset) N. J., and Page's, N. J., 1705-1707; Ep.; d. at sea, Autumn, 1707 (drowned on the voyage to England).

TIMOTHY BROOKS, b. Woburn, Mass., 16 Oct. 1662, son of Henry and Susannah Brooks; came from Swansea, Mass., to Cohansey, N. J., ca. 1687, where he was living 10 Mar. 1711/2; sett. Cohansey (Salem) N. J., 1710-1716 (and perhaps 1687-1716); also Cohansey, N. J., 2nd Bapt. Chh., 1700-1710; Bapt.; d. Cohansey, N. J., 1716, a. 54.

THOMAS BROUWER, came to America, 1715; sett. Schenectady, N.Y., 1715-1728; Dutch Ref.; d. Schenectady, N.Y., 1728.

DAVID BROWN, came from Scotland; was a member of the New Castle Presbytery, 1748-1749; returned to Scotland, 1749; Presb.

GEORGE BROWN, sett. Reading (Adams) Pa., Great Conewago Chh., ca. 1770; Lower Milford (Lehigh) Pa., Great Swamp Chh., ca. 1770; Germ. Bapt.

JAMES BROWN, A.M., prob. b. Windham, Conn., 29 Jan. 1720/1, son of James and Esther (Broughton) Brown; A.B., Y.C., 1747, A.M.; Ord. Bridgehampton, L. I., N.Y., 15 June 1748–27 Mar. 1775; Presb.; d. Southampton, L. I., N.Y., 22 Apr. 1788, a. 68.

THOMAS BROWN, A.B., b. Holywell, Oxford, England, 1731, son of Thomas Brown; matric. Magdalen Hall, Oxford, 20 May 1748, a. 17; A.B., St. Alban's Hall, Oxford, 17 Jan. 1752; Chaplain, 27th Regt., at Albany, N.Y., 1754–1764; Ord. London, 8 July 1764; K.B., 20 Aug. 1764; sett. Albany, N.Y., St. Peter's Chh., 1764–1768; Schenectady, N.Y., St. George's Chh., 1764–1768; induct. Dorchester Parish (Dorchester) Md., 30 May 1772; sett. Dorchester Parish, Md., 1768–1782; St. Luke's Parish (Queen Annes) Md., 1782–1784; Ep.; d. Dorchester, Md., 2 May 1784, a. 53.

ISAAC BROWNE, A.M., b. West Haven, Conn., 20 Mar. 1708/9, son of Daniel and Mary (How) Browne; A.B., Y.C., 1729, A.M.; Ord. London, 1733; K.B. for N.Y., 1 Sept. 1733; sett. Brookhaven, L. I., N.Y., Caroline Chh., at Setauket, 14 Dec. 1733–1744; Newark (Essex) N. J., Trinity Chh., 2 June 1747–1777; Belleville (Essex) N. J., Christ Chh., at Second River, 1750–1777; physician; member, N. J. Medical Soc., 1766; refugee to N.Y., Jan. 1777; sett. Annapolis, Nova Scotia, 1783–1785; Ep.; d. Windsor, N. S., 1787.

JOHN BROWNFIELD, b. Greenwich, England, June 1714; brought up in the family of General Ogelthorpe, and accompanied him to Georgia as his Secretary, Feb. 1737; came to Bethlehem, Pa., Apr. 1745; head steward and Secretary of the Moravian Soc. for the Furtherance of the Gospel, 1745; Ord. deacon, 1749; sett. Bethlehem, Pa., as minister, 1749–1752; Moravian; d. Bethlehem, Pa., Apr. 1752.

ABRAHAM BRUBAKER, sett. Clay (Lanc.) Pa., Chh. at Indiantown, 1750–1811; Mennonite.

DAVID BRUCE, b. Scotland; came from Edinburgh; joined the Moravians in England; Ord. Elder, 24 July 1740; arriv. Bethlehem, Pa., 25 June 1742; sett. Nazareth (Northampton) Pa., Forks of the Delaware Chh., 1740–1742; Philadelphia, Pa., 1742–1742; N.Y., N.Y., 1742–1742; The Minisinks (Delaware Water Gap, Pa., Wallpack, N. J., Paulin's Kill, N. J., and the surrounding region), 1743–1744; Bethlehem, Pa., Brodhead Settlement at Dansbury, Pa., 1743–1744; Wallpack (Sussex) N. J., 1743–1744; Gnadenhuetten, Pa., Indian Chh., 1745 ff.; Indian missionary at Wequodnoc in Sharon, Conn., 1741–1749; first English speaking missionary among the Moravians in America; d. Sharon, Conn., 9 July 1749.

JOHN BRUCKER, arriv. Philadelphia, 7 June 1742; Bethlehem, Pa., 25 June 1742; 1st minister at Nazareth, Pa.; Ord. N.Y., N.Y., 1743;

missionary in N. J.; missionary in the Danish West Indies, May 1743–1765; Moravian; d. West Indies, 1765.

PETER BRUNNHOLTZ, b. Niebuhl, Gluckburg, Schleswig-Holstein; ed. Halle; Ord. Wernigerode, Germany, 12 Apr. 1744; embarked at Gravesend, England, 29 Nov. 1744; arriv. Philadelphia, 26 Jan. 1744/5; sett. Philadelphia, Pa., St. Michael's Luth. Chh., 1745–1758; Germantown, Pa., St. Michael's Chh., 1745–1751; Upper Providence (Montgomery) Pa., Augustus Luth. Chh. at Trappe, 1745–1746; New Hanover (Montgomery) Pa., Falkner's Swamp Chh., 1745–1746; Earl (Lanc.) Pa., Chh. at New Holland, 1747–1748; Luth.; d. Philadelphia, Pa., 7 July 1758, unm.

PAUL DANIEL BRYZELIUS, b. Haeradshammer, Linkoeping, Sweden; ed. Upsala; came to Philadelphia, Pa., 1742; Ord. (Moravian), Jan. 1743; Ord. (Lutheran), 29 Oct. 1760; Ord. (Ep.), London, 1767; sett. Ammasland (Del.) Pa., 1743–45; Bethlehem (Northampton) Pa., 1743–1745; Calkoen's Hook (Del.) Pa., 1743–1745; Bridgeton (Cumberland) N. J., 1743–1745; Cape May (Cape May) N. J., 1743–1745; Little Egg Harbor (Ocean) N. J., 1743–1745; Maurice River (Gloucester) N. J., 1743–1745; Oldmans Creek (Gloucester) N. J., 1743–1745; Swedesborough (Gloucester) N. J., Chh. on Raccoon Creek, 1743–1744; Pennsneck (Salem) N. J., 1743–1745; Pilesgrove (Salem) N. J., 1743–1744; Great Egg Harbor (Atlantic) N. J., 1743–1755; Narraticon, N. J., 1743–1760; went to Europe; arriv. N.Y., N.Y., 15 Apr. 1754; Lutheran ministry: Bedminster (Somerset) N. J., St. Paul's Chh., 1760–1766; Pluckemin (Somerset) N. J., 1761–1766; Raritan (Somerset) N. J., 1761–1766; Fairmount (Hunterdon) N. J., Fox Hill Luth. Chh., Tewksbury, 1761–1766; Whitehouse (Hunterdon) N. J., Chh. at Leslyland, 1761–1766; Potterstown (Hunterdon) N. J., Rockaway Luth. Chh., 1761–1766; German Valley (Morris) N. J., Luth. Chh. at Washington, 1761–1766; New Germantown (Morris) N. J., Zion Luth. Chh. at Tewksbury, 1761–1766; Ep. ministry: sett. Nova Scotia, 1767; Sw. Luth.; Moravian; Luth.; Ep.

JAMES BRUYAS, S.J., sett. Rome, N.Y., St. Francis Xavier's Mission to the Oneida Indians, 1667–1671; Superior, St. Peter's Mohawk Mission, Fonda, N.Y., 1671–1678; Syracuse, N.Y., St. John the Baptist's Mission to the Onondagas, 1700–1702; R.C.; living 1702.

JOHN CONRAD BUCHER, b. Nuenkirch, Schaffhausen, Switzerland, 13 June 1730, son of Landvogt Johann Jacob and Anna Dorothea (Burgauer) Bucher; matric. Marburg, 14 July 1752; also at Basel; arriv. America, 1755; Ord. ca. 20 June 1767; sett. Carlisle (Cumberland) Pa., 1762–1768; Penn (Lanc.) Pa., White Oaks Chh., 1763–1769; Elizabethtown (Lanc.) Pa., 1763–1779; Pittsburgh, Pa., Chh. at Fort Pitt, 1764–1766; Sharpsburg (Allegheny) Pa., 1764–1766; Shippensburg (Cumberland) Pa., 1764–1766; Bedford (Bedford) Pa., 1764–1766; Coxestown (Dauphin) Pa., 1764–1766; Conococheague, Md., St. Paul's Chh., 1765–1768; Middletown (Fredk.) Md., Zion or Kittatinny Mountain Chh.,

1765–1768; Derry (Dauphin) Pa., Hummelstown Chh., 1765–1769; Lebanon (Leb.) Pa., Tabor Chh., 1767–24 Nov. 1768–7 July 1780; Chambersburg (Frank.) Pa., Falling Spring Chh., 1767–1778; East Donegal (Lanc.) Pa., Maytown Chh., 1767–1779; Mt. Joy, Pa., Miller's Chh., 1767–1769; Reading (Berks) Pa., 1769–1770; Manheim (Lanc.) Pa., St. Paul's Chh., 1771–1778; Rapho, Pa., 1771–1778; Warwick, Pa., Kissel Hill Chh., 1771–1778; North Annville (Leb)., Pa., Hill Chh. or Quittopehilla Chh., 1771–1778; Jonestown, Pa., 1771–1778; Swatara, Pa., Little Swatara Chh., 1771–1778; comm. Ensign, 1st Battal. Pa., Regt., 11 Apr. 1758; Lieut., Pa. Troops, 19 Apr. 1760–1764; Capt., 31 July 1764–1765; Chaplain, Rev. War, 1775–1 Aug. 1777; Germ. Ref.; d. Annville, Pa., 15 Aug. 1780.

JEDEDIAH BUCKINGHAM, A.M., b. Saybrook, Conn., 2 Oct. 1696, son of Thomas, Jr. and Margaret (Griswold) Buckingham; A.B., Y.C., 1714, A.M.; preached at Newark, N. J., October 1716–Dec. 1718; Presb.; d. Norwalk, Conn., 28 Mar. 1720, a. 24.

WILLIAM BUCKINGHAM (also spelled Beckingham), b. England; a Friend at Cohansey, N. J.; bapt. ca. 28 Jan. 1697 as a Quaker-Bapt.; sett. Newtown, Upper Providence, Pa., 12 Oct. 1697–1701 (the chh. was incorp., 12 Oct. 1697, and disrupted, 1700); sett. Nottingham, Md., 1700–1701; was living in Chester co., Pa., 1680, 1688, and at Chichester, 14 Feb. 1701; mason; bought house and 150 acres of land at Upper Providence, 7 Apr. 1687, and on 1 Oct. 1696, another 100 acres; 7th Day Bapt.; d. Chester co., Pa., ca. 1701.

THOMAS BUDD, sett. Newtown, Pa., at Upper Providence, 12 Oct. 1697–1701; co-pastor with William Buckingham, Abel Noble, Thomas Martin and Enoch David: too many ministers for one small chh.; sett. Nottingham, Md., after 1701; 7th Day Bapt.

SAMUEL BUELL, D.D., b. Coventry, Conn., 20 Aug. 1716, son of Capt. Peter and Hannah (Welles) Buell; A.B., Y.C., 1741, A.M.; S.T.D., Dart. Coll., 1791; Ord. New Fairfield, Conn., 9 Nov. 1742; itinerant preacher, 1742–1745; inst. East Hampton, L. I., N.Y., 19 Sept. 1746–1798; Cong.-Presb.; d. East Hampton, L. I., N.Y., 19 July 1798, a. 82.

ABRAHAM BUENINGER, b. Bulach, Zurich, Switzerland, 1720; came to Pa., 1742; Ord. 1756; missionary to the Indians; sett. West Indies; sett. Codorus, Pa., 1746–1748; sett. Salem (Washington) N.Y., 1770–1811; Morav.; d. Salem, N.Y., Mar. 1811, a. 91.

GOTTLOB BUETTNER (Bittner), b. 1717; arriv. Bethlehem, Pa., 26 Oct. 1741; Ord. Oley, Pa., 11 Feb. 1741/2; sett. Heidelberg (Berks) Pa., 1742–1742; sett. Marion (Berks) Pa., Chh. at Stouchsburg, Mar. 1742–1742; sett. Shekomeko (Dutchess) N.Y., Indian Chh., 1742–1745; Morav.; d. Pine Plain, Shekomeko, N.Y., 1745, a. 28.

COMER BULLOCK, b. 1734; sett. Stanford (Dutchess) N.Y., Oct. 1759–1778; sett. Stanford (2nd Bapt. Chh.), 9 May 1778–1812; Bapt.; d. Stanford, N.Y., 10 June 1812, a. 78.

EPHRAIM BULLOCK, sett. Stanford, N.Y., Oct. 1759-1778; Bapt.

Bishop CHRISTIAN BURKHOLDER, b. Switzerland, 1 June 1746, son of Christian Burkholder; arriv. Philadelphia, July 1755; Ord. minister, 1770; Ord. Bishop, 1780; sett. West Earl (Lanc.) Pa., Groffdale Chh., 1770-1809; sett. East Earl (Lanc.) Weaverland Chh., 1770-1809; Menn.; d. Groffdale, Pa., 13 May 1809, a. 63.

Bishop HANS BURKHOLDER (Burghholtzer, Burgholzer), preacher in Langnau, Emmenthal, Berne, Switzerland; imprisoned July 1708-18 Mar. 1710; left Mannheim, Germany for Pa., 1717; arriv. Philadelphia, 24 Aug. 1717; sett. Pequea (Lanc.) Pa., New Danville meeting house, 1717-1745; Menn.; d. Pequea, Pa., ca. 1745.

ULRICH BURKHOLDER, brother of Bishop Christian Burkholder of Groffdale; sett. Brecknock (Lanc.) Pa., *before* 1778-1804; Menn.; d. 1804.

MATTHIAS BURNET, D.D., b. Battle Hill, N. J., 24 Jan. 1749, A.B., Princeton, 1769, A.M., 1772, D.D., 1802; A.M., Y.C., 1785; Ord. Jamaica, L. I., N.Y., Apr. 1775; sett. Jamaica, 1774-May 1785; inst. Norwalk, Conn., 2 Nov. 1785-1806; Presb.; d. Norwalk, Conn., 30 June 1806, a. 58.

JAMES BURNSIDE, b. Meath, Leinster, Ireland, June 1708; arriv. Ga., 1743; accountant for the Trustees of the colony of Savannah; minister at The Minisinks (the area between Delaware Water Gap, Pa., Paulin's Kill, N. J., and Wallkill, N. J.), 1745-1749; Bethlehem, Pa., Brodhead Settlement at Dansbury, Pa., 1747-1749; Wallkill (Sussex) N. J., 1747-1749; farmer; member, Provincial Assembly of Pa., 1752; Moravian; d. near Bethlehem, Pa., Aug. 1755.

President AARON BURR, A.M., b. Fairfield, Conn., 4 Jan. 1715/6, son of Daniel and Elizabeth Burr; A.B., Y.C., 1735, A.M.; Ord. Newark, N. J., 25 Jan. 1737/8; sett. Newark, N. J., 1736-1755; Princeton, N. J., 1st. Chh., 1756-1757; Trustee, Princeton, 1746-1748, President, 9 Nov. 1748-1757 (Princeton was then called the College of New Jersey); he was father of Lieut.-Col. Aaron Burr (1756-1836), Vice-President of the United States, 1801-1805; Presb.; d. Princeton, N. J., 24 Sept. 1757, a. 42.

BLACKLEACH BURRITT, b. Huntington, Conn., son of Peleg and Elizabeth (Blackleach) Burritt; Ord. Pound Ridge (Westchester) N.Y., 16 June 1774; sett. Pound Ridge, 1772-1 Apr. 1776; taken prisoner in the Rev. War by the British, 18 June 1779-Aug. 1781; later supplied churches in Conn., N.Y., and Vt.; Cong.; Presb.; d. Winhall, Vt., 1794, a. ca. 50.

JOHN BURROWS, b. Taunton, Somersetshire, England; Ord. Taunton, Eng.; arriv. Philadelphia, Nov. 1711; sett. Middletown (Monmouth) N. J., 1713-1738; d. Middletown, N. J., 1738.

ABNER BUSH, inst. Goshen (Orange) N.Y., Fall of 1758; sett. Goshen, 1758-1766; Marlborough (Ulster) N.Y., 1766-1773; Newburgh (Orange) N.Y., 1774-1774; Presb.

ANDREW BUSSE, arriv. N.Y., N.Y., 2 June 1756; sett. Bethlehem, Pa., as chaplain, 1756–1776; Moravian.

JOACHIM BUSSE, Ord. in Europe; minister at Berlin, Germany; arriv. N.Y., N.Y., 24 Sept. 1751; sett. St. Thomas, West Indies, 1751; Moravian.

WILLIAM BUTCHER, b. Birmingham, Pa., 18 May 1699; sett. Birmingham (Delaware) Pa., and Newlin (Chester) Pa., 1719–1721; sett. Cohansey, N. J., 1721–1724; Bapt.; d. Cohansey, N. J., 12 Dec. 1724, a. 26, s.p.

ELIAB BYRAM, A.B., b. Bridgewater, Mass., son of the Hon. Maj. Ebenezer and Hannah (Hayward) Byram; A.B., H.C., 1740; Ord. Mendham (Morris) N. J., May 1744; sett. Mendham, N. J., Oct. 1743–1751; inst. Amwell (Hunterdon) N. J., Chh. at Reaville, 14 Aug. 1751; sett. Amwell, N. J., 25 June 1751–1754; Presb.; d. Amwell, N. J., Apr. 1754.

JAMES CALDWELL, A.M., b. Cub Creek (Charlotte) Va., 17 Apr. 1734, son of John Caldwell; A.B., Princeton, 1759, A.M., Trustee, 1768–1781, clerk of the Board, 1772–1781, Treasurer, 1777–1779; Ord. New Brunswick Presbytery, 17 Sept. 1760; preached in the Carolinas, 1760–1761; sett. Elizabethtown, N. J., Mar. 1762–1776; Chaplain, 3rd N. J. Battalion, Continental Army, 1776–1781; Assistant Deputy Quartermaster-General of the Continental Army; an eligible member of the Society of the Cincinnati; member, N. J. Senate, 1781; Presb.; d. (killed) Elizabethtown, N. J., 24 Nov. 1781 (GS); his wife was also shot by a British soldier.

Bishop JOHN CHRISTOPHER FREDERICK CAMMERHOFF, b. Hillersleben, near Magdeburg, 28 July 1721; studied at Bergen; grad. U. Jena, 1738; Lindheim, 1744; Prof. at the Theol. Sem. at Marienborn, Wetteravia; Ord. Zeyst, Holland, May 1746; consecrated Bishop at London, Sept. 1746; arriv. Lewes, Del., 28 Dec. 1746; sett. Bethlehem, Pa., 10 Jan. 1746/7–1751, as assistant to Bishop Spangenberg; preached in Pa., N. J., and Md.; Morav.; d. Bethlehem, Pa., 28 Apr. 1751, a. 30.

JOHN CAMPANIUS, b. Stockholm, Sweden, 15 Aug. 1601, son of John Peter Campanius; U. of Upsala; Ord. 19 July 1633; arriv. at Fort Christiana on the Delaware, 15 Feb. 1642/3; sett. Tinicum (Bucks) Pa., New Goeteborg Chh., 1643–1648; Chester, Pa., Upland Chh., 1643–1648; Wilmington, Del., Old Swedes Chh., and New Castle, Del., 1643–1648; returned to Sweden, 16 May 1648; Chaplain to the Admiralty; Rector at Frosthuelt and Hernevi, Sweden, 1648–1683; Sw. Luth.; d. Stockholm, 17 Sept. 1683.

ALEXANDER CAMPBELL, K.B. for Va., 30 Dec. 1725; S.P.G. missionary at Appoquinimink, Del., 1726–1729; Middletown, Del., St. Anne's Chh., 1726–1729; Setauket, L. I., N.Y., Caroline Chh., 1729–1732; Ep.

COLIN CAMPBELL, A.M., b. Earnhill, Scotland, 1707, son of Colin Campbell; ed. Inverness; A.M., Aberdeen, 1729; K.B., Isle of Nevis,

W.I., 9 Feb. 1737/8; sett. Burlington, N. J., St. Mary's Chh., 10 May 1738–1766; S.P.G. missionary; Bristol (Bucks) Pa., Chh. of St. James the Greater, 1741–1766; Mt. Holly (Burlington) N. J., St. Andrew's Chh., 1742–1766; his portrait hangs in St. Mary's Chh., Burlington, N. J.; Ep.; d. Burlington, N. J., 9 Aug. 1766.

JAMES CAMPBELL (See *Colonial Clergy of North Carolina*), b. Campbellton-on-Kintyre, Argyleshire, Scotland; came to America, 1730; lic. 1735; Ord. 3 Aug. 1742; sett. Tinicum (Bucks) Pa., 1738–1749 (inst. 24 May 1744); Tohickon (Bucks) Pa., 1739–1749; Newtown (Bucks) Pa., 1739–1749; Durham (Bucks) Pa., 1742–1749; Forks of the Delaware, Pa., 1742–1749; Greenwich (Warren) N. J., 1742–1749; Oxford (Warren) N. J., 1742–1749; Rocky Spring Chh., Letterkenney (Franklin) Pa., 1749–1757; Conococheague or Falling Spring Chh., Guilford (Franklin) Pa., 1749–1757; in 1757, he removed to N.C.; Presb.; d. Cape Fear, N.C., 1781.

JOHN CAMPBELL, b. Scotland, 1713; came to America, 1734; ed. at the Log College; lic. Presbytery of New Brunswick, 14 Oct. 1747; Ord. New Providence, 21 Nov. 1750; sett. Charlestown (Chester) Pa., 27 Oct. 1747–1753; Lower Providence (Montg.) Pa., 1747–1753; Brandywine Manor, Pa.; Norriton (Montg.) Pa., 1747–1753; Presb.; d. Providence, Pa., 1 May 1753, a. ca. 40 (GS).

JOHN CAMPBELL, b. Scotland, 1718; served on the island of Jamaica; Presb.; d. N.Y., N.Y., 21 June 1770, a. 52 (GS).

ROBERT CAMPBELL, Ord. Canaan (Litchfield) Conn., 20 Oct. 1761; sett. Canaan, 1761–1762; sett. Stillwater (near Bemis Heights), N.Y., 1762–1789; Cong.

DAVID CANDLER, sett. York (York) Pa., Christ Chh., 1743–1744; Hanover (York) Pa., St. Michael's Chh., 1743–1744; Conewago (Adams) Pa., 1743–1744; sett. Frederick (Fredk.), Md., 1743–1744; Monocacy Chh., Md., 1743–1744; his parish extended from the Susquehanna to the Potomac; Luth.; d. Hanover, Pa., Dec. 1744.

RICHARD CANER, A.M., b. Boston, Mass., 4 June 1717, son of Henry and Abigail Caner (brother of Henry Caner, D.D., of King's Chapel, Boston); A.B., Y.C., 1736, A.M.; Ord. London, Eng., Oct. 1741; sett. Norwalk, Conn., June 1742–1745; sett. Staten Island, N.Y., St. Andrew's Chh., 1745; Ep.; d. New York City, 14 Dec. 1745, a. 28, of smallpox.

JEAN CARLE, b. Nimes, France; arriv. N.Y., N.Y., 27 July 1754; original trustee of Columbia U.; inst. New York, N.Y., French Chh. of the Saint Esprit, 4 Aug. 1754–1764; sett. New Rochelle (Westchester) N.Y., French Chh., 1754–1764; resigned 23 May 1763; sailed for London, 17 Apr. 1764; Chaplain, French Hospital, London, England, 1764–1790; French Ref.

HUGH CARLISLE, prob. b. in Ireland; adm. to New Castle Presbytery, bef. Sept. 1735; sett. Newtown (Bucks) Pa. and Plumstead (Bucks)

Pa., June 1736–Nov. 1737; Amwell (Hunterdon) N.J. and Union (Hunterdon) N.J., Bethlehem Chh., Nov. 1737–1738; Lewes Presbytery, 14 Mar. 1738–1742; Presb. (It would seem that Hugh Carlisle who sett. at St. George's Parish (Harford) Md., 1744–1749; Ep. was the same man.)

JAMES CARMAN, b. Cape May, N.J., 1677; Ord. Hightstown (Mercer) N.J., 1745–1756; Bapt.; d. Hightstown, N.J., 28 Oct. 1756, a. 79.

JOHN CARMICHAEL, A.M., b. Tarbert, Argyleshire, Scotland, 17 Oct. 1728, son of Donald and Elizabeth (Alexander) Carmichael; came to America, 1737; A.B., Princeton, 1759, A.M.; Ord. Brandywine Manor (Chester) Pa., Forks of the Brandywine, 21 Apr. 1761–1785; Charlestown (Chester) Pa., 1763–1773; Presb.; d. Forks of the Brandywine, Pa., 15 Nov. 1785, a. 57.

CASPARUS CARPENTIER, prob. son of the Rev. Caspar Carpentier; minister at Amersfoort, Holland, 1650; Amsterdam, Holland, 1650; arriv. in America, 1657; sett. New Castle, Del. (Dutch Ref. Chh.), 1657–1684; he also supplied occasionally the French Chh. in New York City, 1657–1684; Dutch Ref.; d. New Castle, Del., 1684.

EZEKIEL CARRÉ (Carreus), matric. Geneva, 1670; minister of the Huguenot chhs. at Mirambeau and La Roche Chalais in France; came to America ca. 1673; sett. New York City, French Chh., 1673–1678; sett. Huguenot Chh. at Narragansett, R.I., 1686–1691; also occasionally supplied the French Huguenot Chh. in Boston; French Ref.; disappears after 1691.

ROBERT CARTER, A.M., b. 1721, son of William Carter of Kimmel, Flintshire, Wales; matric. Oriel Coll., Oxford, 7 June 1739, a. 18; A.B., 11 Feb. 1742/3, A.M., 1747; K.B. to New Providence, Bahamas, 27 Sept. 1749; sett. Perth Amboy (Middlesex) N.J., St. Peter's Chh., 1760–1762; Ep.

HENRY CARY, sett. Pawling (Dutchess) N.Y., 1766 (and possibly to 1770); Bapt.

WHEELER CASE, A.M., A.B., Princeton, 1755, A.M.; inst. Pleasant Valley (Dutchess) N.Y., 1765–1791; Charlotte, N.Y., near Albany, 1774; Poughkeepsie (Dutchess) N. Y., 1774–1774; Presb.; d. Pleasant Valley, N.Y., 31 Aug. 1791.

ISAAC CASSEL, b. 21 Aug. 1746; sett. Skippack (Montg.) Pa., 1774–1823; Menn.; d. Skippack, Pa., 2 Sept. 1823.

JULIUS CASSEL, b. Kriesheim, Germany, bef. 1681, son of Rev. Yillis Kassel; arriv. Pa., 16 Oct. 1727; Ord. betw. 1725 and 1738; sett. Skippack, Pa., 1730–1750; Menn.; d. Skippack, Pa., 1750.

ROBERT CATHCART, b. Ireland; received in New Castle Presbytery, 15 Apr. 1730; Ord. 1730; sett. Middletown (Del.) Pa., 1730–1754; sett. Brandywine Manor (New Castle) Del., 1730–1754, in Christiania

Hundred; sett. Wilmington, Del., 1740-1754; Presb.; d. Wilmington, Del., 1754.

SAMUEL CAVIN, b. Ireland, 1701; Ord. Greencastle (Franklin) Pa., 16 Nov. 1739; sett. Conococheague (Franklin) Pa., 16 Nov. 1737-Mar. 1738; Antrim, Greencastle, Pa., Mar. 1738/9-1749; Guilford, Falling Spring Chh. at Chambersburg, Mar. 1738/9-May 1741; Montgomery (Orange) N.Y., Good Will Chh., 26 May 1743-1744; Greencastle, Pa., 6 Nov. 1744-1749; North Middleton (Cumberland) Pa., Meeting House Springs Chh., 1745-1750; Lower Pennsborough (Cumberland) Pa., Silver Spring Chh., 1745-1750; Cumberland at Gettysburg, Pa., 1740-1741; Presb.; d. Silver Spring, Pa., 9 Nov. 1750, a. 49 (GS).

ISAAC CHALKER, A.M., b. Saybrook, Conn., 12 Sept. 1707, son of Lieut. Abraham and Deborah (Barber) Chalker; A.B., Y.C., 1728, A.M.; Ord. for Cornwall and Montgomery, N.Y., 1734; sett. Cornwall (Orange) N.Y., Bethlehem Presb. Chh., 1734-1743; Wallkill (Ulster) N.Y., 1734-1740; inst. Buckingham, Conn., Oct. 1744; sett. Buckingham, Dec. 1743-1765; sett. New Paltz (Ulster) N.Y., 1760-1760; Presb.; Dutch Ref.; d. Buckingham, Conn., 28 May 1765, a. 57.

THOMAS BRADBURY CHANDLER, D.D., b. Thompson, Woodstock, Conn., 26 Apr. 1726, son of William and Jemima (Bradbury) Chandler; A.B., Y.C., 1745, A.M.; A.M., Christ Chh. Coll., Oxford, 25 May 1753; D.D., Oxford, 23 Jan. 1766; A.M., Columbia U., 1758, D.D., Columbia U., 1767; Ord. by Bishop of London, 1751; lic., 20 Aug. 1751; K.B., N.J., 4 Sept. 1751; catechist, Elizabethtown, N.J., 1748-1750; sett. Elizabethtown, N.J., St. John's Chh., 3 Nov. 1751-1775; June 1785-1790; refugee to England, May 1775-1785; sett. Woodbridge, N.J., 1752-1763; d. Elizabethtown, N.J., 17 June 1790, a. 64.

JEDEDIAH CHAPMAN, A.M., b. East Haddam, Conn., 27 Sept. 1741, son of Robert and Mary (Church) Chapman; A.B., Y.C., 1762, A.M., Princeton U.; lic. 5 June 1764; Ord. Orange, N.J., at Newark Mountain, 22 July 1766-13 Aug. 1800; inst. Geneva, N.Y., 8 July 1812; sett. Geneva, N.Y., 1800-1813; Chaplain, N.J. regt., 1776; moderator of the synod of N.Y. and Pa., 1787; Presb.; d. Geneva, N.Y., 22 May 1813, a. 72.

RICHARD CHARLTON, A.B., K.B. for Leeward Islands, 4 Apr. 1730; sett. Newburgh (Orange) N.Y., St. George's Chh., 1730-1730; New Windsor, N.Y., 1730; Walden (Orange) N.Y., St. Andrew's Chh., 1732-1747, N.Y., N.Y., Trinity Chh., 1732-1746; Staten Island, N.Y., St. Andrew's Chh., 1747-1777; Ep.; d. Staten Island, N.Y., 1777.

PIERRE JOSEPH CHAUMONOT, S.J., b. Chatillon-sur-Seine, France, 1611; became a Jesuit at Rome, 1632; arriv. Quebec, 1 Aug. 1639; at Lake Huron, Sept. 1639; missionary among the Onondagas of N.Y., 1655-1657; sett. Syracuse, N.Y., St. Mary's Chapel, 1655-1657; founder of Lorette at St. Charles, Quebec; R.C.; d. Quebec, 21 Feb. 1693.

BENJAMIN CHESNUT, A.M., b. England; A.B., Princeton, 1751, A.M.; Ord. Woodbury (Glouc.), N.J., 3 Sept. 1751; sett. Woodbury, N.J., 1749-17 May 1753, 1766-1775; Gloucester (Camden) N.J., Timber Creek Chh. at Blackwood, 1750-1753, 1766-1775; Pennsneck (Salem) N.J., at Quihawken, 1749-1753; Charlestown (Chester) Pa., 1753-May 1763; Lower Providence (Montg.) Pa., Nov. 1753-May 1763; New Londonderry (Chester) Fagg's Manor Chh., 1753 ff.; Forks of the Delaware, Pa., 1753; Norriton (Montg.) Pa., 1758-1763; Berlin (Camden) N.J., at Waterford, 1766-1775; Presb.; d. Gloucester, N.J., 21 July 1775.

JAMES CLARK, sett. Flatbush, L.I., N.Y., at Midwout, 1685-1695; New Utrecht, L.I., N.Y., 1680-1695; Dutch Ref.

JESSE CLARK, A.B., b. New Haven, Conn., 21 Mar. 1728, son of Nathan and Phebe (Lines) Clark; A.B., Y.C., 1756; Ord. Austerlitz (Columbia) N.Y., 16 Apr. 1760-1780, as the 1st minister; Cong.; d. Austerlitz, N.Y., ca. 1800.

PHINEAS CLARK, sett. Pawling (Dutchess) N.Y., 1775 ff.; Bapt.

THOMAS CLARK, M.D., b. Scotland; M.D., U. of Glasgow; fought in the war against the Pretender, 1745-1746; liv. Stirling, Scotland, Apr. 1748; Ord. Ballybay (Monaghan) Ireland, 23 July 1751-1764; arriv. N.Y., N.Y., 28 July 1764; sett. Salem (Washington) N.Y., 1764-1779; Perth (Fulton) N.Y., New Perth Chh., 1764-1779; Cambridge (Washington) N.Y., 1769-1779; Cedar Spring and Long Cane Chhs., S.C., inst. 1786; sett. 1779-1793; physician; Associate Presb.; d. Long Cane, S.C., 25 Dec. 1793.

JOHN CLARKE, A.B., b. 1718; A.B., Princeton, 1759; lic. 1759; Ord. 1760; sett. Allen (Northampton) Pa., 1762-1767; inst. Upper Mount Bethel (Northampton) Pa., Forks North Chh., 13 Oct. 1762-4 Nov. 1767; sett. Bethel (Harford) Md., Upper Node Forest Chh., 1769-1781; sett. Bethel and Lebanon, Pa., 1781-1797; Presb.; d. western Pa., 1797.

JOSIAS CLARKE, A.B., b. Tarvin, Cheshire, England, 1622, son of the Rev. Sabaoth Clarke; matric. New Inn Hall, Oxford, 9 Apr. 1641, a. 19; A.B., Queens' Coll., Oxford, 1644/5; Rector of Tattershall, Cheshire, 1658; Chaplain of the Fort at New York, N.Y., 1684-1686; sett. Boston, Mass., King's Chapel, asst. min., 1686-1687; ret. to England, 7 Apr. 1687; Vicar of Broxbourne, Herts., 1689-1694; Ep.

RICHARD SAMUEL CLARKE, A.M. (See *Colonial Clergy of New England*, p. 57), sett. North Salem (Westchester) N.Y., St. James's Chh., 1764-1766; Ep.

JAMES CLARKSON, b. Scotland, ca. 1738; came to America, 1772; Ord. Chanceford (York) Pa., Guinston Chh., 1773; sett. Chanceford, Pa., 25 Aug. 1773-Mar. 1808; Assoc. Presb.; d. Valley Field, Chanceford, Pa., 30 Oct. 1811, a. 73.

THOMAS CLAYTON, K.B. to Md., 11 Jan. 1697/8; had been Rector of Crofton, Yorkshire; sett. Philadelphia, Pa., Christ Chh., bef.

16 Sept. 1698–1699; 1st Ep. min. to come to Pa.; d. Sassafras, Md., 1699, of yellow fever.

JOHN CLEMENT, b. Great Britain; Ord. Rehoboth (Somerset) Md., June 1719; sett. Rehoboth, 1719–1720; sett. Gloucester (Camden) N.J., Timber Creek Chh. at Blackwood, 1720–1750; sett. Pilesgrove, N.J., 1720–1741; Presb.; d. 1766.

Bishop VALENTINE CLEMMER, Ord. preacher and Bishop in Europe; arriv. in Pa., 1717; sett. Milford (Bucks) Pa., Great Swamp Chh., 1717–1771; Bishop in Pa.,; living 15 June 1771; Menn.; said to have d. in Lancaster co., Pa., and to have been buried at Mellingers.

JOHN CLEVERLY, A.M., b. Braintree, Mass., 9 Mar. 1695/6, son of Lieut. John and Hannah (Savil) Cleverly; A.B., H.C., 1715, A.M., 1718; schoolteacher at Braintree, 1715–1726; Georgetown, Me., 1728; Freetown, 1730; Morristown, N.J. (then West Hanover), Sept. 1735; apparently not ordained; sett. New Providence (Union) N.J., Turkey Christian Chh., 1737–1739; Rahway, N.J., 1741–1742; Presb.; d. Rahway, N.J., 31 Dec. 1776, unm.

DAVID CLOSE, A.M., b. North Salem, N.Y., 1742/3, son of Solomon and Deborah (Brush) Close; A.B., Y.C., 1771, A.M.; Ord. Patterson (Putnam) N.Y., 24 Nov. 1772–1783; sett. Carmel (Putnam) N.Y., 1774–1783; Presb.; d. Patterson, N.Y., 19 Mar. 1783, a. 40 (GS).

JOHN CLOSE, A.M., b. Greenwich, Conn., 1737, son of Solomon Close and brother of David Close, q.v.; A.B., Princeton, 1763, A.M.; A.M. (hon.) Y.C., 1771; Ord. Huntington, L.I., N.Y., 30 Oct. 1766; sett. Huntington, L.I., N.Y., 1766–4 Apr. 1773; New Windsor (Orange) N.Y., 1773–1796; Newburgh, N.Y., 1773–1796; Cornwall (Orange) N.Y., Bethlehem Chh., 1773–1796; sett. Waterford (Saratoga) N.Y. and Middletown, N.Y. (both Dutch Ref. chhs.), 1796–1804; Presb.; d. Waterford, N.Y., 1813.

JOHN CLUBB, b. Wales; K.B. for Pa., 3 Apr. 1704; asst. min. and schoolmaster, Philadelphia, Pa., Christ Chh., 1704–1708; sett. Oxford (Chester) Pa., Trinity Chh., 1708–1710, 1714–1715; S.P.G. missionary; sett. Middletown, Del. and Appoquinimink, Del., 1712–1713; sett. Radnor in Newtown (Del.) Pa., St. David's Chh., Sept. 1714–Dec. 1715, as first minister of the chh.; Ep.; d. Radnor, Pa., 25 Dec. 1715.

GERHARD DANIEL COCK, came to America, 1763; sett. Rhinebeck Flats (Dutchess) N.Y., D.R. Chh., 1763–1790; Kingsbury (Dutchess) N.Y., 1763–1790; Rhinebeck, N.Y., G.R. Chh., 1764–1790; Rhinebeck Flats (Dutchess) N.Y., 1764–1790; Germantown (Columbia) N.Y., D.R. Chh., 1764–1790; New Paltz (Ulster) N.Y., D.R. Chh., 1768–1770; Claverack (Columbia) N.Y., D.R. Chh., 1770–1776; Linlithgow (Columbia) N.Y., D.R. Chh., 1770–1779; Pine Plains (Dutchess) N.Y., Red or Koch's Chh. at Pulvers, 1772–1790; Germ. Ref., but preached mostly in Dutch Ref. chhs.; d. Germantown, N.Y., 1790.

HENRICUS COENS, Ord. Amsterdam, Holland, 4 Sept. 1725; sailed for America, 7 Oct. 1725; sett. Belleville (Essex) N.J., Chh. at Second River, 1725-1730; Passaic (Passaic) N.J., Chh. at Acquackanonk, 1726-1735; Pompton Plains (Morris) N.J., Chh. at Pequannock, 1726-1735; Ponds (Bergen) N.J., Chh. at Oakland, 1726-1735; Dutch Ref.; d. N.J., 14 Feb. 1735.

BENJAMIN COLES, b. Oyster Bay, L.I., N.Y., 6 Apr. 1737; sett. Stratfield, Conn., 1768-1774; Hopewell (Mercer) N.J., 15 Oct. 1774-1781; Scotch Plains (Union) N.J., 1781-1783; Oyster Bay, L.I., N.Y., 1783-1810; Bapt.; d. Oyster Bay, L.I., N.Y., Aug. 1810, a. 73.

THOMAS COLGAN, A.B., b. Dublin, Ireland, 1702, son of John Colgan, weaver; pensioner, Trinity Coll., Dublin, 6 June 1718, a. 16; A.B., Trinity Coll., Dublin, 1722; K.B. for N.Y., 2 June 1726; S.P.G. missionary, 1726; arriv. N.Y., N.Y., 1726; sett. N.Y., N.Y., Trinity Chh., 1726-1732; sett. Jamaica, L.I., N.Y., Grace Chh., 1733-1755; Flushing, L.I., N.Y., St. George's Chh., 1731-1755; Newtown, L.I., N.Y., 1733-1755; Ep.; d. Jamaica, L.I., N.Y., Dec. 1755.

NICHOLAS COLLIN, D.D., b. Sweden, 1745; Ord. Sweden, ca. 1770; D.D., U. of Pa., 1788; Rector, Swedesboro (Glouc.) N.J., Trinity Chh. on Raccoon Creek, now Ep., 1773-1783; Raccoon, N.J., 1773-1783; Pennsneck (Salem) N.J., St. George's Chh., now Ep., 1773-1783; sett. Wicaco, Kingsessing and Upper Merion, all in Pa., 1783-1831; Sw. Luth.; d. Wicaco, Pa., Oct. 1831, a. 86.

BRUIN ROMCAS COMINGOE, Ord. Lunenburg, Nova Scotia, The Dutch Calvinistic Presbyterian Congregation, 3 July 1770-1819; Germ. Ref.

JOHN CONRAD, b. 6 June 1681; sett. Germantown, Pa., 1712-1758; Menn.; d. Germantown, Pa., 1758.

Commissary SAMUEL COOKE, A.M., b. Yarmouth, Eng., 1723, son of Thomas Cooke; pensioner, 9 Nov. 1743, a. 19; A.B., Gonville & Caius, Cambridge U., 1747/8; A.M., U. of Pa. (hon.), 1760; Ord. by Bishop of Norwich, 23 Sept. 1750; lic. 3 June 1751; K.B. for N.J., 6 June 1751; Curate, Beccles, co. Suffolk, England; S.P.G. missionary at Freehold (Monmouth) N.J., St. Peter's Chh., Sept. 1751-1765; Spotswood, N.J., 1751-1765; Shrewsbury (Monmouth) N.J., Christ Chh., 1751-1775; Middletown (Monmouth) N.J., Christ Chh., 1751-1775, and at South River, Cranbury and Matchaponex, N.J.; ret. to Eng., 24 May 1775-1784; sett. St. John's, New Brunswick, 1785-1786; sett. Fredericktown, N.B., Aug. 1786-1795; Commissary to N.B., 1790-1791; Ep.; d. St. John's River, N.B., 23 May 1795 (drowned).

THOMAS COOMBE, D.D., b. Philadelphia, Pa., 12 Oct. 1747, son of Thomas and Sarah (Rutter) Coombe; U. of Pa., 1766; D.D., Trinity Coll., Dublin; Ord. London by the Bishop of London, 1771; K.B. for Pa., 29 Oct. 1771; sett. Philadelphia, Pa., United chhs. (Christ Chh. and St. Peter's Chh.), 30 Nov. 1772-7 July 1778; Chaplain to Lord Carlisle in Ireland; Rector, Donagh Henry, Ireland, 1781–1783; Chaplain to the King, 1794; Prebendary, Canterbury, 1800; Rector, London, England, St. Michael's Queenhithe, and Trinity the Less, 1808–1822; member Am. Phil. Soc., 1773; Ep.; d. London, England, 15 Aug. 1822.

JOHN COOPER, sett. Trenton, N.J., Green Street Chh., 1776–1776; Meth.

MYLES COOPER, D.C.L., LL.D., b. 1737, son of William Cooper of Millum, Cumberland, England; matric. Queen's Coll., Oxford, 27 Feb. 1753, a. 16, A.B., 1756, A.M., 1760; D.C.L., Oxford U., 25 Feb. 1767; LL.D., Columbia, 1768; K.B. to N.Y., 11 Aug. 1762; came to America, 1762; Prof. of Moral Philosophy, Columbia, 1762–1763; President, Columbia, 1763–1775; returned to England, 1775; sett. Edinburgh, Scotland; Ep.; d. Edinburgh, Scotland, 1785.

ROBERT COOPER, D.D., b. Northern Ireland, ca. 1732; A.B., Princeton, 1763; D.D., Dickinson Coll., 1792; Ord. Middle Spring, Pa., 21 Nov. 1765; sett. Southampton (Cumb.) Pa., Middle Spring Chh., 1765–12 Apr. 1797; sett. West Nottingham (Chester) Pa., 1765–1797; sett. Lower West Nottingham (Cecil) Md., Lower Octoraro Chh., 1765–1797; Captain, Pennsylvania Volunteers, 1776; Trustee, Dickinson Coll., 1783–1805; Presb.; d. Middle Spring (near Shippensburg) Pa., 5 Apr. 1805, a. 72.

JOHN CORBLEY, b. Great Britain or Ireland, 1733; sett. western Pa., 1768; sett. Uniontown (Fayette) Pa., 1770–1803; sett. Goshen, Redstone Settlement, Pa., 1775–1803; Bapt.; d. Uniontown, Pa., 9 June 1803, a. 70.

Domine CORNELISON, sett. English Neighborhood (Bergen) N.J., 1770–1776, near Ridgefield, N.J.; Dutch Ref.

JEAN COURDIL, b. Nimes, France; Ord. London, 1683; officiated at the home of the Sieur La Cassagne near Nimes; sett. St. Paul's Cathedral, London, England, 1683–1686; sett. N.Y., N.Y., 1686–1689; returned to England, 1689; taken a prisoner to Nantes; sent to Copenhagen; Fr. Huguenot.

DAVID COWELL, A.M., b. Wrentham, Mass., 12 Dec. 1704, son of Joseph and Martha (Fales) Cowell; A.B., H.C., 1732, A.M.; Trustee, Princeton, 1748–1760; acting President, Princeton, 1757–1758; Ord. Trenton, N.J., 3 Nov. 1736; sett. Trenton, 1st Chh., 1735–11 Mar. 1760; Hopewell, N.J. (Ewing Chh., 1736–1760; Pennington Chh., 1736–1739); New Side Presb.; unm.; d. Trenton, N.J., 1 Dec. 1760, a. 56 (GS).

NICHOLAS COX, b. New Castle co., Del., 24 Mar. 1742; lic. Philadelphia, 1771; Ord. Wantage (Sussex) N.J., 15 Apr. 1772–1783; sett. Kingwood (at Baptistown) N.J., 4 Nov. 1784–1792; Bapt.

CORNELIUS COZINE, b. Long Island, N.Y., 4 Nov. 1718; sett. New Jersey, ca. 1751; was living in Somerset co., N.J., 1762; sett. Conewago (Adams) Pa., 1772–1788; Dutch Ref.

Colonial Clergy of the Middle Colonies

GEORGE CRAIG, A.B., b. Scotland; prob. A.B., U. of Aberdeen 28 May 1750; curate to Dr. Bristowe in England; lic. for N.J., 1 Sept. 1750; K.B. for Pa., 12 Sept. 1750, as an itinerant missionary of the S.P.G. in Pa. and N.J.; landed at Philadelphia, 17 May 1751; missionary at Alexandria (Hunterdon) N.J., St. Andrew's Chh., 1751-1753; Amwell (Hunterdon) N.J., St. Thomas's Chh., at Lambertville, 1751-1753; Lancaster, Pa. (where he resided), St. James's Chh., 1751-1758; Churchtown, 1751-1759; Salisbury, St. John's at Compassville, 1751-1759; Caernarvon, Bangor Chh., 1751-1759; and Carlisle (Cumb.) Pa., St. John's Chh., 1751-1757; Huntington (Adams) Pa., at York Springs, 1751-1757; and he was settled in the following towns in Delaware co., Pa., Chester, St. Paul's Chh., 1759-1781; Chichester, St. Martin's Chh., 1759-1783; Concord, St. John's Chh., 1759-1771; and Marcus Hook, St. Martin's Chh., 1759-1783; Ep.; d. Marcus Hook, Pa., after 1783.

ALEXANDER CRAIGHEAD (See *Colonial Clergy of Virginia*, p. 12), b. ca. 1706, son of the Rev. Thomas Craighead, q.v.; lic. 8 Oct. 1734; Ord. Bart (Lanc.) Pa., Middle Octoraro Chh., 18 Nov. 1735-1741; North Middleton (Cumb.) Pa., Meeting House Springs Chh., 1734-1735; was a Cameronian, 1745-1753; sett. in Va. and N.C., 1749-1766, being the only minister in 1766 betw. the Yadkin and Catawba rivers, and was the third minister to sett. in N.C.; author of a pamphlet on political independence, 1743; Presb.; d. Rocky Creek, N.C., Mar. 1766.

JOHN CRAIGHEAD, A.B., b. 1742, A.B., Princeton, 1763; inst. Letterkenney (Franklin) Pa., Rocky Spring Chh., 13 Apr. 1768-9 Apr. 1799; Chaplain and Captain, Pennsylvania Volunteers, 1776 ff.; Presb., d. Letterkenney, Pa., 20 Apr. 1799.

THOMAS CRAIGHEAD, A.M., b. Donoughmore, co. Donegal, Ireland, son of Rev. Robert and Agnes (Hart) Craighead; studied medicine; A.M., Edinburgh U., 28 July 1691; Ord. Donegal, Ireland, 1698; minister of the Presb. chhs. of Donegal and Ballyshannon, co. Donegal, Ireland, 1698-1714; arriv. at Boston, Oct. 1714, in the ship "Thomas and Jane"; sett. Freetown, Mass., Jan. 1715-1723; sett. Brandywine, Del., 1724-1730; sett. Mill Creek (New Castle) Del., White Clay Creek, Del., inst. 22 Sept. 1724-1731; sett. Salisbury (Lanc.) Pa., Pequea Chh., inst. Oct. 1733-7 Sept. 1736; sett. Newville (Cumb.) Pa., Hopewell Chh. at Big Spring, 1737-inst. Oct. 1738-1739; Southampton (Cumb.) Pa., Middle Spring Chh., 17 Nov. 1737-1739; Letterkenney (Franklin) Pa., Rocky Spring Chh., 1738-1739; physician; Moderator, Presb. synod, 1726; Presb.; d. Newville, Pa., April 1739.

JOHN CROSS, b. Scotland; Ord. 1732; sett. Basking Ridge, Bernard, N.J., 1732-1742; sett. Staten Island, N.Y., 1732-1742; suspended 23 June 1742; in Oct. 1746, he asked to be restored; Presb.; d. bef. 1750.

ROBERT CROSS, b. near Ballykelly, Ireland, 1689; ed. in Ireland; came to America, 1717; Ord. New Castle, Del., 19 Sept. 1719; sett. New Castle, 1st Chh., 1718-May 1722; Jamaica, L.I., N.Y., 1st Chh., 10 Oct.

1723–May 1737; Philadelphia, Pa., 1st Presb. Chh., inst. 10 Nov. 1737–22 June 1758; leader of the Old Side Presb.; d. Philadelphia, Pa., 9 Aug. 1766, s.p. (GS).

HENRY CROSSLEY, Ord. Schooley's Mountain (Morris) N.J., 1753–1755; Woolverton; Knowlton (Warren) N.J., 1763–1766; Mt. Bethel (Warren) N.J., 1769–1770; Manahawkin (Monmouth) N.J., 1774–1775; Bapt.

ALEXANDER CUMMING, A.M., b. Freehold, N.J., 1726, son of Elder Robert Cumming; ed. by his uncle, Rev. Dr. Samuel Blair; A.M. (hon.) Princeton, 1760; A.M. (hon.) H.C., 1761; Ord. New York, N.Y., 1st Presb. Chh., Oct. 1750; sett. N.Y., N.Y., 1750–25 Oct. 1753; New Brunswick (Middlesex) N.J., 1753–1761; inst. Boston, Mass., Old South Chh., 25 Feb. 1761–1763; 1st Presb. minister to preach within the bounds of Tennessee; d. Boston, Mass., 25 Aug. 1763, a. 37.

ARCHIBALD CUMMINGS, K.B. for Pa., 24 Jan. 1725/6; Rector Philadelphia, Pa., Christ Chh., 9 Sept. 1726–Apr. 1741; Ep.; d. Philadelphia, Pa., 19 Apr. 1741.

WILLIAM CURRIE, b. Scotland, 1710; ed. U. of Glasgow; a dissenting minister in Pa.; K.B. to Pa., 7 Oct. 1736; sett. as S.P.G. missionary, Newtown (Del.) Pa., St. David's Chh. at Radnor, 1736–1783; Caernarvon (Lanc.) Pa., Bangor Chh., 23 May 1739–1743; Lower Providence (Montg.) Pa., St. James's Chh. at Evansburg, 1736–1776; resigned 13 May 1776; Whitemarsh (Montg.) Pa., St. Thomas's Chh., 1742–1743; Tredyffryn (Chester) Pa., St. Peter's Chh., Great Valley, 1751–1776; res. 1776; Ep.; d. Radnor (near Valley Forge) Pa., 1803, a. 93.

ANTONIUS CURTENIUS, b. Drenthe, Netherlands, 1698; matric. Groningen, 4 Oct. 1724; matric. Leyden, 23 Aug. 1725, a. 26; Ord. Amsterdam, Holland, 3 Oct. 1729; arriv. N.Y., N.Y., 24 Oct. 1730; sett. Hackensack (Bergen) N.J., Chh. at New Barbadoes, 1730–1755; sett. Schraalenburg (Bergen) N.J., 1737–1755; supply at Paramus (Bergen) N.J., 1737–1748; sett. Brooklyn, Bushwick, Flatbush, Flatlands, Gravesend and New Utrecht, all on L.I., N.Y., 1755–1756; Dutch Ref.; d. L.I., N.Y., 1756.

THOMAS CURTIS, b. 1685; Elder at Baptisttown, 1738–1745; Ord. Kingswood, Baptisttown Chh., 28 Oct. 1745–1749; Bapt.; d. Kingswood, N.J., 28 Apr. 1749, a. 64.

JOHN CUTHBERTSON, b. Scotland, 1719; Ord. Scotland; missionary in Ireland; arriv. New Castle, Delaware, 5 Aug. 1751; sett. Muddy Run (York) Pa., 1751–1791; Cumberland (Adams) Pa., Rock Creek Chh., 1751–1773; Pequea (Lanc.) Pa., 1752–1791; Bart (Lanc.) Pa., Octoraro Chh., 1752–1791; Martic (Lanc.) Pa., Muddy Run Chh., 1752–1791; Lower Chancefield (York) Pa., 26 Mar. 1771–1791; only Assoc. Ref. Presb. minister in America, 1752–1773; Assoc. Ref. Presb.; d. Bart, Pa., 10 Mar. 1791, a. 72 (GS).

LEONARD CUTTING, D.D., b. Great Yarmouth, Norfolk co., England, 1724, son of Leonard Cutting; A.B., Pembroke Coll., Cambridge, 1747/8; A.M., Columbia, 1758; D.D.; Tutor, Columbia Coll., N.Y., 1756–1763; Ord. London, 1763; lic. for N.J., 21 Dec. 1763; K.B. for N.J., 9 Feb. 1764; sett. New Brunswick (Middlesex) N.J., Christ Chh., 1764–1766; sett. Piscataway (Middlesex) N.J., St. James's Chh., 1764–1766; Rector, Hempstead, L.I., N.Y., St. George's Chh., 1766–1782; Rector, Snow Hill, Md., 1784–1785; Rector, Newbern, N.C., Christ Chh., 1785–1793; d. New York, N.Y., 25 Jan. 1794, a. 70.

CLAUDE DABLON, S.J., b. Dieppe, France, Feb. 1618; entered the Jesuit Order, 1639; came to Canada, 1655; missionary to the Onondagas, Syracuse, N.Y., St. Mary's Chapel, 1655–1657; at Hudson Bay, Canada, 1661; went to Lake Superior with Pere Marquette; founded Sault Ste Marie mission; Superior General of all Canadian missions, 1670–1680, 1686–1693; R.C.; d. Quebec, P.Q., 3 May 1697.

NAPHTALI DAGGETT, D.D., b. Attleborough, Mass., 8 Sept. 1727, son of Ebenezer and Mary (Blackinton) Daggett; A.B., Y.C., 1748, A.M.; A.M., (hon.) H.C., 1771; S.T.D., Princeton, 1774; Ord. Smithtown, L.I., N.Y., Chh. at Nissequoque (Presb.), 18 Sept. 1751; sett. Smithtown, 1749–6 Nov. 1755; inst. Prof. of Divinity, Y.C., 4 Mar. 1756–1780; Pres., pro temp., Y.C., Oct. 1766–Mar. 1777; Cong.-Presb.; d. New Haven, Conn., 25 Nov. 1780, a. 54.

PIERRE DAILLÉ, b. ca. 1648; Prof. at Saumur, France; exiled; came to New York, ca. 1683 (said to have been sent out to America by the Bishop of London); sett. N.Y., N.Y., First Fr. Ref. Chh., 1683–1696; New Paltz (Ulster) N.Y., 1683–1696; Hackensack (Bergen) N.J., 1683–1696; Staten Island, N.Y., South Side and Fresh Kills Fr. Ref. Chhs., 1683–1688; N.Y., N.Y., Fr. Ref. Chh. of the Saint Esprit, 1683–1686; sett. Boston, Mass., Fr. Huguenot Chh., 1696–1715; French Ref.-Huguenot; d. Boston, Mass., 20 May 1715, a. ca. 66.

SIMON DAKIN, b. Concord, Mass., 27 Jan. 1720/1, son of Simon and Huldah Dakin; Ord. Northeasttown (Dutchess) N.Y., 1753–1803; Franklin, N.Y., 1751–1773; Bapt.; d. Fishkill, N.Y., 19 Sept. 1803, a. 82.

FREDERICK DALLIKER, b. Zurich, Switzerland, 27 Feb. 1738, son of an artist (possibly of Huguenot descent: De la Cour); Ord. Zurich, 1757; Chaplain of a French regt., 1760–1766; arriv. Philadelphia, Oct. 1767; sett. Lebanon (Hunterdon) N.J., Rockaway Chh., 6 Nov. 1768–1782; sett. Amwell (Hunt.) N.J., 1768–1770; sett. Alexandria, (Hunt.) N.J., 1768–1782; Tewksbury (Hunt.) N.J., Fox Hill Chh. at Fairmount, 1769–1782; sett. German Valley (Morris) N.J., at Washington, 1768–1781, 1782–1784; sett. Stillwater (Sussex) N.J., 12 Oct. 1769–1782; and after the Rev. War: Lower Milford (Lehigh) Pa., Great Swamp Chh., 1781–1784; New Hanover (Montg.) Pa., Falkner's Swamp Chh., 1783–1799; Upper Hanover (Montg.) Pa., New Goshenhoppen Chh., 1782–1784; Vincent (Chester) Pa., 1783–1799; Germ. Ref.; d. Falkner's Swamp, Pa., 15 Jan. 1799, a. 60.

Colonial Clergy of the Middle Colonies

JOHN DARBEE, M.D., perhaps b. Canterbury, Conn., 1723, son of William and Elizabeth (Spalding) Darbee; A.B., Y.C., 1748, A.M., 1753; M.D., Dartmouth Coll., 1782; lic. 18 Apr. 1749; stated supply, Lower Aquebogue and Mattituck (both in Southold) L.I., N.Y., 1749-1751; Ord. Oyster Ponds, L.I., N.Y., 10 Nov. 1757; sett. Connecticut Farms (Union) N.J., 1758-1760; sett. Hanover (Morris) N.J., Parsippany Chh., 1760-1767, 1770-1773; physician; Cong.-Presb.; d. Parsippany, N.J., Dec. 1805, a. 80.

JAMES DAVENPORT, A.M., b. Stamford, Conn., 1716, son of the Rev. John and Elizabeth (Morris) (Maltby) Davenport; A.B., Y.C., 1732, A.M.; A.M., Princeton, 1749; lic. 8 Oct. 1735; Ord. Southold, L.I., N.Y., 1st Chh. at Cutchogue, 26 Oct. 1738-1743; founded the Separatist Chh. in New London, Conn., 6 Mar. 1743-1744; member of the New Brunswick Presbytery, 22 Sept. 1746; sett. Amwell, N. J., 1746-1747; sett. Lawrenceville, N.J. (Chh. at Maidenhead), inst. 22 Oct. 1754, and Pennington, N.J. (Chh. at Hopewell), 1737-1738, 1746-1747, 1753-1757; Connecticut Farms, N.J., 1748-1754; Red Mills, Carmel, with Patterson and Philippi, N.Y., 1750-1754; Phillipsburg (Warren) N.J., 1752-1754; Presb.; d. Pennington, N.J., 10 Nov. 1757, a. 40 (GS).

JOHN DAVENPORT, A.M., b. Philippi, N.Y., 11 Aug. 1752, son of the Rev. James and Parnell Davenport; A.B., Princeton, 1769, A.M.; A.M., Y.C., 1785; A.M., Brown, 1805; Ord. Southold, L.I., N.Y., at Mattituck Chh., 4 June 1775-1777; Lower Aquebogue, L.I., N.Y., 1775-1777; inst. Deerfield, Mass., 12 Aug. 1795-1805; returned to N.Y., 1809; sett. Bedford, N.Y., Deerfield, N.J., and Lysander, N.Y.; Presb.; d. Lysander, N.Y., 13 July 1821.

CHRISTIAN DAVID, b. in Moravia, converted from the R.C. church; sett. Berthelsdorf, Saxony, 1722; sett. Herrnhut; started from Greenland, 19 Jan. 1733; arriv. N.Y., N.Y., 12 May 1749; came to Bethlehem, Pa., 1749, to get timber for the Greenland mission; carpenter; Moravian.

ENOCH DAVID, b. Duck Creek, Delaware, 22 Feb. 1718; called to the ministry at Welsh Tract, Del., 1751; became a Sabbatarian, 1752; Ord. 16 Oct. 1769; sett. Newtown (Del.) Pa., Lower Dublin, Pa., Warwick (Chester), French Creek Chh. at East Nantmeal, Pa., and Nottingham, Md., 1769-1772; he was the only 7th Day Bapt. in Pa., in 1770.

ROBERT DAVIDSON, D.D., b. Elkton, Md., 1750; A.B., U. of Pa., 1771, A.M., 1780; D.D., 1784; Ord. Philadelphia, Pa., 1772; sett. Philadelphia, Pa., 1st Presb. Chh., 1773-1784; Carlisle (Cumb.) Pa., 1784-1812; Prof. of History, U. of Pa., 1773-1784; Prof. of Greek and Latin Languages, U. of Pa., 1780-1782; Vice-Pres. and Prof. of Belles Lettres and History, Dickinson Coll., 1 Nov. 1784-1804; Prof. of Moral Philosophy, Dickinson Coll., 1804-1809; Pres., pro temp., Dickinson Coll., 1785-1786, 1804-1809; member Am. Phil Soc., 1783; Old Light Presb.; d. Carlisle, Pa., 13 Dec. 1812, a. 61.

President SAMUEL DAVIES, A.M. (See *Colonial Clergy of Virginia*, p. 13), b. near Summit Ridge (New Castle) Del., 3 Nov. 1723, son of David Davies; ed. Mr. Blair's Log Coll., at Fagg's Manor; A.M. (hon.) Princeton, 1753; Ord. Hanover, Va., 19 Feb. 1746/7-1759; visited England and Scotland to solicit funds for Princeton U., 1753-1755; arriv. N.Y., N.Y., 13 Feb. 1755; sett. Princeton, N.J., 1st Chh., 1759-1761; Pres., Princeton U., 26 Sept. 1759-1761; Presb.; d. Princeton, N.J., 4 Feb. 1761, a. 36 (GS).

HUGH DAVIS, b. Cardiganshire, Wales, 1665; Ord. Rydwilim, Wales; arriv. Pa., 26 Apr. 1711; sett. Tredyffryn (Chester) Pa., Great Valley Chh., 1711-1753; Bapt.; d. Great Valley, Pa., 13 Oct. 1753.

JOHN DAVIS, b. Llanfernach (Pembroke) Wales, 1 Nov. 1702; arriv. in America, 27 July 1713; called to the ministry, 1722; Ord. Tredyffryn (Chester) Pa., Great Valley Chh., 16 Nov. 1732-1777; Bapt.; d. Yellow Springs, Pa., 15 Feb. 1777, a. 70.

JONATHAN DAVIS, b. Swansea, Mass., 15 May 1675; preached at Trenton, N.J., 1737-1750; Bapt.; d. Trenton, N.J., 1750, a. 75, s.p.

JONATHAN DAVIS, b. 1710, son of Elnathan Davis; sett. Cohansey (Cumb.) N.J., Chh. at Shiloh, 27 Mar. 1737-1769; 7th Day Bapt.; d. Shiloh, Cohansey, N.J., 2 Feb. 1769, a. 59.

JONATHAN DAVIS, b. Newark, Del., 7 July 1734, son of Rev. David and Rachel (Thomas) Davis; Ord. Cohansey, N.J., Chh. at Shiloh (Cumb.) N.J., 12 Nov. 1768-1785; 7th Day Bapt.; d. Shiloh, N.J., 23 July 1785.

PHILIP DAVIS, sett. Warwick (Chester) Pa., French Creek Chh. at Nantmeal, about 1726 ff.; 7th Day Bapt.

PHILIP DAVIS, sett. Warwick (Chester) Pa., French Creek Chh. at East Nantmeal, dates not known, but after 1726 and bef. 1769; 7th Day Bapt.

THOMAS DAVIS, b. Llanfernach (Pembroke) Wales, 1707 (brother of the Rev. John Davis, q.v.); arriv. in America, 27 July 1713; Ord. and sett. Great Valley, Pa.; sett. Hopewell (Mercer) N.J., 1741-1745; Oyster Bay, L.I., N.Y., 1745-1748; Southampton (Bucks) Pa., 1761-1763; Bapt.; d. Yellow Springs, Pa., 15 Feb. 1777, a. 70.

WILLIAM DAVIS, b. Wales, 1664; ed. Oxford U.; became a Quaker; arriv. Philadelphia, 1684; became a Keithian Bapt., 1691; excommunicated for heresy by the Pennypack Bapt. Chh., 17 Feb. 1698/9; sett. Lower Dublin, Pa., 1699-1702, 1727-1734; Oxford (Chester) Pa., 1702-1710; Westerly, R.I., 1711-1727, 1734-1744; Squan (Monmouth) N.J., 1745-1745; Keithian-Bapt.; 7th Day Bapt.; d. Squan, N.J., 1745, a. 81.

WILLIAM DAVIS, b. 1692, son of the Rev. William Davis of Squan; sett. Squan (Montmouth) N.J., 1752, a. 60.

WILLIAM DAVIS, b. Castellneth, Glamorganshire, Wales, 1695; came to America, 1722; returned to Great Britain; sett. Vincent, Pa., 1737; New Britain (Bucks) Pa., 1749-1768; Rockhill (Bucks) Pa., 1749-

1768; Kenton, Del., Old Dutch Creek Chh. or Bryn Zion Chh., 1766–1768; Bapt.; d. Dutch Creek, Del., 3 Oct. 1768.

WILLIAM DEAN, b. 1719; came from the North of Ireland, 1739/1740; ed. at the Log College; lic. by New Brunswick Presbytery, 13 Oct. 1742; Ord. Brandywine Manor (Chester) Pa., Forks of the Brandywine Chh., May 1745; sett. Brandywine Manor, Pa., 1743–1748; Warwick (Bucks) Neshaminy Chh., 1742–1743; Salisbury (Lanc.) Pa., Pequea Chh., 1743–1744; Forks of the Delaware, Lehigh Valley, Pa., 1742–1743, Oct. 1744–1745; Cold Spring (Cape May) N.J., 1744–1745; Cohansey (Cumb.) N.J., 1744–1745; Greenwich (Cumb.) N.J., 1744–1745; Timber Ridge and Forks of the James (Rockbridge) Va., 1747–1748; Presb.; d. Brandywine Manor, Pa., 9 July 1748, a. 29 (GS).

Dr. GEORGE de BENNEVILLE, b. London, England, 26 July 1703; came to America, 1745; taught school; practiced medicine and preached at Oley; preached to the "New Mooners," 4 Jan. 1748; became a Moravian; sett. Oley (Berks) Pa., 1748–1755; removed to Philadelphia, 1755, where he practiced medicine until his death; Huguenot; "New Mooner"; Morav.; d. Philadelphia, Pa., 1793, a. 93.

CARL DE BEVOIS, pre-lector, Brooklyn, N.Y., 1664–1664; carried on the services; Dutch Ref.

DAVID DE BONREPOS, D.D., minister of the Huguenot Chh. on the Island of Saint Christopher, West Indies, 1671–1686; sett. Boston, Mass., Huguenot Chh., 1687–1689; New Rochelle, N.Y., French Protestant Chh., 1689–1696; New Paltz (Ulster) N.Y., 1696–1700; Staten Island N.Y., French Ref. Chhs. at Fresh Kills, 1696–1714, and South Side, 1697–1714; French Ref.; d. Staten Island, N.Y., 1734.

JOHN DEBOW, A.B. (See *Colonial Clergy of North Carolina*, p. 61), A.B., Princeton U., 1772; lic. 1775; Ord. 1776; Oxford (Warren) N.J., 1775–1775; inst. Upper Mount Bethel (Northampton) Pa., Forks North Chh., 19 May 1775–1775; sett. Hawfields, Eno, and Little River, N.C., 1775–1783; Presb.; d. Hawfields (Alamance) N.C., Sept. 1783.

STEPHEN DE CARHEIL, Recollect Father; sett. Auburn, N.Y., Cayuga mission, N.Y., 1668–1684; Michilimackinac mission, 1689–1703; R.C.

JOHN HENRY DECKER, b. Markoebel, Nassau, 17 Aug. 1730; matric. in Latin at Hanau, Germany, 27 Mar. 1750; took the oath of allegiance at Philadelphia, Pa., 21 Sept. 1751; sett. Windsor (Berks) Pa., Lebanon Chh. at the Blue Mountains, now St. Paul's Chh., 1752–1755; Brecknock (Lanc.) Pa., Muddy Creek Chh., 10 Dec. 1754–4 Oct. 1761; Ephrata (Lanc.) Pa., Bethany Chh., Cocalico, 1762–1763; Heidelberg (Berks) Pa., Hain's or Cacusi Chh., 1752–1756; Germ. Ref.; d. prob. at Reading, Pa., ca. 1763.

EVERT TEN HEUVEN (DE HAVEN), b. Muelheim-on-the-Ruhr, Germany; came to America, 1698; Ord. Elder at Whitemarsh (Montg.) Pa., St. Peter's Chh., Barren Hill, 4 Jan. 1710; Dutch Ref.; Germ. Ref.

Colonial Clergy of the Middle Colonies

JAMES D'HEU, sett. Victor, N.Y., Seneca mission, 1707-1709; R.C.

JAMES DE LAMBERVILLE, sett. Syracuse, N.Y., Onondaga mission, 1675-1686, 1702-1709; R.C.

JOHN DE LAMBERVILLE, sett. Syracuse, N.Y., Onondaga mission, 1671-1686; R.C.

GODFRIEDUS DELLIUS, b. 1652; matric. Leyden, 1 Oct. 1672, in philosophy; Ord. Amsterdam, Holland, 20 July 1682; sett. Albany, N.Y., Dutch Ref. Chh. 1683-1699; Schenectady, N.Y., Dutch Ref. Chh., 1690-1699; missionary to the Mohawk Indians, 1683-1699; returned to Holland; sett. Antwerp, Belgium, 1700-1714, et seq.; Dutch Ref.

PETER DE MAREUIL, sett. Syracuse, N.Y., Onondaga mission, 1702-1710; R.C.

JACQUES ADAM DE MARTEL, came from London, 1770; K.B. for Nova Scotia, 8 July 1767; sett. N.Y., N.Y., French Ref. Chh. of the Saint Esprit, 4 Feb. 1770-Aug. 1771; French Ref.

OLIVER DEMING, JR., A.M., b. Wethersfield, Conn., 21 Mar. 1741/2, son of Oliver and Lucy (Hale) Deming; A.B., Y.C., 1760, A.M.; lic. by the Hartford South Assn., Oct. 1769; Ord. by Presbytery of New York, 1771; itinerant; sett. Bermuda Island, 1774; Presb.; d. bef. May 1774.

CHRISTOPHER DEMUTH, came from Kathelsdorf, Moravia; sett. Bethlehem (Northampton) Pa., Feb. 1748; minister of rural churches, 1748-1754; paper box maker; Morav.; d. Nazareth, Pa., Mar. 1754.

JEREMIAH DENCKE, arriv. New York, 19 Oct. 1761; sett. Bethlehem, Pa., May 1772-Oct. 1784, as warden; 1784-1795, as preacher; Morav.; d. Bethlehem, Pa., 28 May 1795.

THOMAS DENHAM, b. ca. 1621; preached in Rye and Bedford (Westchester) N.Y., 15 Oct. 1677-1688; d. Bedford, N.Y., 1688 (will dated 2 May 1688).

RICHARD DENTON, A.B., b. York co., England, 1603; A.B., St. Catherine's Hall, Cambridge, 1623/4; Ord. by the Bishop of Peterborough, 8 June 1623; sett. Coley Chapel, Halifax, co. York, 1623-1630; at Wethersfield, Conn., and Stamford, Conn., 1635-1644, not sett.; sett. Hempstead, L.I., N.Y., 1647-1659; ret. to Eng., 1659; Cong.; d. Essex co. Eng. 1662/3.

JOHN BAPTIST DE RITTER, S.J., b. 1717; sett. Washington (Berks) Pa., St. Paul's Chapel at Bally, 31 May 1765-1787; Washington, Pa., Chh. of the Blessed Sacrament, 1767-1787; Allentown (Lehigh) Pa., 1767-1777; Easton (Northampton) Pa., 1767-1777; Elizabethtown (Lanc.) Pa., 1768-1787; Haycock (Bucks) Pa., 1767-1787; Maxatawny (Berks) Pa., 1767-1777; Philadelphia, Pa., St. Joseph's Chh. and St. Mary's Chh., 1767-1777; R.C.; d. Washington, Pa., 3 Feb. 1787, a. 70.

COLONIAL CLERGY OF THE MIDDLE COLONIES

LAMBERTUS DE RONDE, b. Holland, 1720; sett. Zwilichem, Holland, until 1746; Surinam, Dutch Guiana, South America, 1746–1750; came to America 1750; Trustee of Princeton U., 1764–1769; sett. N.Y., N.Y., 1st or South Dutch Ref. Chh., and Middle Dutch Ref. Chh., 1751–1784; N.Y., N.Y., North Dutch Chh., 1765–1784; Harlem, N.Y., 1750–1784; Schaghticoke (Rensselaer) N.Y., Chh. at Reynolds, 1776–1795; Dutch Ref.; d. Schaghticoke, N.Y., 30 Sept. 1795.

JOHN CHRISTIAN ALEXANDER DE SCHWEINITZ, Ord. in Europe; sett. Bethlehem, Pa., 16 Nov. 1770–1802; Ord. Senior Civilis, 1801; administrator, 1770–1801; v.p. Board of Oversight; 1st treasurer, Unity Elder's Conference, 1787; Morav.; d. Bethlehem, Pa., 1802.

FERDINAND PHILIP JACOB DETTMERS, arriv. N.Y., N.Y., 19 Oct. 1761; sett. Bethlehem, Pa., 1768–1772, as warden; Nazareth, Pa., May 1772, as warden; Lititz, Pa.; Morav.; d. Lititz, Pa., 1803.

Bishop Baron JOHN DE WATTEVILLE (John Michael Languth, Jr.), b. Thuringia, 1718, son of the Rev. John Michael Languth, a Lutheran clergyman; ed. Jena; Ord. 1739; consecrated Bishop, 1747; came to America, 1748; founded the Moravian Chh. in New York, Dec. 1748; he was sett. at N.Y., N.Y., 1748–1749; his first visit to America was 1748–1749; 2nd visit was 1783–1787; he m. the dau. of Count Christian Zinzendorf; Morav.; d. Gnadenfrei, Silesia, 1 Oct. 1788.

PETER DE WINT, came to America, 1749; sett. Bergen (Bergen) N.J., 1st Chh., 1749–1751; Staten Island, N.Y., Port Richmond and Richmond Union Chhs., 1751–1752; an imposter; deposed 1752; went to the West Indies.

EBENEZER DIBBLEE, D.D., b. Danbury, Conn., 1715, son of Wakefield Dibblee; A.B., Y.C., 1734, A.M.; D.D., Columbia, 1793; Ord. London, Sept. 1747; K.B. to America, 14 Sept. 1748; arriv. N.Y., N.Y., 23 Oct. 1748; appointed missionary at Stamford, Conn., 25 Oct. 1748; sett. Stamford, Conn., 1748–1799; Greenwich, Conn., 1748–1799; North Salem (Westchester) N.Y., St. James's Chh., 1750–1764; New Castle (Westchester) N.Y., 1761–1764; South Salem (Westchester) N.Y., St. John's Chh., 1759–1764; Ep.; d. Stamford, Conn., 9 May 1799, a. 84.

President JONATHAN DICKINSON, A.M., b. Hatfield, Mass., 22 Apr. 1688, son of Hezekiah and Abigail (Blakeman) Dickinson; A.B., Y.C., 1706, A.M.; Ord. Fairfield co., Conn., 29 Sept. 1709; sett. Elizabethtown (Union) N.J., 1709–1747; missionary at Rahway, Westfield, Connecticut Farms and Springfield, all in Union co., N.J., at all of which places churches were later established; President, Princeton U., 22 Oct. 1746–Oct. 1747; Presb.; d. Elizabethtown, N.J., 7 Oct. 1747, a. 60 (GS).

MOSES DICKINSON, A.M., b. Springfield, Mass., 12 Dec. 1695, son of Hezekiah and Abigail (Blakeman) Dickinson; A.B., Y.C., 1717, A.M.; Fellow, Y.C., 1758–1777; Ord. Hopewell, N.J., 1719; sett. Hopewell (Mercer) N.J., Chhs. at Ewing and Pennington, 1719–Aug. 1727; Lawrenceville (Mercer) N.J., Maidenhead Chh., 1719–1727; Trenton (Mercer) N.J., 1726–1727; Norwalk, Conn., 1st Chh., 1 Nov. 1727–1778; Cong.-Presb.; d. Norwalk, Conn., 1 May 1778, a. 83.

BERNARD DIDERICK, b. Belgium; sett. Conewago (Adams) Pa., Sacred Heart Chh., 1758–1758; Deer Creek (Harford) Md., St. Joseph's Chapel, 1775–1776; Baltimore (Balt.) Md., St. Peter's Chh., 1775–1782; R.C.; d. Sept. 1793.

JOHN JACOB DILLENBERGER, b. Switzerland; sett. Whitehall (Lehigh) Pa., Egypt Chh., 1754–1755 and perhaps longer; Germ. Ref.

ALEXANDER DOBBIN, b. Londonderry, Ireland, 4 Feb. 1742; Glasgow U. (A.B., A.M.?); Ord. Scotland, 1774; arriv. New Castle, Del., 1774; sett. Cumberland (Adams) Pa., Rock Creek Chh. at Gettysburg, 1774–1808; Assoc. Ref. Presb.; d. Gettysburg, Pa., 1 June 1809, a. 76.

JOHN DODGE, inst. N.Y., N.Y., 2nd or Bethel Bapt. Chh., 14 Jan. 1771–1776; Bapt.

JOHN PHILIP DOERBAUM, b. Mittelhausen, Alsace, 1714; theol. student at Lindheim, near Frankfort-on-the-Main, 1744, a. 30; sett. Bethlehem, Pa., May 1749–1751; Morav.; d. Bethlehem, Pa., 1751.

GEORGE J. L. DOLL, b. Frankfort, Germany, 1739; came to America, ca. 1770; sett. Albany, N.Y. (Germ. Ref. Chh.), 1772–1775; Kingston (Ulster) N.Y., at Esopus, (Dutch Ref. Chh.), 1775–May 1808; Kaatsbaan (Ulster) N.Y., Dutch Ref. Chhs. at Camp, West Camp, Kaatsbaan and Saugerties, 1775–1780; preached in German, French and Dutch; Germ. Ref.; d. Kinderhook, N.Y., 28 Mar. 1811, a. 72.

PETER HENRY DORSIUS, bapt. Moers, Germany, 2 Jan. 1711, son of John Henry and Peternella (Gravers) Dorsius; matric. in theol., Groningen, Holland, 5 Apr. 1734; matric. in theol., Leyden, Holland, 17 Sept. 1736; Ord. Groningen, Holland, 29 May 1737; arriv. Philadelphia, 26 Sept. 1737; Northampton (Bucks) Pa., Neshaminy G.R. Chh., 1737–1748; Northampton (Bucks) Pa., D.R. Chh., 1737–1748; Southampton (Bucks) Pa., North and Southampton G.R. Chhs., 1738–1748; Southampton (Bucks) Pa., Neshaminy D.R. Chh. at Churchville, 1737–1748; Lower Milford (Lehigh) Pa., Great Swamp Chh., 1741–1744; Upper Hanover (Montgomery) Pa., New Goshenhoppen G.R. Chh., 1741–1744; Upper Salford (Montg.) Pa., Old Goshenhoppen G.R. Chh., 1741–1744; visited Holland, May 1743–Jan. 1743/4; returned to Holland, 1748; Germ. Ref.; d. Holland, ca. 1757.

JOHN DOTY, A.M., b. New York City, ca. 1750, son of Joseph Doty; A.B., Columbia, 1770; A.M.; lic. for N.Y., 1 Jan. 1771; K.B. for N.Y., 8 Jan. 1771; sett. Philipstown (Putnam) N.Y., St. Philip's Chh. in the Highlands, 16 July 1771–1773; Peekskill (Westchester) N.Y., St. Peter's Chh. in the Manor of Cortlandt, 16 July 1771–1773; Schenectady, N.Y., St. George's Chh., 1773-1777; removed to Canada; Chaplain, His Maj. Royal regt., of N.Y., 1777-1781; sett. Sorel, Canada, 1783-1803; Ep.; d. prob. in Canada, 1803.

SAMUEL DOUGALL, sett. Metal (Franklin) Pa., Lower Path Valley Presb. Chh. at Fannettsburg, 11 Oct. 1775-4 Oct. 1790; Presb.

JOHN DRAKE, b. Piscataway, N.J., 1655, son of Capt. Francis Drake; Ord. (prob.) Piscataway Bapt. Chh. (at Stilton, Raritan), 1689; sett. Piscataway, N.J., 1689-1739; Bapt.; d. Piscataway, N.J., 7 Apr. 1740.

SAMUEL DRISIUS, b. Middleburg, Holland, 1600, of German parents; matric. Leyden, 23 Sept. 1620, a. 20; matric. in medicine, Leyden, 14 Jan. 1649 (a. 46); minister in England, 1630-1649, preaching in Dutch, English and French; sailed for America, 4 Apr. 1652; sett. N.Y., N.Y. (then New Amsterdam), 1st Chh., D.R., 1652-1673; N.Y., N.Y., French Ref. Chh., 1652-1673; Staten Island, N.Y., Dutch Ref. Chh., 1652-1660; Staten Island, F.R. Chh. at Fresh Kills, 1652-1660; Staten Island, South Side F.R. Chh., 1652-1660; in 1653, he protested against permitting religious services to the Lutherans in N.Y.; sent as a diplomatic agent to the Governor of Virginia; suggested the establishment of a Latin School in N.Y.C., 1658; took the oath of allegiance to England, 1668; Dutch Ref.; d. N.Y., N.Y., 18 Apr. 1673.

Domine DRUMMOND, sett. Saratoga, N.Y., 1771-1777; Dutch Ref.

ABRAHAM Du BOIS (also spelled Duboy), b. Epstein, Germany, 1679; became a Germ. Bapt., 1712; Ord. in Germany; came to America, 1728; sett. Perkiomen (Montgomery) Pa., 1728-1738; Lower Milford (Lehigh) Pa., Great Swamp Chh., 1738-1748; Germ. Bapt.; d. Great Swamp, Pa., 21 Mar. 1748.

BENJAMIN Du BOIS, b. Pittsgrove, N.J., 30 Mar. 1739, son of Lewis Du Bois; Ord. 1764; sett. Freehold (Monmouth) N.J., 1764-1827; Holmdel (Monm.) N.J., 1764-1827; Marlborough (Mon.) N.J., Freehold and Middletown Chh., 1764-1827; elected Trustee of Queen's (now Rutgers) College, 1783; Dutch Ref.

GIDEON Du BOIS, came to America, 1724; sett. Passaic, N. J., Chh. at Acquackanonk, 1724-1726; Dutch Ref.

GUALTERUS Du BOIS, b. Streefkerk, Holland, 1671, son of the Rev. Peter Du Bois of Amsterdam; Ord. Amsterdam, Holland, 1 June 1699; came to America, 1699; N.Y., N.Y., 1st or South Dutch Chh., 1699-1751; North Tarrytown, Mt. Pleasant (Westchester) N.Y., Chh. in Sleepy Hollow, supply, 1699-1750; Hackensack, N.J., Chh. at New Barbadoes, supply, 1728-1730; N.Y., N.Y., Middle Dutch Chh. at Nassau Street, 1729-1751; Dutch Ref.; d. N.Y., N.Y., 9 Oct. 1751.

JONATHAN Du BOIS, b. Pittsgrove, N.J., 3 Dec. 1727, son of Barnet and Amy (Greenman) Du Bois; ed. at the Presb. School, New London, Pa.; an original Trustee of Queen's (now Rutgers) Coll., 1770; lic. 1750; Ord. Lancaster, Pa., 21 Sept. 1752; sett. Northampton (Bucks)

Pa., Dutch Ref. Chh., 1751–1772; Northampton, Pa., Germ. Ref. Chh. at Neshaminy, 1751–1772; sett. Southampton (Bucks) Pa., Neshaminy Dutch Ref. Chh. at Churchville, 1751–1772; Southampton, Pa., North and Southampton Germ. Ref. Chh., 1751–1772; Presb.; Dutch Ref.; Germ. Ref.; d. Southampton, Pa., 16 Dec. 1772.

JACOB DUCHÉ, D.D., b. Philadelphia, Pa., 31 Jan. 1737/8, son of Col. Jacob and Mary (Spencer) Duché; A.B., U. of Pa., 1757, A.M.; D.D., Clare Hall, Cambridge, England, 1780; Prof. of Oratory, U. of Pa., 1759–1782; Trustee, U. of Pa., 1761–1778; Ord. London, 1762; K.B. to Pa., 24 Sept. 1762; asst. minister, Philadelphia, Christ Chh., 1759–1775, and St. Peter's Chh., 1762–1775; sett. Philadelphia, Pa., (United Chhs.: Christ Chh. and St. Peter's Chh.), 25 Sept. 1775– 9 Dec. 1777; went to England, Dec. 1777; sett. as Chaplain at St. George's Fields, Lambeth Asylum, London, England, 1777–1789; returned to Philadelphia, 1792; member, Am. Phil. Soc., 1768; Chaplain to Congress, 8 Sept. 1774–17 Oct. 1776; Ep.; d. Philadelphia, Pa., 3 Jan. 1798, a. 60.

GEORGE DUFFIELD, D.D., b. Pequea, Pa., 7 Oct. 1732, son of George and Margaret Duffield; of Huguenot parentage; A.B., Princeton, 1752, A.B., A.M.; Tutor, 1754–1756; D.D., Y.C., 1785; lic. 1756; Ord. Carlisle, Pa., Old Stone Chh., 25 Sept. 1761–1768; sett. Newville (Cumb.) Pa., Hopewell Chh. at Big Spring, 1761–1768; Carroll (York) Pa., Monahan Chh. at Dillsburg, 1769–1771; Philadelphia, Pa., 3rd Presb. Chh. or Pine Street Chh., 1771–1790; Chaplain, Continental Army, 8 July 1776–1777; Chaplain, Continental Congress; Trustee, Princeton U., 1777–1790; New Side Presb.; d. Philadelphia, Pa., 2 Feb. 1790, a. 57.

DU GUESLIS, see Vaillant du Gueslis.

THOMAS DUNGAN, b. London, England, ca. 1632, son of William and Frances (Latham) (Weston) Dungan; came to Newport, R.I., 1637; Sergeant, R.I., 1678; Deputy, R.I., 1678–1681; first Bapt. minister and founder of the first Bapt. Chh. in Pa., 1684; sett. Bristol (Bucks) Pa., Bapt. Chh. at Coldspring, 1684–1688; Bapt.; d. Bristol, Pa., 1688.

EDMUND DUNHAM, b. England, 1662; came to Piscataway (Middlesex) N.J., 1681; Ord. Westerly, R.I., 11 Oct. 1705; sett. Piscataway, N.J., 1705–1734; 7th Day Bapt.; d. Piscataway, N.J., 7 Mar. 1734, a. 72.

JONATHAN DUNHAM, b. 1682, son of the Rev. Edmund and Elizabeth (Bonham) Dunham; Ord. deacon, 2 Nov. 1734; sett. Piscataway (Middlesex) N.J., 1734–1777; 7th Day Bapt.; d. Piscataway, N.J., 11 Mar. 1777, a. 85, of smallpox.

SAMUEL DUNLAP, sett. Montgomery (Franklin) Pa., Welsh Run Chh., 1773–1773; sett. Cherry Valley (Otsego) N.Y., 1774–1774; Presb.

JOHN DYLANDER, b. Sweden, 1709; minister at Boerstel, Sweden, 1737; arriv. Philadelphia, 2 Nov. 1737; sett. Philadelphia, Pa., Gloria Dei Chh., 6 Nov. 1737–1741; Lancaster, Pa., Holy Trinity Chh., 1740–

1741; preached in German, Swedish, and English, often as many as sixteen times per week; Swed. Luth.; d. Philadelphia, Pa., 2 Nov. 1741, a. 32 (GS).

GEORGE EAGLESFIELD, sett. Philadelphia, Pa., 1723-1725; Hopewell (Mercer) N.J., 1725-1728; Chestnut Ridge (Balt.) Md., ca. 1742; Bapt.

SAMUEL EAKIN, A.M., A.B., Princeton, 1763, A.M.; sett. Salem (Salem) N.J., 1774-1776; Pencader Hundred (New Castle) Del., 1776-1783; Chaplain of New Jersey Militia, Rev. War; Presb.; d. Pencader, Del., 1784.

GEORGE EATON, sett. Lower Dublin (Philadelphia) Pa., Pennypack Bapt. Chh., 1734-1761; lay preacher; Bapt.; d. Lower Dublin, Pa., 1 July 1764.

ISAAC EATON, A.M., b. Montgomery, Pa., 1724, son of the Rev. Joseph Eaton; A.M. (hon.) Princeton, 1756; A.M. (hon.) U. of Pa., 1761; A.M. (hon.) Brown, 1770; Ord. Hopewell (Mercer) N.J., Bapt. Chh., 29 Nov. 1748-1772; Principal, Hopewell Academy, 1756 ff.; Bapt.; d. Hopewell, N.J., 4 July 1772, a. 46.

JOSEPH EATON, b. Nantmeal, Radnor, Wales, 25 Aug. 1679; came to America, 1686; called to the ministry, 1722; Ord. 24 Oct. 1727; sett. Montgomery (Montg.) Pa., 1722-1743; Hopewell (Mercer) N.J., 1722-1730, once a month as supply; New Britain (Bucks) Pa., 1743-1749; Rockhill (Bucks) Pa., 1743-1749; Bapt.; d. New Britain, Pa., 1 Apr. 1749.

NICHOLAS HENRY EBERHARD, b. 2 Jan. 1723; arriv. Bethlehem, Pa., 10 Dec. 1751; sett. Warwick (Lanc.) Pa., St. James's Chh. at Lititz, 1765-1767; sett. Graceham (Fredk.) Md., 1767-1770; Morav.; d. Graceham, Md., 8 Apr. 1770.

SAMUEL EBURNE, b. London, England, ca. 1645, son of Richard Eburne, of St. Antholin's Parish, London; adm. pensioner at St. John's Coll., Cambridge, 3 Oct. 1663, a. 18; Ord. 1 June 1667; Rector of Stocking-Pelham, England, 1667; sett. Setauket, L.I., N.Y., 1685-1688; sett. Bruton Parish (James City co.) Va., 1688-1697; S.P.G. missionary at the Isles of Shoals, N.H., 1703; res. on L.I., N.Y., 1697-1705, with short absences for services; Ep.

EMANUEL ECKERLING, b. Strasbourg, Alsace, son of City Councilor Michael Eckerling; arriv. Pa., 1725; sett. Tulpehocken (Berks) Pa., 1735-1735; remov. to Ephrata, 1735; Amwell (Hunterdon) N.J., 1738-1738; Ephrata (Lanc.), Pa., German Bapt. Chloister, 1738-1745; Dunkard or Germ. Bapt.

GABRIEL ECKERLING, b. Strasbourg, Alsace; son of City Councilor Michael Eckerling; arriv. in Pa., 1725; sett. as prior at Ephrata (Lanc.) Pa., German Bapt. Chloister, 1745 ff.; Dunkard or Germ. Bapt., killed by the Indians, Aug. 1757.

ISRAEL ECKERLING, b. Strasbourg, Alsace, 1705, son of City Councilor Michael Eckerling; arriv. in Pa., 1725; asst. minister, Lower Frederick (Montg.) Pa., at Falkner's Swamp Chh., 1729-1740; Ord. Ephrata (Lanc.) Pa., German Bapt. Chloister, Aug. 1740-1745; prior of the community; ejected 1745; Dunkard or German Bapt.

Dr. SAMUEL ECKERLING, b. Strasbourg, Alsace; son of City Councilor Michael Eckerling; arriv. in Pa., 1725; ejected from the German Bapt. Chloister, 1745; sett. Strasburg (Shenandoah) Va., 1750-July 1764; German Bapt. or Dunkard; d. 15 Jan. 1781.

ADOLPH ECKESPARRE, arriv. in Pa., Dec. 1756; Ord. deacon; sett. Nazareth (Northampton) Pa., 1759 ff.; officiated at the churches at Ephrata, Nazareth, Gnadenthal, Christianspring and Friedenthal; head master of the school at Nazareth; Moravian.

President JONATHAN EDWARDS, A.M., b. East Windsor, Conn., 5 Oct. 1703, son of the Rev. Timothy and Esther (Stoddard) Edwards; A.B., Y.C., 1720, A.M.; Tutor, 1724-1726; sett. N.Y., N.Y., 2nd Presb. Chh., 1722-1722; Ord. Northampton, Mass., 15 Feb. 1726/7-22 June 1750; sett. Stockbridge, Mass., preacher to the Indians, 1750-1758; Princeton, N.J., 1st Chh., 1758-1758; inst. President of Princeton U., Jan. 1758-Mar. 1758; a leading intellect of America; Cong.-Presb.; d. Princeton, N.J., 22 Mar. 1758, a. 55 (GS).

President JONATHAN EDWARDS, D.D., b. Northampton, Mass., 26 May 1745, son of the Rev. Jonathan and Sarah (Pierpont) Edwards; A.B., Princeton, 1765, A.M., Tutor, 1766-1769, D.D., 1785; A.M., Y.C., 1769; Ord. New Haven, Conn., White Haven Chh., 5 Jan. 1769-May 1795; inst. Colebrook, Conn., 1797-July 1799; President, Union College, Schenectady, N.Y., 1799-1801; Presb.; d. Schenectady, N.Y., 1 Aug. 1801, a. 56.

MORGAN EDWARDS, A.M., b. Trevethin, Monmouth, Wales, 9 May 1722; ed. Bapt. Seminary, Bristol, England; A.M. (hon.) U. of Pa., 1762; A.M. (hon.) Brown, 1769; Fellow, Brown, 1764-1789; sett. Boston, co. Lincoln, England, 1746-1753; Ord. Cork, Ireland, 1 June 1757-1759; Rye, Sussex co. England, 1760-1761; arriv. Philadelphia, 23 May 1761; sett. Philadelphia, Pa., 1761-1772; sett. Newark, Del., 1772-1775; Bapt.; d. Pencader, Del., 28 Jan. 1795, a. 72.

WILLIAM EDWARDS, b. co. Gloucester, England, 24 Oct. 1708; came to America, 1736; became a Moravian, 1741; sett. Bethlehem, Pa., 1749; he was Zeisberger's assistant at Lichtenau, Nov. 1776; founder of Goshen; Representative for Northampton co., Pa., 1755; Morav.; d. Goshen, Pa., 8 Oct. 1801.

JACOB EHRENHARDT, b. Marstadt, near Worms, Rhein-Hessen, 1716, son of John and Ann Magdalena Ehrenhardt; came to Pa., 1739; resided at Macungie; joined the Moravians, 1742; Ord. deacon, Salisbury (Lehigh) Pa., 1747; sett. Salisbury, Macungie Chh. at Emaus, 1747-1760; Morav.; d. Macungie, Pa., July 1760.

JACOB CHRISTIAN EICHER, b. 1709; Ord. Ephrata (Lanc.) Pa., German Bapt. Chloister; sett. Ephrata, 1768-1791; prior, 1749-1791; Dunkard or German Bapt.; d. Ephrata, Pa. 20 Aug. 1791, a. 82.

PETER EIZELBERGER, sett. Cocalico (Lanc.) Pa., Conestoga Chh., 1772 ff.; Dunkard or Germ. Bapt.

Colonel JOHN ELDER, b. Edinburgh, Scotland, 26 Jan. 1706, son of Robert and Eleanor Elder; grad. U. of Edinburgh; lic. 1732; came to America, 1736; Ord. Swatara (Dauphin) Pa., Paxton Chh. on Fishing Creek, 22 Dec. 1738-13 Apr. 1791; sett. Pennsboro (Cumb.) Pa., 1737-13 Apr. 1791; sett. Derry (Dauphin) Pa., 1740-13 Apr. 1791; Capt. of Rangers, 1757; Colonel in the militia; Old Side Presb.; d. Swatara, Pa., 17 July 1792, a. 68.

DANIEL ELMER, A.M., b. East Windsor, Conn., ca. 1690, son of Samuel Elmer; A.B., Y.C., 1713, A.M.; supply at Brookfield, Mass., 1714-1715; New Haven, Conn., 1716-1717; Westborough, Mass., 1717-1724; Springfield, Mass., Aug. 1724-1725; remov. to New Jersey, 1727; Ord. Fairfield (Cumb.) N.J., Church of Christ at Cohansey, 1728; sett. Fairfield, 1727-1755; Cong.; Old Side Presb.; d. Fairfield, N.J., 14 Jan. 1755, a. 65 (GS).

JONATHAN ELMER, A.M., b. Norwalk, Conn., 4 June 1727, son of Deacon Jonathan and Mary Elmer; A.B., Y.C., 1747, A.M.; Trustee of Princeton, 1782-1795; Ord. Florida Parish (Goshen, Florida, Warwick), N.Y., Oct. 1750; sett. Goshen (Orange) N.Y., 1750-1754; Florida (Orange) N.Y., 1750-1754; Warwick (Orange) N.Y., 1750-1754; sett. New Providence (Union) N.J., Turkey Christian Chh., 1 Oct. 1757 (inst. 13 Nov. 1765)-3 July 1793-14 Oct. 1793; Presb.; d. New Providence, N.J., 5 June 1807, a. 80.

PHILIP EMBURY, b. Ireland, 1730; sett. Balligarane, Ireland, 1752-1760; came to America, 1760; N.Y., N.Y., John Street Chh., 1764-1769; N.Y. Conference, 1764-1769; Ash Grave (Washington) N.Y., 1769-1775; Meth.; d. Camden, N.Y., Summer, 1775, a. 45.

JOHN ENEBERG, b. Sweden, 1689; ed. Upsala; Ord. England, 1729; Philadelphia, Pa., Gloria Dei or Wicacoa Chh., 1729-1733; Wilmington Del., Old Swedes Chh., 1732-1742; Chester (Del.) Pa., Upland Chh., 1732-1742; Sw. Luth.; returned to Sweden, 1742.

JOHN GODFREY ENGEL, arriv. N.Y., N.Y., 12 May 1749; sett. York (York) Pa., 1753-1756; Salisbury (Lehigh) Pa., Chh. at Emaus, 1756-1758; his wife Margaret was also ord. and served with him; Morav.

JOHN THEOPHILUS ENGELOND (or John Gottlieb Engelland), came from Wurtemberg, Germany; had been minister at Hamburg, Germany; sett. Strasburg (Lanc.) Pa., St. Michael's or Beaver Creek Chh., 1751-1754; Ephrata (Lanc.) Pa., Bergstrasse Chh., 1753-1758; Elizabethtown (Lanc.) Pa., Christ Chh., 1752-1758; Stone Arabia (Montgomery) N.Y., 1763-1773; Middletown, Lower Swatara (Dauphin) Pa., St. Peter's Chh., 1767-1773; Luth.

ROBERT ENGLISH, supply at Crosswicks (Burlington) N.J., 1738; Allentown (Monmouth), 1739; Presb.

JOHN MICHAEL ENTERLEIN, b. Palatinate, Germany, 1726; ed. Leipsic; Ord. 1751; came to America, ca. 1760; sett. Nockamixon (Bucks) Pa., 1763-1771; Springfield (Bucks) Pa., Trinity Chh., 1763-1771; Franconia (Montgomery) Pa., Indian Creek or Zion's Chh., 1768-1770; Rockhill (Bucks) Pa., Indianfield Chh., 1768-1770; Derry (Dauphin) Pa., Zion's Chh., 1769-1779; East Donegal (Lanc.) Pa., at Maytown, 1771-1781; Elizabethtown (Lanc.) Pa., Christ Chh., 1771-1781; Mifflin (Dauphin) Pa., St. John's Chh. at Berrysburg, 1780-1800; Luth.; d. Mifflin, Pa., Mar. 1800.

REINHARDT ERICKZON, b. Groningen, Holland, 1695/1700; matric. at Groningen, 28 Aug. 1714; Ord. Amsterdam, Holland, 4 Sept. 1725; came to America, 1725; sett. Hackensack (Bergen) N.J., New Barbadoes Chh., Paramus (Bergen) N.J., Schraalenburg, N.J., 1725-1728; Schenectady, N.Y., 1728-1736; Schoharie, N.Y., at Huntersfield, 1730-1731; Claverack (Columbia) N.Y., 1731-1732; Freehold (Monmouth) N.J., 1736-1764; Middletown (Monm.) N.J., at Holmdel, 1736-1764; Dutch Ref.; d. 1771.

ANDREW ESCHENBACH, came from Naumburg, Germany; arriv. Philadelphia, Oct. 1740; Ord. in Europe, 1740; sett. Bethlehem, Pa., 1740-28 Sept. 1741-1747; sett. Oley (Berks) Pa., 1740-1742; Philadelphia, 1743-1747; left the church, 1747; farmer at Oley, Pa., 1747; Morav.; d. Oley, Pa., 1763.

Bishop JOHN ETTWEIN, b. Trendenstadt, Wurtemberg, 29 June 1721; Ord. deacon, 1746; arriv. N.Y., N.Y., 15 Apr. 1754; sett. N.Y., N.Y., Moravian Chh., 1754-1755; missionary among the Indians; came to North Carolina, 22 July 1758; sett. Bethabara, N.C., 1759-1766 (at Wacovia); senior pastor at Bethlehem, Pa., 20 Sept. 1766-1802; sett. Hope (Warren) N.J., 1769-1770; "traveled thousands of miles, often on foot, and preached in eleven of the thirteen original colonies"; consecrated Bishop, 25 June 1784-1801, retired 1801; founder of the "Soc. for Prop. the Gospel among the Heathen ... 1787"; Moravian; d. Bethlehem, Pa., 2 Jan. 1802.

DAVID EVANS, A.M., b. Wales, ca. 1690, son of Elder David Evans, Esq., of Welsh Tract; came to America, 1701; A.B., Y.C., 1713, A.M.; Ord. Welsh Tract Chh. (Pencader Hundred), Del., 3 Nov. 1714-1720; sett. Tredyffryn, Pa., Old Side Chh., at Great Valley, 1720-23 Apr. 1740; Sadsbury, Pa., Chh. at Upper Octoraro, 1720-1724; Norriton (Montgomery) Pa., 1727-1731; Pilesgrove, N.J., 30 Apr. 1741-1751; Pennsneck, N.J., Chh. at Quihawken, 1741-1751; Presb.; Old Side; d. Pilesgrove, N.J., 4 Feb. 1750/1.

EDWARD EVANS, sett. Philadelphia, Pa., 1743-1747; Morav.

EVAN EVANS, D.D., b. Carnoe, Montgomery, Wales, 1671, son of Evan David Evans; matric. St. Alban's Hall, Oxford, 12 Mar. 1691/2,

a. 21; A.B., Brasenose Coll., Oxford, 1695, A.M., 1714, B.D., 1714, D.D., 1714; curate, Wrexham, North Wales; Rector, Gwaynysgor, Flintshire, 1697; Ord. 1700; K.B. for Philadelphia, 5 July 1700; sett. Philadelphia, Pa., Christ Chh., 1700-15 Feb. 1717/8; Lower Providence (Montgomery) Pa., St. James's Chh. at Evansburg, 1700-1707, 1709-1716; Newtown (Del.) Pa., St. David's Chh. at Radnor, 1700-1714, 1716-1718; Concord, Pa., St. John's Chh., 1700-1703; Chester, Pa., St. Paul's Chh., 1702-1704; Oxford (Chester) Pa., Trinity Chh., 1716-1718; (also preached in Welsh at Montgomery, 1700-1704, and Radnor, and at Chichester, 1700-1704, Oxford, 1702-1704, Perkiomen and Newcastle, 1700-1705, all in Pa., and Evesham, N.J., 1700-1713); sett. St. George's Parish (Harford) Md., Spesutia Chh. near Perrymans, 1718-1721; Ep.; d. St. George's Parish, Md., Oct. 1721.

ISRAEL EVANS, A.M., A.B., Princeton U., 1772; A.M., Dart. Coll., 1792; Chaplain, 1st N.Y. regt., 1775; Chaplain, 2nd N.Y. regt., 1776; Brigade Chaplain, N.Y. Brigade, Continental Army, 1777-1783; retired June 1783; Presb.; an elligible officer for membership in the Society of the Cincinnati in the State of New York; d. 1807.

JOEL EVANS, A.B., b. Great Valley, Pa., son of the Rev. David and Ann Evans; A.B., Y.C., 1740; lic. 17 Sept. 1741; sett. Woodbury (Gloucester) N.J., 1741-1742; Deerfield (Cumb.), N.J., 1741-1742; Appoquinimink (New Castle) Del., Apr. 1742-1 Apr. 1743; Presb.; d. Appoquinimink, Del., Apr. 1743.

NATHANIEL EVANS, A.M., b. Philadelphia, Pa., 8 June 1742, son of Edward and Rebecca Evans; non grad., U. of Pa., 1762, A.M. (hon.) 1765; Ord. London (Bsp. of London), 1765; lic. 22 Sept. 1765; missionary for S.P.G.; K.B. for N.J., 23 Sept. 1765; Waterford, Colestown (Cumb.) N.J., St. Mary's Chh., 1765-1766; Clarksboro, formerly Berkeley in Greenwich (Cumb.) N.J., St. Peter's Chh., 1765-1766; Gloucester (Greenwich in Cohansey) (Cumb.), St. Stephen's Chh., 1765-1766 (Gloucester, Waterford and Berkeley were within the town of Greenwich in Cumberland co.); Egg Harbor (Atlantic) N.J., 1765-1766; Haddonfield (Camden) N.J., 1765-1766; sett. Mount Holly (Burlington) N.J., St. Andrew's Chh., 1766-1767; Delaware (Camd.) N.J., 1766-1767; poet; Ep.; d. Haddonfield, N.J., 29 Oct. 1767; bur. in Christ Chh., Philadelphia.

SAMUEL EVANS, A.M., b. Great Valley, Pa., son of the Rev. David and Ann Evans; A.B., Y.C., 1739, A.M.; Ord. Tredyffryn, Great Valley, Pa., 5 May 1742-1747; sett. Norriton (Montg.) Pa., 1742-1747; went to Europe for Ep. ordination but failed to receive it; Old Side; Presb.; d. ca. 1766.

JOHN EWING, D.D., b. Nottingham (Cecil) Md., 21 June 1732; A.B., Princeton U., 1754, A.M., Tutor, 1756-1758; A.M., U. of Pa., 1759; D.D., Edinburgh U., 1773; Ord. Philadelphia, Pa., 1st Chh., 1759-1802; v.p., Am. Phil. Soc.; Provost, U. of Pa., 1779-1802; Prof. of

Natural Phil., U. of Pa., 1758-1759; Presb.; d. Philadelphia, Pa., 8 Sept. 1802, a. 70 (GS).

NICHOLAS EYRES (Ayres), b. Chipmanslade, Wiltshire, England, 22 Aug. 1691; came to N.Y., 1711; Ord. N.Y., N.Y., 1st Bapt. Chh., Sept. 1724-1731; resigned Oct. 1731; inst. Newport, R.I., 2nd Bapt. Chh., Oct. 1731-1759; Bapt.; d. Newport, R.I., 13 Feb. 1759.

JOHN CHRISTOPHER FABER, b. Mosbach on the Neckar, Rhein-Pfaltz, 1732, son of a minister at Gimmeldingen, and cousin of the Rev. John Theobald Faber; matric. Heidelberg, 26 Feb. 1752: Ord. in Germany; arriv. Philadelphia, 1767; sett. Worcester (Montg.) Pa., Wentz's or Skippack Chh., Oct. 1767-Oct. 1768; Baltimore, Md., 1st Germ. Ref. Chh., 1768-1771; Pipe Creek, Md., 1768-1775; Taneytown, Md., 1772-1785; West Manheim, Pa., David's or Sherman's Chh., 1772-1776; Codorus (York) Pa., St. Jacob's Chh., 1776-1776; also Zion's Chh., Blimyer's Chh., and Jerusalem Chh., all in Pa., 1776; Germ. Ref.; d. 1796.

JOHN THEOBALD FABER, Sen., b. Zozenheim, Palatinate, 13 Feb. 1739, son of the Rev. John Faber; matric. Heidelberg, 5 Feb. 1760; Ord. Heidelberg, 20 Apr. 1763; arriv. Philadelphia, 24 Oct. 1766; sett. Upper Salford (Montgomery) Pa., Old Goshenhoppen Chh., Nov. 1766-6 Oct. 1779; Upper Hanover (Montg.) Pa., New Goshenhoppen Chh., 24 Oct. 1766-6 Oct. 1779; Lower Milford (Lehigh) Pa., Great Swamp Chh., 1766-1779; Milford (Bucks) Pa., Trumbaur Chh., 1773-1779, 1782-1785; Lancaster, Pa. and New Providence, Pa., Sept. 1779-Sept. 1782; Rockhill (Bucks) Pa., Indianfield Chh., July 1782-1785; Bedminster (Bucks) Pa., Tohickon Chh., 1782-1785; Germ. Ref.; d. Upper Hanover, Pa., 2 Nov. 1788, a. 49 (GS).

JACOB FABRITIUS (a German or Pole), studied at Altdorf; Ord. Grosglogau, Silesia, ca. 1669; sett. N.Y., N.Y., Holy Trinity Luth. Chh., 1669-1671; Chester (Del.) Pa., Chh. at Upland, 1671-1677; Ord. Philadelphia, Pa., Gloria Dei or Wicacoa Sw. Luth. Chh., Trinity Sunday, 1677-1693; Wilmington, Del., Old Swedes Chh., 1677-1691; Tinicum (Bucks) Pa., 1677-1677; Crane Hook (New Castle) Del., Chh. at Tran Hook, 1688-1691; he was suspended for a time, 15 Sept. 1675; preached in Dutch and Swedish; Sw. Luth.; d. Philadelphia, Pa., 1693.

CHRISTIAN FREDERICK FAEHRING, see FOERING.

DANIEL FALKNER (or Falckner) b. Langen-Reinsdorf, Zwichau, Saxony, 25 Dec. 1666, son of the Rev. Daniel Falkner; ed. Erfurth; Ord. Germany, 1693-1700; arriv. Philadelphia, 23 June 1694; returned to Europe, 1698; arriv. in Pa. again, 1700; sett. New Hanover (Montgomery) Pa., Falkner's Swamp Chh. (the first Luth. Chh. in Pa.), 1704-1714; left Pa. in 1709, though he appears to have continued to preach at Falkner's Swamp until 1714; sett. Fairmount (Hunterdon) N.J., Fox Hill Chh. at Tewksbury, 1714-1734; Mahwah (Bergen) N.J., Ramapo Chh. (also called Remmespack), 1714-1734; Millstone (Somerset) N.J. (also called Muehlstein, Millstein) at Hillsborough near

Harlingen, 1714–1734; Bedminster (Somerset) N.J., Pluckemin Chh. (also called Hill Congregation, Pluckemin, Im Gebirge, In the Highlands), 1714–1734; Potterstown (Hunterdon) N.J., Rockaway Chh. (also called Rackeway) two miles from New Germantown, 1714–1734; Raritan (Somerset) N.J., 1714–1734; Montgomery (Orange) N.Y., Chh. on the Wallkill (also called Uylekil and Remrepugh), 1714–1734; and the following Luth. chhs. in N.J. and N.Y., 1723–1734: Albany, N.Y.; Claverack (Columbia) N.Y., St. Thomas's Chh.; Coxsackie (Greene) N.Y.; Four Mile Point, N.Y.; Kinderhook (Columbia) N.Y.; Klickenberg, N.Y.; Langen Rack, N.Y.; Newburgh, N.Y., Quassic Chh.; Newtown, N.Y.; Queensbury (Warren?) N.Y.; Rhinebeck (Dutchess) N.Y.; Rosendale (Ulster) N.Y.; Saddle River (Bergen) N.J.; Shawanggunk (Ulster) N.Y.; and Tarbush, N.Y.; from 1724 to 1725: East Camp, N.Y., Christ Chh.; and from 1724 to 1734: Kaatsbaan (Ulster) N.Y. and West Camp (Ulster) N.Y. at Saugerties—26 congregations in all; bailiff, 1701; physician; Luth.; d. New Germantown (Hunterdon) N.J., ca. 1741.

JUSTUS FALKNER (Falckner), b. Langen-Reinsdorf, Saxony, 22 Nov. 1672, son of the Rev. Daniel Falkner; matric. Halle, 20 Jan. 1693; came to Pa., 1700; Ord. Philadelphia, Pa., 24 Nov. 1723 (the first ordination of a Lutheran minister in America); burgess, Germantown, Pa., 1701; sett. N.Y., N.Y., Holy Trinity Luth. Chh., 2 Dec. 1703–1723; also in 1703: Raritan, N.J., 1703–1714, Kinderhook, N.Y., 1703–1723, Mahwah, N.J., Ramapo Chh., 1703–1714; Coxsackie, N.Y., 1703–1723; added in 1704 were: Saddle River (Bergen) N.J., 1704–1723; Hackensack (Bergen) N.J., 1704–1723; and in 1705: Albany, N.Y., 1705–1723; and in 1712: Athens, N.Y., Loonenburgh Chh., 1712–1723; besides N.Y., N.Y., and Albany, he had in 1715, seven congregations: 3 in N.J. and 4 in N.Y. These were: summer congregations: Hackensack, Raritan, Remmespach, i.e. Ramapo, Piscataway, Elizabethtown and Phillipsburg (Warren), all in N.J.: winter congregations: Athens, i.e. Loonenburgh, Klickenberg, Four Mile Point, Coxsackie, Kinderhook and Claverack, all in N.Y. In 1716 were added as regular congregations: Claverack, N.Y., St. Thomas's Chh., 1716–1723; Four Mile Point, 1716–1723; and Klickenberg, 1716–1723, all in N.Y. In 1719, seven new chhs. were added: Newburgh, i.e. Quassick Chh., 1719–1723; Rosendale, or Rosenthal in Ulster co., 1719–1723; Shawanggunk (Ulster), 1719–1723; Langen Rack, 1719–1723; Newtown, 1719–1723; Tarbush, 1719–1723; Queensbury, 1719–1723; Rhinebeck (Dutchess), 1719–1723; and Schoharie, 1719–1723, all in N.Y. state. Finally in 1720, three more N.Y. chhs. were added: East Camp, Christ Chh., 1720–1723; Kaatsbaan (Ulster), 1720–1723; and West Camp (Ulster), Chh. at Saugerties, 1720–1723. If to the 25 chhs. served by Daniel are added the 27 chhs. served by his brother Justus, we have 52 chhs.; Luth.; d. Newburgh, N.Y., a 51.

GABRIEL FALK, b. West Gothland, Sweden; Ord. Skara Castle, Sweden; sett. Philadelphia, Pa., Gloria Dei or Wicacoa Chh., 7 Jan.

1733-1733; sett. Molatton (Berks) Pa., St. Gabriel's Chh., Manathanim, Douglassville, Pa., 1735-1745; sett. New Hanover (Montgomery) Pa., Falkner's Swamp Chh., 1735-1742; preached at Purrysburg, S.C., 30 Jan. 1739; preached at Savannah, Ga., 24 June 1739; only once at these two places so far as is known; sett. Pelachecola, Ga., 1739-1740, dism., 1740; returned to Charleston, S.C.; Sw. Luth.

FERDINAND FARMER, see Steinmeyer; R.C.

ALEXANDER FARQUHARSON, K.B. for N.J., 12 Aug. 1717; Ep.

JAMES FARQUHARSON, K.B. for Pa., 25 Apr. 1712; Ep.

ROBERT FEEKS, b. Flushing, L.I., N.Y., 22 June 1685, son of John and Elizabeth (Prior) Feeks; Ord. Oyster Bay, L.I., N.Y., 1724; sett. Oyster Bay Bapt. Chh., 1703-1773; Bapt.; d. Oyster Bay, L.I., N.Y., 2 Apr. 1773, a. 88.

JAMES FINLEY (See *Colonial Clergy of Maryland*, p. 42).

President SAMUEL FINLEY, D.D., b. co. Armagh, Ireland, 1715; arriv. Philadelphia, 28 Sept. 1734; ed. at the Log College; D.D., U. of Glasgow, 1763; D.D., Princeton U., 1749; lic. 5 Aug. 1740; Ord. as an evangelist at New Brunswick, N.J., 13 Oct. 1742; sett. Deerfield (Cumb.) N.J., 1740-1743; sett. Greenwich (Cumb.) N.J., 1740-1743; sett. Cape May (Cape May) N.J., Chh. at Cold Spring, 1740-1743; sett. Lower West Nottingham, Md., 1744-14 July 1761, where he established an academy; sett. West Nottingham (Chester) Pa., 1744-1761; sett. Princeton, N.J., 1761-1766; president of Princeton U., July 1761-1766; Presb.; d. Philadelphia, Pa., 17 July 1766, a. ca. 60 (GS).

SETH FLETCHER, son of the Rev. William Fletcher; teacher at Hampton, N.H., 1652-1654; sett. Durham, N.H., 1656-1657; Wells, Me., 1657-1660; Saco, Me., 1661-1675; sett. Southampton, L.I., N.Y., 1677-1679; sett. Elizabeth, N.J., 1680-1682; Cong.; d. Elizabeth, N.J., bef. 18 Sept. 1682 (adm. gr.).

CHRISTIAN FREDERICK FOERING, b. Hanover, Germany, 1736; stud. under the Rev. Dr. Caspar Dietrick Weyberg, and at Princeton U.; Ord. Germantown, Pa., 21 Sept. 1769; sett. Germantown, 1769-1772; sett. Whitpain (Montgomery) Pa., Boehm's Chh., 1769-1772; Worcester (Montg.) Pa., Wentz's or Skippack Chh., 11 June 1769-Feb. 1772; Frankford (Philadelphia) Pa., 1770-1772; N.Y., N.Y., Germ. Ref. Chh., 1773-1774; Hillsborough (Somerset) N.J., D.R. Chh. at Millstone, Oct. 1774-1779; Germ. Ref.; d. Hillsborough, N.J., 29 Mar. 1779.

JOHN FORBES, b. Scotland (poss. the John Forbes of Banff, U. of Aberdeen, 1730); K.B. for East N.J., 1 Sept. 1733; sett. Freehold, St. Peter's Chh.; Middletown, Christ Chh.; Shrewsbury, Christ Chh., all in Monmouth co., N.J., 1733-1736; resided at Toponemus near Christ Chh., Middletown; Ep.; d. Monmouth co., N.J., bef. 9 Nov. 1736 (adm. of his estate gr. that date).

ROBERT FORDHAM, A.M., b. Sacomb, Hertfordshire, England, 1603, son of Philip Fordham; adm. Gonville and Caius Coll., Camb. U., 3 July 1622; matric. 1623; A.B., 1625, A.M., 1629; came from England, 1640; sett. Hempstead, L.I., N.Y., as the 1st min., 1643–1647; sett. Southampton, L.I., N.Y., 1647–1674; Cong.; d. Southampton, L.I., N.Y., Sept. 1674.

JONAH FORDHAM, A.B., b. ca. 1633, son of the Rev. Robert and Elizabeth (Benning) Fordham; A.B., H.C., 1658; sett. Hempstead, L.I., N.Y., 1660–1674; sett. Southampton, L.I., N.Y., 1674–1680; sett. Brookhaven, L.I., N.Y., Setauket Chh., 1691–1696; Cong.-Presb.; d. Southampton, L.I., N.Y., 17 July 1696, a. 63.

WILLIAM FOSTER, A.B., b. Little Britain (Lancaster) Pa., 1739/40, son of Alexander Foster; A.B., Princeton, 1764; lic. 21 Apr. 1767; Ord. Sadsbury (Chester) Pa., Upper Octoraro Chh., 19 Oct. 1768–1780; sett. East Fallowfield (Chester) Pa., Doe Run Chh., 1768–1780; Presb.; d. Upper Octoraro, Pa., 30 Sept. 1780, a. 41.

JAMES FRAMBACH, S.J., sett. Conewago (Adams) Pa., Sacred Heart Chh., ca. 1758 and ff.; R.C.; d. Conewago, Pa., 1795.

JOHN CHRISTOPHER FRANKE, arriv. at Bethlehem, Pa., Sept. 1742; schoolmaster at Nazareth, Pa., 18 July 1743–1745, 1759 ff.; Ord. deacon, 1749; sett. Oley (Berks) Pa., 1751–1752; sett. Salisbury (Lehigh) Pa., at Emaus, 1752–1753; Philadelphia, Pa., 1754–1756; Chaplain at Gnadenthal; his wife Christina was also ordained; sett. Warwick (Lancaster) Pa., St. James's Chh. at Lititz, 1763–1765; Moravian.

THEODORE FRANKENFIELD, b. Herborn, Germany, 25 Nov. 1727, son of Nicholas Herbert Frankenfield; ed. at Herborn, 26 Apr. 1736–27 Apr. 1741; Ord. at The Hague, 1752; arriv. N.Y., N.Y., 27 July 1752; arriv. Frederick, Md., 4 May 1753; sett. Frederick, Md., 1753–1756; sett. Monocacy Chh., near Frederick, 1753–1756; sett. Conococheague, Md., St. Paul's Chh., 1753–1756; sett. Conewago (York) Pa., Zion's or Quickel's Chh., 1753–1756; sett. Union (Adams) Pa., 1753–1756; Germ. Ref.; d. Frederick, Md., June 1756.

Bishop MICHAEL FRANTZ, b. near Basel, Switzerland, 1687; came to America, 1727; Ord. 1737; sett. Cocalico (Lancaster) Pa., Conestoga Chh., 1735–1748; Germ. Bapt.; d. Cocalico, Pa., Dec. 1748.

WILLIAM FRAZER, b. Scotland, 1743, prob. studied at Aberdeen; lic. by the Bsp. of London, 21 Dec. 1767; S.P.G. missionary; K.B. for N.J., 12 Jan. 1766; sett. Amwell (Hunterdon) N.J., St. Andrew's Chh. at Lambertville, May 1768–1776, 1784–1795; Alexandria (Hunterdon) N.J., St. Thomas's Chh., Kingwood, May 1768–1775, 1782–1785; Musconetcong, near Alexandria, 1768–1776; Tory, 1776–1784; sett. Trenton (Mercer) N.J., St. Michael's Chh., 1787–1788; rector of St. Michael's, 1788–1795; Ep.; d. Trenton, N.J., 6 July 1795, a. 52 (GS).

BERNARDUS FREEMAN, b. Westphalia, Germany; Ord. at Westphalia for service at Albany; came to America, 1700; sett. Schenectady,

N.Y., 1700–1705, as missionary to the Mohawks, and minister of the chh.; sett. Brooklyn, Bushwick, Flatbush and New Utrecht, L.I., N.Y., 26 Dec. 1705–1741; Freehold (Monmouth) N.J., 1705–1709; Holmdel (Monmouth) N.J., 1705–1709; Marlborough (Monmouth) N.J., 1705–1709; minister emeritus, 1741–1743; supply at Staten Island, N.Y., Richmond Union Chh. and Port Richmond Chh., 1705–1741; Dutch Ref.; d. 1743.

FERDINANDUS FRELINGHUYSEN, son of Theodorus Jacobus Frelinghuysen; U. of Utrecht, 1752; Ord. Amsterdam, Holland, 3 July 1752; called to Kinderhook, N.Y., but d. on the passage, 1753, of smallpox; Dutch Ref.

HENRICUS FRELINGHUYSEN, son of Theodore Jacob Frelinghuysen; Ord. in America, 1754; sett. Marbletown, Rochester and Wawasing, all in Ulster co., N.Y., 1754–1757; Dutch Ref.; d. Rochester (Ulster) N.Y., 1757.

JACOBUS FRELINGHUYSEN, A.B., son of Theodore Jacob Frelinghuysen, A.B., Princeton, 1750; preached at Wawasing, N.Y., 1752; Rochester (Ulster) N.Y., 1752–1753; Utrecht U.; Ord. Amsterdam, Holland, 3 July 1752; sailed for America, but d. on passage, 1753, of small pox; Dutch Ref.

JOHN FRELINGHUYSEN, b. Three-Mile Run, N.J., 1727, son of the Rev. Theodore Jacob Frelinghuysen; Ord. Amsterdam, Holland, 1749; sett. Raritan, Sourland, near Harlingen, Six Mile Run, at Franklin, Neshanic, North Branch at Redington, and Three Mile Run, all in Somerset co., N.J., 1750–1754; Dutch Ref.; d. L.I., N.Y., Sept. 1754; buried at Raritan.

THEODORUS FRELINGHUYSEN (Freylinghuysen), bapt. 26 May 1723, son of the Rev. Theodore Jacob Frelinghuysen; studied under J. H. Goetschius; Ord. Amsterdam, Holland, 1745; sett. at Albany, N.Y., 1749–1759; Catskill (Greene) N.Y., 1749–1752; Schaghticoke (Rensselaer) N.Y., 1749–1759; Dutch Ref.; d. Holland, 1761.

THEODORUS JACOBUS FRELINGHUYSEN, b. Hagen, Westphalia, 6 Nov. 1692, son of the Rev. Johannes Henricus Frylinghousen; Ord. Embden, Westphalia, 1717; Subrector of the Latin Academy at Enkhuizin, Holland, Sept. 1718–1719; sett. Embden, Westphalia and East Friesland, Holland, 1717–1719; arriv. America, 1719/20; sett. Raritan, 31 Jan. 1719/20–1747, and during the same time, New Brunswick (Middlesex), as well as Six Mile Run, Three Mile Run and North Branch at Readington, all in Somerset co., N.J.; Sourland, near Harlingen, 1729–1747; Northampton (Bucks) Pa., Dutch Ref. Chh., 1721–1730 and Neshaminy Chh., 1721–1730; North and Southampton Chh., occasionally, 1721–1739; he was the first Ref. Chh. minister to settle in central N.J.; Dutch Ref.; d. Raritan, N.J., 1747.

JAMES FREMIN, S.J., sett. Syracuse, N.Y., Onandaga mission, 1656–1658; Fonda, N.Y., Mohawk mission, 1667–1667; Victor, N.Y.,

COLONIAL CLERGY OF THE MIDDLE COLONIES

Seneca mission, 1 Nov. 1668–1669; La Prairie, 1669; Green Bay, Wisc.; R.C.

ANDREAS FREY, Ord. Lower Frederick (Montgomery) Pa., Falkner's Swamp Chh., 8 Mar. 1727/8; sett. Falkner's Swamp, 1728–1743; became a Moravian, 1743; went to Europe, 1743; returned and became a German Bapt. again; d. after 20 Apr. 1750.

JOHN FRICK, sett. Lower Milford (Lehigh) Pa., Great Swamp Chh., 1748–1770; lay preacher, 1770; Germ. Bapt.

JOHN ANDREAS FRIEDERICHS (or Friederici, Friderici), ed. Halle and Goettingen; sett. Williams (Northampton) Pa., at Cedarville, 1756–1760; Lower Milford (Lehigh) Pa., Upper Milford Chh., 1754–1763; Upper Saucon (Lehigh) Pa., St. Paul's, Blue or Organ Chh., 1754–1762; Moore (Northampton) Pa., Emmanuel Chh., 1754–1778; Lehigh (Northampton) Pa., St. Paul's Chh., at Cherryville, 1762–1769; Lynn (Lehigh) Pa., Jerusalem Chh., at Allemaengel, 1770–1774; Allen and Lehigh (Northampton) Pa., 1772–1778; Luth.; he is called "old, bedridden, impoverished", 1778, but the church records show that he was minister again at Williams, Pa., 1783–1793.

JOHN JACOB FRIES, had a collegiate ed.; arriv. N.Y., N.Y., 9 Sept. 1753; in North Carolina, 15 Apr. 1754; sett. Bethabara, N.C., at Wacovia, 1754–1755; Philadelphia, Pa., 1770–1774; chaplain at Bethlehem, Pa., May 1777–1793; Moravian; d. Bethlehem, Pa., 1793.

CHRISTIAN FROELICH, b. Felsburg, Hesse-Cassel, 19 Aug. 1715; came to Pa., with Bishop Nitschmann, Dec. 1740; he was an itinerant preacher in New England, 1745, and a missionary to the West Indies; his trade was sugar-baker; Morav.; d. Bethlehem, Pa., 5 Apr. 1776.

SOLOMON FROELICH, D.D., b. Red Hook, N.J., 29 May 1730; A.M., Princeton, 1774; Trustee, Rutgers, 1783–1810; D.D., Rutgers, 1811; Ord. 11 June 1775; sett. Jamaica, Newtown, Oyster Bay and Success, L.I., N.Y., 1775–1776; Fishkill and Poughkeepsie, N.Y., 1776–1780; also Hillsborough and Neshanic, N.J., 1780–1786; Hackensack and Schraalenburg, N.J., 1786–1822; Lecturer in Theology, 1792–1797; Professor of Theology, 1786–1822; Dutch Ref.; d. Schraalenburg, N.J., 8 Oct. 1827.

JOHN FROMELT, arriv. N.Y., 21 Oct. 1763; sett. Bethlehem, Pa., 1763; general superintendent of all organizations of young men; Moravian.

JOHANNES CASPARUS FRYENMOET, b. Switzerland, 1720; Ord. 16 Dec. 1744; sett. The Minisinks, at Montague (Sussex) N.J., Lower Wallpack Chh., at Flatbrookville (Sussex) N.J., Port Jervis (Orange) N.Y., at Deerpark, Smithfield (Monroe) Pa., Shawanee Chh. at Lower Smithfield: 1 June 1741–Dec. 1756; Lehman (Pike) Pa., Lower Wallpack Chh., at Bushkill, Delaware (Pike) Pa., at Dingman's Ferry, Layton (Sussex) N.J., Wallpack Chh., 1 June 1741–12 Aug. 1756; Wawarsing (Ulster) N.Y., supply, 1745–1751; Claverack (Columbia)

55

COLONIAL CLERGY OF THE MIDDLE COLONIES

N.Y., Germantown (Columbia) N.Y., Linlithgow (Columbia) N.Y., Kingsbury (Dutchess) N.Y.: 30 Oct. 1756–1770; Kinderhook (Columbia) N.Y., 12 Sept. 1756–1778; Gallatin (Dutchess) N.Y., 1759–1766; Red Hook Landing (Dutchess) N.Y. and Schodack (Rensselaer) N.Y., supply, 1770–1778; Germ. Ref. but preached mostly in Dutch Ref. chhs.; d. Kinderhook, N.Y., 1778.

Bishop CHRISTIAN FUNK, b. Franconia township (Montgomery) Pa., 1731, son of Bishop Henry and Anne (Meyer) Funk; Ord. minister at Franconia, Pa., 1756; Ord. Bishop, 1769; sett. Franconia, Pa., 1757–1778; excommunicated, 1778, for his sympathies towards the patriot cause; Menn.; d. Franconia, Pa., 31 May 1811, a. 80.

Bishop HENRY FUNK, arriv. in Pa., 1719; sett. Franconia (Montgomery) Pa., Indian Creek Chh., 1719–1760; sett. Lower Salford (Montg.) Pa., 1719–1760; Bishop; will made 13 June 1759; Menn.; d. Franconia, Pa., 1760.

HENRY FUNK, b. Montgomery co., Pa., 1730, son of Bishop Henry and Anne (Meyer) Funk; Ord. Milford (Bucks) Pa., Great Swamp Chh., 1768–1778; excommunicated, 1778, for same reasons as for his brother; removed to Va., 1786; Menn.; d. Rockingham co. Va., 1817.

JACOB FUNK, b. 30 May 1730, nephew of Bishop Henry Funk; Ord. Franconia (Montgomery) Pa., 1765; sett. Franconia, Pa., Indian Creek Chh., 1765–1774; Germantown, Pa., 1774–1796; resided at Cheltenham, Pa., 1774–1816; Menn.; d. Germantown, Pa., 11 Mar. 1816, a. 86.

MARTIN GABY, Ord. Oley (Berks) Pa., after 1770; sett. Oley, Pa., 1770 and ff.; German Bapt.

CHARLES GAGE, arriv. N.Y., N.Y., 1686; Roman Catholic Chaplain at the Fort, N.Y., N.Y., under the Roman Catholic Governor of N.Y., Thomas Dongan, 1686–1688; R.C.

HECTOR ERNEST GAMBOLD, b. Punchester (Pembroke) South Wales, son of Bishop John and Elizabeth Gambold; in Bethlehem, Pa., 1742; Ord. (deacon) 1755; Ord. minister before 1763; sett. Philadelphia, Pa., 1751–1751; Staten Island, N.Y., as the 1st settled minister, 1763–1784; also sett. between 1743 and 1755 at the following preaching stations: Ammasland (Del.) Pa., Darby Creek Chh., Bridgeton (Cumb.) N.J., Cohansey Chh., Calkoen's Hook (Del.) Pa., Cape May, N.J., Cold Spring Chh., Great Egg Harbor, N.J., Little Egg Harbor, N.J., Maurice River (Cumb.) N.J., N.Y., N.Y., Pennsneck, N.J., Quihawken Chh., and Swedesborough (Glouc.) N.J.; also at Oblong (Dutchess) N.Y., Chh. at Amenia Union; Morav.; d. Bethlehem, Pa., Nov. 1788.

JOHN GANO, b. Hopewell, N.J., 22 July 1727, son of Daniel and Sarah (Britton) Gano; Ord. 29 May 1754, as a missionary for the South; sett. Morristown, N.J., 1754–25 Sept. 1757; sett. Jersey Settlements (Davidson) N.C., 1758–1760; sett. N.Y., N.Y., 1st Bapt. Chh., 1762–1788; sett. Town Fork Chh., near Lexington, Ky., 1788–1798; commissioned Captain in N.C., 1758–1760; Brigade Chaplain, N.Y. Continental Brigade, served to 3 Nov. 1783; an original member of the Society of the Cincinnati in the State of New York; Bapt.; d. Frankfort, Ky., Aug. 1804, a. 77 (GS).

JULIAN GARNIER, S.J., sett. Syracuse, N.Y., Onondaga mission, N.Y., St. John the Baptist Chh., 1667-1670; sett. Victor, N.Y., Seneca mission, N.Y., St. Michael's Chh., 1670-1683, 1702-1709; sett. Rome, N.Y., St. Francis Xavier's mission to the Oneidas, 1667-1667; R.C.

FREEBORN GARRETTSON, b. Md., 15 Aug. 1752; served in Frederick co., Md., 1776-1776; served in the N.Y. Conference, 1776-1827; Meth.; d. N.Y., N.Y., 26 Sept. 1827, a. 66.

JACOB GASS ("brother Jethro"), adm. Ephrata Chloister (Lanc.) Pa., 9 June 1728; prior at Ephrata, 27 Sept. 1745-1746; 5 Sept. 1746-1749; Germ. Bapt.; d. Ephrata, Pa., 12 Oct. 1749.

PHILIP GATCH, b. near Baltimore, Md., 2 Mar. 1751, son of George Gatch; missionary preacher in N.J., Del., and Md., 1773-1788; sett. Frederick, Md., 1774-1774; sett. Va., 1788-1797; Ohio circuit, 1797-1835, part time; assoc. judge, court of common pleas, 1803-1824; Meth.; d. Clermont co., Ohio, 25 Dec. 1835.

JOHN GABRIEL GEBHARD, b. Waldorf, Palatinate, Germany, 2 Feb. 1750; matric. Heidelberg, Jan. 1768; lic. 1771; arriv. N.Y., N.Y., 14 Jan. 1772; sett. Whitpain (Montgomery) Pa., Boehm's Chh. and Worcester (Montg.) Pa., Wentz's or Skippack Chh., 19 Apr. 1772-4 Sept. 1774; Milford (Bucks) Pa., Lower Milford Chh., at Trumbaursville, 1773-1773; N.Y., N.Y., Germ. Ref. Chh., Nov. 1774-1776; Claverack (Columbia) N.Y., Dutch Ref. Chh., 4 July 1776-1826; also at Taghkanic (Columbia) N.Y., 1777-1797; Ghent (Columbia) N.Y., at Squampawmock, 1782-1787; Hillsdale (Columbia) N.Y., 1793-1814; Germ. Ref.; d. Claverack, N.Y., 16 Aug. 1826.

ABRAHAM GEHMAN, son of Christian Gehman; arriv. Philadelphia, 11 Aug. 1732; sett. Rockhill (Bucks) Pa., Bechtel's or Gehman's Chh., 1770-1792; trustee of Rockhill Chh., 1773; Menn.; d. Rockhill, Pa., 1792.

JOHN GEHMAN, b. Pa., 12 Feb. 1741, son of Christian Gehman; Ord. 1773; sett. Upper Milford (Lehigh) Pa., Zionsville Chh., 1773-1806; he was also called Hans Gehman; Menn.; d. Upper Milford, Pa., 23 Dec. 1806.

JOHN GEISINGER, ord. betw. 1773 and 1785; sett. in the Great Swamp Chh. district of Pa.; Menn.

DANIEL GEISSLER, an assistant to Johannes Kelpius, in the Theosophical Community, Wissahickon, Pa.; Pietist; d. Pa., 1745.

ALEXANDER GELLATLY, b. Perth, Scotland, ca. 1720; arriv. in Pa., 1752; inst. Bart (Lancaster) Pa., Middle Octoraro Chh., 23 Oct. 1754; sett. Bart, 1753-1761; sett. Oxford (Chester) Pa., 1753-1758; Assoc. Presb.; d. Warwick, Pa., 12 Mar. 1761, a. 41 (GS).

SAMUEL GELSTON, b. Ireland, 1692; came to New England, 1715; lic. in Md., 21 Sept. 1715; Ord. Southampton, L.I., N.Y., 17 Apr. 1717; sett. Southampton, 1717–1727; sett. New London (Chester) Pa., 27 Aug. 1728–1733; physician; d. 22 Oct. 1782, a. 90.

JOHN SIEGFRIED GEROCK, b. Wuertemberg, Germany; Ord. Darmstadt, Hessen, bef. 1752; arriv. Charleston, S.C., 1753; sett. Lancaster (Lanc.) Pa., Holy Trinity Chh., Mar. 1753–29 Mar. 1767; sett. Strasburg (Lanc.) Pa., St. Michael's or Beaver Creek Chh., 1753–1767; sett. Sharpsburg (Washington) Md., Mt. Calvary Chh., 1758–1767; N.Y., N.Y., Holy Trinity Chh., 1769–1773; Baltimore, Md., Luth. Chh., 1773–1787; Luth.; d. Baltimore, Md., 1787.

Provost LAWRENCE GIRELIUS, arriv. at Wilmington, Del., 21 Oct. 1767; sett. Wilmington, Del., Old Swedes Chh., now Ep., 1767–1791; sett. Chester (Del.) Pa., Chh. at Upland, 1767–1791; Provost of the Swedish Lutheran Church of America, 1767–1791.

JOHN CHRISTOPHER GOBRECHT, b. Angerstein, near Goettingen, Germany, 11 Oct. 1733, son of Daniel Gobrecht; arriv. Philadelphia, 11 Sept. 1753; Ord. Bedminster (Bucks) Pa., Tohickon Chh., 26 Sept. 1766; sett. Bedminister, Pa., 12 Oct. 1766–9 Dec. 1770; Milford (Bucks) Pa., Lower Milford Chh. at Trumbaursville, 1766–1770; Rockhill (Bucks) Pa., Indian Field Chh., 1766–1770; Franconia (Montgomery) Pa., Indian Creek Chh., 1766–1770; sett. West Cocalico (Lanc.) Pa., Swamp or Little Cocalico Chh., 15 Dec. 1770–5 Dec. 1779; Earl (Lanc.) Pa., Zeltenreich Chh., 1770–1779; Brecknock (Lanc.) Pa., Muddy Creek Chh., 15 Dec. 1770–1779; Elizabeth (Lanc.) Pa., Zion Chh., 1770–1779; Ephrata (Lanc.) Pa., Bethany Chh., 1770–1779; Pequea (Lanc.) Pa., 1772–1779; Hanover (York) Pa., 1779–1806; Mt. Joy (York) Pa., 1779–1806; Hamilton (York) Pa., 1779–1806; Latimore (Adams) Pa., 1779–1806; Germ. Ref.; d. Hanover, Pa., 6 Nov. 1815, a. 82.

Bishop JACOB GODSHALK (Gottschalk or Gaedtschalch), b. Gock, Germany, 1670; Ord. Germantown, Pa., 8 Oct. 1702; chosen Bishop, 9 May 1708; sett. Germantown, Pa., 1702–1713; Skippack (Montg.) Pa., 1714–1763; sett. Towamencin (Montg.) Pa., Kulpsville Chh., 1750–1763; Menn.; d. Skippack, Pa., 1763 (will made 26 Dec. 1760; proved 3 June 1763).

ANDREW GOERANSON, sett. Philadelphia, Pa., Gloria Dei or Wicacoa Chh., 1768–1779; Philadelphia, St. James's Chh., Kingsessing, 1768–1779; Upper Merion (Montg.) Pa., Christ Chh., 1768–1779; Sw. Luth.

JACOB GOERING, b. Chanceford, Pa., 17 Jan. 1755, son of Jacob and Margaret Goering; ed. Halle; lic. Lancaster, Pa., 1774; sett. Carlisle (Cumberland) Pa., 1774–1783; Dover (York) Pa., Salem or Strayer's Chh., 1774–1783; Paradise (York) Pa., Holz Schwamm Chh., 1775–1783; Upper Bermudian, Pa., 1774–1783; Latimore (Adams) Pa., Lower Bermudian Chh., 1774–1783; Lower Settlement, Pa., 1774–1783;

Colonial Clergy of the Middle Colonies

sett. York (York) Pa., Christ Chh., 1783–1807; Luth.; d. York, Pa., 1807, a. 53.

JOHN HENRY GOETSCHIUS (or Goetschy), b. Bernegg, Zurich, Switzerland, 8 Mar. 1717/8, son of the Rev. Maurice and Esther (Werndli) Goetschius; matric. 23 Mar. 1734, at the Latin School at Zurich; arriv. Philadelphia, 29 May 1735, in the "Mercury"; lic. 28 May 1736; Ord. 7 Apr. 1741; reordained 1748; German Ref. ministry: sett. Lower Salford (Montg.) Pa., Reiff's or Skippack Chh., 1735–1739; Upper Salford (Montg.) Pa., Old Goshenhoppen Chh., 1735–1740; Upper Hanover (Montg.) Pa., New Goshenhoppen Chh., Jan. 1735/6–1740; Lower Milford (Lehigh) Pa., Great Swamp Chh., 1735–1740; Whitehall (Lehigh) Pa., Egypt Chh., 1735–26 Oct. 1736; Lower Saucon (Northampton) Pa., Saucon Chh., 1735–1739; Maxatawny (Berks) Pa., De Long Chh., 1735–1739; Oley (Berks) Pa., 1736–1736; Bern (Berks) Pa., Bern Chh., 24 Mar. 1739–1741; Mill Creek (Lebanon) Pa., Tulpehocken or Trinity Chh., 1736–1741; Heidelberg (Berks) Pa., Hain's or Cacusi Chh., 1736–1739; Salisbury (Lehigh) Pa., Jerusalem Chh., 1737–1739; Worcester (Montg.) Pa., Wentz's or Skippack Chh., 1735–1741; Northampton (Bucks) Pa., Dutch Ref. Chh., 1738–1740; Richmond (Berks) Pa., Moselem Chh., 1739–1740; Southampton (Bucks) Pa., North and Southampton Chh., 1739–1741; also Neshaminy Chh. at Churchville, 1739–1741. Dutch Ref. ministry; Jamaica, Oyster Bay, Newtown, Success, all L.I., N.Y., 1741–1748; Hackensack, N.J., New Barbadoes Chh., 1748–1774; Schraalenburg (Bergen) N.J., 1748–1774; Germ. Ref.; Dutch Ref.; d. Schraalenburg, N.J., 14 Nov. 1774.

Dr. JOHN MAURITIUS GOETSCHIUS, A.M., b. Thurgau, Switzerland, July 1724; ed. as a physician; came to America, 1744; A.M. (hon.) Princeton, 1773; Trustee, Rutgers, 1770–1771; lic. 1754; sett. Schoharie, N.Y., German and Dutch Ref., 1757–1760; Shawangunk (Ulster) N.Y., Chh. at Bruynswick, Dutch Ref.; 1760–1771; New Palz (Ulster) N.Y., Fr. Ref. Chh., 1760–1771; Dutch Ref.; d. Mar. 1771.

MAURICE GOETSCHIUS, b. Zurich, Switzerland, 1686; matric. Zurich Latin School, 4 Dec. 1702; Ord. St. Gall, 1710; sett. Bernegg, St. Gall, Switzerland, 1712–1720; sett. Saletz, Switzerland, 1720–1731; deposed, 1731; arriv. Philadelphia, 29 May 1735; d. same day; Germ. Ref.; d. Philadelphia, Pa., 29 May 1735.

STEPHEN GOETSCHIUS, A.B., b. ca. 1752, son of John Henry Goetschius; studied under his father; A.B. (hon.) Princeton, 1774; lic. 1775; Ord. June 1777; sett. New Palz (Ulster) N.Y., 1775–1796; sett. New Hurley (Ulster) N.Y., Chh. at Plattekill, 1775–1796; Marbletown (Ulster) N.Y., 1796–1814; Shokan, N.Y., 1796–1814; Saddle River and Pascack, 1814–1835; he org. 9 chhs. in Ulster co.; Dutch Ref.; d. Bergen co., N.J., 1837.

JOHN ERNST GOETWASSER, Ord. Holland, 10 Apr. 1657; arriv. N.Y., N.Y., 6 June 1657; sett. N.Y., N.Y., Holy Trinity Chh., as the 1st minister, 1657–1658; sett. Albany, N.Y., 1657–1658; Luth.

BENJAMIN GOLDSMITH, A.M., b. Southold, L.I., N.Y., 5 Nov. 1736, son of John Goldsmith; A.B., Y.C., 1760, A.M., 1765; Ord. Lower Aquebogue, at Riverhead, L.I., N.Y., 28 June 1764; sett. Lower Aquebogue, 1764–1810; sett. Southold, L.I., N.Y., Mattituck Chh., 1777–1810; Presb.; d. Lower Aquebogue, L.I., N.Y., 19 Nov. 1810, a. 74.

FRANCIS GOODHUE, A.B., b. Essex, Mass., 4 Oct. 1678, son of Dea. William and Hannah (Dane) Goodhue; A.B., H.C., 1699; sett. Jamaica, L.I., N.Y., 1705–1707; Presb.; d. Rehoboth, Mass., 15 Sept. 1707.

Dr. JOHN GORDON, Chaplain at the Fort, N.Y., N.Y., 25 Aug. 1683–1683; Ep.

JOHN GORDON, sett. Penn (Chester) Pa., St. John's Chh., 1744–(1750); Frederick (Frederick) Md., 17(38)–(1765): Ep.

PATRICK GORDON, Chaplain, Royal Navy, arriv. N.Y., N.Y., Apr. 1702; sett. Jamaica, L.I., N.Y., Grace Chh., 1702–1702; Flushing, L.I., N.Y., 1702–1702; 2nd S.P.G. missionary and the 1st in N.Y.; d. Jamaica, L.I., N.Y., July 1702.

PETER GORDON, mentioned in Pa., ca. 1708; Scotch Franciscan; R.C.

JOHN GORGAS, sett. Germantown, Pa., 1712–1725; Menn.; d. after 1725.

MATTHEW GOTTLIEB GOTTSCHALK, b. Arnswalde, Brandenburg, 1716; theol. student at Lindheim, 1744, a. 28; came to Bethlehem, Pa., Jan. 1747; itinerant minister in Md., 1745; sett. Antietam (Washington) Md., 1745–1747; Conococheague, Md., 1745–1747; Monocacy, Md., 1745–1747; South Branch of the Potomac, West Virginia, 1745–1747; sett. Bethlehem, Pa., 1747–1748 as an itinerant minister in Pa. at Alsace, Coventry, Goshenhoppen, Neshaminy, Oley and Skippack, 1747–1748; Morav.; d. Bethlehem, Pa., Aug. 1748.

EBENEZER GOULD, A.M., b. Guilford, Conn., son of Benjamin and Elizabeth Gould; A.B., Y.C., 1723, A.M.; Ord. Greenwich (Cumberland) N.J., 1728–1739; inst. Southold, L.I., N.Y., chhs. at Cutchogue and Mattituck, Sept. 1740; sett. Cutchogue and Mattituck, 1740–1747; sett. Orient, L.I., N.Y., 1740–1747; sett. Middlefield, Conn., 10 Oct. 1747–1756; Cong.; Presb.; d. East Granville, Mass., 1778.

WILLIAM GRAF, b. Liningen, Germany; ed. Giessen; Ord. Hackensack, N.J., 1760–1775; sett. Saddle River (Bergen) N.J., Zion's Chh., 1760–1775; Spruce Run (Hunterdon) N.J., 16 July 1775–1808; Whitehouse (Hunterdon) N.J., at Leslyland, 1775–1808; New Germantown (Hunterdon) N.J., Zion's Chh. at Tewksbury, 1775–1808; Potterstown (Hunterdon) N.J., Rockaway Chh., 1775–1808; Bedminster (Somerset) N.J., St. Paul's Chh., 1775–1808; Raritan (Somerset) N.J., 1775–1808; Pluckemin (Somerset) N.J., 1775–1808; Luth.; d. Spruce Run, N.J., 1808.

Bishop JOHN MICHAEL GRAFF, ed. Jena, 1738; U. of Koenigsberg; Ord. in Europe; arriv. N.Y., N.Y., 24 Sept. 1751; consecrated Bishop, 1773; sett. Nazareth, Pa., 1755–1762; sett. Philadelphia and New York, 1762–1762; went to North Carolina, 20 Apr. 1762; sett. Bethabara, N.C., 1762–1773; Salem, N.C., 1774–1782; hymn writer; Morav.; d. Salem, N.C., 29 Aug. 1782.

CHAUNCEY GRAHAM, A.M., b. Lebanon, Conn., 13 Nov. 1731, son of the Rev. John and Abigail (Chauncey) Graham; A.B., Y.C., 1747, A.M.; A.M., Princeton, 1752; Ord. Fishkill (Dutchess) N.Y., 25 Jan. 1749/50; sett. Fishkill, Rumbout Chh., 1750–1773; sett. Poughkeepsie (Dutchess) N.Y., 1750–29 Sept. 1752; physician; Chaplain, 1760, in the expedition to Canada; ran an ordinary in Fishkill; Presb.; d. Fishkill, N.Y., 30 Mar. 1784, a. 53.

JOHN GRANT, A.M., b. ca. 1716 (parentage unknown), A.B., Y.C., 1741, A.M.; sett. Charleston, S.C., Scotch Chh., ca. 1745; Ord. Westfield (Union) N.J., Sept. 1746–1753; Presb.; d. Westfield, N.J., 16 Sept. 1753, a. ca. 37.

WILHELMUS GRASMEER, minister at Graftdyck, Holland, 1647–1650, but deserted his chh. there; m. a dau. of the Rev. Johannes Megapolensis; arriv. N.Y., N.Y., 1650; preached at Rensselaerwyck, N.Y., Feb. 1651–Aug. 1651; sett. Albany, N.Y., 1651–1652; excommunicated; returned to Holland, 1652; restored to good standing; sett. Ursem, Holland, 4 Aug. 1679; Dutch Ref.

Bishop JOHN GRAYBILL, son of (Rev.) John Graybill; came to Lancaster co., Pa., 1772; sett. Monroe (Juniata) Pa., 1772 ff.; Bishop; Menn.

JOHN GRAYBILL (perhaps the same), sett. Woodstock (Shenandoah) Va., ca. 1754; Menn.

JAMES GREATON, A.M., b. Roxbury, Mass., 10 July 1730, son of James and Catherine Greaton; A.B., Y.C., 1754, A.M., A.M. (hon.) H.C., 1760; inst. Boston, Mass., Christ Chh., 30 May 1760–1767; left 31. Aug. 1767; sett. Huntington, L.I., N.Y., St. John's Chh., 1768–1773; Brookhaven, L.I., Setauket, Caroline Chh., 1768–1773; Islip, L.I., N.Y., St. John's Chh., 1768–1773; Oyster Bay, L.I., N.Y., Christ Chh., 1768–1773; Ep.; d. Huntington, L.I., N.Y., 17 Apr. 1773, a. 42.

JOSEPH GREATON, S.J., b. London, England, 12 Feb. 1679; adm. S.J., 5 July 1708; at Liege, Belgium, 1710; St. Omer's, France, 1711; sett. St. Chad, Staffordshire, England, 1715–1720; arriv. in Md., 1721; sett. Conewago (Adams) Pa., Sacred Heart Chh., 1721–1752; Philadelphia, Pa., St. Joseph's Chh., 1729–1752; Bohemia, Md., 1750–1752; took up a patent of 373 acres at Washington, Pa., 1748; Superior, 1740–1753; R.C.; d. Bohemia Manor, Md., 9 Aug. 1753.

JACOB GREDER, came from the Palatinate, Germany; arriv. Philadelphia, 17 Aug. 1733; sett. Skippack (Montgomery) Pa., 1733–1759; res. near Graterford, Pa.; Menn.

ENOCH GREEN, A.B., A.B., Princeton, 1760; inst. Deerfield (Cumberland) N.J., 9 June 1767-1776; Chaplain, Continental Army, 1775-1776; Presb.; d. Greenfield, N.J., 2 Nov. 1776.

Dr. JACOB GREEN, A.M., b. Malden, Mass., 22 Jan. 1722, son of Jacob and Dorothy (Lynde) Green; A.B., H.C., 1744, A.M.; A.M. (hon.) Princeton, 1749; taught school at Sutton, Mass., 1744; lic. Sept. 1745; Ord. Hanover (Morris) N.J., Whippany Chh., Nov. 1746-1790; sett. Hanover (Morris) N.J., Parsippany Chh., 1746-1760; v.p., Princeton, 1758-1759; physician; Presb.; d. Hanover, N.J., 24 May 1790, a. 68 (GS).

THOMAS GREENING, sett. Philadelphia, Pa., 1743-1747; Morav.

NEHEMIAH GREENMAN, A.M., prob. b. Norwalk, Conn., July 1721, perhaps son of Nehemiah Groman; A.B., Y.C., 1748, A.M.; lic. 20 Oct. 1748; sett. Moriches, Brookhaven, L.I., N.Y., 1748-1749; Little Quogue, Westhampton, L.I., N.Y., 1748-1749; sett. Madison (Morris) N.J., Bottle Hill Chh., Apr. 1750-1752; Ord. Pilesgrove, N.J., 5 Dec. 1753; sett. Pilesgrove, 1753-9 Apr. 1779; sett. Logtown (Salem) N.J., Lower Alloway's Creek Chh., 1753-1779; Pennsneck (Salem) N.J., Chh. at Quihawken, 1753-1779; Presb.; d. Pittsgrove, N.J., 25 July 1779, a. 58 y. 21 d.

Bishop CHRISTIAN GREGOR, Ord. in Europe; arriv. Bethlehem, 16 Nov. 1770; sett. Bethlehem, 1770-1772; returned to Europe, 6 May 1772; made an official visit to the Moravian chhs.; consecrated Bishop, 1789; hymn writer; Morav.

ELNATHAN GREGORY, A.B., b. prob. at Norwalk, Conn., 1734; A.B., Princeton, 1757; sett. Carmel (Putnam) N.Y., 1760-1773; Cong.; d. Carmel, N.Y., 1816, a. 82.

JAMES GREIR, A.B., b. Plumstead, Pa., 1750, son of John and Agnes (Caldwell) Greir; A.B., Princeton, 1772; Tutor, 1773-1774; lic. 1775; Ord. Bedminster (Bucks) Pa., Deep Run Chh., June 1776; sett. Bedminster, Pa., 1776-1791; Presb.; d. Deep Run, Bedminster, Pa., 19 Oct. 1791.

DAVID GRIFFITH, D.D., M.D., b. N.Y., N.Y., 1742; physician, 1763-1770; M.D., D.D., U. of Pa., 1786; Ord. London, England, 19 Aug. 1770; K.B. for N.J., 3 Sept. 1770; S.P.G. missionary at Gloucester and Waterford, N.J., 1770-1771 (i.e. Gloucester, Waterford, and Berkeley in the town of Greenwich, N.J.); sett. Greenwich, formerly Waterford, N.J., 1770-1771; Clarksboro, formerly Berkeley, St. Peter's Chh., 1770-1771; Gloucester City (Cumb.) N.J., 1770-1771; Delaware (Camden) N.J., St. James's Chh., 1770-1771; sett. Shelburne Parish (Loudoun) Va., 1771-1776; Chaplain and Surgeon, 3rd Va. regt., Continental Army, 1776-1779; res. 18 Mar. 1779; an original member of the Society of the Cincinnati in the State of Virginia, 1783; sett. Fairfax Parish (Fairfax) Va., 1780-1789; Bishop elect of the Diocese of Va., May 1786; Ep.; d. Philadelphia, Pa., 3 Aug. 1789, a. 48.

JOHN GRIFFITH, Ord. Charlestown (Chester) Pa., 1753-1763; preached in Welsh; Presb.; d. Charlestown, Pa., ca. 1763.

ABEL GRIFFITHS, b. Montgomery, Pa., 23 Dec. 1723, son of the Rev. Benjamin and Sarah (Miles) Griffiths; Ord. 1761; sett. Birmingham (Delaware) Pa., Brandywine Chh., 12 Apr. 1761-1767, 1775-1791; Newlin (Chester) Pa., Hephzibah Chh., 1761-1767, 1775-1791; Vincent (Chester) Pa., 1761-1767, 1775-1791; sett. Salem (Salem) N.J., 1767-1771; Bapt.; removed to Ky., 1791.

BENJAMIN GRIFFITHS, b. Llanllwyni, Cardiganshire, Wales, 16 Oct. 1688, half brother of Abel and Enoch Morgan; came to America, 1710; Ord. Montgomery (Montgomery) Pa., 23 Oct. 1725; sett. Montgomery, Pa., 1722-1768; sett. Hilltown (Bucks) Pa., Perkasie Chh., 1737-1768; sett. New Britain (Bucks) Pa., Upper Perkasie Chh., 1754-1768; Bapt.; d. Montgomery, Pa., 5 Oct. 1768, a. 80.

JOHN DANIEL GROS, D.D., bapt.. Webenheim, Zweibruecken, Germany, 22 June 1738, son of Lorenz and Anna Magdalena Gros; matric. Marburg, 20 Apr. 1758; matric. Heidelberg, 21 Apr. 1761; Regent, New York U., 1784-1787; Trustee, Columbia, 1787-1792; S.T.D., Columbia, 1789; Prof. of German and Geography, Columbia, 1784-1795; arriv. Philadelphia, 4 Dec. 1764; Ord. Whitehall (Lehigh) Pa., 1765; sett. Whitehall, Pa., Egypt Chh., 20 Dec. 1764-1770; Allentown (Lehigh) Pa., Zion Chh., 1765-1770; North Whitehall (Lehigh) Pa., Schlosser's or Scrub Oak (Grund Eichel) Chh., 1765-1771; South Whitehall (Lehigh) Pa., Jordan Chh., 1765-1770; Lehigh (Northampton) Pa., Driesbach Chh., 1765-1770; Lower Saucon (Northampton) Pa., 1770-1773; Northampton (Bucks) Pa., Neshaminy Chh., 1765-1770; Rockhill (Bucks) Pa., Indianfield Chh., 1770-1773; Southampton (Bucks) Pa., North and Southampton Chh., 1765-1770; Springfield (Bucks) Pa., Trinity Chh., 1770-1773; Kingston (Ulster) N.Y., 1773-1783; Chaplain, Rev. War, 1781-1782; N.Y., N.Y., Germ. Ref. Chh., 1783-1795; Stone Arabia, N.Y., 1796-1800; Canajoharie, N.Y., 1796-1800; Germ. Ref.; d. Canajoharie, N.Y., 27 May 1812.

JOSEPH GROVER, A.M., b. Tolland, Conn., 1742, son of Joseph Grover; A.B., Dartmouth Coll., 1773, A.M.; Ord. Hanover, N.J., Parsippany Chh., 1774; sett. Parsippany, N.J., 1773-1798; sett. Bristol, N.Y.; Presb.; d. Bristol, N.Y., 1826, a. 84.

BERNARD ADAM GRUBE, b. near Erfurth, Germany, 1715; grad. U. of Jena; arriv. Bethlehem, Pa., 26 June 1746: Indian missionary in Monroe co., Pa., 1752; sett. Bethabara, North Carolina (at Wacovia), Oct. 1753-1754, as the first Moravian minister in N.C.; sett. Kent, Conn., 1758-Oct. 1760; sett. Province Island, Nov. 1763-Mar. 1765; sett. Warwick (Lancaster) Pa., St. James's Chh. at Lititz, 1765-1780; sett. Bethlehem, Pa., May 1787-1808; sett. Hope (Warren) N.J., 1791-1793; sett. Emaus (Lehigh) Pa., 1791-1808; Morav.; his wife Sarah was his assistant; d. Bethlehem, Pa., 20 Mar. 1808, a. 93.

JOHN GUILD, A.B., b. prob. at Wrentham, Mass., 23 Nov. 1712, son of John and Mercy (Foster) Guild; A.B., H.C., 1734; lic. 19 Sept. 1737; Ord. Hopewell, N.J., 11 Nov. 1741; sett. Hopewell, Pennington Chh., 1739-1787; sett. Lawrenceville, N.J., Maidenhead Chh., 1739-1766; Presb.; d. Pennington, N.J., 10 July 1787.

SAMUEL GULDIN, bapt. Bern, Switzerland, 8 Apr. 1664, son of Hans Joachim and Anna Maria (Koch) Gueldi; matric. U. of Bern, 1679; minister at Stettlen, Switzerland, Aug. 1692-1696; assistant minister at the Cathedral of Bern, 21 Dec. 1696-9 June 1699; but was dism. for Pietistic views; sett. Boltigen, Switzerland, 1701-1701; came in the ship "Maria Hope"; arriv. at Philadelphia, 23 Sept. 1710; preached at Philadelphia, Oley, Roxborough, and Germantown, Pa.; sett. 1 Dec. 1710, as magister and chaplain of the Pietist Community at Wissahickon, Pa.; later he resided at Roxborough, Philadelphia, Pa., as a farmer and preacher; he was the first recorded minister of the German Reformed faith to settle permanently in Pennsylvania, 1710; Germ. Ref.; d. Philadelphia, Pa., 31 Dec. 1745, a. 81.

GOTTFRIED HABERECHT, b. Schoenheide, Lower Silesia, Germany, May 1700, of Lutheran parents; arriv. Savannah, Ga., 1735; came to Pa., 1738; sett. Nazareth (Northampton) Pa., Forks of the Delaware Chh., 1738-1739, as a Moravian; sett. Ephrata (Lancaster) Pa., 1739-Sept. 1741, as a Germ. Bapt. or Dunkard; sett. Bethlehem (Northampton) Pa., 1741-1743, as a Moravian, and was restored to full membership, 23 June 1742, in the Morav. fold; returned to Europe, Jan. 1743; missionary at Algiers, 1747-1748; at London, 1749; at Jamaica, W.I., 1754-1759; sett. Bethlehem, Pa., 1759-1767; Germ. Bapt.; Morav.; d. Christian Spring, Pa., 26 Feb. 1767.

JOHN FREDERICK HAEGER, bapt. Siegen, Westphalia, Germany, 28 Sept. 1684, son of the Rev. Prof. John Henry and Anna Catharine (Friesenhagen) Haeger (his father having been the Germ. Ref. minister at Massanutton Chh., Germania Ford (Orange) Va., 1714-1718, and at Weaverville (Fauquier) Va., 1718-1733); matric. Herborn, 5 July 1703; matric. Lingen, 1705; at U. of Lingen, 1705-14 Nov. 1707; lic. Siegen, 14 Feb. 1708; came to N.Y. with 2138 Palatine settlers, May 1709; Ord. (Bsp. of London) 20 Dec. 1709, as an Ep.; K.B. for N.Y., 5 Jan. 1709/10; arriv. N.Y., N.Y., 19 June 1710; sett. East Camp (Ulster) N.Y., 1710-1721; Kaatsbaan (Ulster) N.Y., 1710-1721; Rhinebeck (Dutchess) N.Y., 1715-1721; West Camp (Ulster) N.Y., 1710-1721; Schoharie (Schoharie) N.Y., 1710-1721; chaplain, expedition to Canada, 1712; pioneer Germ. Ref. minister in N.Y. state; Germ. Ref.; Ep.; d. Albany, N.Y., 1721.

GERARDUS HAEGHOORT, Ord. Amsterdam, Holland, 2 Apr. 1731; arriv. N.Y., N.Y., 24 July 1731; sett. Freehold (Monmouth) N.J., 1731-1735; Holmdel (Monm.) N.J., 1731-1735; Marlborough (Monm.) N.J., 1731-1735; Belleville (Essex) N.J., at Second River, 1735-1776; Dutch Ref.; d. ca. 1783.

JOHN HAGEN, arriv. Savannah, Ga., 18 May 1740; came to Pa., Feb. 1742; Ord. Bethlehem, Pa., 1742; missionary to the Indians; sett. Nazareth (Northampton) Pa., Chh. at the Forks of the Delaware, 24 July 1742-1747; Morav.; d. Shamokin, Sunbury (Northampton) Pa., 1747.

JOHN VALENTINE HAIDT, arriv. N.Y., N.Y., 15 Apr. 1754; sett. Philadelphia, Pa., 1754-1756; sett. Graceham (Frederick) Md., 1757-1758; sett. Bethlehem, Pa., 1758-1780, as minister; painter; Morav.; d. Bethlehem, Pa., Jan. 1780.

BENJAMIN HAIT, A.M., (or Hoit), b. Norwalk, Conn.; A.B., Princeton, 1754, A.M.; Ord. and inst. Amwell (Hunterdon) N.J., Chh. at Reaville, 4 Dec. 1755; sett. Amwell, 1755-29 May 1765; Montgomery (Orange) N.Y., Good Will Chh., Nov. 1765-1769; Connecticut Farms (Union) N.J., 1769-1779; Presb.; d. Connecticut Farms, N.J., 27 June 1779.

THOMAS HALIDAY (or Halliday) (prob. A.M., U. of Edinburgh, 1702), K.B. to N.J., 10 Oct. 1710; sett. Perth Amboy (Middlesex) N.J., St. Peter's Chh., 1711-1713, 1717-1718; Hopewell (Mercer) N.J., 1714-1717; Elizabethtown (Union) N.J., St. John's Chh., 1714-1717; Piscataway (Middlesex) N.J., St. James's Chh., 1714-1718; Woodbridge (Middlesex) N.J., Trinity Chh., 1714-1718; Trenton (Mercer) N.J., 1711-1717 and Shrewsbury (Monmouth) N.J., 1711-1717 occasional services at both places; he was removed from his office as a trouble maker by Commissary Barclay, 1718; removed to Appoquinimink (New Castle) Del., 1718-1722; Ep.; d. bef. 22 May 1722.

JEREMIAH HALSEY, A.M., b. 1733; A.B., Princeton, 1752, A.M.; Tutor, 1757-1767; Trustee, Princeton, 1770-1780; Clerk, Board of Trustees, 1772; sett. Lamington (Somerset) N.J., Chh. at Bedminster, 17 Apr. 1770-1780; Presb.; d. Lamington, N.J., 2 Oct. 1780, a. 47.

Mr. HALSTEAD, see Holstead.

ADAM HAMMAKER, sett. Mt. Joy (Lancaster) Pa., Great Swatara Chh., 1770 ff.; Germ. Bapt.; lay preacher.

NOAH HAMMOND, b. Newton, Mass., 14 Feb. 1718, son of Isaac and Mary (Chamberlain) Hammond; Ord. New London, Conn., ca. 1748; sett. Brookhaven, L.I., N.Y., Coram Chh., 1749-1774; Bapt.; d. Coram, L.I., N.Y., 14 Nov. 1774, a. 56.

JOHN FREDERICK HANDSCHUCH, b. Halle, Saxony, Germany, 14 Jan. 1714; ed. Halle, 1733-1737; U. of Leipzig, 1737; Ord. Altenberg, 1744; sett. Graba, Germany, 1744-1746; arriv. Philadelphia, 5 Apr. 1748; sett. Lancaster (Lanc.) Pa., Holy Trinity Chh., 3 May 1748-May 1750; Earl (Lanc.) Pa., Chh. at New Holland, 1748-1749; Strasburg (Lanc.) Pa., St. Michael's or Beaver Creek Chh., 1748-1751; Germantown, Pa., St. Michael's Chh., 20 May 1751-1764; Upper Dublin (Montgomery) Pa., Puff's Chh., 1754-1757; Philadelphia, Pa., St. Michael's Chh., 1756-1764; taught French and German at Philadelphia Academy, 1755-1758; Luth.; d. Philadelphia, Pa., 9 Oct. 1764, a. 50.

JOHN HANNA, A.M., M.D., A.B., Princeton, 1755, A.M.; M.D.; sett. Alexandria (Hunterdon) N.J., Mt. Pleasant Chh., May 1760-1801; Union (Hunterdon) N.J., Bethlehem Chh., 1761-1801; Kingwood (Hunterdon) N.J., Mt. Bethel Chh., 1763-1801; physician; Presb.; d. Alexandria, N.J., 4 Nov. 1801.

WILLIAM HANNA, A.M., b. Litchfield, Conn., ca. 1738; A.B., Columbia, 1759, A.M., 1765; A.M., Y.C., 1768; Ord. Albany, N.Y. (Presb.), 1761-May 1767; became an Ep.; Ord. (Ep.) by Bsp. of London, 1772; lic. for Culpeper co., Va., 11 June 1772; K.B. for Va., 18 June 1772; sett. Culpeper co., Va., 1772-1775; sett. Christ Chh. Parish (Queen Annes) Md., 1775; Westminster Parish, Md., 1778-1785; Annapolis, Md., St. Anne's Chh., 1779-1780; attorney and physician; Presb.-Ep.; d. Westminster Parish (Anne Arundel) Md., 1785, a. 48.

President JACOB RUTSEN HARDENBURGH, D.D., b. Rosendale (Ulster) N.Y., 1736, son of Col. Johannes and Maria (DuBois) Hardenburgh; A.M., Princeton, 1770; S.T.D., 1771; S.T.D., Columbia, 1789; original trustee of Rutgers Coll., 1770-1785; President, Rutgers Coll., 1785-1790; Ord. in America, 1758; sett. Raritan (Somerset), N.J., 1st Chh. at Bridgewater, now Somerville, 1 May 1758-Oct. 1761, 1763-1781; Bedminster (Som.) N.J., 1758-1761, 1763-1781; Harlingen (Som.) N.J., Chh. at Montgomery, 1758-1761; Neshanic (Som.) N.J., Chh. at Hillsborough, 1758-1761; Hillsborough (Som.) N.J., Chh. at Millstone, 1758-1781; Readington (Hunterdon) N.J., North Branch Chh., 1758-1761, 1763-1781; supply at Conewago (Adams) Pa., Chh. at Hunterstown, 1770-1770; Marbletown, Rochester, Wawarsing and Rosendale, all in Ulster co., N.Y., 1781-1786; New Brunswick (Middlesex) N.J., 1785-1790; member, Prov. Cong., N.J., 10 June 1776; Dutch Ref.; d. New Brunswick, N.J., 30 Oct. 1790, a. 52 (GS).

ROBERT HARDING, S.J., b. Nottingham, England, 6 Oct. 1701; adm. S.J., 1722; came to America, 1732; sett. St. Thomas's Manor, Md., 1732-1749; arriv. Philadelphia from England, Aug. 1749; sett. Concord (Chester) Pa., Chh. at Ivy Mills, 1749-1772; sett. Philadelphia, Pa., St. Joseph's Chh., 1749-1772; Macopin (Passaic) N.J., Chh. at Echo Lake, and missionary to N.J., 1762-1772; Philadelphia, Pa., St. Mary's Chh., 1763-1772; R.C.; d. Philadelphia, Pa., 1 Sept. 1772, a. 70.

SAMUEL HARKER (or Harcour), of Huguenot extraction; Princeton U., non grad.; lic. 6 Nov. 1751; Ord. Roxbury (Morris) N.J., Succasunna Chh., 31 Oct. 1752-1763; Mount Olive (Morris) N.J., at Schooley's Mt., 1752-1763; Chester (Morris) N.J., at Black River, 1752-1763; Succasunna (Morris) N.J., see Roxbury above; chaplain; Arminian; Presb.; will dated 22 Mar. 1764; d. at sea enroute to England.

JOHN HARRIMAN, A.M., bapt. New Haven, Conn., 24 Jan. 1647/8, son of John and Elizabeth Harriman; A.B., H.C., 1667, A.M.; sett. New Haven, Conn., 1670-1674, 1676-1682, 1683-1687; Southampton, L.I., N.Y., 1675-1676; East Haven, Conn., 1683; inst. Elizabethtown (Union)

N.J., 30 Sept. 1687; sett. Elizabethtown, 1687-1705; Cong.; d. Elizabethtown, N.J., 20 Aug. 1705.

HENRY HARRISON, b. Netherlands, of English parents; arriv. N.Y., N.Y., 1685; R.C. chaplain at the Fort, N.Y., N.Y., 1685-1688, under Gov. Thomas Dongan; R.C.

WILLIAM HARRISON, b. ca. 1678; Ord. Mar. 1720/1; S.P.G. missionary in N.J., 31 Aug. 1721; supply, Philadelphia, Pa., Christ Chh., May 1722-1722, while Mr. Vicary was sick; Hopewell (Mercer) N.J., S.P.G. missionary, 1722-1723; Lawrence (Mercer) N.J., Maidenhead Chh., 1722-1723; Amwell (Hunterdon) N.J., St. Anne's Chh., 1722-1723; Alexandria (Hunterdon) N.J., St. Thomas's Chh., Kingwood, S.P.G. missionary, 1722-1723; Trenton, N.J., 1722-1723; sett. Staten Island, N.Y., St. Andrew's Chh., 1723-1739; Ep.; d. Staten Island, N.Y., 4 Oct. 1739.

CONSTANT HART, sett. Wantage (Sussex) N.J., prob. from 1763 to 1772, certainly in 1770; Bapt.

JOHN HART, b. Whitney, co. Oxford, England, 16 Nov. 1651; came to Pa., preached among the Indians until 1691; sett. Southampton (Bucks) Pa., Keithian Bapt. Chh., 1697-1702; may have preached at Lower Dublin, Pa., Pennepack Bapt. Chh., 1702 ff.; Keithian Bapt.; Bapt.; lay preacher.

JOSHUA HART, A.M. (or Hartt), b. Huntington, L.I., N.Y., 17 Sept. 1738; A.B., Princeton, 1770, A.M.; Ord. 2 Apr. 1772; sett. Hempstead, L.I., N.Y., 1772-1776, 1787-1807; inst. Smithtown, L.I., N.Y., Chh. at Nissequoque, 29 Apr. 1774; sett. Smithtown, 1774-1787; dism. 6 Sept. 1787; sett. Fresh Ponds, L.I., N.Y., 1787-1829; Presb.; d. Fresh Ponds, L.I., N.Y., 3 Oct. 1829, a. 91.

OLIVER HART, A.M., b. Warminster (Bucks) Pa., 5 July 1723; A.M. (hon.) Brown, 1769; lic. 20 Dec. 1746; Ord. 18 Oct. 1749; inst. Charleston, S.C., 15 Feb. 1749/50; sett. Charleston, 1750-1780; inst. Hopewell, N.J., 16 Dec. 1780; sett. Hopewell, 1780-1795; Bapt.; d. Hopewell, N.J., 31 Dec. 1795, a. 72.

JACOB HARTMAN, b. 1714; Ord. East Lampeter (Lancaster) Pa., Mellingers meeting house, 1760; sett. East Lampeter, 1760-1796; Menn.; d. East Lampeter, Pa., 18 Mar. 1796, a. 82.

JOHN CHRISTOPHER HARTWIG, b. Thueringen, Saxe Gotha, Germany, 6 Jan. 1714; Ord. London, England, 24 Nov. 1745; sett. Bedminster (Som.) N.J., St. Paul's Chh., 1745-1748; Raritan (Som.) N.J., 1745-1748; New Germantown (Hunterdon) N.J., Zion's Chh. at Tewksbury, 1745-1748; East Camp (Ulster) N.Y., Christ Chh., 1746-1760; Hackensack (Bergen) N.J., 1748-1749; Mahway (Bergen) N.J., Ramapo Chh., 1748-1749; N.Y., N.Y., Holy Trinity Chh., 1748-1749, 1761, 1782; Saddle River (Bergen) N.J., Zion's Chh., 1748-1749; Rhinebeck (Dutchess) N.Y., 1749-1750; Hyde Park (Dutchess) N.Y., Wuertemberg Chh., 1749-1750; Upper Hanover (Montgomery) Pa., New Goshenhoppen Chh., 1750–1751; Upper Providence (Montg.) Pa., Augustus Chh. at Trappe, 1751–1751; Exeter (Berks) Pa., Schwartzwald Chh., 1757–1759; Muhlenberg (Berks) Pa., Alsace Chh., 1757–1759; Reading (Berks) Pa., 1757–1759; Frederick, Md., 1762–1763, 1768–1769; Winchester (Frederick) Va., Strasburg Chh., 1762, 1769, 1781; Boston, Mass., 1784; Waldoborough, Maine, 1784; chaplain in a German regt., 1st French War and the French and Indian Wars; he left his large estate to found Hartwig Seminary, at Hartwig, Otsego co., N.Y., 1816; Luth.; d. Clermont, N.Y., 17 July 1796, a. 82.

THOMAS HARVEY, S.J., arriv. N.Y., N.Y., Aug. 1683; sett. N.Y., N.Y., 30 Oct. 1683–1688, as Jesuit Chaplain to Gov. Col. Thomas Dongan of N.Y.; sett. St. Mary's City (St. Mary's) Md., 1688–1696; assumed name Smith occasionally to escape the penal code; R.C., d. St. Mary's City, Md., 1696, a. 84.

BERNARD MICHAEL HAUSIL, b. Heilbronn, Wuertemberg, Germany, 1727, son of the Rev. Bernard Hausil; arriv. Annapolis, Md., 1752; Ord. Luth.; sett. Frederick, Md., 1752–1759; Antietam (Washington) Md., 1754–1759; Chhs. in Berks co., Pa., as follows: Exeter, Schwartzwald Chh., 1759–1762, Muhlenberg, Alsace Chh., 1759–1762, Perry, Zion's Chh., 1759–1763, Reading, Trinity Chh., 1759–1762; Easton (Northampton) Pa., St. John's Chh., 1763–1769; Upper Saucon (Lehigh) Pa., St. Paul's, Organ or Blue Chh., 1764–1769; Elizabethtown (Lanc.) Pa., Christ Chh., 1766–1768; N.Y., N.Y., Holy Trinity Chh., 1770–1783, senior minister; Tory; became an Ep.; Ord. by Bsp. of London, 1785; sett. Halifax, Nova Scotia, St. George's Parish, 1795–1799; Luth.-Ep.; d. Halifax, N.S., 9 Mar. 1799.

Domine HAYGER (Hege or Haeger), arriv. at Bethlehem, Pa., June 1749; Morav.

SAMUEL HEATON, b. New Haven, Conn., 9 Dec. 1709, son of Nathaniel Heaton; lic. North Castle (Westchester) N.Y., 28 May 1734; Presb.; d. Norwalk, Conn., Jan. 1736.

SAMUEL HEATON, b. Wrentham, Mass., 18 Nov. 1711, son of Samuel and Sarah Heaton; sett. N.J., ca. 1734; Ord. 1751; sett. Opequon Creek (Berkeley) now West Virginia, at Mill Creek, 1751–1754; Konolowa (Cumb.) Pa., 1754–1756; Cape May (Cape May) N.J., 1756–1760; Dividing Creek (Cumb.) N.J., 1761–1777; Bapt.; d. Dividing Creek, N.J., 26 Sept. 1777, a. 65.

JOHN EGIDIUS HECKER, b. Dillenburg, Nassau, Germany, 26 Jan. 1726, son of Johann Wigand and Anna Juliana Hecker; ed. Herborn U.; arriv. Philadelphia, 23 Sept. 1751; sett. Bedminster (Bucks) Pa., Tohickon Chh., 19 Apr. 1756–Feb. 1762; Lehigh (Northampton) Pa., St. Paul's Chh., 1756–1765; and Driesbach Chh., 1756–1763; Lower Saucon (Northampton) Pa., 1756–1766; Moore (Northampton) Pa., Emmanuel Chh., 1756–1773; Springfield (Bucks) Pa., Trinity Chh., 1756–1766; Upper Milford (Lehigh) Pa., Zionsville Chh., 1757–1762; Allentown (Lehigh) Pa., Zion Chh., 1762–1765; Milford (Bucks) Pa.,

Lower Milford Chh. at Trumbaursville, 1762-1766; and prob. Heidelberg (Berks) Pa., Hain's or Cacusi Chh., 1762-1766; Germ. Ref.; d. Moore, Pa., Nov. 1773.

JOHN GOTTLIEB ERNESTUS HECKEWELDER, b. Bedford, England, 12 Mar. 1743, son of David and Regina Heckewelder; arriv. N.Y., N.Y., 15 Apr. 1754; Indian missionary at Muskingum, Ohio, 1762; in the Susquehanna valley, Pa., 1765; and in charge of the Mackiwihilusing mission; for 19 years he was a fellow laborer among the Indians with David Zeisberger; he was the founder of Salem, on the Tuscarawas, and his was prob. the first marriage of white people in the present state of Ohio; his name stands second only to that of David Zeisberger as a missionary to the Indians; Morav.; d. Bethlehem, Pa., 31 Jan. 1823.

PETER HECKMAN, Ord. and sett. Tulpehocken (Berks) Pa., Little Swatara Chh., 1770 ff.; Germ. Bapt.

Bishop MATTHEW G. HEHL, b. 1708; grad. Tuebingen U.; arriv. Bethlehem, 10 Dec. 1751; consecrated Bishop, 1751; assistant to Bishop Spangenberg, 1751-1752; Bishop in charge of the Moravian church in America, 1752; missionary in North Carolina, 22 Aug. 1756; sett. Warwick (Lancaster) Pa., St. James's Chh. at Lititz, Nov. 1756-1787; he also supervised Lititz; Allemaengel, in Lynn (Northampton) Pa.; Mill Creek, 12 miles from Heidelberg, Pa.; Muddy Creek, now Reamstown; Donegal, now Mt. Joy; Heidelberg, Oley, Lancaster and York, Pa.; Graceham and Carroll's Manor, Md.; Morav.; d. Lititz, Pa., 4 Dec. 1787, a. 79.

JOHN DIETRICH MATTHIAS HEINTZELMAN, b. Salswedel, Altenmark, Brandenburg, Germany, 1726, son of Dr. Heintzelman; ed. U. of Halle; Ord. Wernigerode, Saxony, 11 July 1751; arriv. Philadelphia, 1 Dec. 1751; sett. Philadelphia, Pa., St. Michael's Chh., 1751-1756; Luth.; d. Philadelphia, Pa., 9 Feb. 1756, a. 30.

JOHN CONRAD ALBERTUS HELFFENSTEIN, b. Mosbach, Palatinate, Germany, 16 Feb. 1748, son of the Rev. Peter and Anna Margaretha (Dietz) (Helffrich) Helffenstein; matric. Heidelberg, 7 May 1764; Ord. 1771; arriv. N.Y., N.Y., 14 Jan. 1772; sett. Germantown, Pa., 1772-27 Dec. 1775, 1779-1790; Frankford, Pa., 1772-1775; sett. Lancaster, Pa., Jan. 1776-July 1779; clerk of the Coetus, 1779, 1787; president of the Coetus, 1781, 1788; Germ. Ref.; d. Germantown, Pa., 17 May 1790, a. 42.

JOHN HENRY HELFFRICH, b. Mosbach, Hessen, 22 Oct. 1739, son of the Hon. John Peter and Anna Margaretha (Dietz) Helffrich; matric. Heidelberg, 2 Feb. 1758; Ord. 22 Sept. 1761; sett. at Sinsheim, Rohrbach, Reyen, Kirchhard, Steinfurth, 1761-1771; arriv. N.Y., N.Y., 14 Jan. 1772; sett. the ff. chhs. in Berks co. Pa., Mar. 1772-1810: Maxatawny, De Longe Chh., and St. John's Chh. at Kutztown, Oley, Manatawny Chh.; and the ff. chhs. in Lehigh co. Pa., Mar. 1772-1810: Lowhill, Heidelberg, and Weisenberg, Ziegel's and Weisenberg Chhs.;

Longswamp (Berks) Pa., 1775-1810; and the following chhs. in Lehigh co. Pa.: Salisbury, Jerusalem Chh., 1779-1785; Upper Milford, Zionsville Chh., 1779-1810; Upper Macungie, St. Paul's Chh. at Trexlerstown, 1784-1810; Lower Macungie, Little Lehigh Chh. at Macungie, 1785-1810; and Lynn, Lynntown Chh. at Lynnville, 1804-1810; Germ. Ref.; d. Maxatawny (Berks) Pa., 5 Dec. 1810, a. 77 (GS).

JUSTUS HENRY CHRISTIAN HELMUTH, D.D., b. Helmstadt, Brunswick, Germany, 16 May 1745, son of John Christopher and Justina Helmuth; ed. Halle; A.M. (hon.) Princeton, 1787, D.D. (hon.) 1787; A.M. (hon.) U. of Pa., 1780; D.D. (hon.) 1785; Prof. of German, U. of Pa., 1784 ff.; Ord. Wernigerode, 1768; arriv. Philadelphia, 2 Apr. 1769; sett. Lancaster (Lanc.) Pa., Holy Trinity Chh., Whitsuntide, 1769-25 May 1779; Elizabethtown (Lanc.) Pa., Christ Chh., 1769-1771; Elizabeth (Lanc.) Pa., Emmanuel Chh., 1774-1775; Strasburg (Lanc.) Pa., St. Michael's or Beaver Creek Chh., 1769-1775; Philadelphia, Pa., Zion's and St. Michael's Chhs., Mar. 1780-1820; member, Am. Phil. Soc., 1784; Luth.; d. Philadelphia, Pa., 5 Feb. 1825, a. 80.

SAMUEL HEMPHILL, came from the Presbytery of Strabane, Ireland, 1734; sett. Philadelphia, Pa., 1st Presb. Chh., May 1734-1734; tried and dropped for Arminianism in his sermons; Presb.

JOHN WILLIAM HENDEL, D.D., b. Duerkheim, Palatinate, Germany, 20 Nov. 1740, son of John Jacob and Anna Sybilla (Otten) Hendel; matric. Heidelberg, 10 May 1759-10 Feb. 1762; D.D. (hon.) Princeton, 1787; came to America, 1764; sett. Lancaster (Lanc.) Pa., Jan. 1765-Sept. 1769; Pequea (Lanc.) Pa., 1765-1769; Mt. Joy (Lanc.) Pa., Miller's Chh., 1765-1769; Stephenstown (Frederick) Va., 1766-1770; North Annville (Lebanon) Pa., Hill or Quittopehilla Chh., 1765-1769; he preached, 1769-1782, to the ff. chhs. in Berks co. Pa.: Center, Lower Heidelberg, St. John's Chh., Tulpehocken, Host Chh., Upper Tulpehocken, Blue Mountain or North Kill Chh.; and during the same period, 1769-1782, to the ff. chhs. in Lebanon co. Pa.: Jackson, Muhlbach or Millbach Chh., Mill Creek, Tulpehocken or Trinity Chh., Bethel, Heidelberg, Schaeffer's Chh.; also North Lebanon (Lebanon) Pa., St. Jacob's or Kimmerling Chh., and Swatara (Lebanon) Pa., 1771-1782; thus in 1773, he was preaching to ten congregations; sett. Lancaster, Pa., Holy Trinity Chh., 1782-Feb. 1794; sett. Philadelphia, Pa., 9 Feb. 1794-1798; v.p., Franklin Coll., 1787-1794; Pres. Council, Germ. Ref. Chhs., 1768, 1779, 1789 and 1791; Germ. Ref.; d. Philadelphia, Pa., 29 Sept. 1798, of yellow fever.

Commissary JACOB HENDERSON (See *Colonial Clergy of Delaware*, pp. 76-77), S.P.G. missionary at Trenton, N.J., 1710-1714; Ep.

MATTHEW HENDERSON, b. Fifeshire, Scotland, 1735; Ord. Scotland, 1758; sett. Oxford (Chester) Pa., 1758-1775; Pencader (New Castle) Del., 1758-1775; later he went to Washington co. Pa., where he was preaching in Chartiers, Buffalo in Hopewell, Mingo in Union, and at

Mill Creek, in 1782; Associate Presb.; d. Washington co. Pa., 2 Oct. 1795, a. 60.

JAMES HENDRICKS, sett. Hanover (York) Little Conewago, Pa., ca. 1770; Germ. Bapt.; lay preacher.

GERHARD ANTHONY JACOB HENKEL, bapt. (as Anthony Jacob Henckel), at Mehrenberg, Germany, 27 Oct. 1668, son of George and Anna Eulalia (Dentzer) Henckel; a descendant of Count Henkel of Poeltzig; grad. in theol., U. of Giessen, 16 Mar. 1692; Ord. Eschelbronn, Germany, 28 Feb. 1692; sett. near Frankfort-on-the-Main, Germany; sett. Germanna (Orange) Va., Massanutton Chh., 1714–1716; returned to Germany, 1716; came to America, 1717; sett. Germantown, Pa., St. Michael's Chh., 1717–1728; new Hanover (Montgomery) Pa., Falkner's Swamp Chh., 1717–1728; Richmond (Berks) Moselem Chh., 1723–1728; Mill Creek (Lebanon) Pa., Reed's or Old Tulpehocken Chh., 1723–1728; Oley (Berks) Pa., Manatawny Chh., 1723–1728; Oley (Berks) Pa., Christ or Hill Chh., 1723–1728; Washington (Berks) Coldbrookdale Chh., 1723–1728; Rockland (Berks) Pa., Bieber Creek Chh., 1723–1728; in one or two instances, these were preaching stations before the chh. named above was organized; Luth.; d. Germantown, Pa., 12 Aug. 1728 (will dated the same day).

FREDERICK LEWIS HENOP, b. Kaiserslautern, Palatinate, 7 Oct. 1740, son of a minister; matric. Heidelberg, 29 Nov. 1758; arriv. in America, 1765; sett. Chhs. in Pa., 1765–1769: Durham (Bucks), Greenwich (Berks) Dunkel Chh.; and in Northampton co., Dryland, Easton, Lehigh, St. Peter's Chh. and Plainfield, St. Peter's Chh.; Greenwich, N.J., 1765–1769; Frederick, Md., 8 Oct. 1769–Sept. 1784; Middletown (Frederick) Md., Zion or Kittatinny Mountain Chh., 1770–1784; Glades, Md., 1770–1784; Lovettsville (Loudoun) Va., 1770–1784; Stephenstown (Frederick) Va., 1770–1784; Strasburg (Shenandoah) Va., at Stauffers town, 1770–1784; Timberville, Va., Roeder's Chh., 1770–1784; Winchester (Frederick) Va., 1770–1784; Woodstock (Shenandoah) Va., at Millerstown, 1770–1784; Germ. Ref.; d. Frederick, Md., late in Sept. 1784.

ARVID HERNBORN, sett. Philadelphia, Pa., Gloria Dei or Wicacoa Chh., ca. 1720; Sw. Luth.

FREDERICK EMANUEL HERMANN (or Herrmann), came from Herrnhay, Germany; arriv. N.Y., N.Y., 12 June 1748; sett. Bethlehem, Pa., 1748–1755; Philadelphia, Pa., ca. 1760; warden, 1752; Moravian.

Bishop CHRISTIAN HERR, b. Switzerland, son of the Rev. Hans and Elizabeth (Kendig) Herr; Ord. in Europe; arriv. Philadelphia, Sept. 1710; sett. West Lampeter (Lanc.) Pa., at Willow Street, 1710–1735; Menn.; d. after 1735.

Bishop HANS HERR, b. Switzerland, 17 Sept. 1639, son of Emanuel Herr; came to Pa., Sept. 1710, with his four sons; sett. West Lampeter, Pa., 1710–1725; he patented land at Pequea, Pa., 23 Oct. 1710; 1st Bishop on the Pequea River; Menn.; d. Pa., 11 Oct. 1725, a. 86.

HANS HERR, son of Hans Herr and grandson of Bishop Hans Herr; Ord. Strasburg (Lanc.) Pa., 1739; sett. Strasburg, Pa., 1739-1783; Providence (Lanc.) Pa., Black Horse Chh., 1739-1783; Menn.; d. Pequea, Pa., 1783.

Bishop JOHN HERR, son of Emanuel and Maudlin (Brackbill) Herr, and grandson of Bishop Hans Herr; Ord. 1740; sett. Strasburg (Lanc.) Pa., 1740-1797; Menn.; d. Strasburg, Pa., 1797.

SAMUEL HERR, arriv. N.Y., N.Y., 22 June 1748; sett. Bethel (Lebanon) Pa., 1752-1756; sett. York (York) Pa., 1758-1760; Moravian.

ABRAHAM HERSHEY, brother of Bishop Benjamin Hershey and Benedict Hershey; came to Lancaster co. Pa., 1719; sett. East Hempfield (Lanc.) Pa., Chh. at Rohrerstown, 1719-1733; West Lampeter (Lanc.) Pa., Chh. at Willow Street, 1719-1733; Menn.; d. after 1733.

ANDREW HERSHEY, b. Switzerland, 1702, brother of Bishop Christian Hershey, removed to the Palatinate, Germany; came to Lancaster, Pa., 1719; sett. East Hempfield, Pa., Rohrerstown, Chh. (perhaps 1719-1792, but certainly before 1775-1792); sett. East Hempfield, Millersville Chh., 1757-1792; sett. Manor (Lanc.) Pa., 1775-1792; Menn.; d. Rohrerstown, Pa., 1792, a. 90.

BENEDICT HERSHEY, brother of Bishop Benjamin Hershey and Abraham Hershey, sett. West Lampeter (Lanc.) Pa., 1719-1733; Menn.; d. after 1733.

Bishop BENJAMIN HERSHEY, Senior, b. 1697, son of Bishop Christian Hershey; minister and Bishop in Europe; came to Lancaster co. Pa., 1717; sett. East Hempfield (Lanc.) Pa., Rohrerstown Chh., 1717-1789; East Hempfield, Millerstown Chh., 1757-1789; Manor (Lanc.) Pa., Masonville Chh., 1739-1789; Menn.; d. Rohrerstown, Pa., 29 July 1789, a. 92.

Bishop BENJAMIN HERSHEY, Junior, son of Bishop Benjamin Hershey; sett. East Hempfield (Lanc.) Pa., at Rohrerstown, before 1775-1812; Ord. Bishop, 1789, to succeed his father; Menn.; d. Rohrerstown, Pa., 1812.

Bishop CHRISTIAN HERSHEY, brother of Bishop Benjamin and Andrew Hershey, appears to have come over perhaps in 1708, and to be sett. at Manor in 1725 as minister; he certainly came over, perhaps the second time, arriving at Philadelphia, 3 Sept. 1739; sett. East Hempfield (Lanc.) Pa., Chh. at Rohrerstown, 1708-1725; Manor (Lanc.) Pa., at Habeckers meeting house, 1739-1799; Manor, Masonville Chh., before 1757-1799; he was the first minister at East Hempfield; Menn.; d. Manor, Pa., ca. 1799.

JOHN HENRY HERTZER, b. Wuertemberg, Germany; came to America from Herrnhut, and arriv. N.Y., N.Y., 26 Nov. 1743; sett. Graceham (Frederick) Md., 1745-1745; Warwick (Lanc.) Pa., 1745, at Lititz, minister in rural districts; Lynn (Lehigh) Pa., Allemaengel Chh., 1747-1747; Morav.; d. Quittopehille (Lebanon) Pa., May 1748.

Colonial Clergy of the Middle Colonies

Bishop JACOB HERTZLER, b. Switzerland, 1709; Ord. in Switzerland; came to Pa., 1749; sett. Upper Bern (Berks) Pa., North Kill or Blue Mountain Chh., near Hamburg, 1749-1770; first Amish Bishop in America; d. near Hamburg, Pa., 1770.

ANDREW HESSELIUS, nephew of Bishop Svedberg; sett. Chester (Del.) Pa., Chh. at Upland, 1713-1723; Wilmington, Delaware, Old Swedes Chh., 1713-1723; Hwitler Kill, Pa., St. James's Chh., 1720-1723, as S.P.G. missionary; sett. Gagnef, Sweden, 1723 ff.; Sw. Luth.

SAMUEL HESSELIUS, b. Delacarlien, Sweden; nephew of Bishop Svedberg; Ord. Skara, Sweden, 27 Apr. 1718; arriv. Philadelphia, 3 Dec. 1719; sett. Philadelphia, Pa., Gloria Dei or Wicacoa Chh., 1719-1723; Southampton (Bucks) Pa., Neshaminy Dutch Ref. Chh., at Churchville, 1719-1721; Molatton (Berks) Pa., Sw. Luth. Chh., now St. Gabriel's Ep. Chh. at Manathanim, Douglassville, 1720-inst. Oct. 1723-1731; New Hanover (Montgomery) Pa., Falkner's Swamp Luth. Chh., 1720-1723; Wilmington, Del., Old Swedes Chh., 1723-1731; Chester (Del.) Pa., Sw. Luth. Chh. at Upland, 1723-1731; Chester, Pa., St. Paul's Ep. Chh., 1726-1728; returned to Sweden after 10 Oct. 1731; sett. Rumfertuna (Westeras) Sweden, 1731; Sw. Luth.

JOHN GEORGE HEYDECKER, arriv. Bethlehem, Pa., 25 June 1742; sett. Falkner's Swamp Chh., 1742-1742; Morav.; d. Falkner's Swamp, Pa., 10 Sept. 1742; buried at Bethlehem.

JOHANNES HILDEBRAND, b. Germany, 1679; well educated; came early to Germantown, Pa.; sett. Ephrata (Lanc.) Pa., 1739-1765; wrote pamphlets against the Moravians, 1743; Germ. Bapt.; d. Ephrata, Pa., 1765.

HENRY HIRTZEL, sett. Maxatawny (Berks) Pa., St. John's Chh. at Kutztown, 1770-1772; Lynn (Lehigh) Pa., Ebenezer Congregation and Jacob's Chh., 1772 ff.; Long Swamp (Berks) Pa., and Little Lehigh, 1774-1780; he was a mason by trade; Germ. Ref.

JEREMIAH HOBART, A.M., b. Hingham, England, 6 Apr. 1631, son of the Rev. Peter Hobart; A.B., H.C., 1650, A.M.; sett. Wells, Me., 1667; Ord. Topsfield, Mass., 2 Oct. 1672-1680; dism. 21 Sept. 1680; inst. Hempstead, L.I., N.Y., 17 Oct. 1683-1691; inst. Haddam, Conn., 14 Nov. 1700, as the 1st minister; Haddam, Conn., 1691-1715; Cong.; d. Haddam, Conn., 6 Nov. 1715, a. 84.

JONATHAN HOBART, Y.C., 1724; sett. Trenton (Mercer) N.J., ca. 1724; Presb.

JOSHUA HOBART, A.M., b. England, ca. 1628, son of the Rev. Peter Hobart; A.B., H.C., 1650, A.M.; preached at Beverly, Mass., 1650-1655; preached at Barbadoes, and then went to London; returned and was Ord. Southold, L.I., N.Y., 7 Oct. 1674-1717; Cong.; d. Southold, L.I., N.Y., 28 Feb. 1716/7, a. 88.

JOHN JACOB HOCH, prob. came from Rotenberg, Hessen; matric. Marburg 22 Sept. 1712; Ruling Elder and lay preacher at Lancaster,

1733-1736; Ord. Lancaster (Lanc.) Pa., 20 June 1736-1737; sett. Ephrata (Lanc.) Pa., 1736-1737; Germ. Ref.

GEORGE LEWIS HOCHHEIMER, arriv. America, 1 Nov. 1755; sett. York (York) Pa., Christ Chh., 1756-1758; Sandy Run (Lexington) S.C., Chh. at Saxe Gotha, 1765-1774; Luth.; d. after 1774.

JOHN JACOB HOCHREUTINER, b. St. Gall, Switzerland, 27 Apr. 1721, son of a minister; ed. St. Gall; lic. 16 Dec. 1743; Ord. Amsterdam, Holland, 15 Nov. 1747; arriv. Philadelphia, 13 Aug. 1748; assigned to Lancaster, Pa., 1748; Germ. Ref.; d. Philadelphia, Pa., 14 Oct. 1748, by the explosion of a gun.

CHRISTOPHER HOEPFNER, came from Halle, Germany, to Bethlehem, Pa., ca. 1 Feb. 1748; Ord. deacon, 1756; Morav.; d. Santa Cruz, Dec. 1760.

BALTHASAR HOFFMAN, b. Harpersdorf, Silesia, 1687, son of Christopher and Ursula (Anders) Hoffman; sett. Vienna, 5 May 1721-1726; came to Pa., 12 Sept. 1734; sett. Lower Salford (Montgomery) Pa., Schwenkfelder Community, 1740-1775; 2nd Schwenkfelder minister in America; d. Salford, Pa., 11 July 1775, a. 89.

JOHN HOLBROOKE, grandson of the Rev. John Holbrooke, A.M., of Oriel Coll., Oxford, 1661; Ord. by Bsp. of Coventry and Litchfield, 1722; curate of Chilcot, Derbyshire, England, 1722; K.B. for N.J., 23 Dec. 1723; arriv. in N.J., 1724; S.P.G. missionary at Salem (Salem) N.J., St. John's Chh., 1724-1728, 1736; Maurice River (Cumb.) N.J. and Greenwich in Cohansey, N.J., 1724-1728; St. George's Parish (Harford) Md., 1725-1726; Hungar's Parish (Northampton) Va., Oct. 1729-1747; Ep.; d. Hungar's Parish, Va., 1747.

ISRAEL HOLGH, sett. Wilmington, Del., Old Swedes Chh., 1644-1646; Tinicum (Bucks) Pa., New Goeteborg Chh., 1647-1650; Sw. Luth.

WILLIAM HOLLINGSHEAD, D.D., b. Philadelphia, Pa., 8 Oct. 1748, son of William Hollingshead; A.B., U. of Pa., 1770; D.D., Princeton, 1793; Ord. Fairfield (Cumberland) N.J., chh. at Cohansey, 1773-1783; sett. Charleston, S.C., Independent Cong. Chh., 1783-1817; Cong.; d. Charleston, S.C., 26 Jan. 1817, a. 67 (GS).

ELKANA HOLMES, lic. Kingwood (Hunterdon) N.J., 2 Apr. 1774; Ord. Kingwood, N.J., 1775; sett. Knowlton (Warren) N.J., 22 Aug. 1775 ff.; sett. North River (Warren) N.Y.; Bapt.

Mr. HOLSTEAD (or Halstead), sett. Fishkill (Dutchess) N.Y., 1745 ff.; Bapt.

MICHAEL HOLZHAUSEN, sett. Upper Milford (Lehigh) Pa., Zionsville Chh., 1740-1773; Menn.; d. Upper Milford, Pa., ca. 1773.

JAMES HONEYMAN, b. Kinneff, Kincardinshire, Scotland, ca. 1675, son of the Rev. James and Mary (Leask) Honeyman; Ord. bef. 22 Mar. 1702/3; Chaplain, British Navy, 1704; missionary, S.P.G., at Jamaica, L.I., N.Y., Grace Chh., 1704-1704; sett. Newport, R.I.,

Trinity Chh., 1704-1750; his portrait hangs in Trinity Chh.; Ep.; d. Newport, R.I., 2 July 1750.

HENRY HOOK, b. Ireland; Ord. Ireland, 1718; sett. Fairfield (Cumberland) N.J., Cohansey Chh., 1718-1722; Greenwich (Cumb.) N.J., 1718-1722; New Castle, Del., 1st Chh., 1723-1726; inst. Drawyer's Creek, Del., 14 Sept. 1724-1741; Appoquinimink (New Castle) Del., 1724-1741; Chester Town (Kent) Md., 1737-1741; Presb.; d. Drawyer's Creek, Del., 1741.

ANDREW HORNE, arriv. N.Y., N.Y., 25 Oct. 1744; Ord. deacon, 1755; sett. Salisbury (Lehigh) Pa., Chh. at Emaus, 1751-1752; at Crown Inn, 15 Sept. 1757 ff.; wife Dorothy also ordained; Moravian.

NICHOLAS HORNELL, b. Sweden; sett. Hoeoer, Scania, Sweden; Ord. London, England, 1747; arriv. York, Pa., 8 July 1763; sett. York (York) Pa., Christ Chh., 8 July 1763-30 June 1765; Hellam (York) Pa., Kreutz Creek Chh., 1763-1765; Lower Windsor (York) Pa., 1763-1765; West Manchester (York) Pa., St. Paul's or Wolf's Chh., 1763-1765; retired from the ministry, 1765; Luth.

AZARIAH HORTON, A.M., b. Southold, L.I., N.Y., 20 Mar. 1715, son of Jonathan and Mary (Tuthill) Horton; A.B., Y.C., 1735, A.M.; Ord. by Presbytery of N.Y., 1741; sett. New Providence (Union) N.J., 1740-1741; Southampton, L.I., N.Y., missionary to the Shinnecock Indians, 1741-1751; supply, Southampton, L.I., N.Y., 1750-1751; Smithfield (Monroe) Pa., Indian missionary at Shawnee, 1741-1750; sett. Madison (Morris) N.J., Bottle Hill Chh., 1752-Nov. 1776; res. Chatham, N.J.; Presb.; d. Chatham, N.J., of smallpox, 27 Mar. 1777, a. 62 (GS).

SIMON HORTON, A.M., b. Southold, L.I., N.Y., 30 Mar. 1711, son of Joshua and Elizabeth (Grover) Horton; A.B., Y.C., 1731, A.M.; Ord. Connecticut Farms (Union) N.J., Sept. 1735; sett. Connecticut Farms, N.J., Sept. 1734-1746; sett. Newtown, L.I., N.Y., 1746-1772, 1775-1786; sett. West Indies, 1774; Presb.; d. Newtown, L.I., N.Y., 8 May 1786, a. 75.

NATHANIEL HORWOOD, A.M., b. 1680, son of Edward Horwood of Westminster, London; matric. Trinity Coll., Oxford, 13 Oct. 1699, a. 19; A.B., 1703, A.M., 1706; Rector, Bundleigh, Devonshire, England, 1712-1726; K.B. for N.Y., 30 Aug. 1726; was to have been settled at Salem, N.J., 1726, but the incumbent remained; sett. Burlington (Burlington) N.J., St. Anne's, now St. Mary's, Chh., 1727-1730; Ep.; d. Burlington, N.J., 28 July 1730.

Bishop JACOB HOSTETTER, b. ca. 1682; Ord. Switzerland; preacher and Bishop in Europe; came to America, ca. 1712; sett. East Hempfield (Lanc.) Pa., Rohrerstown Chh., 1712-1761; East Hempfield, Millersville Chh., 1757-1761; Pequea (Lanc.) Pa., Chh. at New Danville, 1717-1761; Pequea, Byerland Chh., 1747-1761; Menn.; d. Manor township (Lanc.) Pa., 1761.

MICHAEL HOUDIN, A.M., b. France, 1705; Ord. priest by the Archbishop of Trèves, Easter, 1730; Superior at a Convent of Franciscans, Montreal, Canada; became an Ep., Easter, 1747; sett. Trenton (Mercer) N.J., St. Michael's Chh., June 1750-1757; S.P.G. missionary, 1 Nov. 1750; Amwell (Hunterdon) N.J., St. Andrew's Chh., 1753-1755; Allentown (Monmouth) N.J., Christ Chh., 1750-1753; Alexandria (Hunterdon) N.J., St. Thomas's Chh., Kingwood, 1750-1757; missionary visits also to Burlington, Bethlehem, and Greenwich (Cumb.), N.J., 1750-1757; chaplain and interpreter at the taking of Quebec, 29 Apr. 1757-28 Nov. 1758; also chaplain, 6 Feb. 1759-June 1761; New Rochelle (Westchester) N.Y., Trinity Chh., 20 Aug. 1761-1766; R.C.; Fr. Huguenot; Ep.; d. New Rochelle, N.Y., Sept. 1766.

WILLIAM HOUSEL, b. Neuritt, Germany, 1728; sett. Amwell (Hunterdon) N.J., after 1760; Germ. Bapt.

JOSEPH HOUSTON, b. Ireland; ed. in Scotland; Ord. Elk River (Cecil) Md., The Rock Chh., 15 Oct. 1724; sett. Elk River, 1724-1739; sett. Montgomery (Orange) N.Y., at Wallkill, Good Will Chh., Jan. 1739/40-1740; Presb.; d. Wallkill, N.Y., 29 Oct. 1740.

ALEXANDER HOWIE, K.B. for Pa., 11 Feb. 1730/1; S.P.G. missionary; sett. Whitemarsh (Montgomery) Pa., St. Thomas's Chh., 24 June 1733-1741; Oxford (Chester) Pa., Trinity Chh., 1733-1741; resigned 1741; Lower Providence (Montg.) Pa., St. James's Chh. at Evansburg, 1734-1741; went to the West Indies, 1741; Ep.

JOHN HUBBARD, A.M., b. Boston, Mass., 9 Jan. 1676/7, son of John and Ann (Leverett) Hubbard; A.B., H.C., 1695, A.M.; Ord. 1698; sett. Jamaica, L.I., N.Y., 1702-1705; Presb.; d. Jamaica, L.I., N.Y., 5 Oct. 1705, a. 28.

NATHANIEL HUBBELL, A.M., b. Fairfield, Conn., 11 Aug. 1702, son of Richard and Hannah (Sillaway) Hubbell; A.B., Y.C., 1723, A.M.; sett. Westfield (Union) N.J., 1727-1745; Hanover (Morris) N.J., Whippany Chh., 1727-1730; and the following missionary stations (later chhs.) in Morris co., N.J., 1727-1730: Morristown, chh. org. 1742; Chatham, at Madison, chh. org. 1747; and Hanover, at Parsippany, chh. org. 1760; Presb.; d. Lebanon (Hunterdon) N.J., 1760.

GRIFFITH HUGHES, A.M., b. Merionethshire, Great Britain, 1707, son of Edward Hughes of Towyn; matric. St. John's Coll., Oxford, 16 May 1729, a. 22; A.B., A.M., 1748; came to Pa., 1732/3; sett. Caernarvon (Lanc.) Pa., Bangor Chh., 1732/3-25 June 1736; S.P.G. missionary at Newtown (Del.) Pa., St. David's Chh. at Radnor, 1733-1736; and Lower Providence (Montgomery) Pa., St. James's Chh. at Evansburg, 1733-1736; Ep.; returned to England, 1736.

JOHN HUGHES, sett. Newtown (Del.) Pa., St. David's Chh. at Radnor, 1733-1736, perhaps as an asst. to Griffith Hughes; Ep.

HUGSTON HUGHES, sett. Cape May (Cape May) N.J., Chh. at Cold Spring, 1726-1727; Presb.

PHILIP HUGHES, came from the diocese of Waterford, Ireland; appointed to serve at Perth Amboy (Middlesex) N.J., 1759, but declined; Chaplain of the 44th regt. of Foot, 1759. (See Philip Hughes, D.D., in *Colonial Clergy of Maryland*, p. 49; there may be some connection here.)

JOHN HUMPHREY(S), A.B., b. Limerick, Ireland, 1683, son of Dr. Thomas Humphreys; sizar, Trinity Coll., Dublin, 13 Nov. 1699, a. 16; A.B., 1704; schoolmaster, N.Y., 1706-1710; Ord. by Bsp. of London, 1710; K.B. for Pa., 3 Nov. 1710; sett. Oxford (Chester) Pa., Trinity Chh., 1711-1713, 1718-1719; S.P.G. missionary at Chichester (Delaware) Pa., 1713-1714, Marlborough (Chester) Pa., 1715-1726, Newtown (Del.) Pa., St. David's Chh. at Radnor, 1717-1718; sett. Chester (Del.) Pa., St. Paul's Chh., 1714-1726; Concord (Del.) Pa., St. John's Chh., 1714-1726; Marcus Hook (Del.) Pa., St. Martin's Chh., 1724-1729; St. George's Parish (Harford) Md., 1724-1725; Annapolis (Anne Arundel) Md., St. Anne's Chh., 11 Feb. 1724/5-1739; Ep.; d. Annapolis, Md., 8 July 1739, a. 53.

ANDREW HUNTER, Ord. Greenwich (Cumberland) N.J., 4 Sept. 1746; sett. Greenwich, 1746-1775; Deerfield (Cumb.) N.J., 1746-1760; New Side Presb.; d. Greenwich, N.J., 28 July 1775.

JONATHAN HUNTING, bapt. Easthampton, L.I., N.Y., 24 Oct. 1714, son of the Rev. Nathaniel and Mary (Green) Hunting; Y.C., 1735; asst. to his father at Easthampton, L.I., N.Y., but not sett. on account of ill health; Presb.; d. Hartford, Conn., 3 Sept. 1750, a. 36.

NATHANIEL HUNTING, A.M., b. Dedham, Mass., 15 Nov. 1675, son of John and Elizabeth (Payne) Hunting; A.B., H.C., 1693, A.M.; Ord. Easthampton, L.I., N.Y., 13 Sept. 1699; sett. Easthampton, 1696-1746; dism. 19 Sept. 1746; Presb.; d. Easthampton, L.I., N.Y., 21 Sept. 1753.

NATHANIEL HUNTTING, 3rd., A.M., bapt. Easthampton, L.I., N.Y., 6 Sept. 1702, son of the Rev. Nathaniel and Mary (Green) Hunting, A.B., 1722, A.M.; he began preaching but ill health required the relinquishment of his ministry; Captain, N.Y., militia; Presb.; d. Easthampton, L.I., N.Y., 18 July 1770, a. 68 (GS).

SAMUEL HUNTINGTON, b. Cape May, N.J., 1677; Ord. Hightstown (Mercer) N.J., 1745; sett. Hightstown, 1745-1756; Bapt.; d. Hightstown, N.J., 1756, a. 79 (cf. James Carman).

CLEMENT HYSLOP, Scotch Franciscan; came to Pa., 1708; R.C.

TRAUGOTT FREDERICK ILLING, sett. Elizabethtown (Lanc.) Pa., Christ Chh., 1758-1766; he is said to have become an Ep., and did receive K.B. for Pa., 11 Sept. 1772, but continued to serve Lutheran chhs.; sett. Lower Swatara (Dauphin) Pa., St. Peter's Chh. at Middletown, 1773-1788; Pequea (Lanc.) Pa., St. John's Chh., 15 Apr. 1784-1788; Luth.; Ep.

Bishop CHARLES INGLIS, D.D., b. Glenkilcar, Donegal, Ireland, ca. 1734, son of the Rev. Archibald Inglis; came to America, 1755; A.B. (hon.) Columbia, 1767, A.M., Oxford, 6 Apr. 1770; D.D., Oxford, 25 Feb. 1778; schoolmaster in America, 1756; Ord. London, 1759; K.B. for Pa., 10 Jan. 1759; sett. Kent co. Delaware chhs., 1759-1765: Dover, Christ Chh., Smyrna, St. Peter's Chh., Mispillion, Christ Chh., and Milford, Christ Chh.; sett. N.Y., N.Y., Trinity Chh., 6 Dec. 1765-1783; 1st Bsp. of Nova Scotia, 12 Aug. 1787-1816; Ep.; d. Halifax, N.S., 24 Feb. 1816, a. 82.

JOHN WILLIAM INGOLD, b. Simmern, near Coblenz, Germany, 4 Oct. 1734, son of the Rev. John William Ingold, senior; matric. Heidelberg, 4 Aug. 1754; Ord. Heidelberg, 10 May 1762; sett. London, Eng., 1774; arriv. Pa., 1774; sett. Lower Salford (Montgomery) Pa., Reiff's or Skippack Chh., 1774-1775; Whitpain (Montg.) Pa., Boehm's Chh., 7 Nov. 1774-13 Aug. 1775; Worcester (Montg.) Pa., Wentz's or Skippack Chh., 1774-1775; Greenwich (Warren) N.J., 1775-1785; Easton (Northampton) Pa., 1775-1785; Dryland (Northampton) Pa., 1776-1786; Lehigh (Northampton) Pa., St. Paul's Chh., 1776-1786; Plainfield (Northampton) Pa., St. Peter's Chh., 1776-1780; Upper Salford (Montgomery) Pa., Old Goshenhoppen Chh., 1780-1781; Reading (Berks) Pa., Nov. 1786-Apr. 1788; Rockhill (Bucks) Pa., Indianfield Chh., Apr. 1788-1790; Bedminster (Bucks) Pa., Tohickon Chh., Apr. 1788-1790; Milford (Bucks) Pa., Lower Milford Chh. at Trumbauersville, Apr. 1788-1790; Spier's Chh. (Berks) Pa., 1790-1793; Amity (Berks) Pa., 1791-1796; excluded, 1801; Germ. Ref.; d. after 1801.

Dr. ALEXANDER INNIS, b. Aberdeenshire, Scotland; prob. grad. of the U. of Aberdeen, 1666/1683; arriv. N.J., 1686; Chaplain to the English chh. at the Fort, N.Y., N.Y., 20 Apr. 1686-20 Aug. 1689; sett. Middletown (Monmouth) N.J., Christ Chh., 28 Oct. 1700-1713; Perth Amboy (Middlesex) N.J., St. Peter's Chh., 1709-1713; Freehold (Monm.) N.J., 28 Oct. 1700-1713; Shrewsbury (Monm.) N.J., Christ Chh., 28 Oct. 1700-1713; called doctor, prob. a physician; will made 27 July 1713; Ep.; d. Perth Amboy, N.J., ca. 1. Aug. 1713.

NATHANIEL IRWIN, A.M., b. Fagg's Manor (Chester) Pa., 17 Oct. 1756; William & Mary Coll., Va.; A.B., Princeton, 1770, A.M.; Ord. Warwick (Bucks) Pa., Neshaminy Chh., 3 Nov. 1774-1812; moderator of the General Assembly, 1801; Presb.; d. Neshaminy, Pa., 3 Mar. 1812, a. 56.

JESSE IVES, A.M., b. Meriden, Conn., 2 Apr. 1738, son of John and Hannah (Royce) Ives; A.B., Y.C., 1758, A.M.; Ord. Sprague, Conn., Norwich, 8th Society, 1766; sett. Sprague, Conn., 1766-1770; inst. Southold, L.I., N.Y., 14 Oct. 1772-1773; inst. Monson, Mass., 23 June 1773; sett. Monson, 1773-1805; Cong.; d. Monson, Mass., 31 Dec. 1805, a. 68.

WILLIAM JACKSON, A.M., b. 1732; A.M., U. of Utrecht; A.M., Columbia, 1761; A.M., Y.C., 1763; A.M., Princeton, 1771; original trustee of Rutgers C.; Ord. Amsterdam, Holland, 10 Sept. 1757; sett. Bergen, N.J., and Staten Island, N.Y., Chh. at Port Richmond, 1757-10 Dec. 1789; and Staten Island, Richmond Chh. (Union of French, Dutch and English Reformed Chhs.), 1757-1776; emeritus, 1789-1813; Dutch Ref.; d. Bergen, N. J., 25 July 1813.

THOMAS JAMES, Jr., b. England, ca. 1620, son of the Rev. Thomas and Elizabeth James; sett. Easthampton, L.I., N.Y., 1651-1696; Cong.; d. Easthampton, L.I., N.Y., 1696.

NATHANIEL JENKINS, b. Cardigan, Wales, 25 Mar. 1678; came to America, 1710; sett. Cape May (Cape May) N.J., 1712-1747; Cohansey (Salem) N.J., 1st Bapt. Chh., 1730-1754; Bapt.; d. Cohansey, N.J., 2 Jan. 1754.

NATHANIEL JENKINS, Jr., b. Wales, 11 Apr. 1710, son of the Rev. Nathaniel and Esther (Jones) Jenkins; Ord. 1747; sett. Cape May, N.J., 1747-1769; Bapt.; d. Cape May, N.J., 1769.

Commissary ROBERT JENNEY, LL.D., b. Waneytown, co. Armagh, Ireland, 1687, son of Archdeacon Henry Jenney, D.D., of Dromore; pensioner, Trinity Coll., Dublin, 13 Oct. 1704, a. 16; A.B., 7 Mar. 1709/10; Ord. 8 June 1710; Chaplain, Royal Navy, 1710-1714; K.B. for Pa., 27 June 1714; Philadelphia, Pa., Christ Chh., 1714-June 1715; S.P.G. missionary to N.Y., 1715-1717; asst., N.Y., N.Y., Trinity Chh., appointed, 5 Mar. 1714/5; sett. Trinity Chh., 29 June 1715-1722; Chaplain at the Fort, N.Y., N.Y., 1715-1722; Rector, Rye, N.Y., Christ Chh., 17 June 1722-19 May 1726; Bedford (Westchester) N.Y., St. Matthew's Chh., 1722-1726; Greenwich, Conn., 1722-1725; Hempstead, L.I., N.Y., St. George's Chh., 1 July 1726-1742; Philadelphia, Pa., Christ Chh., 8 Nov. 1742-1762; Bishop's Commissary in Pa., 4 Jan. 1742/3-1762; Ep.; d. Philadelphia, Pa., 5 Jan. 1762, a. 75.

RASMUS JENSEN, b. Denmark; Chaplain of a Danish expedition from Denmark, which sailed for America, 9 May 1619; 1st Lutheran minister in America; d. 20 Feb. 1619/20, buried on American soil.

JONATHAN JERMAN, b. Cohansey, N.J., 20 Oct. 1740; Ord. Piscataway, N.J., 4 July 1772; sett. Warwick (Chester) Pa., at French Creek, chh. at East Nantmeal, 1772-1778; sett. Cohansey, N.J., 1778-1789 ff.; 7th Day Bapt.; d. Cohansey, N.J., after 1789.

JACOB JODER (or Yoder), lay preacher, sett. Oley (Berks) Pa., 1770 ff.; Germ. Bapt.

ISAAC JOGUES, S.J., b. Orleans, France, 10 Jan. 1607; adm. S.J., 24 Oct. 1624; Prof. at Rouen; Ord. 1636; missionary to Canada, 1636; tried to establish a mission among the Mohawks, but was taken prisoner by them, 3 Aug. 1643 at Ossernenon (now Auriesville, Montgomery co. N.Y.); escaped; rescued by the Dutch; to Albany, N.Y., where assisted by Dutch traders, he reached New Amsterdam (now New York City), and was sent by the Dutch to France, 1643; he returned to Canada, 1644; established near Fonda (Montgomery) N.Y., the "Mission of the

Martyrs," among the Mohawks; then visited Canada; returning to his mission, he was captured, tortured and killed, the first of many martyrs; R.C.; killed by the Indians at Auriesville on the Mohawk River, N.Y., 18 Oct. 1646.

TIMOTHY JOHNES, D.D., b. Southampton, L.I., N.Y., 24 May 1717, son of Deacon Samuel and Esther (Stephens) Johnes; A.B., Y.C., 1737, A.M., D.D., 1783; Trustee, Princeton, 1748-1788; Ord. Morristown (Morris) N.J., 9 Feb. 1742/3-1794; sett. Newburgh (Orange) N.Y., 1766-1767; New Windsor (Orange) N.Y., 1766-1767; Presb.; d. Morristown, N.J., 15 Sept. 1794, a. 78 (GS).

JACOB JOHNSON, A.M., b. Wallingford, Conn., 7 Apr. 1713, son of Sgt. Jacob and Abigail (Hitchcock) Johnson; A.B., Y.C., 1740, A.M., 1763; Ord. Ledyard, Conn. (2nd Chh. in Groton), 10 June 1749-Oct. 1772; Indian missionary; sett. Wilkes-Barre (Luzerne) Pa., 11 Dec. 1772-1778, 1781-1797; Cong.; Presb.; d. Wilkes-Barre, Pa., 15 Mar. 1797. (See *N.E.H.G. Register*, 55: 370-371).

NICHOLAS JOHNSON (Claus Jansen), b. 1658; came to Germantown, 1686; sett. Skippack (Montgomery) Pa., 1702-1745; Menn.; d. Skippack, Pa., 1745.

President SAMUEL JOHNSON, D.D., b. Guilford, Conn., 14 Oct. 1696, son of Deacon Samuel and Mary (Sage) Johnson; A.B., Y.C., 1714, A.M.; Tutor, 1715-1719; A.M., U. of Cambridge, 1723; A.M., U. of Oxford, 1723, D.D., 1743; Ord. West Haven, Conn. (Cong. Chh. at Orange), 20 Mar. 1719/20-1722; became an Ep.; Ord. London, Eng., 31 Mar. 1723; K.B. for N.E., 28 June 1723; sett. Stratford, Conn., Christ Chh., 1723-1754, 1764-1772; Huntington, Conn., Chh. at Ripton, 1740-1754; first President, Columbia U., 1754-1763; sett. N.Y., N.Y., Trinity Chh., 1753-1763; Cong.; Ep.; d. Stratford, Conn., 6 Jan. 1772, a. 76.

SAMUEL JOHNSON, A.M., b. near Durham, Conn., Sept. 1744; A.B., Y.C., 1769, A.M.; Ord. New Lebanon (Columbia) N.Y., Cong. Chh. of Christ, Nov. 1772-1776; sett. West Stockbridge, Mass., 1776-1779; became a Shaker, 1780; Cong.; Shaker; d. New Lebanon, N.Y., 14 May 1835, a. 91.

WILLIAM JOHNSON, A.M., b. Stratford, Conn., 9 Mar. 1730/1, son of the Rev. Samuel Johnson, D.D.; A.B., Y.C., 1748, A.M.; A.M., H.C., 1753; A.M., Oxford, 1756; A.M., Cambridge, 1756; Ord. London, Eng. (Bsp. of Carlisle), 25 Mar. 1756; K.B. for N.Y., 14 Apr. 1756; Ep.; d. London, England, 20 June 1756, a. 25.

DAVID JONES, A.M., b. White Clay Creek, Del., 12 May 1736, son of Morgan and Eleanor (Evans) Jones; ed. Hopewell School; A.M. (hon.) Brown, 1774; lic. 1761; Ord. Upper Freehold, N.J., Crosswicks Bapt. Chh., 12 Dec. 1766-1775; sett. Tredyffryn (Chester) Pa., Great Valley Bapt. Chh., Apr. 1775-1776, 1792-1820; Chaplain, 3rd regt. Pa. Continental Line, 1776-1781, and eligible officer of the Society of the

Cincinnati in the state of Pa.; chaplain, 1794, and in the War of 1812; Bapt.; d. East Town (Chester) Pa., 5 Feb. 1820, a. 83.

ELIPHALET JONES, b. Concord, Mass., 9 Jan. 1640, son of the Rev. John and Susannah Jones; H.C., but did not graduate; sett. Greenwich, Conn., 2 Feb. 1669/70–1672; Ord. Stamford, Conn., 1673; sett. Huntington, L.I., N.Y., Jan. 1676–1731; Cong.; d. Huntington, L.I., N.Y., 5 June 1731, a. 90.

JENKIN JONES, b. Llanfernach, Pembroke, Wales, 1690; came to America, 1710; sett. Welsh Tract, Del., 1724–1725; sett. Lower Dublin, Pa., Pennypack Bapt. Chh., 1725–1746; sett. Philadelphia, Pa., Bapt. Chh., 1725–1761; the Bapt. Chh. of Philadelphia was constituted 14 May 1746; Bapt.; d. Philadelphia, Pa., 16 July 1761.

JOSHUA JONES, b. Newcastle, Pembroke, Wales, 1721; came to America, 1726; Ord. New Britain (Bucks) Pa., 1761–1795; resigned 1795; sett. Rockhill (Bucks) Pa., 1761–1795; Bapt.; d. New Britain, Pa., 26 Dec. 1802.

MALACHI JONES, b. Wales, 1651; adm. Presbytery of Philadelphia, 9 Sept. 1714; Ord. Wales bef. Sept. 1714; inst. Bensalem (Bucks) Pa., and Northampton (Bucks) Pa., 22 Apr. 1719; sett. Bensalem (Bucks) Pa., Dutch Ref. Chh., 1714–1719, 1719–1723; Northampton (Bucks) Pa., D.R. Chh., 1714–1723; Southampton (Bucks) Pa., Neshaminy D.R. Chh. at Churchville, 1714–1721; Tredyffryn (Chester) Pa.; Great Valley Chh., 1714–1720; Abingdon (Montgomery) Pa., Presb. Chh., 1714–1729; Norriton (Montgomery) Pa., Presb. Chh., 1714–1727; Germantown, Pa., D.R. Chh., 1714–1719; will proved 25 Mar. 1729; Dutch Ref. and Presb.; d. Abingdon, Pa., 25 Feb. 1729, a. 79.

MORGAN JONES, A.B., b. 1618, son of John David of Trethuen, co. Monmouth, Wales, matric. Jesus Coll., Oxford, 1 June 1636, a. 16; A.B., 12 Dec. 1639; vicar in Undy, co. Monmouth, Wales, 1661; lived among the Indians on the Virginia coast, 1669; on 8 Apr. 1670, set sail for Port Royal, S.C., but eight months later started back for Virginia, but fell in with Maj. Gen. Richard Bennett of Nansemond co. Va., and served as his chaplain; was in Somerset co. Md., 1678, having been a member of Maj. Samuel Appleton's co., King Philip's War, July 1676; sett. Staten Island, N.Y., 1676–1682; East Chester and West Chester, N.Y., 1678–1688; sett. Newtown, L.I., N.Y., 17 Dec. 1678–1704, when he resigned; Presb.; living 1704.

SAMUEL JONES, b. Llanddewi, Radnor, Wales, 9 July 1657; came to America, 1686; called to the ministry, 1697; Ord. Lower Dublin, Pa., Pennypack Bapt. Chh., 23 Oct. 1706; sett. Lower Dublin, 1697–1722; sett. Philadelphia, Pa., Bapt. Chh., 1698–1722; Bapt.; d. Bristol, Pa., 16 Dec. 1722 (GS).

SAMUEL JONES, D.D., b. Cefyn-y-Gelli, Bettws Parish, Glamorgan, Wales, 14 Jan. 1735, son of the Rev. Thomas and Martha (Morris) Jones; came to America, 1737; A.B., U. Pa., 1762, A.M.; A.M. (hon.)

COLONIAL CLERGY OF THE MIDDLE COLONIES

Brown, 1769, D.D., Brown, 1786; D.D., U. of Pa., 1788; a founder of Brown U.; Ord. Philadelphia, Pa., 2 Jan. 1763; sett. Lower Dublin, Pa., Pennypack Bapt. Chh., 8 Jan. 1763-1814; Southampton (Bucks) Pa., 1763-1770; Chaplain of a Pa. regt. in the Rev. War; Bapt.; d. Philadelphia, Pa., 7 Feb. 1814.

THOMAS JONES, b. Newton Notage, Glamorgan, Wales, 1701; arriv. in America, 22 July 1737; Ord. Cumru (Berks) Pa., Tulpehocken Chh. 1740; sett. Cumru, Pa., 1738-1774; Spring (Berks) Pa., Bapt. Chh. at Sinking Spring, 1740-1744; Bapt.; d. Great Valley, Pa., 22 Mar. 1788, a. 87 (GS).

WILLIAM JONES, asst. minister at Easthampton, L.I., N.Y.,1693-1696; Cong.

Mr. JOTTER, a Baumanite minister, 1727, in Pa.

JOHN GEORGE JUNG, ed. at Halle; arriv. in America, 1768; sett. Heidelberg (Lehigh) Pa., 1768-1768; North Whitehall (Lehigh) Pa., Schlosser's Chh., 1769-1772; South Whitehall (Lehigh) Jordan Chh., 1769-1772; Chambersburg (Franklin) Pa., St. John's Chh., 1770-1783; Whitehall (Lehigh) Pa., Egypt Chh., 1771-1773; Guilford (Franklin) Pa., Grindstone Hill Chh., 1772-1783; Antietam (Washington) Md., 1773-1785; Hagerstown (Washington) Md., St. John's Chh., 1773-1793; Luth.; living 1793.

MICHAEL JUNG, b. 5 Jan. 1743; came to America, 1751, and to Bethlehem (Northampton) Pa., 1767; sent as Indian missionary to New Gnadenhuetten (Tuscarawas) Ohio; Morav.; d. Lititz, Pa., 1828.

JOHN GEORGE JUNGMAN, b. Hochenheim, Baden, Germany, 19 Apr. 1720, son of Johann Dietrich Jungman; came as a boy to Oley (Berks) Pa., 1731; res. Bethlehem (Northampton) Pa., 1745; Indian missionary, 1770-1785; sett. Gnadenhuetten (Tuscarawas) Ohio, 1746-1754; sett. Pachgatgoch (near Kent, Connecticut), 1754-1758; sett. Christiansbrunn, near Nazareth, Pa., Wyalusing (Bradford) Pa., and Lanuntutenmunk; and Schoenbrunn, Ohio, 1770-1777, 1781-1785; his wife, Anna Margaret (Bechtel) Buettner, was his assistant; Morav.; d. Bethlehem, Pa., 17 July 1808, a. 88.

Professor PETER KALM, b. Finland, 1715; sett. Swedesborough (Gloucester) N.J., 1748-1749; Swedish botonist; author: "A Journey to North America."; Sw. Luth.; d. Abo, Finland, 16 Nov. 1779.

JOHN WILLIAM KALS, b. 1700; came from Julich; matric. Leyden U., 25 Aug. 1745, a. 45; minister in Surinam; arriv. Philadelphia, 1756; stated supply, Philadelphia, Pa., 1756-1757; Amwell (Hunterdon) N.J., 1757-1759; Lebanon (Hunterdon) N.J., Rockaway Chh. at Clinton, 1757-1759; Fairmount (Hunterdon) Fox Hill, Tewksbury, Raritan Chh., 1757-1759; N.Y., N.Y., Germ. Ref. Chh., 1759-1760; Germ. Ref.; d. Reading, Pa., 1763.

HERMAN KASDORF, came from Altona, Germany, 4 Mar. 1700; Ord. Germantown, Pa., 20 Apr. 1708; sett. Germantown, Pa., 1708-1725; Menn.; d. Germantown, Pa., bef. 20 Apr. 1725.

GEORGE KASKE, Ord. Bethlehem, Pa., 1747; missionary at Berbice, South America, 1745-1752; sett. Bethlehem, 1742; returned to Pa.; Morav.; d. Nazareth, Pa., 1795.

ELIAS KEACH, b. 1667, son of the Rev. Benjamin Keach of London; came to America, 1686; Ord. by Mr. Dungan; sett. Lower Dublin, Pa., Pennypack Bapt. Chh., 1688-1692; Burlington, N.J., Bapt. Chh., 1690-1692; returned to England, 1692; sett. London, England, 1692-1699; Bapt.; d. London, England, 1699.

JACOB KEAGY, sett. Heidelberg (York) Pa.; was a minister before 14 May 1775, as shown by a deed of that date; Menn.

GEORGE KEITH, A.M., b. Peterhead, Aberdeenshire, Scotland, ca. 1638/9, (poss. a grandson of the Rev. George Keith of Kecoughtan Parish, Va., ca. 1636), ed. U. of Aberdeen, ca. 1653-1657; A.M.; Ord. minister of the Chh. of Scotland, ca. 1663; became a member of the Society of Friends (Quakers), 1674; came to N.E., N.J., and other colonies, 1682, 1688, 1690; schoolmaster and preacher in Philadelphia, Pa., 1689, 1691; in 1692 he instigated a separatist faction among the Society of Friends called Christian Quakers, or Keithian or Anglican Quakers; and was disowned by the Society of Friends, 1692; returned to London, 1694; became an Ep.; Ord. by the Bishop of London, as an Ep. priest, March 1702; returned to America as one of the first S.P.G. missionaries, 1702-1704; preached at Perth Amboy, 3 Oct. 1702-2 Jan. 1704; Shrewsbury, 1702; Piscataway, 1702; Elizabethtown, 1703; Woodbridge, 1703-1703, all in N.J.; and at Kecoughtan Chh., Elizabeth River Parish, Va., 1703; as well as at many other places in the colonies; his faction was of no permanent importance, except that it gave a strong impetus towards integration among the Society of Friends; returned to England; vicar of St. Andrew's Chh., Edburton, Sussex, England, 1705-1711; Presb.; Friend; Ep.; d. Edburton, Sussex, England, 27 Mar. 1716.

ERASMUS KELLEY, A.M., b. Perkasie (Bucks) Pa., 24 July 1748; A.B., U. of Pa., 1769, A.M., 1783; A.M., Brown, 1772; sett. Southampton (Bucks) Pa., 13 May 1770-Aug. 1771; Ord. Newport, R.I., 1st Bapt. Chh., 9 Oct. 1771; sett. Newport, R.I., 1771-1783; preached in Conn., Warren, R.I.; and Pa., 1783-1784; Bapt.; d. Newport, R.I., 7 Nov. 1784.

JOHANNES KELPIUS, A.M., b. Halwegen, Segesvar, Transylvania, 1673, son of the Rev. George Kelp; A.M. (Ph.D.), U. of Altdorf, 1689; arriv. Philadelphia, Pa., 23 June 1694; sett. Theosophical Community, Wissahickon, Pa., 1694-1708; Pietist; d. bef. 1 Mar. 1708/9, a. 35.

ROBERT KELSEY, b. near Drummore, Ireland, 1711; arriv. in Md., 1734; came to Cohansey, N.J., 1738; lic. 1743; Ord. Cohansey (Salem) N.J., 1st Bapt. Chh., 1750; sett. Cohansey, 1756-1789; Bapt., d. Cohansey, N.J., 30 May 1789.

SAMUEL KENNEDY, A.M., M.D., b. Scotland, 1720; ed. U. of Edinburgh; A.B., Princeton, 1754, A.M., 1760; lic. 1748; Ord. Basking Ridge (Somerset) N.J., at Bernard, 26 June 1751-1787; Amwell (Hunterdon) N.J., at Reaville, 1769-1787; Cumberland (Adams) Pa., Upper Marsh Creek Chh., at Gettysburg, 1771-1772; physician and teacher; Presb.; d. Basking Ridge, N.J., 31 Aug. 1787, a. 67 (GS).

Domine KENNIPE, sett. Canajoharie (Montgomery) N.Y., D.R. Chh. at Minden, 1775-1779; Dutch Ref.

ELISHA KENT, A.M., b. Suffield, Conn., 9 July 1704, son of John and Abigail (Dudley) Kent; A.B., Y.C., 1729, A.M.; Ord. Newtown, Conn., 27 Sept. 1732; sett. Newtown, 1732-1743; dism., 25 Feb. 1742/3; sett. Carmel (Putnam) N.Y., 1743-1749; sett. South East (Putnam) N.Y., Philippi Chh., 1743-1776; Cong.; d. South East, N.Y., 17 July 1776, a. 72 (GS).

NATHAN KER, A.B., b. Basking Ridge, N.J., ca. 1735, of Scotch descent; A.B., Princeton, 1761; sett. Springfield (Union) N.J., 1763-1765; sett. Goshen (Orange) N.Y., 1766-1804; Chaplain, Continental Army, Rev. War; Presb.; d. Goshen, N.Y., 14 Dec. 1804, a. 69 (GS).

JOHN MICHAEL KERN, b. Mannheim, Germany, 31 Aug. 1730, son of John Leonard and Anna Eva Kern; matric. Heidelberg, 21 Nov. 1753; sett. Heidelberg, Germany, 1763; arriv. N.Y., N.Y., Sept. 1763; sett. N.Y., N.Y., Germ. Ref. Chh., 1763-inst.-27 Jan. 1764-1771; Montgomery (Orange) N.Y., D.R. Chh., 1771-1778; Hanover (Ulster) N.Y., 1775-1775; Halifax, Nova Scotia, 1778-1787; Rhinebeck (Dutchess) N.Y., G.R. Chh., 1787-1787; Bedminster (Bucks) Pa., Tohicon Chh., May 1787-1788; Rockhill (Bucks) Pa., Indianfield Chh., 1782-1788; Germ. Ref.; d. Rockhill, Pa., 22 Mar. 1788.

ABRAHAM KETTELTAS, A.M., (or Keteltas), b. N.Y., N.Y., 26 Dec. 1732, son of Abraham and Jane (Jacobs) Ketteltas; A.B., Y.C., 1752, A.M.; A.M., Princeton; Ord. Elizabethtown (Union) N.J., Presb. Chh., 14 Sept. 1757; sett. Elizabethtown, N.J., 1757-Sept. 1760; Hempstead, L.I., N.Y., Presb. Chh., 1760-1765; Jamaica, L.I., N.Y., D.R. Chh., 1760-1762; N.Y., N.Y., French Ref. Chh. of the Saint Esprit, Sept. 1766-Apr. 1776; Chairman, Committee of Correspondence, Dec. 1774; delegate to N.Y. State Congress, 1777; preached in English, Dutch and French; French Ref.; Presb.; d. Jamaica, L.I., N.Y., 30 Sept. 1798, a. 65 (GS).

THOMAS KILLINGSWORTH, b. (prob.) Norwich, England; Ord. in England; sett. Cohansey (Salem) N.J., 1st Bapt. Chh., 1690-1708; Bapt.; Judge of the Salem Court; d. Cohansey, N.J., 1708, s.p.

ROBERT KILLPATRICK, K.B. for Newfoundland, 25 June 1730; sett. Trinity Bay, Newfoundland, 1730-1731; sett. Newburgh (Orange) N.Y., St. George's Chh., 1731-1733; S.P.G. missionary at New Windsor (Orange) N.Y., 1731-1733; sett. Trinity Bay, Newfoundland, 1734-1741; Ep.; d. Trinity Bay, Newfoundland, 19 Aug. 1741.

JOHANN JACOB KIMMEL, b. Gimsheim, Germany; arriv. Philadelphia, 14 Sept. 1751; adm. Ephrata (Lancaster) Pa., German Bapt. Chloister, Dec. 1751; sett. Latimore (Adams) Pa., Bermudian Chh., 1752–1753; Ephrata Chloister, 1753–1784; Germ. Bapt.; d. Ephrata, Pa., 25 Nov. 1784.

ANDREW KING, A.M., A.B., Princeton, 1773, A.M., 1786; inst. Montgomery (Orange) N.Y., Good Will Chh., 11 June 1777; sett. Montgomery, N.Y., 1776–1815; Presb.; d. Montgomery, N.Y., 16 Nov. 1815.

JOHN KING, D.D., b. Chestnut Level, Drumore (Lancaster) Pa., 5 Dec. 1740, son of Elder Robert King; A.B., U. of Pa., 1766; D.D., Dickinson Coll., 1792; taught school at West Conococheague, Pa., 1760–1763; sett. New London (Chester) Pa., 1762–1769; Ord. Upper West Conococheague, now Mercersburg (Franklin) Pa., May 1769–1809; Montgomery, Hill Chh., at Mercersburg, 1769–1809; Presb.; d. Mercersburg, Pa., 5 July 1811, a. 70.

JOHN KING, came from London, 1769; itinerant minister in Del., N.J., Va., Md., and N.C., 1772–1800; preached, Eastern Shore of Md., 24 Dec. 1772; Frederick, Md., 1773; sett. Trenton, N.J., Green St. Chh., 1773–1775; Meth.; d. near Raleigh, N.C., ca. 1800.

JOHN KINKEAD, b. Ireland, lic. 1732; Ord. ca. 1753; sett. Norriton (Montgomery) Pa., 1752–1757; Tredyffryn (Chester) Pa., Great Valley Chh., 1752–1757; Middletown (Del.) Pa., 1757–1758; Windham, New Hampshire, Oct. 1760–Apr. 1765; a contemporary deed mentions the "Calfpasture" of 250 acres, "near the home of Rev. Mr. Kinkead" in 1762, at Beverly Manor (possibly in Beverly, Upper Darby (Del.) Pa.); Presb.; d. after 1769.

EBENEZER KINNERSLEY, A.M., b. Gloucester, England, 30 Nov. 1711, son of the Rev. William Kinnersley; arriv. in America, 12 Sept. 1714; A.M., U. of Pa. (hon.) 1757; Ord. Philadelphia, Pa., 1743–1754; preached but was never settled; member of the 1st Bapt. Chh. in Philadelphia; experimenter in electricity with Benjamin Franklin; Prof. of English, U. of Pa., 11 July 1755–17 Oct. 1772; member, Am. Phil. Soc.; Bapt.; d. Lower Dublin, Pa., 4 July 1778, a. 67.

WILLIAM KINNERSLEY, b. Lynch, near Leominster, Hereford co. England, 1669; came to America, 12 Sept. 1714; lived in Lower Dublin; sett. Lower Dublin, Pa., Pennypack Bapt. Chh., 1714–1734; Bapt.; d. Lower Dublin, Pa., 13 Feb. 1734.

JOHN CASPAR KIRCHNER, sett. Baltimore, Md., 1762–1773; York (York) Pa., Christ Chh., 1763–1767; Springfield (York) Pa., Frieden Saal or Shuster's Chh., 1763–1767; Luth.; d. Baltimore, Md., 1773.

WILLIAM KIRKPATRICK, A.M., b. 1726; A.B., Princeton, 1757, A.M.; Trustee, Princeton, 1767–1769; lic. 15 Aug. 1758; Ord. Cranbury (Middlesex) N.J., 4 July 1759; supply, Trenton (Mercer) N.J., 1st Presb. Chh., 28 Apr. 1761–1766; Hopewell (Mercer) N.J., Ewing Chh.,

1760–1766; sett. Amwell (Hunterdon) N.J., chh. at Reaville, June 1766– inst. Aug. 1766–1769; Treasurer and Clerk of the Presbytery, 1769; Moderator of the Synod of Philadelphia, 1769; d. Amwell, N.J., 8 Sept. 1769, a. 43.

SAMUEL KIRKLAND, A.M., b. Norwich, Conn., 1 Dec. 1741, son of the Rev. Daniel and Hannah (Perkins) Kirtland; A.B., Princeton, 1765; A.M., Y.C., 1768; Ord. Lebanon, Conn., 19 June 1766; Indian missionary near Oneida Lake, N.Y., 1766–1808; Chaplain, Continental Army, 1775–1783; an eligible member, Society of the Cincinnati; Cong.; d. Clinton, N.Y., 28 Feb. 1808.

JOHN RUDOLPH KITTWEILER (or Kidenweiler, Kindweiler), b. Basel, Switzerland, 26 May 1716, son of Hans Jacob and Catherine (Spoerin) Kittweiler; Ord. Switzerland; arriv. Philadelphia, 28 Sept. 1749; sett. Weisenberg (Lehigh) Pa., 1749–1761; Long Swamp (Berks) Pa., 1754–1763; Salisbury (Lehigh) Pa., New Jerusalem Chh., 1759–1764; Lower Milford (Lehigh) Pa., Great Swamp Chh., 1762–1764; Germ. Ref.; d. Long Swamp, Pa., 2 Oct. 1764, a. 47 y. 9 m. (GS).

GEORGE KLEINE, b. Zweibruecken, France, 9 Oct. 1715; came to America, 1738; Ord. 1757; sett. Bern (Berks) Pa., Northkill Chh., 1750–1770; Tulpehocken (Berks) Pa., Little Swatara Chh., 1757–1770; Oley (Berks) Pa., 1757–1770; Germ. Bapt.; d. after 1770.

SEBASTIAN HENRY KNAUSS, b. Tittelsheim, near Frankfort-on-the-Main, Germany, Oct. 1714, son of Louis and Ann Margaret (Goerlach) Knauss; came to Pa., 1732; Ord. deacon, Salisbury (Lehigh) Pa., 1747; sett. Salisbury, Macungie Chh., 1743–1747 ff.; Morav.

EBENEZER KNIBLOE, b. Scotland; ed. Edinburgh; came to America, 1752; Ord. Carmel (Putnam) N.Y., 18 Feb. 1756–11 July 1759; sett. Amenia (Dutchess) N.Y., Smithfield Chh., 1760–1775; Cong.; d. Amenia, N. Y.

MICHAEL CHRISTIAN KNOLL, b. Holstein, 1696; Ord. London, England, 1732; sett. Newburgh (Orange) N.Y., Quassick Chh., 1733–1748; N.Y., N.Y., Holy Trinity Chh., 1732–1748; Hackensack, N.J., 1734–1748; he also preached in the Berckenmeyer congregations at Coxsackie, Claverick, St. Thomas's Chh., and Athens, Loonenburgh Chh. in Greene co. N.Y.; Rhinebeck (Dutchess) N.Y.; and East Camp, Christ Chh., Kaatsbaan, West Camp at Saugerties, Four Mile Point and Rosendale, all in Ulster co. N.Y., 1732–1748; Luth.

STEPHEN KOCH, Ord. Krefeld, Rhine, Germany, ca. 1715; sett. Krefeld, 1715–1719; came to Germantown, Pa., 1719; sett. Wissahickon, Pa., 1733–1739; Ephrata (Lanc.) Pa., Germ. Bapt. Chloister, 1739–1763; Germ. Bapt.; d. Ephrata, Pa., 7 July 1763.

JOSHUA von KOCKERTHAL, b. near Bretton, Baden, 1669; sett. Landau, Palatinate, 1704; came to America, 1708, bringing with him many Palatine settlers; arriv. N.Y., N.Y., 1 Jan. 1707/8; returned to England; was Ep. ordained; K.B., N.Y., 28 Jan. 1709/10; arriv. N.Y.,

N.Y., 2nd time, 14 June 1710; sett. Newburgh (Orange) N.Y., Quassick Chh., 1708–1719; East Camp (Ulster) N.Y., Christ Chh., 1708–1719; Rhinebeck (Dutchess) N.Y., 1709–1719; West Camp (Ulster) N.Y., at Saugerties, 1710–1719; Kaatsbaan (Ulster) 1710–1719; Newtown (Ulster) N.Y., 1711–1719; Schoharie (Schoharie) N.Y., 1715–1719; Shawangunk (Ulster) N.Y., 1716–1719; Langen Rack (Ulster) N.Y., 1716–1719; Rosendale (Ulster) N.Y., 1716–1719; Tarbush, N.Y., 1716–1719; Queensboro, N.Y., 1716–1719; Elizabethtown, N.J., bef. 1719; Luth.; d. West Camp, N.Y., 27 Dec. 1719.

HEINRICH BERNHARD KOESTER, b. Blumenberg, Lippe, Westphalia, Nov. 1662, son of Burgomaster Ludolph and Ann Catherina (Blumen von Schwalenberg) Koester; ed. U. of Frankfort-on-the-Oder, 1681–1684; teacher in Berlin, 1685–1692; was at first a Pietist, then a Lutheran preacher; sett. Germantown, Pa., 1694–1699; held the first Lutheran service in Pa., 1694; arriv. London, England, Jan. 1700; visited Stockholm, 1702; sett. Eingfleish, near Berlin, 1714–1724; Luth.; d. Hanover, Germany, 1749, a. 87.

JACOB KOHN, arriv. Bethlehem, Pa., Sept. 1742; sett. Oley (Berks) Pa., 1743–1744; sett. Mount Joy (Lancaster) Pa., Donegal Chh., May 1745–Nov. 1745; returned to Europe, Nov. 1745; Morav.

DIELMAN KOLB, b. Wolfsheim, Palatinate, Germany, 10 Nov. 1691, son of Dielman and —— (Schumacher) Kolb; minister at Mannheim, Germany, 27 Aug. 1710; arriv. Philadelphia, 10 Aug. 1717; sett. Lower Salford (Montgomery) Pa., 1718–1756; trustee at Salford, 1738; will proved 30 Apr. 1757; Menn.; d. Lower Salford, Pa., 29 Dec. 1756.

DIELMAN KOLB, b. 2 Mar. 1719 (prob. son of Dielman Kolb); Ord. Skippack (Montg.) Pa., 1752–1779; Menn.; d. Skippack, Pa., 19 Oct. 1779.

HENRY KOLB, b. Wolfsheim, Palatinate, Germany, son of the Rev. Dielman Kolb; came to Pa., 1707; sett. Germantown, Pa., 1707–1709; Skippack (Montg.) Pa., 1709–1730; Menn.; d. Skippack, Pa., 1730.

HENRY KOLB, Jr., b. 1721; Ord. Skippack (Montgomery) Pa., 1752; sett. Skippack, Pa., 1753–1781; Menn.; d. Skippack, Pa., 1783.

Bishop ISAAC KOLB, b. 28 Mar. 1711, son of Dea. Jacob and Sarah (Van Sintern) Kolb; Ord. Rockhill (Bucks) Pa., 1744; Ord. Bishop, Franconia (Montgomery) Pa., 1761; sett. Franconia, Pa., Indian Creek Chh., 1744–1766; Rockhill, Pa., Bechtel's or Gehman's Chh., 1744–1766; Hatfield (Montg.) Pa., chh. at Lansdale, 1764–1766; Menn.; d. Gwynned (Montgomery) Pa., 1766.

MARTIN KOLB, b. Wolfsheim, Palatinate, Germany, 1680; came to Pa., 1707; Ord. Germantown, Pa., 20 Apr. 1708–1709; sett. Skippack (Montg.) Pa., 1709–1761; Menn.; d. Skippack, Pa., 23 Aug. 1761.

PETER KOLB, b. Wolfsheim, Palatinate, Germany, son of Dielman Kolb; minister at Mannheim, Germany; came from Mannheim, 1707;

sett. Lower Salford (Montgomery) Pa., 1718-1757; Menn.; will proved 30 Apr. 1757; d. Salford, Pa., 1757.

JOHN VALENTINE KRAFT, minister at Zweibruecken, Palatinate, Germany; arriv. Philadelphia, 25 Aug. 1742; sett. Germantown, Pa., St. Michael's Chh., 1742-1742; Philadelphia, Pa., St. Michael's Chh., 1742-1742; Richmond (Berks) Pa., Zion or Moselem Chh., 20 Jan. 1742/3-1745; Mill Creek (Lebanon) Pa., Reed's or Old Tulpehocken Chh., 1742-1743; Marion (Berks) Pa., Zion or Rieth's Chh., the original Old Tulpehocken Chh. at Stouchsburg, 1742-1743; Lancaster (Lanc.) Pa., Holy Trinity Chh., 1742-1743, May 1747-Mar. 1747/8; Hanover (York) Pa., St. Michael's Chh., 1747-1749; living, not settled, in Frederick, Md., 1749; Monocacy (Frederick) Md., 1750-1751; Luth.; d. Frederick, Md., 1751, in extreme poverty.

MATTHEW KRAUSE, in Pa., 1745; Morav.

SAMUEL KRAUSE, Ord. abroad before 1749; arriv. N.Y., N.Y., 12 May 1749; sett. Bethlehem (Northampton) Pa., 1749-1753; returned to Europe, 1753; Morav.

CHRISTOPHER KRIEBEL, b. Harpersdorf, Silesia, 1724, son of Christopher and Maria (Heydrich) Kriebel; came to Pa., 1734; religious teacher, Lower Salford (Montgomery) Pa., 1764-1797; minister, 1782-1796; Schwenkfelder; d. Lower Salford, Pa., 31 Dec. 1800.

OTTO CHRISTIAN KROGSTRUP, had a university education; arriv. N.Y., N.Y., 9 Sept. 1753; sett. Lancaster (Lanc.) Pa., 1754-1755, 1773-1776; Philadelphia, Pa., 1756-1762; Warwick (Lanc.) Pa., St. James's Chh. at Lititz, 1762-1763; Graceham (Frederick) Md., 1764-1767; York (York) Pa., 1767-1773; Morav.; d. Bethlehem, Pa., 1785.

JOHN ANDREW KRUG, b. Saxony, 19 Mar. 1732; taught at the Orphan House at Halle, at Wasserleben, and at Wernigerode; Ord. 1763; arriv. Philadelphia, 1 Apr. 1764; sett. Reading (Berks) Pa., Trinity Chh., 1764-1771; Exeter (Berks) Pa., Schwartzwald Chh., 1764-1771; Muhlenberg (Berks) Pa., Alsace Chh., 1764-1771; Perry (Berks) Pa., Zion's Chh., 1765-1771; Frederick (Frederick) Md., 28 Apr. 1771-1796; Middletown (Fred.) Md., 1771-1779; Luth.; d. Frederick, Md., 30 Mar. 1796.

TOBIAS KRYTER, Menn.; (no further record).

—— KUHLWEIN, in Pa., 1727; Baumanite.

DANIEL KUHN, son of Adam Simon Kuhn of Lancaster, Pa.; sett. Elizabeth (Lancaster) Pa., Emmanuel Chh., 1769-1770; Middletown, Pa., 1770 ff. (perhaps Lower Swatara (Dauphin) Pa., St. Peter's Chh. at Middletown, as an assistant); Luth.; d. ca. 1779.

JOHN CHRISTOPHER KUNZE, D.D., b. Artern, Mansfield, Saxony, 5 Aug. 1744; matric. U. of Leipzic, 21 Sept. 1763; A.B., Halle; A.M., U. of Pa., 1780, D.D., 1783; sett. Closter Bergen and at the Orphan House at Greitz; Ord. Wernigerode, May 1770; arriv. N.Y., N.Y., 22 Sept. 1770; sett. Philadelphia, Pa., St. Michael's and Zion's

Chhs., 8 Oct. 1770-1784; sett. N.Y., N.Y., Christ Chh., 1780-1784; Prof. of German, U. of Pa., 1780-1784; Prof. of Oriental Languages, Columbia U., 1784-1787, 1792-1799; Luth.; d. N.Y., N.Y., 24 July 1807, a. 64 (GS).

JOHN NICHOLAS KURTZ, D.D., b. Luetzellinden, Nassau-Weilburg, Germany, Oct. 1722; ed. U. of Giessen and Halle; arriv. Philadelphia, 26 Jan. 1744/5; Ord. 15 Aug. 1748, the first Lutheran minister to be ordained in America; sett. New Hanover (Montgomery) Pa., Falkner's Swamp Chh., as assistant, 1745-1746; Lynn (Lehigh) Pa., Jerusalem Chh. at Allemaengel, 1745-1745; Mahwah (Bergen) N.J., Ramapo Chh., 1746-1748; Marion (Berks) Pa., Zion's, Rieth's, or Old Tulpehocken Chh., at Stouchsburg, 13 Sept. 1747-Apr. 1770; also Marion, Christ Chh. at Stouchsburg, Old Tulpehocken, 5 Sept. 1747-1770; Mill Creek (Lebanon) Pa., Reed's or Old Tulpehocken Chh., 1747-1770 (these are offshoots of the original Old Tulpehocken, which is Rieth's noted above); Upper Saucon (Lehigh) Pa., St. Paul's, Blue or Organ Chh., 1749-1749; Heidelberg (Berks) Pa., St. Daniel's Chh., 1757-1770; Elizabeth (Lancaster) Pa., Emmanuel Chh., 1762-1769; Upper Dublin (Montgomery) Pa., Puff's Chh., 1763-1764; Lower Windsor (Berks) Pa., 1770-1789; York (York) Pa., Christ Chh., Apr. 1770-1789; West Manchester (York) Pa., St. Paul's or Wolf's Chh., 1770-1789; Baltimore, Md., 1772-1794; Luth.; brother of William Kurtz; d. Baltimore, Md., 12 May 1794, a. 72 (GS).

JOHN WILLIAM KURTZ, b. prob. at Luetzellinden, Germany, son of John George Kurtz; ed. Halle, 15 yrs.; arriv. America, 1754; lic. 1760; Ord. Lancaster, Pa., May 1761; teacher at York, Pa., 1756; sett. Douglass (Berks) Pa., Oley Hill Chh., 1756-1758; Pike (Berks) Pa., St. John's or Hill Chh., 1756-1758; New Hanover (Montgomery) Pa., Falkner's Swamp Chh., 1757-1758; Upper Dublin (Montgomery) Pa., Puff's Chh., 1757-1758; Bedminster (Bucks) Pa., Keller's Chh., 1763-1781; Brecknock (Lancaster) Pa., Muddy Creek or East Cocalico Chh., 1763-1781; Earl (Lanc.) Pa., Chh. at New Holland, 1763-1779; Ephrata (Lanc.) Pa., Bergstrasse Chh., 1763-1779; Lebanon (Lebanon) Pa., Salem or Kruppe's Chh., 1775-1794; Strasburg (Lanc.) Pa., St. Michael's or Beaver Creek Chh., 1775-1779; Hummelstown (Dauphin) Pa., 1781-1799; Jonestown (Lebanon) Pa., Zion's Chh., 1781-1799; Luth.; d. Jonestown, Pa., 27 May 1799.

WARMOLDUS KUYPERS, b. Holland, 1732; ed. U. Gronigen, 1753; came to America from Curacoa, 1768; sett. Rhinebeck Flats (Dutchess) N.Y., 1769-1771; Upper Red Hook Landing (Dutchess) N.Y., 1769-1771; Hackensack (Bergen) N.J., Second Chh., 1771-1797; Schraalenburg (Bergen) N.J., DuMont Chh., 1771-1797; Dutch Ref.; d. 1797.

JACQUES (James) LABOURIE, b. Cardaillac, Lot, France; grad. U. Geneva, Switzerland, 12 Mar. 1688, in theology; Ord. Zurich (or Geneva) 30 Oct. 1688; sett. London, England, French Chh., 1688-1698; came to America; sett. Oxford, Mass., Huguenot Chh., 1699-1704;

sett. N.Y., N.Y., French Ref. Chh. of the Saint Esprit, 15 Oct. 1704-25 Aug. 1706; became an Ep.; practiced medicine and surgery; sett. Fairfield co. Conn., 1716, as a physician; Fr. Ref.; Ep.; d. Fairfield, Conn., ca. 1731.

ARCHIBALD LAIDLIE, D.D., b. Kelso, co. Roxburgh, Scotland, 4 Dec. 1727; ed. U. of Edinburgh, 1730; S.T.D., Princeton, 1770; Ord. 1759; sett. Flushing, Holland, 1759-1763; arriv. N.Y., N.Y., 29 Mar. 1734; sett. N.Y., N.Y., 1st or South Dutch Chh., 1764-1779; 2nd or Middle Dutch Chh. at Nassau Street, 1764-1779; 3rd or North Dutch Chh. at Fulton Street, inst., 14 Apr. 1764-1776; Presb.; Dutch Ref.; d. Red Hook, N.Y., 1779, a. 52.

ROBERT LAING (or Lenig) (poss. son of the Rev. Henry Laing (Layng), D.D., of Wells, England; b. 1697; matric. Trinity Coll., Oxford, 28 Mar. 1713, a. 16, A.B., Balliol Coll., 1716, A.M., 1719); came from Great Britain to Md., 1722; member of New Castle Presbytery, Del.; sett. Snow Hill, Md., 1722; Brandywine and White Clay Creek, Del., Mar. 1722-Aug. 1722; sett. Bensalem (Bucks) Pa. and Warwick (Bucks) Pa., Neshaminy Chh., 22 Dec. 1723-1726; Presb.; suspended for bathing on Sunday, 19 Sept. 1724, and again 24 Sept. 1726; the Presbytery advised him to quit the ministry.

JOSEPH LAMB, A.M., b. Stonington, Conn., son of John Lamb, Jr.; A.B., Y.C., 1717, A.M.; Ord. Southold, L.I., N.Y., Mattituck Chh., 6 Dec. 1717-1734; sett. Hempstead, L.I., N.Y., 1717-1725; Guilford, Conn., 4th Chh., 1735-1741; New Providence (Union) N. J., Turkey Christian Chh., 1741-1743; Basking Ridge (Somerset) N.J., 25 July 1744-1749; Presb.; d. Basking Ridge, N.J., 28 July 1749, a. 60 (GS).

JOSEPH LAMSON, A.M., b. Stratford, Conn., 28 Mar. 1718, son of William and Elizabeth (Burch) Lamson; A.B., Y.C., 1741, A.M.; A.M. (hon.) Columbia, 1773; Ord. London, England, 1744/5; K.B. for N.Y., 3 July 1745; Bedford (Westchester) N.Y., St. Matthew's Chh., 18 June 1745-1747; New Castle (Westchester) N.Y., 1745-1747; Rye (Westchester) N.Y., 1745-1746; Fairfield, Conn., Trinity Chh., 1747-1773; Ridgefield, Conn., 1747-1773; Stratford, Conn., 1747-1773; Norwalk, Conn., 1747-1773; physician; Ep.; d. Fairfield, Conn., 1773, a. 55. (will made 1 June 1773; proved 7 Sept. 1773).

ABRAHAM LANDES (or Landis), Ord. Bedminster (Bucks) Pa., Deep Run Chh., 1758-1773; Menn.

BENJAMIN LANDIS, b. Switzerland, 1710, son of Jacob Landis; came from Switzerland, 1718; sett. East Lampeter (Lanc.) Pa., at Mellingers meeting house, 1746-1781; was a minister there before 1746; Menn.; d. East Lampeter, Pa., 1791, a. 81.

JACOB LANDIS, sett. Franconia (Montgomery) Pa., Indian Creek Chh., 1773-1778; Franconia circuit; Menn.

JOHN LANDIS, sett. Cocalico (Lanc.) Pa., Conestoga Chh., 1770 ff.; lay preacher; Germ. Bapt.

JAMES LANG, A.M., son of Patrick Lang of Lancaster co. Pa.; A.B., U. of Pa., 1763, A.M. (hon.), 1765, Tutor, 1763; Ord. Guilford (Franklin) Pa., Falling Spring Chh., at Chambersburg, 1767-1794; Cumberland (Adams) Pa., Upper Marsh Creek Chh., at Gettysburg, 1767-1770; Antrim (Franklin) Pa., Old Red Chh., 1767-1794; Presb.

ANDREW LANGGARD, arriv. N.Y., N.Y., 19 Oct. 1761; sett. Lancaster (Lanc.) Pa., 1766-1773; Salisbury (Lehigh) Pa., Chh. at Emaus, 1773-1777; his wife Maria was his assistant; Morav.; d. Emaus, Pa.

Bishop DANIEL LANGENECKER, came from Switzerland to America, 1719/1722; sett. Washington (Berks) Pa., Manatant Chh., 1725-1756; Hereford (Berks) Pa., Hereford Chh., 1727-1756; East Vincent (Chester) Pa., 1727-1756; Upper Providence (Montgomery) Pa., 1742-1756, at Mingo near Royersford; trustee of Coventry, 1751; Menn.; d. ca. 1756.

DAVID LANGENECKER (Langanecker, Langanacre, Longaker, Longacre), prob. son of Bishop Daniel Langenecker; sett. East Coventry (Chester) Pa., 1750-1773; East Vincent (Chester) Pa., 1750-1773; Phoenixville (Chester) Pa., 1750-1773; Menn.

JOHN LANGENECKER, Ord. 1770; sett. East Coventry (Chester) Pa., 1770-1773; Phoenixville (Chester) Pa., 1772-1773; East Vincent (Chester) Pa., 1772-1773; Menn.

JOHN CASPAR LAPP, b. Windecken, near Hanau, 1724, son of Dr. Francis Lapp; matric. U. of Marburg, 16 Apr. 1744; Ord. Marburg, 20 Dec. 1744; sett. Neukirchen, 20 Dec. 1744-10 Jan. 1746; Dillenburg, Solms Hohenzollern and Niederweissel, Germany, 1746-1753; arriv. Philadelphia, 2 Oct. 1753; inst. Amwell (Hunterdon) N.J., 1753-1756; Lebanon (Hunterdon) N.J., Rockaway Chh. at Clinton, 1755-1756; German Valley (Morris) N.J., 1755-1756; Germ. Ref.; d. Amwell, N. J., after 1 Apr. 1756.

JAMES LATTA, D.D., b. Ireland, 1732, son of James and Mary (Alison) Latta; A.B., U. of Pa., 1757, A.M., D.D., 1799; Tutor, 1756-1759; Ord. 19 Feb. 1762; sett. Bedminster (Bucks) Pa., Deep Run Chh., 1762-12 Apr. 1770; John's Island (Charleston) S.C., 1768-1770; Drumore (Lanc.) Pa., Chestnut Level Chh., Nov. 1771-1801; pvt. and chaplain, Pa. militia, Rev. War; Presb.; d. Chestnut Level, Pa., 29 Jan. 1801, a. 68.

ABRAHAM LAUSHÉ, b. Crayfelt, Germany, 1732; sett. Amwell, N.J.; Germ. Bapt.

ANDREW ANTHONY LAWATSCH, arriv. in America, 17 May 1752; sett. Bethlehem (Northampton) Pa., 1752-1762, as warden; returned to Europe, 1 July 1762; Morav.

DANIEL LAWRENCE, b. Long Island, 1718; ed. Log Coll., Pa.; lic. Philadelphia, Pa., 28 May 1745; Ord. Forks of the Delaware (Northampton) Pa., 2 Apr. 1747; sett. Forks, 24 May 1746-1751; Upper Mount

Bethel (Northampton) Pa., Forks North Chh., 1746–1751; Allen (Northampton) Pa., 1747–1752 (North: Hunter's at Lower Mt. Bethel; South: Craig's, now Bath); Cape May (Cape May) N.J., Cold Spring Chh., 1751–inst. 20 June 1754–1766; Presb.; d. Cape May, N.J., 11 Apr. 1766 (GS).

JOHN LAWRENCE, sett. Pawling (Dutchess) N.Y., 1770–1782; Phillips' Patent (Dutchess) N.Y., 1774–1782; Bapt.

DANIEL LEATHERMAN, sett. Hanover (York) Pa., Little Conewago Chh., 1738–1770; Monocasy (Frederick) Md., 1738–1770; Germ. Bapt.

DANIEL LEATHERMAN, JR., sett. Reading (Adams) Pa., Great Conewago Chh., 1770–1789; Germ. Bapt.

DANIEL LEHMAN, b. Strasbourg, Alsace, France, 15 Apr. 1754; ed. at Halle U.; came to America, 1773; lic. 1775; Ord. 1778; sett. Heidelberg (Lehigh) Pa., Heidelberg Chh., 1773–1778; Maxatawny (Berks) Pa., St. John's Chh. at Kutztown, 1773–1778; Weisenberg (Lehigh) Pa., Ziegel Chh., 1773–1778; Lynn (Lehigh) Pa., Jerusalem Chh. at Allemaengel, 1773–1810; Whitehall (Lehigh) Pa., Egypt Chh., 1774–1778; South Whitehall (Lehigh) Pa., Jordan Chh., 1775–1778; Reading (Berks) Pa., Trinity Chh., Oct. 1778–1780; Upper Macungie- (Lehigh) Pa., St. Paul's Chh. at Trexlertown, 1778–1784; in 1793, he served: Oley Hill in Douglass, Moselem in Richmond, Bieber Creek in Rockland, St. John's Kutztown in Maxatawny, St. Paul's in Windsor, Hamburg, St. Michael's in Bern, Braunschweig, Greenwich, and two congregations in Albany; Luth., d. Richmond, Pa., at Moselem, 1 Oct. 1810.

Bishop JOHN LEHMAN, Ord. ca. 22 May 1745; Ord. Bishop, bef. 1775; sett. Rapho (Lancaster) Pa., Hernley's Chh., 1745–1790; East Hempfield (Lanc.) Pa., Chh. at Landisville, 1745–1790; Menn.; d. Rapho, Pa., 1790.

PETER LEHMAN, minister at Oberpfalz, Germany, 1699; came to Pa., 1700; Menn.

JOHN LEIGHTON, came from Dundee, Scotland; schoolteacher and preacher; Morav.; d. Bethlehem, Pa., Aug. 1756.

FRANCIS CHRISTIAN LEMBKE, b. Bodensingen, Baden-Durlach, July 1704; grad. Jena, 1739; Prof. at Jena and Strasbourg; arriv. N.Y., N.Y., 15 Apr. 1754; sett. Warwick (Lancaster) Pa., St. James's Chh. at Lititz, 1755–1756; Nazareth (Northampton) Pa., Forks of the Delaware, Jan. 1757–1784; resigned 1784; Morav.; d. Old Nazareth, Pa., July 1785.

SIMON LE MOYNE, S.J., b. Beauvais, France, 1601; adm. S.J., 1622; came to Canada, 1638; Huron-Iroquois missionary in N.Y. and Canada; sett. Syracuse (Onondaga) N.Y., St. Mary's Mission to the Onondagas, July 1654; Fonda (Montgomery) N.Y., St. Peter's Mission to the Mohawks, Sept. 1656–1665; R.C.; d. Cap de la Madeleine, near Three Rivers, 24 Nov. 1665.

SILAS LEONARD, A.M., b. Taunton, Mass., son of Judge Stephen Leonard; A.B., Y.C., 1736, A.M., 1740; Ord. Goshen (Orange) N.Y., 1738-1754; Presb.; will dated 27 Mar. 1764; d. Goshen, N.Y., 1764.

CASPAR LEUTBECKER, Ord. Marion (Berks) Pa., Zion's or Rieth's Chh., the original Old Tulpehocken Chh., at Stouchsburg, 1734; sett. Marion, 1733-1738; Luth.; d. Marion, Pa., 1738.

WILLIAM LEVERICH, A.M. (Leverick or Leveridge), b. Drawlington, co. Warwick, England, 1603, son of Saville Leverich; A.B., Emmanuel Coll., Camb., 1625/6, A.M., 1632; Ord. Peterborough, 1 Nov. 1627; Rector of Great Livermere, Suffolk, 1631; came to N.E. in the ship "James," 10 Oct. 1633; sett. Dover, N.H., 1633-1635; adm. 1st Chh. in Boston, 9 Aug. 1635; Duxbury, Mass., 1637-1639; Sandwich, Mass., the first minister, 1639-1653; Oyster Bay, L.I., N.Y., 1653-1658; missionary to the Indians at Huntington, L.I., N.Y., 1658-1669; sett. Newtown, L.I., N.Y., 1669-1677; Greenwich, Conn., 1673-1677; Cong.; d. Newtown, L.I., N.Y., 1677.

AMZI LEWIS, A.M., b. Waterbury, Conn., 29 Oct. 1746, son of Deacon Samuel and Hannah (Rew) Lewis, A.B., Y.C., 1768, A.M.; Ord. Blooming Grove (Orange) N.Y., 9 Apr. 1772, for Florida and Warwick, these two chhs. being 5 miles apart; sett. Warwick (Orange) N.Y., 1772-1777; Florida (Orange) N.Y., 1772-Nov. 1787; North Salem (Westchester) N.Y., 1787-June 1795; inst. Stamford, Conn., Presb. Chh., 26 Dec. 1795-1819; Cong.; Presb.; d. Stamford, Conn., 5 Apr. 1819, a. 72.

ICHABOD LEWIS, A.M., b. Stratford, Conn., 4 Apr. 1744, son of Ichabod and Sarah (Beardslee) Lewis; A.B., Y.C., 1765, A.M.; lic. 29 Oct. 1766; supply, Southbury, Conn., 1767-1768; Ord. White Plains (Westchester) N.Y., 11 Oct. 1769-1776; Rye and Sing Sing, N.Y., 1769-1774; South East (Putnam) N.Y., Chh., at Philippi, 1777-1790; Presb.; d. South East, N.Y., 8 Apr. 1793, a. 49.

THOMAS LEWIS, A.M., b. Waterbury, Conn., 6 Aug. 1716, son of Deacon Joseph and Sarah (Andrews) Lewis; A.B., Y.C., 1741, A.M.; A.M., Princeton, 1750; Ord. New Fairfield, Conn., (North Parish at Sherman), 28 Mar. 1744, as the 1st minister; sett. Sherman, 1744-7 Oct. 1746; Union (Hunterdon) N.J., Bethlehem Chh., 27 Oct. 1747-May 1761; Oxford, N.J., 27 Oct. 1747-1754; Alexandria (Hunterdon) N.J., Mt. Pleasant Chh., 1747-1754; Kingwood (Hunterdon) N.J., Mt. Bethel Chh., 1752-25 May 1756; Hopewell, N.J., 13 June 1758-20 May 1760; Smithtown, L.I., N.Y., 1763-1769; Mendham (Morris) N.J., 1769-1777; New Side Presb.; Cong.; d. Mendham, N.J., 20 Aug. 1777, a. 61.

GARRET (Gerhardus) LEYDEKKER, A.B., b. in the American colonies, 1729; A.B., Princeton, 1755; Ord. 1765; sett. Readington (Hunterdon) N.J., North Branch Chh., 1767-1767; English Neighborhood (Bergen) N.J., 1770-1776 (but note he must have served with Domine Cornelison); Tory; fled to N.Y., N.Y.; officiated at the Dutch

Chh., during the Rev.; D.R.; d. Pentonville (Salem) N.J., May 1794, a. 65.

JOHN PHILIP LEYDICH, b. Girkhausen, Westphalia, Germany, 28 Apr. 1715, son of the Rev. Leonhard Leydich; arriv. Philadelphia, 15 Sept. 1748; sett. New Hanover (Montgomery) Pa., Falkner's Swamp Chh., 9 Oct. 1748-1765; Upper Providence (Montg.) Pa., St. Luke's Chh. at Trappe, 9 Oct. 1748-1780; Pottstown (Montg.) Pa., 1748-1760, 1770-1784; East Vincent (Chester) Pa., Zion's Chh., 1758-1765; Exeter (Berks) Pa., Schwartzwald Chh., 1762-1770; Muhlenberg (Berks) Pa., Alsace Chh., 1762-1770; Reading (Berks) Pa., Trinity Chh., 1762-1766; Worcester (Montg.) Pa., Wentz's or Skippack Chh., 1762-1762; Upper Salford (Montg.) Pa., Old Goshenhoppen Chh., 1762-1763; Upper Milford (Lehigh) Pa., Zionsville Chh., 1762-1770; Upper Hanover (Montg.) Pa., New Goshenhoppen Chh., 1763-1764; Oley (Berks) Pa., 1766-1766; Salisbury (Lehigh) Pa., Jerusalem Chh., 1766-1771 (and poss. 1748-1771); East Coventry (Chester) Pa., 1769-1784, Brownback's Chh., 1769-1784; Germ. Ref.; d. Frederick, Pa., 14 Jan. 1784, a. 69 (GS).

JOHANNES LEYDT, b. Holland, 1718; ed. by Frelinghuysen and Goetschius; Trustee, Princeton, 1760-1760; original Trustee, Rutgers, 1770-1783; Ord. N.J., 1748; sett. New Brunswick (Middlesex) N.J., 27 Sept. 1748-1783; Six Mile Run (Somerset) N.J., at Franklin, 27 Sept. 1748-1783; Hillsborough (Sussex) N.J., 1766-1774; Conewago (Adams) Pa., Chh. at Hunterstown, 1771-1771; Pres., Gen. Synod, D.R. Chhs., 1778; Dutch Ref.; d. Three Mile Run, Franklin, N.J., 2 June 1783, a. 64 (GS).

JOHN ABRAHAM LIDENIUS, sett. Swedesborough (Gloucester) N.J., Trinity Chh. on Raccoon Creek, 1713-1724, 1751-1762; Pennsneck (Salem) N.J., St. George's Chh., 1713-1724, 1751-1762; Wilmington, Del., Old Swedes Chh., 1713-1724; Chester (Delaware) Pa., Sw. Luth. Chh., at Upland, 1713-1716; went to Sweden, 1724, returned ca. 1751; Molatton (Berks) Pa., St. Gabriel's Chh., Manathanim, 1752-1755; Penn (Chester) Pa., St. John's Chh., 1755-1760; Marcus Hook (Del.) Pa., St. Martin's Chh., 1756-1759; Sw. Luth.

JONAS LIDMAN, came from West Gothland, Sweden; sett. Philadelphia, Pa., Gloria Dei or Wicacoa Chh., 1719-1729; Caernarvon (Lancaster) Pa., Bangor Chh., 1728-1729; Colesville (Colestown?) Sussex, N.J., St. Mary's Chh., 1728-1728; Sw. Luth.; returned to Ekesjoe, Sweden, 1729.

MATTHEW LIND, b. Antrim co. Ireland, 1732; ed. at Glasgow; sett. Coleraine, Ireland, 1760-1774; arriv. New Castle, Del., 1774; sett. Dauphin co., Pa., 1774-1783; Greencastle, Chambersburg, West Conococheague, and Great Cove, all in Franklin co. Pa., 1783-1800; Associate Ref. Presb.; d. Franklin co. Pa., 21 Apr. 1800.

HENRY LINDENMEYER, arriv. N.Y., N.Y., 21 June 1743; sett. York (York) Pa., 1760-1766, 1773-1778; Salisbury (Lehigh) Pa., Chh.

at Emaus, 1766-1773; Bethlehem, Pa., 1778-1791; his wife Elizabeth was his helper; member, Board of External Supervision, 1791; Morav.

ROBERT LINDSAY, sett. Trenton (Mercer) N.J., Green Street Chh., 1776-1776; Meth.

WILLIAM LINDSAY, A.M., b. Ireland, of Scots parentage; A.M., Glasgow, 30 Apr. 1723; came to America, 3 Aug. 1733; returned to England, 14 Mar. 1734/5; Ord. 1735; arriv. Philadelphia, 28 May 1735; traveling missionary in Pa. and N.J., every 3rd Sunday; London Grove (Chester) Pa., 1735-1745; Concord (Chester) Pa., 1735-1745; S.P.G. missionary at Lancaster (Lanc.) Pa., 1734-21 Feb. 1734/5; Bristol (Bucks) Pa., St. James the Greater Chh., 8 June 1734-1745; Mill Creek (New Castle) Del., St. James's Chh. at Stanton, 1735-1745; Penn (Chester) Pa., St. John's Chh., 1735-1745; White Clay Creek, Del., 1735-1735; Alexandria (Hunterdon) N.J., St. Thomas's Chh., 1735-1745; Amwell (Hunterdon) N.J., St. Andrew's Chh., 1735-1735; Hopewell (Mercer) N.J., 1735-1735; Trenton (Mercer) N.J., St. Michael's Chh., 1735-1745; dism. by the S.P.G., 19 July 1745; Ep.; prob. d. in Philadelphia.

WILLIAM LINN, D.D., b. near Shippensburgh, Pa., 27 Feb. 1752, son of William Linn; A.B., Princeton, 1772; D.D., Columbia, 1789; Regent, U.S.N.Y., 1787-1808; Trustee, Rutgers Coll., 1787-1808; Pres., 1791-1794; Pres., Washington Coll., Chestertown, Md., 1784-1787; lic. 1775; Chaplain, Penn. Battalion, Cont. Army, 1776; Chaplain and Lieutenant, 3rd Regt., Conn. Continental Line, 1776-Nov. 1783; sett. Newville, Pa., 1777-1784; N.Y., N.Y., Dutch Ref. Chh., 1785-1805; Elizabethtown, N.J., 1786-1787; Chaplain, U.S. Ho. of Rep., 1789-1790; supply, Albany, N.Y., 1805-1806; an original member of the Society of the Cincinnati; Presb.; d. Albany, N.Y., 8 Jan. 1808.

JOHN JACOB LISCHY, b. Mulhouse, Alsace, France, 28 May 1719; was a Moravian at Mulhouse and Basel, 1733-1742; arriv. N.Y., NY., 28 May 1742; according to his own diaries, he settled in Lancaster co. Pa., 1743; Ord. as a Moravian, by Bishop David Nitschmann, Jan. 1742/3; was sett. in the following Moravian chhs. in Pa.; Lancaster co.: East Cocalico, Muddy Creek Chh. at Reamstown, 1743-1747; Lancaster, 1743-1746; Mt. Joy, Donegal Chh., 1743-1745; Warwick, St. James's Chh. at Lititz, 1743-1744; York co.: Hellam, 1746-1747; York, 1744-1746; Lebanon co.: Bethel, 1743-1744; Mill Creek, Muehlbach Chh., 1743-1747; Swatara, Hebron Chh., South Lebanon, 1743-1745; Berks co.: Heidelberg, 1742-1743; left the Moravian communion, 1747; Ord. York, Pa., Germ. Ref. Chh., 29 Sept. 1747, and was sett. over the ff. chhs. in Pa.: Lancaster co.: Brecknock, Muddy Creek Chh., Mar. 1743-Oct. 1745; Penn, White Oak Chh., 1745-1746; Ephrata, Cocalico or Bethany Chh., 1743-1744; Mt. Joy, Donegal Chh., 1743-1746; Warwick, Kissel Hill Chh., 1743-1745; West Cocalico, Swamp or Little Cocalico Chh., 1743-1748; York co.: Codorus, St. Jacob's Chh., 1747-1761;

Dover, Salem Chh., 1763-1781; Hellam, Kreutz Creek Chh., 1751-1757; Latimore, Mt. Olivet Chh. at Long Green, Lower Bermudian, 1747-1761; Lower Windsor, 1764-1765; North Codorus, St. Peter's or Lischy's Chh., 1765-1775; Paradise, Holz Schwamm Chh., 1775-1781; West Manchester, St. Paul's or Wolf's Chh., 1763-1781; Lebanon co.: Jackson, Muhlbach or Millbach Chh., 1743-1744; Mill Creek, Tulpehocken or Trinity Chh., 1743-1744; Berks co.: Bern, Bern Chh., 1743-1746; Chester co.: East Coventry, Brownback's Chh., 19 May 1743-1744; and in Westminster, Maryland, St. Benjamin's or Kreiger's Chh., 1763-1773; he also preached at Earl (Lanc.) Zeltenreich Chh., 1743-1745; North Annville (Leb.) Hill or Quittopehilla Chh., 1743-1745; East Vincent (Chester) Zion Chh., 1743-1745; Berwick (Adams) 1743-1744; and at Maiden Creek (Berks) 1743-1744; he was thus sett. over 10 Moravian and 25 Germ. Ref. chhs., 35 in all, and in several he preached from ten to twenty years; when challenged by chh. officials, he declared his connection with the Moravians, 21 Mar. 1744/5, and he took Christian Henry Rauch as his assistant in 1745; he was deposed as a Germ. Ref. minister in 1760, but continued to hold many of his congregations, and was accepted after a time; Swiss Ref.; Morav.; Germ. Ref.; Independent; d. North Codorus, Pa., Feb. 1781. (GS).

President JOHN HENRY LIVINGSTON, D.D., b. Poughkeepsie, N.Y., 30 May 1746, son of Henry and Susan (Conklin) Livingston; A.B., Y.C., 1762, A.M.; U. of Utrecht, 1770; S.T.D., U. Utrecht, 1769; Trustee, Rutgers, 1784, 1809; Trustee, Columbia, 1787; Prof. of Theol. and Pres., Rutgers, 1810-1825; Ord. Amsterdam, Holland, 2 Apr. 1770; arriv. N.Y., N.Y., 3 Sept. 1770; sett. N.Y., N.Y., South, Middle and North Dutch Ref. Chhs., 1770-1810; during the Rev. he was sett. at Kingston, 1776-1776; Albany, Nov. 1776-1779; Livingston Manor, 1779-1781; Poughkeepsie, 1781-1783; Red Hook, 1781-1783; his portrait was painted by Gilbert Stuart; Dutch Ref.; d. New Brunswick, N.J., 20 Jan. 1825, a. 78 (GS).

JOHN WOLF LIZEL (also called John Wolfgang Leitzel), b. 1723; came from Nuremberg, Germany; prob. Ord. by Andreae; arriv. Philadelphia, 24 Sept. 1753; schoolmaster, 1754; sett. Bedminster (Bucks) Pa., Tohickon Chh., 1760-1765; Tinicum (Bucks) Pa., Christ Church, 1760-1767; Rockhill (Bucks) Pa., Indianfield Chh., 1767-1769; Salisbury (Lehigh) Pa., 1769-1769; disappears, 1769; Luth.

LARS LOCK (Lawrence Karlsson Lock or Lawrence Charles's son Lock), b. Finland, son of Charles Lock; ed. U. of Upsala; sett. Wilmington, Del., Old Swedes' Chh., 1647-1688; Tinicum (Bucks) Pa., New Goeteborg Chh., 1647-1688; Chester (Del.) Pa., Chh. at Upland, 1647-1669; Philadelphia, Pa., Gloria Dei or Wicacoa Chh., 1677-1688; Crane Hook (New Castle) Del., Chh. at Tran Hook, 1677-1688; for many years after 1650 he was the only clergyman in Pa.; preached both in Swedish and Dutch; Sw. Luth.; d. Wilmington, Del., 1688.

WILLIAM LOCK, b. Dublin; Ord. Deacon, at Kingwood (Hunterdon) N.J., 16 Oct. 1762; Ord. (minister), Tuckahoe (Cape May) N.J., 20 July 1773-1779; Bapt.

RICHARD LOCKE, is said to have had distinguished connections in England; K.B. for Bermuda, 4 July 1743; sett. there 1743-1744; S.P.G. missionary in N.J. and Pa., 1744-1754; sett. Alexandria (Hunterdon) N.J., St. Thomas's Chh., 1744-1748; Amwell (Hunterdon) N.J., 1744-1748; Lancaster (Lanc.) Pa., St. James's Chh., 3 Oct. 1744-1749; Caernarvon (Lanc.) Pa., Bangor Chh., 1744-1751; Pequea (Lanc.) Pa., 1744-1748; went to England for a short visit, 1748; lic. for Va., 10 May 1749; Kingston Parish (Mathews) Va., 24 Oct. 1749-1750; Newtown (Del.) Pa., St. David's Chh. at Radnor, 1753-1753; returned to England, 1754, for a short visit; Lewes (Sussex) Del., St. Peter's Chh., 1754-1755; Ep.; d. Lewes, Del., bef. 28 July 1755.

JOHN JACOB LOESCH, b. Schoharie, N.Y., Ord. Tulpehocken, Pa., as a deacon, 1751; itinerant minister and husbandman; Morav.; d. Nazareth, Pa., Nov. 1782.

JOHN JACOB LOESER, sett. Lower Milford (Lehigh) Pa., Upper Milford Chh., 1748-1748; schoolmaster; Luth.

JOHN HEINRICH LOHMAN (or Lowman), b. Gimbsheim, Germany, where he was a prominent merchant; arriv. Philadelphia, 14 Sept. 1751; entered the Ephrata Chloister, Dec. 1751; sett. Latimore (Adams) Pa., Bermudian Chh., 1758-1770; Germ. Bapt.; d. Ephrata, Pa., 24 Jan. 1782.

Domine LOHRSPACH, sett. Upper Saucon (Northampton) Pa., 1749-1750; Springfield (Bucks) Pa., Trinity Chh., 1751-1755; enlisted in the French and Indian Wars, 1755; Germ. Ref.

Bishop CHRISTIAN LONGANACRE (also see Langenecker), b. Rapho, Pa., 11 Nov. 1732; Ord. Bishop, 15 May 1769; sett. Warwick (Lanc.) Pa., White Oak Chh., 1769-4 May 1772; Cocalico (Lanc.) Pa., Conestoga Chh., 1769-1772; Germ. Bapt.

LUDWIG LOPPIUS (or Lewis Lupp), sett. Canajoharie (Montgomery) N.Y., Chh. at Minden, 1760-1765; Dutch Ref.

JOHN LORETZ, came from Europe to Bethlehem, Pa., 1770; sett. Bethlehem (Northampton) Pa., 16 Nov. 1770-6 May 1772; returned to Europe, 6 May 1772; Morav.

HENRY LOVEALL, b. Cambridge, England, 1694 (his real name was Desolate Baker), sett. Newport, R.I., 1729-1730; Ord. Piscataway (Middlesex) N.J., Chh. at Stilton, Raritan, 1730; sett. Piscataway, 1730-1739, poss. until 1742; Chestnut Ridge (Baltimore) Md., Sater's Bapt. Chh., Fall's Road, 1742-1772; Opequon (Berkeley) West Va., Mill Creek Chh., 1743-1751; General Bapt.; was living at Chestnut Ridge, Md., 1772, a. 78 years.

WILHELMUS LUPARDUS, ed. U. of Leyden 1684; came to America, 1695; sett. Brooklyn, Bushwick, Flatbush, Flatlands, Gravesend, and New Utrecht, all on Long Island, N.Y., 1695-1702; Freehold (Monmouth) with Marlborough, N.J., 1699-1699; Middletown (Monmouth) with Holmdel, N.J., 1699-1699; Dutch Ref.; d. prob. on Long Island, N.Y., 1702.

CHARLES LUTE, sett. Upper Merion (Montgomery) Pa., Christ Chh., 1774-1777; Sw. Luth.; Ep.

AEGIDIUS LUYCK, came to America, 1661; teacher of the grammar school, N.Y., N.Y., 1662-1672; supply, South Dutch or First Chh., 1671-1671; he afterwards became burgomaster; his classical school held a splendid reputation; Dutch Ref.

Lydekker, see LEYDEKKER.

JOHANNES LYDIUS, son of the Rev. Henricus Lydius of Maesdam, South Holland; sett. Antwerp, Belgium, 1692-1700; came to America, 1700; sett. Albany, N.Y., 1700-1709; Schenectady, N.Y., 1705-1709; missionary to the Mohawks, 1702-1709; Dutch Ref.; d. Albany, N.Y., 1 Mar. 1709.

JAMES LYON, A.M., son of Matthew Lyon of Warrington, Lancashire, England; K.B. to N.E., 28 Apr. 1743; sett. Derby, Conn., St. James's Chh., and Waterbury, Conn., 1743-1747; S.P.G. missionary, Brookhaven, L.I., N.Y., Caroline Chh., at Setauket, 1745-1755; A.B., Princeton, 1759, A.M.; Ord. Brunswick, N.J., 1764, as a Presb.; assistant minister perhaps at Bedminster, Lamington, Lebanon, Peapack in Lamington, Readington and Bethlehem in Somerset and Hunterdon cos. N.J., ca. 1760-1764; sett. Onslow, Nova Scotia, 1764-1770; Machias, Me., 1771-1794; Ep.; Presb.; d. Machias, Maine, 12 Oct. 1794.

Bishop ALEXANDER MACK, b. Schreisheim, Palatinate, Germany, 1679/80; Ord. Schwartzenau, 1708; arriv. Philadelphia, Sept. 1729; sett. Germantown, at Beggarstown, 1729-1735; Cocalico (Lancaster) Pa., Conestoga Chh., 1729-1735; miller; pioneer of the Pennsylvania Tunkers; Germ. Bapt.; d. Germantown, Pa., 19 Feb. 1735, a. 56 (GS).

Bishop ALEXANDER MACK, Jr., b. Schwartzenau, Germany, 28 Jan. 1712, son of Bishop Alexander and Anna Margareta (Kling) Mack; arriv. Philadelphia, 15 Sept. 1729; Ord. Elder, 7 June 1748; Ord. Bishop, at Germantown, Pa., 10 June 1753; sett. Ephrata Chloister, 1739-1748; sett. Germantown, Pa., 1 June 1748-1803; left Ephrata Chloister, 4 Sept. 1745; sett. Mahanaim, Va., 1745-1748; returned to Ephrata, Pa., 1748; Tunker, Dunkard, or Germ. Bapt.; d. Germantown, Pa., 20 Mar. 1803, a. 91.

Bishop JOHN MARTIN MACK, b. Leysingen, Wurtemberg, Germany, 13 Apr. 1715; arriv. Savannah, Ga., 20 Feb. 1735/6; Ord. 13 Nov. 1742; Indian missionary, 1736-1762; sett. Sunbury (Northampton) Pa., Shamokin Indian Chh., 1742-1761; Gnadenhuetten, Pa., Indian Chh., 1746-1755; Nain (Lehigh) Pa., Indian Chh., 1760-1762; consecrated Bishop, 18 Oct. 1770, at Bethlehem, Pa., the first Moravian

Bishop to be consecrated in America; sett. St. Thomas, West Indies, 1762-1784; Morav.; d. St. Thomas, W.I., 9 June 1784.

ENEAS MACKENZIE, b.⁄ 1675, ed. Aberdeen and Edinburgh; Chaplain to the Earl of Cromarty, 1700-1705; K.B. to N.J., 2 May 1705; sett. Staten Island, N.Y., St. Andrew's Chh., 1705-1722, as S.P.G. missionary at Staten Island; Ep.

GEORGE MACNISH, ed. in Scotland; sett. Va., 1705; lic. 1706; sett. Princess Anne (Somerset) Md., Manokin Chh., 1710-1711; Salisbury (Wicomico) Md., Wicomico Chh., 1710-1711; Jamaica, L.I., N.Y., 25 Jan. 1712-1723; Father of Presbyterianism in America; d. Newtown, L.I., N.Y., 10 Mar. 1722/3.

GEORGE MACNISH, Jr., A.B., b. Jamaica, L.I., N.Y., 1714, son of the Rev. George and —— (Smith) Macnish; A.B., Y.C., 1736; stated supply, Newtown, L.I., N.Y., 1744-1746; Presb.; d. Wallkill, N.Y., 1779.

ALEXANDER MACWHORTER, D.D., b. New Castle, Del., 15 July 1734, son of Hugh and Jane Macwhorter; A.B., Princeton, 1757, A.M.; Trustee, 1772-1807; D.D., Y.C., 1776; lic. to preach, 1758; Ord. Cranbury, N.J., 4 July 1759; sett. Newark, N.J., 1st Presb. Chh., 1759-1779, 1781-1807; Chaplain in the Army, Am. Rev., 1778-1779; Pres., Charlotte Academy, N.C., 1779-1780; sett. Charlotte (Mecklenburg) N.C., 1779-1779; Abington (Montgomery) Pa., 1780-1780; Presb.; d. Newark, N.J., 20 July 1807, a. 73. (GS).

DANIEL McCALLA, D.D., b. Neshaminy (Bucks) Pa., 1748; A.B., Princeton, 1766; D.D., U. of S.C., 1808; lic. 1772; Ord. Nov. 1772; sett. Lower Providence (Montgomery) Pa., 1774-1776; Norriton (Montgomery) Pa., 1774-1776; Charlestown (Chester) Pa., 1774-1776; Hanover (Hanover) Va., 1776-1788; Chaplain, Am. Rev., 1775-1776; sett. near Charleston, S.C., Cong. Chh., 1788-1809; Presb.; d. Christ Chh. Parish, S.C., May 1809.

JOHN McCALLOH, sett. Marlborough (Ulster) N.Y., 25 Sept. 1773-Nov. 1774; Newburgh (Orange) N.Y., 1773-1773; New Windsor (Orange) N.Y., 1773-1773; Presb.

WILLIAM McCLANACHAN, A.B., b. Ireland, 1714; A.B., U. of Edinburgh, 1730; came to N.E. before 1734; inst. Georgetown, Me., 15 Nov. 1736-1738; inst. South Portland, Me., 2nd Chh., Presb., at Cape Elizabeth, 15 Nov. 1739-1742; inst. Blandford, Mass., 5 Oct. 1744-1746; Chaplain, in the Army, 1745; Ord. (Cong.), Chelsea, Mass., 1st Chh. in Revere, 21 Dec. 1748; sett. Chelsea, 1747-1754; dism. 18 Dec. 1754; Ord. (Ep.) London, Eng., 1755; K.B. for N.E., 4 Apr. 1755; Ep. missionary, 1754-1758; sett. Philadelphia, Pa., St. Paul's Chh. (Ep.), 1758-1765; Presb.; Cong.; Ep.; liv. 1765.

JAMES McCREA, b. Ireland, 1711, son of Elder William McCrea; ed. at Log Coll.; lic. New Brunswick, 6 Nov. 1739; Ord. New Brunswick, N.J., 4 Aug. 1741; sett. Lamington (Somerset) N.J., Chh. at Bedminster, 1 Apr. 1740-11 Nov. 1755; inst. 1 May 1757-21 Oct. 1766; Lebanon

(Hunterdon) N.J., 1740-1755, 1757-1766; Peapack (Somerset) N.J., 1740-1755; Readington (Hunterdon) N.J., White House Chh., 1740-1766; Union (Hunterdon) N.J., Bethlehem Chh., 1740-1747; Amwell (Hunterdon) N.J., 2 Aug. 1742-28 May 1745; Presb.; d. Lamington, N.J., 10 May 1769, a. 58 (GS).

ALEXANDER McDOWALL, b. Ireland; lic. 30 July 1740; Ord. 20 Oct. 1741, by the Donegal Presbytery, as an evangelist to Va.; prob. preached at Peaked Mountain (Rockingham) Va., Peaked Mt. Chh., 1741; sett. Nottingham (Chester) Pa., 1743-1744; principal of a school at Elk, Pa., and Newark, Del.; sett. Elk River (Cecil) Md., Rock Chh. at Lewisville, 1744-1760; Pencader (New Castle) Del., 1767-1773; Bethel (Harford) Md., Chh. at Upper Node Forest, 1774-1782; Presb.; d. Newark, Del., 12 Jan. 1792, unm.

FRANCIS McHENRY, came from Monaghan, Ireland, 1710; lic. 10 Nov. 1737; Ord. Neshaminy, Pa., 18 Sept. 1739; sett. Warwick (Bucks) Pa., 1738-1742, 1743-1757; West Nottingham (Chester) Pa., May 1742-1743; Neshaminy, Pa., 1738-1742; Neshaminy (Bucks) Pa., 2nd Presb. Chh., 16 Mar. 1743-1757; Bedminster (Bucks) Pa., Deep Run Chh., 16 Mar. 1743-1757; Old Side; Presb.; d. Neshaminy, Pa., 23 Jan. 1757.

ROBERT McKEAN, A.M., b. Pa., 13 July 1732, son of William and Letitia (Finney) McKean; A.M. (hon.) U. of Pa., 1760; A.M. (hon.) Columbia, 1763; Ord. by Bsp. of Chester; lic. 26 Apr. 1757; K.B. for N.J., 10 May 1757; sett. New Brunswick (Middlesex) N.J., Christ Chh., 16 Dec. 1757-1762; Piscataway, 1761-1763; Woodbridge (Middlesex) N.J., Trinity Chh., 1763-1767, 1/3 time; Perth Amboy (Middlesex) N.J., St. Peter's Chh., Feb. 1763-1767, 2/3 time; physician and S.P.G. missionary; Pres., N.J. Medical Soc., 1766; Ep.; d. Raritan Landing, N.J., 17 Oct. 1767; (GS) at Perth Amboy.

CHARLES McKNIGHT, b. Ireland, ca. 1720, son of Rev. Malcolm and Catherine McKnight; ed. Log Coll.; Trustee, Princeton, 1757-1778; Ord. Basking Ridge (Somerset) N.J., 12 Oct. 1742; sett. Basking Ridge, 1742-1744; Staten Island, 1742-1744; inst. Cranbury (Middlesex) N.J., 16 Oct. 1744-Oct. 1756; inst. Allentown (Monmouth) N.J., 11 Oct. 1744-Oct. 1766; Bordentown (Burlington) N.J., 1758-1766; Shrewsbury (Monmouth) N.J., 12 Apr. 1767-1776; Middletown Point (Monmouth) N.J., at Matawan, 12 Apr. 1767-1776; Shark River (Monmouth) N.J., 12 Apr. 1767-1776; Chaplain, Continental Army, and British prisoner of war, 1777; Presb.; d. in prison, 1 Jan. 1778 (Memorial Stone, N.Y., N.Y.).

JOHN McKNIGHT, D.D. (See *Colonial Clergy of Virginia*, p. 34) Presb.

JOHN McMILLAN, D.D., b. Fagg's Manor (Chester) Pa., 11 Nov. 1752, son of William and Margaret (Rea) McMillan; A.B., Princeton, 1772; A.M., Washington and Jefferson Coll., 1805, D.D., 1808; lic.

East Nottingham (Chester) Pa., 26 Oct. 1774; preached in New Castle and Donegal Presbyteries, 1774-1775; missionary to Va. and Pa., 1775-1776; Ord. Chambersburg (Franklin) Pa., 19 June 1776; sett. Chartiers (Washington) Pa., 1775-1833; Pigeon Creek (Washington) Pa., 1775-1800; founder and Trustee, Washington Academy, Washington (Washington) Pa., 1787; founder and Trustee, Washington and Jefferson College, 1802; Prof. of Divinity, 1802-1833; Vice-president, 1805-1833; Presb.; d. Canonsburg (Washington) Pa., 16 Nov. 1833, a. 81.

ROBERT McMORDIE, Ord. Cumberland (Adams) Pa., Upper Marsh Creek Chh., Gettysburg, 1754-Jan. 1761; Hopewell (York) Pa., Shrewsbury Chh., Round Hill, 1754-Jan. 1761; East Hanover (Lebanon) Pa., 1762-1766; Baltimore, Md., 1774-1774; missionary to Va. and Carolina, 1772-1784; Chaplain, Pa. Continental Brigade, Rev. War, served to June 1782; original member, Society of the Cincinnati, 1783; Presb.; d. 22 May 1796.

THOMAS McPHERRIN, A.M., A.B., Princeton, 1770, A.M., 1773; sett. Montgomery (Franklin) Pa., Welch Run Chh., 1774-1779; Presb.; d. 1802.

JOHN MADOWELL, came from the Presbytery of Temple-Patrick, Ireland, 1736; sett. Philadelphia, Pa., 1st Presb. Chh., Oct.-Nov. 1736; Presb.

HUGH MAGILL, sett. Bedminster (Bucks) Pa., Deep Run Chh., 1773-1776; Presb.

OLAF MALANDER, sett. Swedesborough (Gloucester) N.J., Trinity Chh. on Raccoon Creek, 1725-1725; Sw. Luth.

GEORGE WILHELMUS MANCIUS, b. Duchy of Nassau, Germany, 1706; Herborn Theol. Sem., 1728-1730; Ord. Germany, 1730; came to America, 1730; sett. Kaatsbaan (Ulster) N.Y., Nov. 1730-1762; West Camp (Ulster) N.Y., Chh. at Saugerties, 1730-1762; Kingsbury (Dutchess) N.Y., 1730-1762; Schraalenburg (Bergen) N.J., 19 Sept. 1731-1732; Paramus (Bergen) N.J., 1731-1732; Kingston (Ulster) N.Y., Chh. at Esopus, 16 May 1732-1762; Germantown (Columbia) N.Y., 1736-1762; Port Jervis (Orange) N.Y., Chh. at Deerpark, 1737-1741; Lehman (Pike) Pa., Lower Wallpack Chh. at Bushkill, 1737-1741; Delaware (Pike) Pa., 1737-1741; Layton (Sussex) N.J., Upper Wallpack Chh., 1737-1741; Flatbrookville (Sussex) N.J., Wallpack Center Chh., 1737-1741; Minisink (Sussex) N.J., at Montague, 1737-1741; Smithfield (Monroe) Pa., Shawnee Chh. at Lower Smithfield, 1737-1741; Catskill (Greene) N.Y., 1738-1738; Rhinebeck (Dutchess) N.Y., Germ. Ref. Chh., 1732-1742, 1748-1755, 1759-1762; Rhinebeck Flatts (Dutchess) N.Y., Dutch Ref. Chh., 1732-1742, 1746-1750; Dutch Ref.; d. Kingston, N.Y., 6 Sept. 1762 (GS).

Matthew Manners, see SITTENSPERGER.

President JAMES MANNING, D.D., b. Elizabeth, N.J., 22 Oct. 1738, son of James and Christian Manning; A.B., Princeton, 1762, A.M.,

D.D., 1786; D.D., U. of Pa., 1785; Morristown (Morris) N.J., 1762–1763; Ord. Warren, R.I., 15 Oct. 1764; sett. Warren, R.I., 1763-1770; inst. Providence, R.I., 1st Bapt. Chh., 31 July 1771–1791; inst. Pres., Brown U., 5 Sept. 1765–1791; member, Cont. Congress, 1785–1786; Bapt.; d. Providence, R.I., 29 July 1791, s.p.

DAVID MARINUS, ed. in Pa.; lic. 1752; sett. Passaic (Passaic) N.J., Chh. at Acquackanonk, 1752–1773; Pompton Plains (Morris) N.J., Chh. at Pequannock, 1752–1773; Paterson (Passaic) N.J., Totowa Chh., 1756–1773; Fairfield (Cumberland) N.J., Chh. at Horseneck, 1756–1773; Montville (Morris) N.J., Parsippany or Boonton Chh., 1756–1768, supply; West New Hempstead (Rockland) N.Y., D.R. Chh. at Kakiat, Spring Valley, 1773–1778; Clarkstown (Rutland) N.Y., 1773–1778; Germ. Ref.; Dutch Ref.

WILLIAM MARSH, b. Wrentham, Mass.; Ord. Mansfield, Conn.; sett. Dover (Dutchess) N.Y., Oblong Chh., 1755–1758; Wantage (Sussex) N.J., 1756–1763; Wilkes-Barre (Luzerne) Pa., 1762–1762, Cong. Chh., where he was murdered by the Indians in the Wyoming massacre, 3 July 1778; Bapt., perhaps later Cong.

WILLIAM MARSHALL, A.M., b. Abernethy, Fifeshire, Scotland, ca. 1740, son of Elder Marshall; arriv. Philadelphia, 1763; A.M. (hon.) Princeton, 1780; Ord. Bedminster (Bucks) Pa., Deep Run Chh., at Dyertown, 30 Aug. 1765–1768; Philadelphia, Pa., inst. Associate Presb. Chh., 30 Apr. 1771; sett. Philadelphia, 1768–1802; Assoc. Presb.; d. Philadelphia, Pa., 17 Nov. 1802, a. 62 (GS).

Bishop FREDERICK MARTIN, arriv. Philadelphia, 1740; sent out later as a missionary Bishop to the West Indies; Morav.; d. West Indies, bef. 1754.

GEORGE ADAM MARTIN, b. Landstuhl, Germany, 1715; Ord. 1739; sett. Reading (Adams) Pa., Great Conewago Chh., 1741–1770; Latimore (Adams) Pa., Bermudian Chh., 1762–1770; Antietam, Md., 1763–1770; Brothertown (Somerset) Pa., Stony Creek Chh., 1770–1776; Dunkard, Tunker, or Germ. Bapt.; d. Ephrata, Pa., 29 Apr. 1794.

HENRY MARTIN, A.M., A.B., Princeton, 1751, A.M.; Ord. Newtown (Bucks) Pa., 9 Apr. 1754–1764; Salisbury (Bucks) Pa., 1754–1764; Presb.; d. Newtown, Pa., 11 Apr. 1764.

Bishop HENRY MARTIN, b. 1741, son of David Martin; Ord. West Earl (Lancaster) Pa., Groffdale Chh., 1770–1825; Ord. Bishop, 1809; sett. East Earl (Lancaster) Pa., Weaverland Chh., 1770–1825; Menn.; d. East Earl, Pa., 27 Apr. 1825, a. 84.

NICHOLAS MARTIN, sett. Conococheague, Md., ca. 1770; Hanover (York) Pa., Little Conewago Chh., ca. 1770; Reading (Adams) Pa., Great Conewago Chh., ca. 1770; Germ. Bapt.

THOMAS MARTIN, Ord. 12 Oct. 1697; sett. Upper Providence (Montgomery) Pa., 1697–1700; Newtown (Del.) Pa., 1697–1701; Nottingham, Md., 1700; Keithian or Seventh Day Bapt.

JOHN MASON, D.D., b. near Mid-Calder, Linlithgow co. Scotland, 1734; Asst. Prof. of Logic and Moral Philosophy, 1758; Ord. Scotland, 1761; arriv. in America, 1761; sett. N.Y., N.Y., Scotch Presb. Chh., 1761-1792; Trustee, Princeton, 1779-1785; D.D., 1786; Chaplain to Posts on the Hudson River, served until the close of the Rev. War; eligible officer, Society of the Cincinnati; Associate Presb.; d. N.Y., N.Y., 19 Apr. 1792, a. 58 (GS).

Bishop JACOB MAST, b. 1738, came to Bucks co. 1750, aged 12 years; began preaching in 1765; Ord. Bishop of Berks, Chester, and Lancaster counties; sett. Caernarvon (Lanc.) Pa., Conestoga Chh., near Morgantown, 1765-1808; Amish; d. Elverson, West Nantmeal (Chester) Pa., 1808, a. 70.

NATHANIEL MATHER, A.B., b. Windsor, Conn., 30 May 1695, son of the Rev. Samuel and Hannah (Treat) Mather; A.B., Y.C., 1715; Ord. Lower Aquebogue, L.I., N.Y., Jonesport at Riverhead, 22 May 1728-1748; Presb.; d. Aquebogue, L.I., N.Y., 20 Mar. 1748, a. 53.

WARHAM MATHER, A.M., b. Northampton, Mass., 7 Sept. 1666, son of the Rev. Eleazer and Esther (Warham) Mather, A.B., H.C., 1685, A.M.; sett. East Chester (Westchester) N.Y., 1683-1684; Northfield, Mass., 1688-1690; Killingworth, Conn., 1691-1693; Farmington, Conn., 1704-1704; not ordained; Justice of the Peace and Quorum, Conn., 1710-1716; Judge of Probate, 1716-1727; Cong.; d. New Haven, Conn., 12 Aug. 1745, a. 79.

JOHN CONRAD MATTHAEI, b. Bern, Switzerland; bailiff at Wangen, 1674-1680; came to Pa., 1704; Hermit of the Pietistic Community at Wissahickon, Pa., 1708-1748; Pietist; d. near Germantown, Pa., Aug. 1748 (buried 1 Sept. 1748).

J. L. MAYOR, b. Nimes, France; arriv. N.Y., N.Y., 27 July 1754; sett. N.Y., N.Y., French Ref. Chh. of the Saint Esprit, 4 Aug. 1754-Apr. 1764; went to London; Chaplain of the French Hospital, London, for many years; Fr. Ref.

ABRAHAM MEAD, A.B., b. Greenwich, Conn., 15 June 1721, son of Ebenezer and Hannah Mead; A.B., Y.C., 1739; lic. 3 Feb. 1741/2; sett. Easthampton, L.I., N.Y., 1742-1743; Presb.; d. East Hampton, L.I., N.Y., 1743, a. 22.

SOLOMON MEAD, A.M., b. Greenwich, Conn., 2 Jan. 1726, son of Ebenezer and Hannah Mead; A.B., Y.C., 1748, A.M.; lic. 31 July 1750; Ord. South Salem (Westchester) N.Y., Chh. at Lewesborough, 20 May 1752-1812; Presb.; d. South Salem, N.Y., 4 Sept. 1812, a. 86.

JOHANNES MEGAPOLENSIS, b. 1601, son of the Rev. Johannes Megapolensis, minister at Coedych, Holland; was a Roman Catholic; studied at Cologne U. 1624; converted to Protestantism, 1624; Ord. ca. 1629; sett. Wieringerweert, North Holland, 14 Aug. 1634-1638; sett. Schoorl and Bergen, 1638-1642; came to America, 1642; contracted to preach for the patroon Van Rensselaer at Rensselaerwyck for six years,

1642-1648; sett. Albany, N.Y., then Fort Orange, 1642-1649; inst. N.Y., N.Y., D.R. or 1st Chh. in N.Y., then New Amsterdam, 6 Aug. 1649-1669; Flatbush and Flatlands, L.I., N.Y., 1664-1669; Dutch Ref.; d. N.Y., N.Y., 24 Jan. 1669/70.

SAMUEL MEGAPOLENSIS, M.D., b. 1634, son of the Rev. Johannes and Machteld (Willemsen) Megapolensis; H.C., 1653-1656; matric. U. of Utrecht, Sept. 1656; matric. Leyden, 14 Nov. 1661; M.D., Utrecht, 1663; Ord. Amsterdam, Holland, 3 Oct. 1662; left Holland, 20 Jan. 1663/4; sett. N.Y., N.Y., 1st or South Dutch Chh., 1664-1668; St. Mark's in the Bowery, N.Y., N.Y., 1664-1668; Brooklyn, N.Y., 1664-1668; returned to Holland; sett. Wernigerode, Holland, 1669-1677; Flushing, Holland, 1677-1685; Dordrecht, Holland, 1685-1700; preached at the English chhs. at Flushing and Dordrecht; Dutch Ref.; d. Dordrecht, Holland, 1706.

BENJAMIN MEINEMA, lic. 1727; sett. Kollum, Friesland, Holland, to 1745; came to America, 1745; sett. Fishkill (Dutchess) N.Y., 1745-1756; Poughkeepsie (Dutchess) N.Y., 1745-1756; Dutch Ref.

ABRAHAM M. MEINUNG, arriv. N.Y., N.Y., 30 Nov. 1741; Ord. deacon, 1745; sett. Oley (Berks) Pa., 1744-1745; St. Thomas, Danish West Indies, Aug. 1746-1749; Morav.; d. St. Thomas, W.I., Oct. 1749.

SAMUEL MELYEN, A.M., b. N.Y., N.Y., 1675; bapt. 7 Aug. 1677, son of Jacob Melyen; A.B., H.C., 1696, A.M.; Ord. Elizabethtown (Union) N.J., 20 May 1704-1707; Presb.; d. Elizabethtown, N.J., between May and July 1711.

RENÉ MENARD, S.J., sett. Auburn (Cayuga) N.Y., St. Joseph's Mission to the Cayugas, 1656-1658; Ottawa mission, 15 Oct. 1660-1661; R.C.; d. Ottawa mission, ca. 10 Aug. 1661.

Bishop VALENTINE METZLER, b. Switzerland, 14 Feb. 1726; minister and bishop in Europe; came to America, 1738; sett. West Lampeter (Lanc.) Pa., Willow Street Chh., 1738-1783; East Hempfield (Lanc.) Pa., Chh. at Rohrerstown, 1738-1783; East Hempfield, Pa., Chh. at Millersville, 1757-1783; Menn.; d. Pequea District (Lanc.) Pa., 24 July 1783, a. 57.

JOHN PHILIP MEURER (or Maurer), b. Alsace, France; arriv. Philadelphia, 7 Jan. 1741/2; Ord. Bethlehem, Pa., 9 Dec. 1742; sett. Marion (Berks) Pa., Chh. at Stouchsburg, Sept. 1742-Jan. 1747; Mount Joy (Lanc.) Pa., Chh. at Donegal, Jan. 1746-1747; Bethlehem, Pa., Jan. 1747-1751; York (York) Pa., 1751-1753; also minister at Lebanon, Swatara, York, Macungie, Oley, and Allemaengel; kept a diary at Bethlehem, Pa.; his wife Christiana was also ordained and assisted him; Luth.; Morav.; d. Bethlehem, Pa., Apr. 1760.

Bishop CHRISTIAN MEYER, b. ca. 1705, son of Christian and Magdalena Meyer; sett. Franconia (Montgomery) Pa., Indian Creek Chh., 1738-1787; Lower Salford (Montg.) Pa., 1738-1787; Bishop; Treasurer, 1756; Menn.; d. 1787.

HERMANN MEYER, D.D., b. Bremen, Germany, 27 July 1733, son of Jacob and Rebecca (Schlichting) Meyer; matric. Groningen, Holland, 6 Sept. 1747, in theol.; Ord. Groningen, Holland, 31 Mar. 1763; arriv. America, Oct. 1763; D.D., Rutgers, 1789; Prof. of Divinity, Rutgers, 1789-1791; Fellow of the German Soc., of Bremen; sett. Kingston (Ulster) N.Y., Chh. at Esopus, 2 Nov. 1763-Nov. 1772; Paterson (Passaic) N.J., Totowa Chh., 1772-1791; Fairfield (Cumberland) N.J., Chh. at Horseneck, 1772-1785; Pompton Plains (Morris) N.J., Chh. at Pequannock, 1772-1791; Montville (Morris) N.J., Parsippany or Boonton Chh., 1772-1791; all these chhs. were Dutch Ref.; Germ. Ref.; d. Pompton Plains, N.J., 27 Oct. 1791.

Bishop JACOB MEYER, b. Switzerland, 1721; came to America, 1741; Ord. minister, 1752; Ord. Bishop, 1763; sett. Upper Saucon (Lehigh) Pa., near Coopersburg, 1752-1790; Milford (Bucks) Pa., Great Swamp Chh., 1752-1790; Milford, Pa., East Swamp Chh., 1771-1790; Menn.; d. Upper Saucon, Pa., 4 May 1790.

JACOB MEYER, b. 28 Jan. 1730, brother of Christian Meyer; Ord. Hilltown (Bucks) Pa., Perkasie or Blooming Glen Chh., 1758-1778; Menn.; d. 1778, of yellow fever.

Dr. JOHN ADOLPH MEYER, son of Dr. Meyer; physician at Bethlehem, Pa., and in the Lehigh Valley; Ord. Bethlehem, Pa., 1748; Nazareth (Northampton) Pa., 1st warden, 1744-1749; Frederick (Montgomery) Pa., Falkner's Swamp Chh., 1746-1749; physician later at Philadelphia and Lititz, Pa.; Morav.; d. Lititz, Pa.

PETER MEYER, b. Switzerland, ca. 1723; brother of Bishop Jacob Meyer; came to America, ca. 1741; Ord. Swamp District (Milford, Bucks co.), Pa., 1773; sett. Springfield (Bucks) Pa., 1773 ff.; Menn.

SAMUEL MEYER, b. 10 June 1734; Ord. Bedminster (Bucks) Pa., Deep Run Chh., 1769; sett. Bedminster (Bucks) Pa., 1769 ff.; Hilltown (Bucks) Pa., Perkasie or Blooming Glen Chh., 1769 ff.; Menn.

JAN MEYLE (or Johannes Meyle), b. Germany, 1701; was an Anabaptist, Dec. 1723; rebaptized as a Dunkard or Germ. Bapt., Dec. 1728; sett. Lower Frederick (Montgomery) Pa., Falkner's Swamp Chh., as an assistant, 1729-1735; sett. Ephrata (Lanc.) Pa., as a member of the German Baptist Chloister at Ephrata, 1753-1783; deeded 180 acres of land to the Eckerling brothers for a Chloister, 13 Aug. 1739; Germ. Bapt.; d. Ephrata, Pa., 6 Aug. 1783, a. 82.

PHILIP JACOB MICHAEL, b. in Europe, 1716; arriv. Philadelphia, 14 Oct. 1731; not ordained; began to preach in Berks co. Pa., 1750; sett. Heidelberg (Lehigh) Pa., 1750-1770; Weisenberg (Lehigh) Pa., Ziegel Chh., 29 June 1750-1760; Lynn (Lehigh) Pa., Jacob's Chh., 1750-1770; Long Swamp (Berks) Pa., 1752-1753, 1762-1774, 1781-1786; Reading (Berks) Pa., 1753-1754; Maxatawny (Berks) Pa., De Long Chh., 1759-1770; Maxatawny, St. John's Chh. at Kutztown, 1759-1770; Lynn (Lehigh) Pa., Ebenezer or Organ Chh., 1760-1770; Upper

Hanover (Montgomery) Pa., New Goshenhoppen Chh., 1763-1764; Upper Salford (Montg.) Pa., Old Goshenhoppen Chh., 1763-1764; Weisenberg (Lehigh) Pa., Weisenberg Chh., 1761-1775; Lynn (Lehigh) Pa., Tresbacker Chh., 1766-1770; Lowhill (Lehigh) Pa., 1769-1770; Upper Bern (Berks) Pa., St. Michael's Chh., 1769-1770; Perry (Berks) Pa., Zion's Chh., 1771-1786; founder of Ziegel's and Jacob's Chhs., noted above; weaver; Chaplain, Am. Rev. War, 17 May 1777 ff.; Germ. Ref.; d. Rockland (Berks) Pa., June 1786 (will dated 6 May 1786; proved 17 June 1786).

JONAS JOHANNES MICHAELIUS, b. Hoorn, Netherlands, 1577, son of Johannes Michaelius (U. Leyden, 1583); matric. U. Leyden, 6 Sept. 1600, a. 23; minister at Nieuwbokswoude, 1612-1614; Hem, St. Luke's Chh., 1614-1624; Naval Chaplain at San Salvador and Brazil, 1624-1625; Fort St. George d'Elmina, Guinea, 1626-1627; returned to Netherlands, 1627; arriv. N.Y., N.Y., then called Niew Amsterdam, 1628; sett. N.Y., N.Y. (Niew Amsterdam), South Dutch Ref. Chh., Jan. 1628-1631, as the first minister of the first church in N.Y. State; sett. French Ref. Chh., N.Y., N.Y., 1628-1631; returned to Holland, 1637-1638; Dutch Chh., Yarmouth, England, 1641; sett. Zealand; Dutch Ref.

JOHN WOLFGANG MICHLER, b. Wuertemberg; arriv. N.Y., N.Y., 26 Nov. 1743; sett. Nazareth (Northampton) Pa., 1743-1745; Oley (Berks) Pa., 1745-1748, 1752-1753; Salisbury (Lehigh) Pa., Chh. at Emaus, 1750-1751; Ord. Deacon, 1762; minister in rural chhs. and at St. Thomas, West Indies; shoemaker; his wife Rosina was also ordained; Morav.

MICHAEL MIKSCH, came from Kunwald, Moravia; missionary among the Samoydes, Arctic Ocean, 1737; sett. Bethlehem, Pa., 1742 ff.; Indian missionary at Gnadenhuetten, Nazareth and Grandenthal; Morav.; d. Gnadenthal, Pa., June 1792.

PETER MILET, sett. Auburn (Cayuga) N.Y., St. John's Mission to the Cayugas, 1668-1671; Rome (Oneida) N.Y., St. Francis Xavier's mission to the Oneidas, 1671-Oct. 1694; R.C.

ALEXANDER MILLER, A.M., A.B., Princeton, 1764, A.M., 1768; Trustee, 1785-1795; lic. 1767; Ord. N.Y., 1770; sett. Schenectady, N.Y., 1770-1781; Princetown (Schenectady) N.Y., Chh. at Currie's Bush, 1770-1781; Remsen's Bush, N.Y., 1770-1781; Presb.; d. after 1795.

BENJAMIN MILLER, b. Scotch Plains, N.J., 1716; Ord. Scotch Plains (Union) N.J., Chh. at Fanwood, 13 Feb. 1748-1781; sett. Jersey Settlements (Davidson) N.C., 1754-1756; Bapt.; d. Fanwood, N.J., 14 Nov. 1781, a. 65 (GS).

FREDERICK CASIMIR MILLER (or Mueller), came from Steticheim, near Mayence; schoolteacher at Mayence; arriv. Philadelphia, 20 Oct. 1744; sett. Upper Salford (Montgomery) Pa., Old Goshenhoppen Chh., 1745-1748; Upper Hanover (Montg.) Pa., New Goshenhoppen Chh., 1745-1748; Lower Milford (Lehigh) Pa., Great Swamp Chh.,

1745-1748; sett. Bern (Berks) Pa., Bern Chh., 1746-1752; Oley (Berks) Pa., Manatawny Chh., 1748-1768; Oley, Pa., Germ. Ref. Chh., 1746-1768; Long Swamp (Berks) Pa., 1748-1752; Brecknock (Lanc.) Pa., Muddy Creek Chh., 29 May 1751-Aug. 1752-1754; East Coventry (Chester) Brownback's Chh., 1751-Nov. 1761 (chh. records); Heidelberg (Berks) Pa., Hain's or Cacusi Chh., 1762-1762; Lebanon (Lebanon) Pa., Tabor Chh., 1762-1766; Swatara (Lebanon) Pa., Little Swatara Chh., 1762-1768; Swatara, Pa., Swatara Chh., 1762-1765; North Annville (Lebanon) Pa., Hill or Quitopehilla Chh., 1762-1765; Tinicum (Bucks) Pa., Christ Chh., 1762-1768; Ephrata (Lanc.) Pa., Bethany Chh., 1763-1765; Germ. Ref.; d. Lebanon, Pa., after 3 July 1768.

GEORGE MILLER, Ord. ca. 1770; sett. Mount Joy (Lanc.) Pa., Great Swatara Chh., 1756-1770; Germ. Bapt.

JOHN MILLER, Chaplain in the Fort, N.Y., N.Y., 1689 ff.; K.B. for N.Y., 1692; Ep.

JOHN PETER MILLER (or Mueller), b. Zweikirchen, near Kaiserslauten, Palatinate, Germany, 25 Dec. 1709, son of the Rev. John Miller; matric. Heidelberg, 29 Dec. 1725; lic. 1725; arriv. Philadelphia, 29 Aug. 1730, on the "Thistle," of Glasgow; Ord. Philadelphia, Pa., 20 Nov. 1730 (Germ. Ref. ministry): Germantown, Pa., 1730-1731; Philadelphia, 1730-1731, 1733-1735; Worcester (Montgomery) Pa., Wentz's or Skippack Chh., 1730-1731; Lower Milford (Lehigh) Pa., Great Swamp Chh., 1730-1734; North Annville (Lebanon) Pa., Hill or Quitopehilla Chh., 1730-1735; Brecknock (Lanc.) Pa., Muddy Creek Chh., 1731-1734; Ephrata (Lanc.) Pa., Bethany Chh., 1731-1734; Penn (Lanc.) Pa., Reyer's Chh. at White Oak, 1731-1734; Earl (Lanc.) Pa., Zeltenreich Chh., 1731-1734; Lancaster (Lanc.) Pa., 1730-1735; Upper Leacock (Lanc.) Pa., Heller's, Hill, Conestoga, or Salem Chh. (variously named at different times but the same chh.), 1731-1734; Mill Creek (Lebanon) Pa., Tulpehocken or Trinity Chh., 1730-1735; Upper Hanover (Montgomery) Pa., New Goshenhoppen Chh., July 1731-July 1734; Upper Salford (Montg.) Pa., Old Tulpehocken Chh., July 1731-July 1734; became a 7th Day Bapt., Tunker or German Bapt., May 1735; as such called Brother Jabez; Ord. Ephrata, Pa., Aug. 1740 (German Bapt. ministry): Oley (Bucks) Pa., Germ. Bapt. Chh., 1732-1735; sett. Ephrata, Pa., Germ. Bapt. Chloister, 1735-1796, prior, 23 Mar. 1746-1768; head of Ephrata, 6 July 1766-1780; sett. Latimore (Adams) Pa., Bermudian Chh., 1758-1762; member, Am. Phil. Soc.; Germ. Ref.; Germ Bapt.; d. Ephrata, Pa., 25 Sept. 1796, a. 86 y. 9 m. (GS).

JOHN PETER MILLER, sett. Weisenberg (Lehigh) Pa., Ziegel's Chh., 1760-1772; Heidelberg (Lehigh) Pa., ca. 1770; Lynn (Lehigh) Pa., Ebenezer Chh. at New Tripoli, 1774-1778; Lynn, Pa., Allemaengel Chh. at Tripoli, 1774-1778;Lynn, Pa., Jacob's Chh., 1774-1778; Germ. Ref.; d. New Tripoli, Lynn, Pa., in or after 1778.

SAMUEL MILLS, A.M., b. Huntington, Conn., son of the Rev. Jedediah and Abigail (Treat) Mills; A.B., Y.C., 1765, A.M.; lic. (Cong.),

31 May 1768; Ord. Bedford (Westchester) N.Y., 13 Dec. 1769; sett. Bedford, N.Y., 1769-2 July 1779; sett. Patterson, N.Y., 1783-1789; became a Baptist; sett. Livingston co., N.Y., as an itinerant; Cong.; Presb.; Bapt.; d. Sparta, N.Y., bef. 7 Oct. 1806.

WILLIAM MILLS, A.M., b. Smithtown, L.I., N.Y., 13 Mar. 1739; A.B., Princeton, 1756, A.M.; A.M. (hon.), Y.C., 1771; sett. Jamaica, L.I., N.Y., 1762-1774; Presb.; d. Jamaica, L.I., N.Y., 18 Mar. 1774.

JOHN MILNE, K.B., for N.Y., 26 Sept. 1727; sett. Albany, N.Y., St. Peter's Chh., 9 Dec. 1727-1736; also served as an Indian missionary; Schenectady, N.Y., St. George's Chh., 1727-1736; S.P.G. missionary in Monmouth co. N.J., 1736-1745; preached at: Freehold, St. Peter's Chh., 1736-1745; Shrewsbury, Christ Chh., 1736-1745; Middletown, Christ Chh., 1738-1745; discharged as a S.P.G. missionary, 20 Apr. 1744; separated, 25 Mar. 1744/5; Ep.

JOHN MILNER, A.B., b. Westchester co., N.Y., 1738, son of Nathaniel Milner; A.B., Princeton, 1758; Ord. England, 1760; lic. for N.Y., 25 Feb. 1761; K.B. for N.Y., 5 Mar. 1761; induct. Rector, Westchester (Westchester) N.Y., St. Peter's Chh., 12 June 1761-1766; East Chester (Westchester) N.Y., St. Paul's Chh., 1761-1766; Yonkers (Westchester) N.Y., St. John's Chh., 1761-1764; sett. Warwisqueake Parish (Isle of Wight) Va., 1766-1775; Ep.; d. Newport Parish, Va., 1775.

PETER MISCHLER, sett. Windsor (Berks) Pa., Lebanon Chh. at the Blue Mountains, now St. Paul's Chh., 1765-1767; Upper Bern (Berks) Pa., St. Michael's Chh., 1769-1770; Luth.

ALEXANDER MITCHELL, A.B., b. 1731; A.B., Princeton, 1765; lic. 1767; Ord. Tinicum (Bucks) Pa., 1769; sett. Tinicum, Pa., 1768-1785; Plumstead (Bucks) Pa., 1768-1785; Octoraro (Chester) Pa., 1785-1808; Doe Run (Chester) Pa., 1785-1808; Presb.; d. 1812.

HENRY MOELLER, A.M. (Miller or Moller), b. Hamburg, Germany, 1749, son of John and Barbara Moeller; ed. Halle; arriv. Philadelphia, 1764; A.M. (hon.) Columbia, 1790; Trustee of Hartwig Seminary; lic. 1774; sett. over the following chhs. in Berks co. Pa.: Reading, Trinity Chh., Aug. 1775-Aug. 1777; Muhlenberg, Alsace Chh., 1775-1777; Exeter, Schwartzwald Chh., 1775-1777; Perry, Zion's Chh., 1775-1777; Upper Bern, St. Michael's Chh., 1775-1777; Windsor, Lebanon Chh. at the Blue Mountains, now St. Paul's Chh., 1775-1777; sett. Albany, N.Y., 1777-1789, 1802-1808; New Holland, Pa., 1789-1795; Harrisburg, Pa., 1795-1802; Sharon, N.Y., and New Rhinebeck (Schoharie co.) N.Y., 1808-1823; Luth.; d. Sharon, N.Y., 16 Sept. 1829, a. 79.

JOHN HENRY MOELLER, sett. Lynn (Lehigh) Pa., 1754-1754; Morav.

JOHN MOFFAT, A.B., b. Ireland; A.B., Princeton, 1749; Ord. Montgomery (Orange) N.Y., Good Will Chh., 1751-1765; teacher; Presb.; d. Little Britain (Orange) N.Y., 22 Apr. 1788.

PETER MOLL, landed at Philadelphia, 19 Aug. 1729; sett. Washington (Berks) Pa., chhs. at Hereford and Manatant, 1729-1759; Menn., d. Hereford, Pa., 19 Mar. 1759.

RICHARD MOLYNEUX, b. London, England, 26 Mar. 1696; arriv. Maryland, 1733; sett. Lancaster (Lanc.) Pa., St. John Nepomucene Chh., 1740-1749; returned to England, 1749; Superior in Md., 1736, 1743; R.C.; d. Bonham, England, 18 May 1766.

ROBERT MOLYNEAUX, sett. Philadelphia, Pa., St. Joseph's Chh., June 1772-1786; R.C.; d. Philadelphia, Pa., after 1786.

JOHN MONTAIGNE, came to America, 1696; sett. Fordham, N.Y., 1696 ff.; Fr. Ref.

Bishop BENJAMIN MOORE, D.D., b. Newtown, L.I., N.Y., 5 Oct. 1748, son of Samuel and Sarah (Fish) Moore; A.M., Columbia, 1768, D.D., 1789; Pres., pro temp., 1775-1784; Prof., 1786-1800; Trustee, 1802-1813; President, 1801-1811; Regent, U. of State of N.Y., 1784-1787; Ord. London, 25 June 1774; K.B., N.Y., 6 July 1774; sett. N.Y., N.Y., Trinity Chh., 1774-1801; Ep. Bishop of N.Y., 1801-1816; Ep.; d. Greenwich, 27 Feb. 1816, a. 68.

JOHN MOORE, may have been at H.C., 1646; came to Southampton, L.I., N.Y., 1641; sett. Newtown, L.I., N.Y., 1651-1661; Cong.; d. Newtown, L.I., N.Y., 17 June 1661.

JOHN MOORE, A.B., perhaps b. Windsor, Conn.; A.B., Y.C., 1741; schoolteacher at Jamaica, L.I., N.Y., 1742; prob. Ord. 1745; Ep.; d. perhaps in 1799.

THOROUGHGOOD MOORE, A.M., b. Biggleswade, co. Beford, England, 1672, son of John Moore; matric. Magdalene Coll. Cambridge, 1692; A.B., 1694/5, A.M., 1698; incorp., 9 July 1700; Ord. (Bsp. of London), 25 Feb. 1703/4; K.B. for America, 19 Feb. 1703/4; arriv. N.Y., N.Y., autumn, 1704; sett. Albany, N.Y., 1704-Oct. 1705, and Indian missionary, 1705-1705; S.P.G. missionary in N.J.: Burlington (Burlington) N.J., St. Mary's Chh., 1705-1706; Hopewell (Mercer) N.J., 1705-1706; Trenton, N.J., 1705-1706; Ep.; set sail for England, but the ship sank with all on board, 1707.

JAMES MOREHEAD, sett. West Jersey and New Castle co. Del., ca. 1735; not received by the Presbytery; Presb.

ABEL MORGAN, Senior, b. Alltgoch, Llanwenog, Cardigan, South Wales, 1637, son of the Rev. Morgan Ryddarch; Ord. Blaenegwent, co. Monmouth, Wales, 1656; arriv. in America, 14 Feb. 1711; sett. Lower Dublin, Pa., Pennypack Bapt. Chh., 1711-1722; sett. Philadelphia, Pa., 1st Bapt. Chh., 1711-1722; Bapt.; d. Philadelphia, Pa., 16 Dec. 1722, a. 85.

ABEL MORGAN, Jr., A.M., b. Welsh Tract, Newark, Del., 18 Apr. 1713, son of the Rev. Enoch Morgan; bapt. 31 Mar. 1733; A.M. (hon.) Brown, 1769; Ord. Welsh Tract (Newark) Del., 1734; sett. Middletown

(Monmouth) N.J., 1738-1785; Bapt.; d. Middletown, N.J., 24 Nov. 1785, unm.

EVAN MORGAN, came from Wales; was called to the ministry, 1702; Ord. Lower Dublin, Pa., Pennypack Bapt. Chh., 23 Oct. 1706; sett. Lower Dublin, Pa., 1702-1709; Philadelphia, Pa., 1st Bapt. Chh., 1702-1709; Bapt.; d. Lower Dublin, Pa., 16 Feb. 1709.

JOSEPH MORGAN, A.M., b. Preston, Conn., 6 Nov. 1671, son of Lieut. Joseph and Dorothy (Parke) Morgan; A.B., Y.C., 1702, A.M., 1720; Ord. Fairfield, Conn., ca. 12 June 1700; sett. Greenwich, Conn., 1st Chh., 1697-1700, 2nd Chh. at Horseneck, 1705-17 Oct. 1708; sett. Bedford (Westchester) N.Y., 26 Dec. 1699-1704; sett. Mt. Vernon, East Chester (Westchester) N.Y., 1702-1704; Presb. chhs.: Middletown (Monmouth) N.J., Chh. at Middletown Point, 1709-1731; Tennent (Monmouth) N.J., at Freehold, 19 Oct. 1708-1729; Freehold, N.J., Dutch Ref. Chh., 1709-1729; Holmdel (Monmouth) N.J., at Middletown, Dutch Ref. Chh., 1709-1729; Marlborough (Monmouth) N.J., Chhs. at Freehold and Middletown, both Dutch Ref., 19 Oct. 1709-1729; Presb. Chhs.: Hopewell (Mercer) Chh. at Ewing, 1728-1736; Hopewell (Mercer) N.J., Pennington Chh., 1728-1738; Lawrenceville (Mercer) N.J., Maidenhead Chh., 1728-1738; Presb.; may also have preached at Trenton, N.J., 1728-1738, as given by some authorities.

ISAAC MORRIS, lic. 21 May 1775; Presb.; no further record.

EVANDER MORRISON, came from Scotland; supply, East Hartford, Conn., 1748-1749; supply, Bedminster (Bucks) Pa., Tohickon Chh., and Forks of the Delaware, Pa., Sept. 1752-1753; sett. Bart (Lanc.) Pa., Middle Octoraro Chh., 1753-1756; Peach Bottom (York) Pa., Slate Ridge Chh., 1753-1756; Presb.

JOHN MORSE, A.M., b. Dedham, Mass., 31 Mar. 1674, son of Ezra and Joanna (Hoare) Morse; A.B., H.C., 1692, A.M.; sett. Newtown, L.I., N.Y., 15 Sept. 1694-1700; Cong.; d. Newtown, L.I., N.Y., Oct. 1700.

ANDREW MORTON (or Moreton), lic. for N.J., 17 Mar. 1760; K.B. for N.J., 18 Mar. 1760; S.P.G. missionary in N.J. and N.C.; sett. Amwell (Hunterdon) N.J., now Lambertville, St. Andrew's Chh., June 1760-1765; Alexandria (Hunterdon) N.J., St. Thomas's Chh., June 1760-1765; St. George's Parish (Northampton) N.C., 1766-1766, and Mecklenburg co. N.C., 1766-1766; left in 1766 on account of ill health; sett. Drysdale Parish (Caroline) Va., bef. 20 Apr. 1774-1775; King and Queen co. Va., 1774-1775; dismissed, 1775; Ep.

EBENEZER MOSELEY, A.M., b. Hampton, Conn., 19 Feb. 1740/1, son of the Rev. Samuel and Bethia (Otis) Moseley; A.B., Y.C., 1763, A.M., 1768; lic. 19 June 1765; sett. Brookfield, Mass., 1765-1767; Ord. Sept. 1767, as an Indian missionary for the New England Company for Propagating the Gospel Among the Indians, at Onohoquaga on the Susquehanna near Binghamton, N.Y., 1767-1772; Capt., Am. Rev., 1775-1777; Col. 1791; Repres., 1776-1806, for 20 sessions; Deacon,

1788; Town Clerk, 1797 ff. for many years; Cong.; d. Hampton, Conn., 20 Mar. 1825, a. 84.

RICHARD MOSELEY, Chaplain of the man-of-war "Salisbury"; S.P.G. missionary, Brooklyn, Conn., 1771–1772; Litchfield, Conn., 1771–1772; Johnstown (Fulton) N.Y., 1772–1773; Ep.

EDMOND MOTT, Chaplain in the Fort, N.Y., N.Y., 1696 ff; K.B. for N.Y., 10 Feb. 1701/2; Ep.

JACOB MOYER, sett. Hanover (York) Little Conewago Chh., ca. 1770; Coopersburg (Lehigh) Pa., at Upper Saucon; lay preacher; Germ. Bapt.

JEAN JOSEPH BRUMAULD MOULINARS, arriv. in America, 1718; sett. N.Y., N.Y., French Chh. of the Saint Esprit, 12 Nov. 1718–1726; New Rochelle (Westchester) N.Y., French Chh., 1726–1741; French Ref.; d. New Rochelle, N.Y., Oct. 1741.

JOHN JACOB MUELLER, came from Nuremberg, Germany; Ord. 1760; joined the Moravian Chh., 1740; Secretary to David Zeisberger, 1740–1742; portrait painter; Morav.; d. Niskey, Prussia, 1781.

FREDERICK AUGUSTUS CONRAD MUHLENBERG, b. Trappe, Pa., 1 Jan. 1750, son of the Rev. Dr. Henry Melchior and Anna Maria (Weiser) Muhlenberg; ed. Halle, 1763–1768; arriv. N.Y., N.Y., 22 Sept. 1770; Ord. Reading (Berks) Pa., 26 Oct. 1770; sett. Douglas (Berks) Pa., Oley Hill Chh., 1770–1775; Elizabeth (Lanc.) Pa., Emmanuel Chh., 1770–1773; Manheim (Lanc.) Pa., 1770–1775; New Hanover (Montgomery) Pa., Falkner's Swamp Chh., 1770–1775; Schoefferstown (Lebanon) Pa., 1770–1771; Exeter (Berks) Pa., Schwartzwald Chh., 1772–1775; Muhlenberg (Berks) Pa., Alsace Chh., 1772–1775; Pike (Berks) St. John's or Hill Chh., 1772–1775; Reading (Berks) Pa., Trinity Chh., 1772–1775; Marion (Berks) Pa., Christ Chh. at Stouchsburg, Old Tulpehocken Chh., 1772–1775; Lebanon (Lebanon) Pa., Salem or Kruppe Chh., 1773–1775; N.Y., N.Y., Holy Trinity Chh., 1775–1775; N.Y., N.Y., Old Swamp Chh., 1775–1775; member, Continental Congress, for Pa., 1779, 1780; Speaker, 1780–1783; Registrar and Recorder, Montgomery co.; Judge, 1784; Congressman, 1787–1793, Speaker; Luth.; d. Lancaster, Pa., 4 June 1801.

GOTTHILF HENRY ERNST MUHLENBERG, D.D., b. Trappe, Pa., 17 Nov. 1753, son of the Rev. Dr. Henry Melchior and Anna Maria (Weiser) Muhlenberg; student at Halle, 1763–1768; matric. Halle, 1769; A.M., U. of Pa., 1780, D.D.; arriv. N.Y., N.Y., 22 Sept. 1770; Ord. Reading (Berks) Pa., 25 Oct. 1770–4 Apr. 1774; Philadelphia, Pa., 1770–Apr. 1779, asst. min.; Bedminster (Somerset) N.J., St. Paul's Chh., 1770–1774; German Valley (Morris) N.J., Fox Hill Chh., at Fairmount, Tewksbury, 1770–1774; German Valley (Morris) N.J., Chh. at Washington, 1770–1774; New Germantown (Morris) N.J., Zion Chh., Tewksbury, 1770–1774; Philadelphia, Pa., Zion's Chh., 1770–1779; Pluckemin (Somerset) N.J., 1770–1774; Potterstown (Hunterdon) N.J.,

Rockaway Chh., 1770–1774; Raritan (Somerset) N.J., Raritan Chh., 1770–1774; Whitehouse (Hunterdon) N.J., Chh. at Leslyland, 1770–1774; Lancaster (Lanc.) Pa., Trinity Chh., 1780–1815; member, Am. Phil. Soc.; first Pres. of Franklin Coll., 1787; Luth.; d. Lancaster, Pa., 23 May 1815.

HENRY MELCHIOR MUEHLENBERG, D.D., b. Einbeck, Hanover, Germany, 6 Sept. 1711, son of the Hon. Nicholaus Melchior and Anna Maria (Kleinschmied) Muehlenberg; matric. U. of Goettingen, Mar. 1735, a. 24; matric. in theol., 1737; grad. 1738; taught at Halle, 1738; D.D., U. of Pa., 1784; Ord. Leipzig, Germany, 24 Aug. 1739, sett. as asst. minister, Gross-Hennersdorf, Upper Lusatia, July 1739–1741; arriv. in America, 22 Sept. 1742; sett. Ebenezer, near Savannah, Ga., 1742; Charleston, S.C., 1742; arriv. Philadelphia, 12 Nov. 1742; he was qualified to preach in German, Dutch, Swedish, English, French and Latin, and did so as frequently as necessary; he preached at Swede's Chh., Oley, Hill, Alsace, Longswamp, Albany, Hain's at Heidelberg, Northkill and Tulpehocken Chhs., as well as at his regular settled parishes: New Hanover (Montgomery) Pa., Falkner's Swamp Chh., Nov. 1742–Oct. 1762; Upper Providence (Montg.) Pa., Augustus Chh. at Trappe, 1742–1787; Lynn (Lehigh) Pa., Jerusalem Chh., at Allemaengel, 1742–1742; Douglass (Berks) Pa., Oley Hill Chh., 1742–1762; Philadelphia, Pa., St. Michael's Chh., 1743–1787; Germantown, Pa., St. Michael's Chh., 1743–1744; Lower Milford (Lehigh) Pa., Upper Milford Chh., 1745–1748; Cohansey (Cumberland) N.J., 1745–1746; Upper Saucon (Lehigh) Pa., St. Paul's, Blue or Organ Chh., 1749–1750; N.Y., N.Y., May–Aug. 1751, May–Aug. 1752; Amity (Berks) Pa., St. Paul's Chh., 1753–1753; Bedminster (Somerset) N.J., St. Paul's Chh., 1757–1769; German Valley (Morris) N.J., Fox Hill Chh., Fairmount, Tewksbury, 1757–1759; German Valley (Morris) N.J., Chh. at Washington, 1757–1759; New Germantown (Morris) N.J., Zion Chh., Tewksbury, 1757–1759; Pluckemin (Somerset) N.J., near Bedminster, 1757–1759; Potterstown (Hunterdon) N.J., at Rockaway, 1757–1759; Raritan (Somerset) N.J., 1757–1759; Upper Dublin (Philadelphia) Pa., Puff's Chh., 1757–1758; Whitehouse (Hunterdon) N.J., Chh. at Leslyland, 1757–1759; Whitemarsh (Montgomery) Pa., St. Peter's Chh., Barren Hill, 1761–1777; Philadelphia, Pa., Zion's Chh., 1769–1787; Strasburg (Lanc.) Pa., St. Michael's or Beaver Creek Chh., 1767–1769; Lynn (Lehigh) Pa., Ebenezer or Organ Chh., 1770–1780; Luth.; d. Trappe, New Providence, Pa., 7 Oct. 1787.

Major-General JOHN PETER GABRIEL MUHLENBERG, b. Trappe, Pa., 1 Oct. 1746, son of the Rev. Dr. Henry Melchior and Anna Maria (Weiser) Muhlenberg; U. of Pa., 1763; U. of Halle, 1763; soldier in colonial wars, 1764–1767; Ord. Lutheran, 1768: sett. New Germantown (Morris) Pa., Zion's Chh., 12 May 1768–1772; Bedminster (Somerset) N.J., St. Paul's Chh., 12 May 1768–1772; Greenwich (Warren) N.J., St. James's Chh., 1769–1772; German Valley (Morris) N.J., at

Washington, 1768-1772; German Valley, N.J., Fox Hill Chh. at Fairmount, Tewksbury, (Hunterdon co.), 1768-1772; Pluckemin (Somerset) N.J., 1768-1772; Raritan (Somerset) N.J., 1768-1772; Potterstown (Hunterdon) N.J., Chh. at Rockaway, 1768-1772; Whitehouse (Hunterdon) N.J., Chh. at Leslyland, 1768-1772; Ord. Ep. (Bsp. of London), 23 Apr. 1772; K.B. for Va., 7 May 1772; sett. Beckford Parish (Shenandoah) Va., Ep., 1772-1775; Madison (Madison) Va., Old Hebron Luth. Chh., 1772-1775; Woodstock (Shenandoah) Va., Luth. Chh., 1772-1775; member, Va. House of Burgesses, 1774; at the Battle of Sullivan's Island, June 1776; Brig.-Gen., 21 Feb. 1777; in command at the Battles of Brandywine, Monmouth, Stony Point, and Yorktown; Maj.-Gen., 1800-1807; member of Congress, 1789-1801; U.S. Senator, 1802; Collector of the Port of Philadelphia, 1802-1807; an original member of the Society of the Cincinnati; Luth.; Ep.; d. Philadelphia, Pa., 1 Oct. 1807, a. 60.

JOHN MUENSTER, sett. Lynn (Lehigh) Pa., Allemaengel Chh., 1747-1747; Morav.

PAUL MUENSTER, arriv. N.Y., N.Y., 19 Oct. 1761; sett. Bethlehem, Pa., 1761-1792; warden; member of the General Executive Board; and Asst. Pastor, 1776-1792; Morav.; d. Bethlehem, Pa., 15 Oct. 1792.

GEORGE MUIRSON, b. Scotland, ca. 1675; schoolmaster at Albany, N.Y., 1703; Ord. London, by Bishop Compton, 1705; S.P.G. missionary; sett. Rye (Westchester) N.Y., Christ Chh., 31 July 1705-1708; Bedford (Westchester) N.Y., St. Mary's Chh., 1705-1708; Greenwich, Conn., 1705-1707; Stratford, Conn., Christ Chh., organized, Apr. 1707, sett. 1706-1707; Ep.; d. Rye, N.Y., 12 Oct. 1708.

HARRY MUNRO, D.D., b. Scotland, 1730, son of Dr. Robert and Anne (Munro) Munro, of Dingwall, Scotland; A.B., St. Andrews, A.M., D.D., 13 Jan. 1782; Edinburgh; A.M. (hon.) Columbia, 1773; Ord. (Presb.), 1757; Chaplain, 12 Jan. 1757-1764: 1st Highland Battalion of Foot, at South Carolina, Fort Duquesne, Ticonderoga, Crown Point, Montreal, and Bahamas, resigned, 1764; Ord. (Ep.), London, 10 Feb. 1765; lic. for N.Y., 11 Feb. 1765; K.B. for N.Y., 20 Feb. 1765; sett. Yonkers (Westchester) N.Y., St. John's Chh., 11 Feb. 1765-1768; Albany, N.Y., St. Peter's Chh., 20 July 1770-1777; Chaplain, Ft. Hunter, Albany, N.Y., 20 July 1770-1777; became a British Chaplain in the Am. Rev.; returned to England; Presb.; Ep.; d. 1801.

JONATHAN MURDOCK, A.M., b. Westbrook, Conn., 7 Apr. 1745, son of John and Frances (Conkling) Murdock; A.B., Y.C., 1766, A.M.; sett. Guilford, Conn., 4th Chh., 1768-1769; Ord. Rye, N.Y., bef. 21 Jan. 1771; sett. Rye, 1771-1774; inst. Greenwich, Conn., 2nd Chh., 20 Oct. 1774-1785; Bozrah, Conn., 12 Oct. 1786-1813; Cong.; Presb.; d. Bozrah, Conn., 17 Jan. 1813, a. 67.

ALEXANDER MURRAY, K.B. for Pa., 16 June 1762; arriv. Molatton, Pa., 9 Apr. 1763; S.P.G. missionary; sett. Reading (Berks) Pa., St. Mary's Chh., 1762-1778; Molatton, or Amity (Berks) Pa.,

St. Gabriel's Chh., Manathanim, at Douglassville, Pa., 1763-1778; 1790-1792; refugee to England, 1778; Ep.

JOHN MURRAY, b. Alton, Hampshire, England, 10 Dec. 1741; arriv. in New Jersey, 28 Sept. 1770; sett. Goodluck, N.J., at Potter's Farm, 1770-1772; Philadelphia, Pa., Meth. Chh., 1770-1771; itinerant preacher in N.E., 1772-1774; Chaplain to R.I. regts., 1775-1777; Ord. Gloucester, Mass., Jan. 1779; re-Ord. 25 Dec. 1788; sett. Gloucester, Mass., Universalist Chh., 1779-1793; Boston, Mass., 1793-1809; Universalist; d. Boston, 3 Sept. 1815.

JOHN MURRAY, A.M., b. Antrim, Ireland, 22 May 1742; A.B., U. of Edinburgh, 1761, A.M.; arriv. in N.E., 1763; sett. Boothbay, Maine, 1763, 1766-1779; dism. from Boothbay, Maine, June 1781; Ord. Philadelphia, Pa., 2nd Presb. Chh., May 1765; sett. Philadelphia, 1765-1766; inst. Newburyport, Mass., 4 June 1781-1793; delegate from Boothbay, Me., to the Provincial Congress, 1775; Presb.; d. Newburyport, 13 Mar. 1793, a. 51.

JACOB MUSSELMAN, came from Germany, 1743; prob. had been ordained there; sett. Milford (Bucks) Pa., Great Swamp Chh., 1743 ff.; Menn.

MICHAEL MUSSELMAN, son of the Rev. Jacob Musselman; Ord. prior to 1773; sett. Milford (Bucks) Pa., Great Swamp Chh., 1771-1773; Milford (Bucks) Pa., East Swamp Chh., 1771-1773; Menn.

FREDERICK MUZELIUS, b. Germany, 5 Jan. 1704; came to America, 1726; sett. Tappan (Rockland) N.Y., Dutch Ref. Chh. at Orangetown, 1726-1749; Tappan, N.Y., 2nd Dutch Ref. Chh., 1767-1778; Germ. Ref.; d. Tappan, N.Y., 7 Apr. 1782, a. 78 (GS).

JEREMIAH NAASS, sett. Amwell (Hunterdon) N.J., 1738 ff.; Germ. Bapt.

JOHANN NAASS, b. Norten, near Cassel, Germany, ca. 1671; Ord. ca. 1715; sett. Marienborn and Crefeld, Germany, 1715-1717; member of the Crefeld community, 1729-1733; sett. Amwell (Hunterdon) N.J., 1733-1741; sett. Lower Frederick (Montgomery) Pa., Falkner's Swamp Chh., 1733-1741; Germ. Bapt.; d. Amwell, N.J., 1741.

HANS RUDOLPH NAEGELE, son of Rudolph Naegele; sett. West Earl (Lanc.) Pa., Groffdale Mennonite Chh., 1717-9 Nov. 1724; became a German Bapt. and entered the Ephrata Chloister, 1725-1749; Menn.; Germ. Bapt.; d. Ephrata, Pa., 29 Jan. 1749.

GABRIEL NAESMAN, Ord. Upsala, Sweden, May 1742; sett. Philadelphia, Pa., Gloria Dei Chh., 1743-1750; Sw. Luth.

HENRY NEALE, S.J., arriv. in Maryland, 21 Apr. 1741; sett. Philadelphia, Pa., St. Joseph's Chh., 1741-1748; Lancaster (Lanc.) Pa., St. John Nepomucene's Chh., 1748-1748; Conewago (Adams) Pa., Sacred Heart Chh., 1748-1748; R.C.; d. Philadelphia, Pa., 5 May 1748.

G. FREDERICK NEIMAYER (Neimeier or Naymeyer); sett. Upper Hanover (Montgomery) Pa., New Goshenhoppen Chh., 1764-

1771; Upper Salford (Montg.) Pa., Old Goshenhoppen Chh., 1771-1771; Franconia (Montg.) Pa., Indian Creek or Zion's Chh., 1771-1771; Rockhill (Bucks) Pa., Indianfield Chh., 1771-1771; Luth.

HENRY NEFF, Ord. ca. 1770; sett. Codorus (York) Pa., 1770-1776; Germ. Bapt.; living in 1789.

JACOB NEFF, son of Dr. John Henry Neff; sett. Providence (Lanc.) Pa., Black Horse Chh., 1764-1814; Menn.; d. Providence, Pa., 16 Feb. 1814.

HUGH NEILL, A.M., A.M. (hon.) Columbia, 1767; sett. N.J. as a Presb.; became an Ep.; Ord. London, 1749; lic. 26 Mar. 1750; K.B. for Pa., 2 May 1750; sett. Dover (Kent) Del., Christ Chh., 1749-1756; Milford (Kent) Del., Christ Chh., 1749-1757; Mispillion (Kent) Del., Christ Chh., 1749-1757; Smyrna (Kent) Del., St. Peter's Chh., 1749-1757; Whitemarsh (Montgomery) Pa., St. Thomas's Chh., 1758-1766; Oxford (Chester) Pa., Trinity Chh., 1758-1765; St. Paul's Parish (Queen Annes) Md., 1765-1781; Presb.; Ep.; d. Oxford, Pa., 1781.

GEORGE NEISSER, b. Sehlen, Moravia, 11 Apr. 1715; arriv. Savannah, Ga., 16 Feb. 1735/6; arriv. Philadelphia, Feb. 1737; arriv. Bethlehem (Northampton) Pa., 25 June 1742, where he was the first schoolmaster, diarist, clerk, post-master, lawyer and musician; sett. N.Y., N.Y., 1742-1748, 1765-1777; Ord. 1748; sett. Graceham (Frederick) Md., 1748-1748; Lancaster (Lanc.) Pa., 1751-1753; York (York) Pa., 1756-1757; Warwick (Lanc.) Pa., St. James's Chh. at Lititz, 1757-1759; Philadelphia, Pa., 1762-1774; Morav.; d. Philadelphia, Pa., Nov. 1784.

JOSEPH NEISSER, Ord. in Europe; arriv. Bethlehem, Pa., 28 Nov. 1765; sett. Graceham (Frederick) Md., 1771-1775; Hope (Warren) N.J., 1775-1776; Morav.

MATTHIAS NERTUNIUS, was stranded near Puerto Rico, 1649; sett. Chester (Del.) Pa., Chh. at Upland, 1654 ff.; Sw. Luth.

DANIEL NEUBERT (or Neibert), b. Koenigswalde, Saxony; had been an active preacher in Holstein and Holland; arriv. Bethlehem, Pa., Sept. 1742; Philadelphia, Pa., 1743-1747; Ord. Dec. 1754; sett. Heidelberg (Berks) Pa., 9 Apr. 1745-1745, 1748-1752; Warwick (Lanc.) Pa., St. James's Chh. at Lititz, 1745-1747, 1756-1757; Salisbury (Lehigh) Pa., Chh. at Emaus, 1753-1755, 1760-1762; Lynn (Lehigh) Pa., Allemaengel Chh., 1751-1753; miller; minister in rural chhs.; his wife Hannah (or Christianna) was also ordained; Morav.; d. Bethlehem, Pa., Jan. 1785.

HANS NEUSS (Nice or Neiss), came from Crefeld, Germany, to Germantown, 1698; Ord. Germantown, Pa., 8 Oct. 1702-1702; withdrew; silversmith; Menn.; d. Frederick (Montgomery) Pa., 19 July 1736.

JOHN WESLEY GILBERT NEVELLING, b. Westphalia, Germany, 1750; he was a relative of the Weybergs; Ord. Lancaster, Pa., 17 June 1772; sett. Amwell (Hunterdon) N.J., 1770-1783; Reading (Berks)

Pa., 1783-1783; by an accident to his throat his speech was permanently affected, 1783; Germ. Ref.; d. Philadelphia, Pa., 18 Jan. 1844, a. 94 years.

HENRY NICOLS, A.M. (Nichols or Nicholls), b. 1 Apr. 1678, son of Jonathan Nicols, of Cowbridge, Glamorgan; matric. Jesus Coll., Oxford, 11 Mar. 1696/7, a. 16; A.B., 1701, A.M., 28 Mar. 1715; Fellow; K.B., 5 May 1703; S.P.G. missionary; sett. Concord (Del.) Pa., St. John's Chh., 1703-1708; Marcus Hook (Del.) Pa., St. Martin's Chh., 1703-1708; Chester (Del.) Pa., St. Paul's Chh., 1704-1708; Newtown (Del.) Pa., St. David's Chh. at Radnor, 1704-1708; St. Michael's Parish (Talbot) Md., 1708-1749; the first resident S.P.G. missionary in Pa.; Ep.; d. St. Michael's Parish, Talbot, Md., 12 Feb. 1749.

GEORGE NIEKE, came from Herrnhut, Moravia; arriv. N.Y., N.Y., 26 Nov. 1743; Ord. Oley, Pa., as deacon, 1 Mar. 1744; sett. Graceham (Frederick) Md., 1746-1748; Monocacy, Md., 1746-1748; minister in rural districts; Morav.

DAVID NITSCHMANN, Senior, b. Zauchtenthal, Moravia, 29 Sept. 1676; sett. Herrnhut, Moravia, 1725; Island of St. Croix, 1734; arriv. Philadelphia, 18 Dec. 1739; sett. Bethlehem, Pa., 1740-1758; naturalized as a citizen of Pa., Oct. 1750; Trustee of the Moravian Estates; called "Father David"; wheelwright and joiner; Moravian; d. Bethlehem, Pa., 14 Apr. 1758, a. 82.

Bishop DAVID NITSCHMANN, b. Zauchtenthal, Moravia, 27 Dec. 1696, nephew of David Nitschmann, Senior; sett. St. Thomas, West Indies, 21 Aug. 1731; St. Croix, 1734; Ord. Berlin, Germany, 13 Mar. 1735; arriv. Savannah, Georgia, 20 Feb. 1736; in Pa., Apr. 1736-June 1736; in Europe, 1736-1740; returned to America, 15 Dec. 1740; sett. Bethlehem, Pa., 1740-1772; absent in Europe, 1744-1751; missionary Bishop, 1751-1772; arriv. N.Y., N.Y., again, 15 Apr. 1754; sett. Warwick (Lanc.) Pa., 1756-1761; took at least 50 sea voyages; his official labors extended over various parts of Germany, Denmark, Sweden, Norway, Livonia, England, Wales, Danish West Indies, Savannah, Ga., Pa., N.Y., and N.C.; he was the first Moravian missionary to the heathen; sett. Herrnhut, Saxony, 1722-1732; 1st American Moravian Bishop and a founder of Bethlehem; d. Bethlehem, Pa., 8 Oct. 1772.

Bishop DAVID NITSCHMANN, Jr., son of the Rev. David and Rosina Nitschmann; Ord. Bishop, 1746; came to America, 1765; arriv. Bethlehem, Pa., 28 Nov. 1765; sett. Bethlehem, Pa., 1765-1766; returned to Europe, 15 Sept. 1766; called the "Syndic"; Morav.

IMMANUEL NITSCHMANN, son of Bishop John and Anna (Haberland) Nitschmann; arriv. N.Y., N.Y., 19 Oct. 1761; sett. Bethlehem, Pa., 1761-1790; kept the records at Bethlehem; Morav.; d. Bethlehem, Pa., 1790.

Bishop JOHN NITSCHMANN, Senior, went to Lapland, 24 Feb. 1734; Ord. Bishop, 1741; arriv. Bethlehem, Pa., 21 May 1749; sett. Bethlehem, 1749-1751; succeeded Bishop Spangenberg, 1749; left for Europe, 4 Dec. 1751; Morav.

JOHN G. NIXDORF, b. Silesia; sett. Lancaster (Lanc.) Pa., 1745-1745; Ord. deacon, 1758; minister, preacher and teacher in rural districts; sett. Lynn (Lehigh) Pa., Allemaengel Chh., 1746-1746; Morav.; d. Bethlehem, Pa., Sept. 1775.

ABEL NOBLE, b. Bristol, R.I., son of William and Frances Noble from Bristol, England; brought up as a Quaker; came to Pa., ca. 1684, as a Friend; became a 7th Day Bapt. or Keithian Bapt., 1691; only 7th Day Bapt. minister in Pa., ca. 1700; sett. Newtown, Pa., 1697-1701; Nottingham, Md., 1697-1700; he served for many years; 7th Day Bapt.

JOHN PETRUS NUCELLA, Ord. Amsterdam, Holland, 13 Apr. 1694; came to America, 1695; arriv. Kingston, N.Y., 15 Dec. 1695; sett. Kingston (Ulster) N.Y., Chh. at Esopus, 1695-1704; resigned 7 Mar. 1704; sett. Hurley (Ulster) N.Y., 1695-1704; Marbletown (Ulster) N.Y., 1685-1704; Rochester (Ulster) N.Y., 1695-1704; supply at Albany, N.Y., 1698-1700; in 1704, he went to London, England, to take charge of Queen Anne's Dutch Chapel there; Dutch Ref.; d. Jan. 1722.

JOHN NUTMAN, A.M., b. Newark, N.J., 1703, son of James and Hannah (Prudden) Nutman; A.B., Y.C., 1727, A.M.; Ord. Hanover (Morris) N.J., Whippany Chh., 1730-1745; teacher at Newark, N.J.; Presb.; d. Newark, N.J., 1 Sept. 1751, a. 48. (GS).

LAWRENCE (Lorenz or Laurentius) THORSTANSEA NYBERG, ed. at Upsala; Ord. Sweden, 1743; excluded from the Swedish Lutheran ministry; preached in Lutheran chhs. as ff: Hanover (York) Pa., St. Michael's Chh., 1744-1746; Warwick (Lanc.) Pa., St. James's Chh., 1744-1746; Lancaster (Lanc.) Pa., Holy Trinity Chh., 1744-1746; York (York) Pa., Christ Chh., 1744-1748; Monocacy (Frederick) Md., 1745-1746; Conewago (Adams) Pa., 1744-1748; had been preaching in Moravian chhs., and on 13 Aug. 1748, he became a Moravian; preached in Moravian chhs. as ff: Warwick, Pa., 1744-1745; Graceham, Md., 1745-1745; York, Pa., 1744-1748; Swatara, Pa., South Lebanon Chh., Mar. 1745-1750; Lancaster, Pa., 1746-1748; Oldmans Creek (Gloucester) N.J., at Pilesgrove, Woolwich, 1747-1749; returned to England, 1750; Ord. England, 1754; Sw. Luth.; Luth.; Morav.

JACOB OBERHOLTZER, sett. Hatfield (Montgomery) Pa., Chh. at Landsdale, 1774-1813; Franconia (Montgomery) Pa., Indian Creek Chh., 1775-1813; supply, Germantown, Pa., 23 Apr. 1797; Menn.; d. Franconia, Pa., 13 Dec. 1813.

JONATHAN ODELL, A.M., M.D., b. Newark, N.J., 25 Sept. 1737; A.B., Princeton, 1754, A.M., 1759; M.D.; studied medicine; Ord. by Bishop of London, Jan. 1767; K.B. for N.J., 23 Jan. 1767; sett. Mount Holly (Burlington) N.J., St. Andrew's Chh., 25 July 1767-1774; Burlington (Burl.) N.J., St. Anne's, now St. Mary's Chh., 26 July 1767-1777; Bristol (Bucks) Pa., St. James the Greater Chh., 1768-1777; elected member, N.J. Medical Soc., 8 Nov. 1774; member, Am. Phil. Soc.; surgeon, British Army, 1776; refugee and Br. Army Chaplain, 1777; to England, 1783; New Brunswick, Canada, 1784; Councillor and Secretary of the Province of New Brunswick, 1785-1818; Ep.; d. Frederickton, N.B., 25 Nov. 1818, a. 81.

JOHN JACOB OEHL (Oel or Ehlig), Ord. London (Bsp. of London), 1722; K.B. for N.Y., 5 Oct. 1722; came to America with a company of Germans, 1722; sett. Kaatsbaan (Ulster) N.Y., 1722-1724; East Camp (Ulster) N.Y., 1722-1724; Kinderhook (Columbia) N.Y., 1722-1727; Schoharie (Schoharie) N.Y., D.R. Chh. at Huntersfield, 1724-1730; West Camp (Ulster) N.Y., Chh. at Saugerties, 1722-1730; asst. missionary to the Mohawk Indians, 1750-1776; Albany, N.Y., Germ. Ref. Chh., 1770-1772; Germ. Ref.; Ep.; d. N.Y., ca. 1780.

UZAL OGDEN, Jr., b. Newark, N.J., 1744, son of Uzal and Charlotte (Thébaut) Ogden; Ord. (Bsp. of London) 1773; K.B. for N.J., 25 Sept. 1773; sett. Sussex, Morris, and Bergen counties, N.J., 1769-1783, stations not given; S.P.G. catechist in Sussex co. 1770-1772; Newtown (Sussex) N.J., Christ Chh., 1773-1776; refugee to N.Y., 1776; returned Jan. 1777; perhaps at Newtown, 1777-1784; Elizabethtown, N.J., 1784-1788; Rector, Newark, N.J., Trinity Chh., 1788-1805; asst., N.Y., N.Y., 1784-18 Aug. 1788; Bishop elect of N.J., 16 Aug. 1798, and Oct. 1799, but not consecrated; he joined the Presb. Chh., 16 Oct. 1805; Ep.; Presb.; d. 4 Nov. 1822.

JOHN OGILVIE, D.D., b. N.Y., N.Y., 1724, of Scottish parents; A.B., Y.C., 1748; D.D., Aberdeen, 1770; A.M., Columbia, 1767, D.D., 1770; sett. Norwalk, Conn., 1748-1749; Ord. London, England, 24 June 1749; K.B. for N.Y., 12 July 1749; S.P.G. missionary to the Indians; sett. Albany, N.Y., St. Peter's Chh., 1 Mar. 1749/50-1760; Schenectady, N.Y., St. George's Chh., 1750-1760; Fort Hunter, Albany, N.Y., Queen Anne's Chapel, 1749-1762; Chaplain in Canada, 1759-1763; N.Y., N.Y., Trinity Chh., Aug. 1764-1774; Peekskill (Westchester) N.Y., St. Peter's Chh. in the Manor of Cortlandt, 1767-1771; Ep. ; d. N.Y., N.Y., 26 Nov. 1774, a. 50.

JOHN GEORGE A. OHNEBERG, b. Hildersheim, Germany, 1721; theol. student at Lindheim, 1744, a. 23; arriv. N.Y., N.Y., 26 Nov. 1743; sett. Nazareth (Northampton) Pa., chhs. at Ephrata, Gnadenthal, Christianspring and Friedenthal, 1747-1750; missionary at Santa Cruz, 1750-1758; sett. Bethlehem, Pa., 1758-1759; glazier; Morav.; d. Bethlehem, Pa., Apr. 1760.

JOHN OKELY, came from Bedford, England; Ord. deacon, 1751; sett. Southampton (Bucks) Pa., Neshaminy Chh., 1746-1747; Philadelphia, Pa., 1743-1747; missionary in Bucks and Philadelphia counties; Justice of the Peace, 1774; asst. Commissary, Continental Army, Rev. War, Aug. 1780; Morav.; d. Lancaster, Pa., 1792.

CHRISTIAN GEORGE ANDREW OLDENDORP, arriv. Bethlehem, Pa., 26 Nov. 1768; sett. Bethlehem, 1768-1769; sett. Danish West Indies, 1766-1768; Morav.; sailed to Europe, 17 Apr. 1769.

JAMES OREM (or Overn), K.B. to N.E., 19 Oct. 1721; N.Y., N.Y., Chaplain in the Fort, 1723; Ep.

ROBERT ORR, b. British Isles; Ord. Lawrenceville (Mercer), N.J., 20 Oct. 1715; sett. Lawrenceville, 1715-1719; Amwell (Hunterdon) N.J., Chh. at Reaville, 1715-1719; Hopewell (Mercer) N.J., at Ewing, 1715-1719; Trenton (Mercer) N.J., 1st Chh., 1715-1719; Titusville (Mercer) N.J., 1715-1719; Pennington, 1715-1719; Presb.

ANDREW OSTROM, sett. Bethlehem (Northampton) Pa., Brodhead Settlement at Dansbury, 1748-1749; Wallpack (Sussex) N.J., 1748-1748; Paulin's Kill (Warren) N.J., 1748-1749; Morav.

Bishop PHILIP WILHELM OTTERBEIN, b. Dillenburg, Nassau, Germany, 3 June 1726, son of the Rev. John Daniel and Wilhelmina Henrietta (Hoerlen) Otterbein; ed. Herborn Seminary, 1742; Ord. Ockersdorf, Germany, 13 June 1749, where he was sett. as a Germ. Ref. vicar; arriv. N.Y., N.Y., 28 July 1752; sett. Lancaster (Lanc.) Pa., Aug. 1752-1758; Pequea (Lanc.) Pa., 1752-1758; Mill Creek (Lebanon) Pa., Tulpehocken or Trinity Chh., 1758-1760; Tulpehocken (Berks) Pa., Host Chh., 1758-1760; Conococheague (Washington) Md., St. Paul's Chh., 1760-1765; Frederick (Frederick) Md., 1760-Nov. 1765; Middletown (Fredk.) Md., Zion or Kittatinny Mountain Chh., 1760-1765; Conewago (York) Pa., Zion's or Quickel's Chh., 1765-1774; Hellam (York) Pa., Kreutz Chh., 1765-1770; Lower Windsor (York) Pa., 1765-1774; Paradise (York) Pa., Holz Schwamm Chh., 1765-1774; Union (Adams) Pa., 1765-1774; York (York) Pa., Nov. 1765-1774; Hopewell (York) Pa., 1767-1774; Antietam (Washington) Md., 1774-1783; Baltimore, Md., 2nd Chh., 1774-1813; founder of the United Brethren in Christ; Germ. Ref.; d. Baltimore, Md., 17 Oct. 1813, a. 87.

BERNARD PAGE, Ord. (Bsp. of London) 24 Aug. 1772; lic. for Wyoming, Pa., 24 Aug. 1772; K.B. for Pa., 11 Sept. 1772; sett. Wyoming, Pa. (now Wilkes-Barre), 1772-1775; Phillipstown (Putnam) N.Y., St. Philip's Chh. in the Highlands, 1775-1776; Peekskill (Westchester) N.Y., St. Peter's Chh. in the Manor of Cortlandt, 1775-1776; Fairfax Parish (Fairfax) Va., 1786-1792; Norbourne Parish (Berkeley) W.Va., 1792-1795; resided at Mount Eagle, near Hunting Creek Bridge; Ep.; d. lower Va., soon after 1795.

ELISHA PAINE, b. Eastham, Mass., 29 Dec. 1693, son of Elisha and Rebecca (Doane) Paine; imprisoned in Conn., for preaching without authority; Bapt. minister; Bridgehampton, L.I., N.Y., 1758 ff; Riverhead, L.I., N.Y., Separatist Chh. of Southold, 26 May 1758 ff.; Bapt.; d. Southold, L.I., N.Y., 26 Aug. 1775.

JOHN PAINE, sett. Bridgehampton, L.I., N.Y., 2nd or Separatist Chh., 1749-1753; Bapt.; d. Southold, L.I., N.Y., Apr. 1753; shot!

THOMAS PAINE, A.M., b. Canterbury, Conn., 1724, son of Abraham and Ruth (Adams) Paine; A.B., Y.C., 1748, A.M., 1754; lic. 20 Dec. 1748; Ord. Southold, L.I., N.Y., Chh. at Cutchogue, 24 Oct. 1750–1766; Cong.; d. Southold, L.I., N.Y., 15 Oct. 1766, a. 42 (GS).

SOLOMON PALMER, A.M., b. Branford, Conn., 6 Apr. 1709, son of Daniel and Elizabeth Palmer; A.B., Y.C., 1729, A.M.; lic., 27 May 1735; Ord. Huntington, L.I., N.Y., 1735–1741; inst. Cornwall, Conn., 19 Aug. 1741–Mar. 1754; became an Ep.; Ord. London, England, Oct. 1765; sett. New Milford, Conn., Ep. Chh., 1755–1760, 1766–1771; Litchfield, Conn., St. Michael's Ep. Chh., 1755–1760, 1766–1771; Great Barrington, Mass., St. James's Chh., 1763–1766; Goshen, Conn., 1667–1771; S.P.G. missionary; Perth Amboy, N.J., St. Peter's Chh., 1760–1762; Cong.; Ep.; d. Litchfield, Conn., 2 Nov. 1771, a. 63.

HENRY PANNEBECKER (Pennypacker), b. 1719; sett. Skippack (Montgomery) Pa., 1775–1792; Menn.; d. Skippack, Pa., 1792.

GEORGE PANTON, A.M., b. in America of Scots parentage; A.B., Aberdeen, A.M.; A.M. (hon.) Columbia, 1774; Ord. by the Bishop of Down and Connor, in Ireland, 1770; returned to America, 1770; sett. Trenton, N.J., St. Michael's Chh., 11 Apr. 1774–7 July 1776; Lawrenceville, N.J., Maidenhead Chh., 1774–1776; Princeton, N.J., 1774–1776; refugee to N.Y., N.Y.; sett. Phillipstown, Yonkers (Westchester) N.Y., St. Philip's Chh. in the Highlands, Dec. 1777–1783; Chaplain, Prince of Wales American Regt., 18 Jan. 1778–13 Oct. 1783; S.P.G., Yarmouth, Nova Scotia, 1785–1786; Ep.; d. in England, after 1786.

JOSEPH PARK, A.M., b. Newton, Mass., 12 Mar. 1705, son of John and Elizabeth (Miller) Park; A.B., H.C., 1724, A.M.; Ord. Westerly, R.I., 13 Aug. 1742; Cong. minister and Indian missionary; sett. Westerly, R.I., 1742–1752, 1756–1777; inst. Southold, L.I., N.Y., Mattituck Chh., 10 June 1752–11 Feb. 1756; Lower Aquebogue, L.I., N.Y., 1752–11 Feb. 1756; Presb. at L.I.; d. Westerly, R.I., 1 Mar. 1772, a. 72.

SAMUEL PARKHURST, A.M., A.B., Princeton, 1757, A.M.; sett. Florida (Orange) N.Y., 1762–1768; Warwick (Orange) N.Y., 1762–1768; Presb.; d. Orange co., N.Y., 1768.

Provost OLOF PARLIN, sett. Philadelphia, Pa., Gloria Dei Chh., July 1750–1757; Provost of the Sw. Luth. chhs. in America, 1756–1757; Sw. Luth.; d. Philadelphia, Pa., 22 Dec. 1757.

NOYES PARRIS, A.M., b. Newton, Mass., 22 Aug. 1699, son of the Rev. Samuel and Dorothy (Noyes) Parris; A.B., H.C., 1721, A.M.; sett. Cohansey, now Fairfield (Cumberland) N.J., 1724–1729; returned to N.E., Sept. 1729; Chaplain, Castle Island, Boston Harbor, for a time; d. perhaps in Sudbury, Mass., ca. 1748.

JOHN PAUL, b. Ireland, 1706; lic. 10 Dec. 1735; inst. Lower West Nottingham (Cecil) Md., Lower Octoraro Chh., Oct. 1736–1739; Presb.; d. Lower West Nottingham, Pa., 1739, a. 33.

Colonial Clergy of the Middle Colonies

ABRAHAM PAYN, sett. Nine Partners (Dutchess) N.Y., ca. 1752; Cong.

JASPER PAYNE, b. Twickenham, Middlesex, England, son of Elizabeth (Bannister) Payne; arriv. Staten Island, N.Y., 26 Nov. 1743; Ord. deacon, 1753; sett. Bethlehem, Pa., 1745-1748; steward, 1752; schoolmaster; L.I., N.Y., 1750-1752; Staten Island, N.Y., 1754-1754; Brodhead Settlement at Dansbury, Pa., 1754-1755; Paulin's Kill (Warren) N.J., 1754-1755; Wallpack (Sussex) N.J., 1754-1755; Philadelphia, Pa., 1760; innkeeper, Aug. 1762-1766; minister in rural churches; Morav.; d. Lititz, Warwick, Pa.

THOMAS PAYTON, S.J., sett. Md., 1658-1659; S.J., R.C., d. N.Y., N.Y., 12 Jan. 1660.

JEREMIAH PECK, b. London, England, 1628, son of William and Elizabeth Peck; came to Boston, 1637; H.C., 1653-1656, non-grad.; teacher at Guilford, Conn., 1656-1660; Ord. Old Saybrook, Conn., 25 Sept. 1661-30 Jan. 1665/6; sett. Newark, N.J., 1666/7-1 Oct. 1667; Elizabethtown, N.J., 1674-1678, as the first minister; West Greenwich, Conn., 3 Sept. 1678-1689; inst. Waterbury, Conn., 1690-1699; Cong.; Presb.; d. Waterbury, Conn., 7 June 1699, a. 71.

PIERRE PEIRET, b. 1645, came from Foix, southern France; sett. London, England, 1687; came to America, 1687; sett. N.Y., N.Y., Fr. Ref. Chh. of the Saint Esprit, 1687-1704; Fr. Ref.; d. N.Y., N.Y., 1 Sept. 1704.

JAMES PELLENTZ, sett. Lancaster (Lanc.) Pa., St. John Nepomucene's Chh., 1758-1800; Conewago (Adams) Pa., Chh. of the Sacred Heart, 1758-1800; Paradise (York) Pa., St. Mary's Chh., 1761-1800; Fredericktown (Frederick) Md., St. Stanislaus's Chh., 1768-1800; vicar-general to Bishop Carroll; R.C.; d. Conewago, Pa., 13 Mar. 1800.

EBENEZER PEMBERTON, D.D., b. Boston, Mass., 6 Feb. 1704/5, son of the Rev. Ebenezer and Mary (Clark) Pemberton; A.B., H.C., 1721, A.M.; D.D., Princeton, 1770; sett. N.Y., N.Y., 1st Presb. Chh., 1727-Oct. 1753; inst. Boston, Mass., New Brick Chh., 6 Mar. 1754-1777; Artillery Election Sermon, 1756; Election Sermon, 1757; Convention Sermon, 1759; Dudleian Lecture, 1766; Fellow, Am. Acad. of Arts and Sciences; Presb.; Cong.; d. Boston, Mass., 9 Sept. 1777, a. 73.

FRANCIS PEPPARD, A.B., A.B., Princeton, 1762; lic. 1764; Ord. 1764; sett. Mendham (Morris) N.J., 1764-1769; New Windsor (Orange) N.Y., 1769-1773; Newburgh (Orange) N.Y., 1769-1773; Cornwall (Orange) N.Y., Bethlehem Chh., 1769-1773; Frelinghuysen (Warren) N.J., Yellow Frame Chh., Apr. 1773-May 1783; Knowlton (Warren) N.J., 27 Apr. 1773-1775; Hackettstown (Warren) N.J., Apr. 1773-May 1783; sett. Allen, Pa., 1781-inst. Aug. 1783-May 1795; Presb.; d. Hardwick, Yellow Frame, N.J., 30 Mar. 1797.

JOHN FREDERICK PETER, Senior, sett. Hernndyck, Holland, 1746-1760; arriv. N.Y., N.Y., 19 Oct. 1761; sett. Bethlehem, Pa., 1761-

1784; as principal pastor, Bethlehem, Pa., Oct. 1784-1813; Morav.; d. Bethlehem, Pa., ca. 1813.

JOHN FREDERICK PETER, Jr., b. Hernndyck, Holland, 19 May 1746, son of the Rev. John Frederick and Susanna Peter; ed. Gros Hennersdorf, Barby, and Niesky; arriv. in America, 1769; teacher at Nazareth, Pa., 1769-1770; sett. Bethlehem, Pa., 1770-1785, as accountant, secretary and organizer; sett. Hope, N.J., Lititz, Pa., Graceham, Md., and Salem, N.C., 1786-1793; sett. Bethlehem, Pa., 1793-1813; noted composer and musician; Morav.; d. Bethlehem, Pa., 19 July 1813.

RICHARD PETERS, D.D., b. Liverpool, Lancashire, England, 1704, son of Ralph Peter, Town Clerk of Liverpool; matric. Wadham Coll., Oxford, 8 Apr. 1731, a. 20; D.D., Oxford, 2 May 1770; Trustee of the U. of Pa., 1749-1776; Ord. Chelsea, England, 1731; arriv. in Penna., 1735; sett. Philadelphia, Pa., Christ Chh., 1735-July1737; Philadelphia, United Chhs., Christ Chh. and St. Peter's Chh., 6 Dec. 1762-23 Sept. 1775; Clerk of the Provincial Council, 14 Feb. 1743-1762; Secretary of the Pennsylvania Land Office, 1737 ff.; member of the Council, 1749; Ep.; d. Philadelphia, Pa., 10 July 1776, a. 72.

JOHN GOTTLIEB PEZOLD, b. Bischofswerda, Saxony; was at Bethlehem, Pa., 1742; Ord. Deacon, 1748; sett. Salisbury (Lehigh) Pa., Chh. at Emaus, 1742-1748, founder of Emaus; General Superintendent of the work of the single men in America; sett. Macungie (Lehigh) Pa.; returned to Europe, 1753-1754; Chaplain at Bethlehem, 1754 ff.; "one of the most devoted and valuable Moravians of his time"; Morav.; d. Lititz, Pa., 1 Apr. 1762.

Bishop MICHAEL PFFAUTZ, b. Germany, 1709; came to America, 1727; Ord. minister, 1735; Ord. Bishop, 1747; sett. Warwick (Lanc.) Pa., White Oak Chh., 1736-1769; Cocalico (Lanc.) Pa., Conestoga Chh., 1748-1769; Bern (Berks) Pa., Northkill Chh., 1748-1769; Mount Joy (Lanc.) Pa., Great Swatara Chh., 1756-1769; German Bapt.; d. Lancaster co. Pa., 21 May 1769, a. 60.

FRANCIS PHILLIPS (or Philips), ed. St. John's Coll., Camb.; no matriculation or degrees found; Ord. deacon, London, England, 4 Mar. 1704/5; Chaplain, British Navy, 1711-1712; K.B. for Md., 10 Dec. 1711; inst. Stratford, Conn., 1712-1713; sett. Philadelphia, Pa., Christ Chh., 1714-1715; unfrocked; Ep.

GEORGE PHILLIPS, A.M., b. Rowley, Mass., 3 June 1664, son of the Rev. Samuel and Sarah (Appleton) Phillips; A.B., H.C., 1686, A.M.; sett. Suffield, Conn., 1690-1692; Jamaica, L.I., N.Y., 1693-1697; Ord. Brookhaven, L.I., N.Y., Chh. at Setauket, 13 Apr. 1702; sett. Setauket, L.I., N.Y., 1697-1739; he was a founder of the Long Island Presbytery, 1717; Cong.; Presb.; d. Setauket, L.I., N.Y., 3 Apr. 1739, a. 75.

JAMES PHILLIPS, sett. Philips' Patent (Dutchess) N.Y., 1773-1774; Fishkill (Dutchess) N.Y., 1774-1793; Bapt.; d. Fishkill, N.Y., 3 Feb. 1793.

JEAN PIERRON, b. Dun-sur-Meuse, France, 28 Sept. 1631; Jesuit nov. at Nancy, France, 21 Nov. 1650; ed. Pont-a-Mousson; instructor at Rheims, Verdun and Metz, 1665–1667; arriv. in Canada, June 1667; sett. among the Mohawks where he replaced Father Fremin, 7 Oct. 1668; Iroquois Mission of Sainte Marie, 1667–1677 (also called the Mission of the Martyrs and the Mohawk Mission of St. Peter's at Fonda, N.Y.); travelled through Acadia, N.E., Md. and Va.; returned to France, 1677; R.C.; date and place of death unknown.

ABRAHAM PIERSON, A.B., b. Yorkshire, England, ca. 1608; A.B., Trinity Coll., Camb., 1632; Ord. in England, where he was minister at Newark, co. Nottingham; came to N.E., 1639; sett. Lynn, Mass., Nov.–Dec. 1640; Southampton, L.I., N.Y., Dec. 1640–1644; Branford, Conn., 7 Mar. 1644–1666; Newark, N.J., June 1667–1678; Chaplain, 1654; Cong.; d. Newark, N.J., 9 Aug. 1678.

President ABRAHAM PIERSON, A.B., b. prob. at Branford, Conn., ca. 1645; A.B., H.C., 1668; Ord. Newark, N.J., 4 Mar. 1672; sett. (asst.) Newark, N.J., 1669–1678; sett. Newark, N.J., 9 Aug. 1678–1692; Greenwich, Conn., 1692–1694; inst. Killingworth, Conn. (now Clinton, Conn.), 1694–1707; Trustee and founder, Y.C., 1700; induct. Y.C., 1st Pres., 11 Nov. 1701–1707; Cong.; d. Killingworth, Conn., 5 May 1707, a. 61.

JOHN PIERSON, A.M., b. Newark, N.J., 1689, son of the Rev. Abraham and Abigail (Clark) Pierson; A.B., Y.C., 1711, A.M.; Trustee, Princeton, 1746–1765; Ord. Woodbridge, N.J., 29 Apr. 1717; sett. Woodbridge, N.J., 1714–1752; Mendham, N.J., 1753–1762; Presb.; d. Hanover, N.J., 23 Aug. 1770, a. 80.

JOHN PIERSON, A.M., b. Newark, N.J., son of Abraham and Hannah Pierson; A.B., Y.C., 1729, A.M.; Ord. London, England, 1733; K.B. for N.J., 1 Sept. 1733; arriv. N.J., 30 Jan. 1733/4; sett. Salem (Salem) N.J., St. John's Chh., 30 Jan. 1733/4–1747; S.P.G. missionary in N.J., at Greenwich in Cohansey (Cumberland) N.J., St. Stephen's Chh., 1734–1747; sett. Maurice River (Cumb.) N.J., 1734–1747; Ep.; d. Salem, N.J., 1747.

JOSEPH PILMORE, D.D., b. Tadmouth, Yorkshire, England, 1734; arriv. Gloucester Point, N.J., 24 Oct. 1769, as a Methodist preacher; D.D., U. of Pa., 1807; Ord. Conn., 27 Dec. 1785; itinerant preacher in the Colonies, 1769–1785; sett. Philadelphia, Pa., St. George's Chh., 1769–1785; United Chhs.: Oxford, Pa., Trinity Chh.; Lower Dublin, Pa., All Saints Chh.; Whitmarsh, Pa., St. Thomas's Chh., 1785–1789; became an Ep.; sett. Philadelphia, Pa., St. Paul's Chh., 1789–1794, 1804–1825; N.Y., N.Y., Christ Chh., 1794–1804; Meth.; Ep.; d. Philadelphia, Pa., 24 July 1825, a. 91.

JOHN PINE, not ordained; preached at N.Y., N.Y., 1745–1750; Bapt.; d. N.Y., N.Y., 1750.

Abbe FRANCIS PIQUET, b. Bresse, France, 6 Dec. 1708; sett. Ogdensburg (St. Lawrence) N.Y., Mission of Our Lady; Sulpician; R.C.; d. Verjon, France, 15 July 1781, a. 73.

GEORGE PITSCHMANN, sett. Salisbury (Lehigh) Pa., Chh. at Emaus, 1762–1763; his wife, Maria, was his helper; Morav.

JOHANNES THEODORUS POLHEMUS, b. Switzerland, 1598; ed. Switzerland; sett. Palatinate, Germany, 1625–1628; Meppel, Overyssel, Netherlands, 1628–1630; Palatinate, 1630–1635; Olinda, Brazil, 1637–1645; Itamacus, Brazil, 1645–1654; arriv. in America, 1654; sett. Flatlands, L.I., N.Y., at Midwout, 1655–1676; Brooklyn, 1655–1660, 1664–1676; Flatlands, at Niew Amersfoordt, 1655–1676; Bushwick, 1655–1676; Gravesend, L.I., N.Y., 1655–1676; Dutch Ref.; d. Brooklyn, L.I., N.Y., 8 June 1676.

SAMUEL POMEROY, A.B., b. Northampton, Mass., 16 Sept. 1687, son of Deacon Medad and Abigail (Strong) Pomeroy; A.B., Y.C., 1705; Ord. Northampton, Mass., 30 Nov. 1709; sett. Newtown, L.I., N.Y., July 1708–1744; Cong.; Presb.; d. Newtown, L.I., N.Y., 30 June 1744, a. 57.

JOHN NICHOLAS POMP, b. Mambaechel, Zweibruecken, Germany, 20 Jan. 1734, son of Peter and Anna Elizabeth (Thomser) Pomp; matric. Marburg, 25 Apr. 1757; Ord. Cassel, Germany; arriv. Philadelphia, 5 Dec. 1765; sett. New Hanover (Montgomery) Pa., Falkner's Swamp Chh., 1765–1783; Pottstown (Montgomery) Pa., Zion's Chh., 1765–1783; East Vincent (Chester) Pa., Zion Chh., 1765–1783; Baltimore, Md., 1 Sept. 1783–15 Nov. 1789; Upper Salford (Montgomery) Pa., Old Goshenhoppen Chh.,1790–1791; Upper Hanover (Montgomery) Pa., New Goshenhoppen Chh., 1790–1791; Franconia (Montgomery) Pa., Indian Creek Chh., 1789–1796; Whitpain (Montgomery) Pa., Boehm's Chh., 1794–1797; Worcester (Montgomery) Pa., Wentz's or Skippack Chh., 1794–1797; lived at Skippack; Germ. Ref.; d. Easton, Pa., 1 Sept. 1819, a. 85 y.

EDWARD PORTLOCK (or Perthuck), Ord. Deacon, 11 May 1691; Ord. Priest, 3 Apr. 1698; came to America, 1698; sett. Perth Amboy (Middlesex) N.J., St. Peter's Chh., 22 Feb. 1698–1700; Elizabethtown (Union) N.J., St. John's Chh., 1698–1700; Burlington (Burlington) N.J., met in the Town House, 1698–1700; Piscataway (Middlesex) N.J., 1698–1700; Woodbridge (Middlesex) N.J., Trinity Chh., 1698–1700; Philadelphia, Pa., Christ Chh., 29 Nov. 1699–1700; sett. Stratton-Major Parish (King and Queen) Va., 1701–1705 and prob. to 1715; Ep.; d. ca. 1715 (bef. 1719).

FREDERICK CHRISTIAN POST, b. Conitz, Polish Prussia, 1710; arriv. Bethlehem, Pa., 25 June 1742; not ordained; Indian missionary in N.Y. and Conn., 1743–1749; went to Europe, 1751–1754; arriv. N.Y., N.Y., 15 Apr. 1754; sett. Labrador, 1752; Wyoming Valley, Pa., 1754; his important services to the Government of Pennsylvania in treating with the western Indians, 1758, made his name celebrated in the history of Pa.; sett. Tuscarawas Valley, Stark co., Ohio, as missionary, Sept. 1761–1764; Moskito Coast, 1764–1784; carpenter; returned to Germantown, 1784; Morav.; d. Germantown, Pa., Apr. 1785.

ELAM POTTER, A.M., b. New Haven, Conn., 1 Jan. 1741/2, son of Dea. Daniel, Jr. and Martha (Ives) Potter; A.B., Y.C., 1765, A.M.; Ord. Shelter Island, L.I., N.Y., Cong. Chh., 12 June 1766; sett. Shelter Island, 1766-1767; inst. Enfield, Conn., 1st Cong. Chh., 1 Mar. 1769-17 Apr. 1776; sett. Southold, L.I., N.Y., Nov. 1792-1794; Cong.; Presb.; d. Southold, L.I., N.Y., 5 Jan. 1794, a. 52.

JOSHUA POTTS, b. Mansfield, N.J., 4 Jan. 1719; Ord. 29 May 1746; sett. Southampton (Bucks) Pa., 1746-1761; Bapt.; d. Southampton, Pa., 18 June 1761.

HOWELL POWELL (Howell ap Howell). came from Wales; Ord. Fairfield (Cumberland) N.J., Cohansey Presb. Chh., 15 Oct. 1714-1717; Presb.; d. Cohansey, N.J., bef. Sept. 1717.

JOSEPH POWELL, b. Pennypack, Pa., 6 Mar. 1734; ed. Hopewell, N.J., Ord. 1764; sett. Konolowa (Cumberland) Pa., Bapt. Chh., 1764-1771; Bapt.

JOSEPH POWELL, came from Whitechurch, Shropshire, England; arriv. Philadelphia, 7 June 1742; sett. Bethlehem, Pa., 1742; Bethlehem, Broadhead Settlement at Dansbury, 1755-1756; Wallpack (Sussex) N.J., 1755-1755; chh. burned by the Indians, 1755; Paulin's Kill (Warren) N.J., 1755-1755; Neshaminy (Bucks) Pa., Sunbury (Northampton) Pa., Indian Chh. at Shamokin, 1745; Staten Island; Carroll's Manor, Md.; Amenia Union (Dutchess) N.Y., Indian mission at "The Oblong"; Ord. Deacon, 1756; sett. Jamaica, West Indies, 1759-1765; Maryland, 1765-1772; Graceham, Md., 1770-1770; Sichem, North East Center (Dutchess) N.Y., 1772-1774; Sharon, Conn., Gnadensee Mission at Wequodnoc; Mr. Powell was the last missionary here; at his death the mission was discontinued; Morav.; d. Sichem, North East Center, N.Y., Sept. 1774.

JAMES POWER, D.D., b. Nottingham (Chester) Pa., 1746; A.B., Princeton, 1766; D.D., Jefferson Coll., 1808; lic. 24 June 1772; sett. Mill Creek (Lebanon) Pa., June 1772-23 Dec. 1772; missionary in Botetourt co., Va., 1773, and in western Pa., 1774; sett. West Nottingham (Chester) Pa., 1774-1776; Ord. 23 May 1776; Dunlap's Creek (Fayette) Pa., near Brownsville, 1776-1779; Mt. Pleasant (Westmoreland) Pa. and Sewickley (Allegheny) Pa., 1779-22 Apr. 1817; Presb.; d. Mt. Pleasant, Pa., 5 Aug. 1830, a. 85.

THOMAS POYER, b. 1685, son of Thomas Poyer of Haverfordwest, co. Pembroke, Wales; matric. Brasenose Coll., Oxford, 6 Apr. 1704, a. 19; Ord. (Bsp. of St. David's) 1706; curate, Haverfordwest, and Chaplain, H.M.S. "Antelope"; K.B. for N.Y., 28 Dec. 1709; sett. Flushing, L.I., N.Y., St. George's Chh., 1710-1731; induct. Jamaica, L.I., N.Y., Grace Chh., 18 July 1710-1732; supplied Trinity Chh., N.Y., N.Y., 1714, during the absence of Mr. Vesey; Ep.; d. Jamaica, L.I., N.Y., Jan. 1732.

WILLIAM PRESTON, A.B., b. 1718, son of George Preston, baronet, of Edinburgh, Scotland; matric. Balliol Coll., Oxford, 26 Aug. 1735, a.

17; A.B., 1739; Chaplain, 26th Regt., 23 Feb. 1741–1781; S.P.G. missionary at Woodbridge (Middlesex) N.J., Trinity Chh., 1767–1774; Perth Amboy (Middlesex) N.J., St. Peter's Chh., Dec. 1768–1777; mission broken up by the Rev. War; rejoined his regt. as Chaplain; Ep.; d. Shrewsbury, N.J., 7 Mar. 1781.

JACOB PRICE (or Preus), came from Wittgenstein, 1719; had been a missionary in Germany; arriv. at Lower Salford, Pa., 1721; sett. Lower Salford (Montgomery) Pa., 1723–1734; Germ. Bapt.

EBENEZER PRIME, A.M., b. Milford, Conn., 21 July 1700; A.B., Y.C., 1718, A.M.; Ord. Huntington, L.I., N.Y., 5 June 1723; sett. Huntington, 1719–1779; Presb.; d. Huntington, L.I., N.Y., 25 Sept. 1779, a. 79.

THOMAS PRITCHARD, A.B., b. Machynlleth, co. Montgomery, Wales, 1677, son of Edward Pritchard; matric. Jesus Coll., Camb., 2 Mar. 1698/9, a. 22; A.B., 1702; K.B. for N.Y., 30 Nov. 1703; arriv. N.Y., N.Y., Apr. 1704; S.P.G. missionary; Rye (Westchester) N.Y., Christ's Chh., 1704–1705; Bedford (Westchester) N.Y., St. Matthew's Chh., 1704–1705; Greenwich, Conn., Apr. 1704–1705; Ep.; d. Rye, N.Y., Mar./Apr. 1705.

JAMES PROUDFIT, A.M. (or Proudfoot), b. Perth, Scotland, 1732; Ord. Scotland, July 1754; arriv. Boston, Mass., Sept. 1754; A.M. (hon.) Columbia, 1790; sett. Brandywine Manor (Chester) Pa., Forks of the Brandywine, 1757–1783; Pequea (Lanc.) Pa., 1757–1783; Salem, Cambridge, Hebron and Argyle (all in Washington co.) N.Y., 1783–1799; Associate Presb.; d. Salem, N.Y., 22 Oct. 1802, a. 69.

Bishop SAMUEL PROVOOST, D.D., b. N.Y., N.Y., 26 Feb. 1742, son of John and Eve (Rutgers) Provoost; A.B., Columbia, 1758, A.M., Trustee, 1787–1801; chairman of the board, 1795–1801; St. Peter's Coll., Camb.; D.D., U. of Pa., 1786; Regent, U. of State of N.Y., 1784–1787; Ord. London, 25 Mar. 1766; sett. N.Y., N.Y., Trinity Chh., Dec. 1766–1768; Rector, 1784–8 Sept. 1800; St. George's Chapel, 1766–1800; St. Paul's Chapel, 1766–1768; Bishop of N.Y., 4 Feb. 1786–1815; Chaplain, U.S. Senate, 1789–3 Sept. 1801; Ep.; d. N.Y., N.Y., 6 Sept. 1815, a. 73.

JOB PRUDDEN, A.M. (See *Colonial Clergy of New England*, p. 170), Ord. Newark, N.J., 19 May 1747; Presb.

JOHN PRUDDEN, A.B., b. Milford, Conn., 9 Nov. 1645, son of the Rev. John and Joanna Prudden; A.B., H.C., 1668; sett. Jamaica, L.I., N.Y., 8 Mar. 1670–Jan. 1674, 19 June 1676–1691; Rye, N.Y., 1675–1676; Newark, N.J., 23 Aug. 1692–9 June 1699; taught school, 1706 ff.; not known to have been ordained; Presb.; d. Newark, N.J., 11 Dec. 1725, a. 80 (GS).

EBENEZER PUNDERSON, A.M., b. New Haven, Conn., 12 Sept. 1705, son of Thomas and Lydia (Bradley) Punderson; A.B., Y.C., 1726, A.M.; Ord. Ledyard, Conn. (2nd Cong. Chh. in Groton) 25 Dec. 1729–5 Feb. 1733/4; became an Ep.; Ord. London, England, 1734; sett.

Ledyard, Conn., Ep. Chh., 1734-1753; Norwich, Conn., Christ Chh., 1736; Hebron, Conn., 1746-1752; New Haven, Conn., Trinity Chh., 1753-1762; Rye (Westchester) N.Y., Christ's Chh., 1762-1764; Bedford (Westchester) N.Y., St. Matthew's Chh., 1762-1764; Ep.; d. Rye, N.Y., 22 Sept. 1764, a. 59.

JOHN CHRISTOPHER PYRLAEUS, b. Pausa, Voigtland, 1713; ed. U. of Leipsic, 1733-1738; arriv. Bethlehem, Pa., 19 Oct. 1740; Ord. Oley, Pa., 11 Feb. 1742; sett. Bethlehem, 1742-1742; Philadelphia, Pa., 1742-1743; commenced the study of the Mohawk language, Jan. 1743/4, under Conrad Weiser; taught the Indian School at Freehold, N.J., 4 Feb. 1744-Nov. 1751; was also itinerant preacher at Burlington, Cranbury, Lawrence, Middletown, Princeton, Swedish Settlements, and Trenton, all in N.J.; at Dover, Duck Creek and Lewes in Del.; and at Durham (Bucks), Lower Salford (Montgomery), Manatawny (Berks), Southampton (Bucks) and Upper Providence (Montgomery) at Trappe, all in Pa., 1743-1749; returned to England, where he remained, 1751-1770, and to Germany, 1771; student and teacher of the Indian languages, especially the Mohawk and Mohican dialects; Morav.; d. Herrnhut, Germany, 28 May 1785.

JOHN WILLIAM PYTHAN, b. Oberingelheim, Palatinate, Germany, 3 May 1740, son of Lieutenant John Pythan; matric. Heidelberg, 30 Jan. 1759; was a minister in the Palatinate; arriv. Philadelphia, 1 Sept. 1769; took oath of allegiance, Philadelphia, 1 Sept. 1769; sett. Dryland, Easton, Lehigh, St. Paul's Chh., Plainfield, St. Peter's Chh., all in Northampton co., Pa., 1769-1774; Greenwich (Warren) N.J., 1769-1774; and Greenwich (Berks) Pa., Dunkel Chh., 1769-1770, where he is said to have been deposed, 1770; sett. Lower Saucon (Northampton) Pa., 8 Aug. 1773-1779; Springfield (Bucks) Pa., 2 May 1773-1779, either in conjunction with or opposition to Caspar Wack, who was also sett. over these last two chhs.; went to North Carolina, 1780; Germ. Ref.; d. Brick Church, N.C., 1789.

Father RAFFEIX, S.J., sett. Fonda (Montgomery) N.Y., St. Mary's Mission to the Mohawks, 1667-1671; Auburn (Cayuga) N.Y., Mission of St. Joseph to the Cayugas, 1671-1671; Victor (Ontario) N.Y., Mission of the Conception to the Senecas, 1671-1675; R. C.

JOHN BERNARD RAHNER, sett. Philadelphia, Pa., 1742; Luth.

WILLIAM RAMSEY, A.M., b. Lancaster co., Pa., 1732, son of James Ramsey; A.B., Princeton, 1754, A.M., 1765; Ord. Fairfield (Cumberland) N.J., Cohansey Chh., 1 Dec. 1756-1771; Presb.; d. Fairfield, N.J., 5 Nov. 1771, a. 39 (GS).

THOMAS RANKIN, b. Dunbar, Scotland, ca. 1738; Methodist preacher appointed to the Sheffield circuit, 1762; Devonshire, 1763; Cornwall, 1764; Epworth, 1766-1767; West Cornwall, 1768; London and Sussex, 1769; Cornwall, 1771; arriv. Philadelphia, 1 June 1773; sett. Philadelphia Conference, 1773-1778; returned to England, arriv. London, June 1778; Meth.; d. London, England, 17 May 1810, a. 72.

PHILIP HENRY RAPP, merchant; Ord. by the Notoria Andrea; came to Pa., 1750; sett. Lower Macungie (Lehigh) Pa., Holy Trinity or Zion Chh., 1750–18 Dec. 1751; called to Christ Chh., N.Y., 29 Oct. 1751; sett. N.Y., N.Y., Christ Chh. or Old Swamp Chh., 1751–1753; Germantown, Pa., St. Michael's Chh., 1 Jan. 1754–1762; Bedminster (Bucks) Pa., Tohickon Chh., 22 Oct. 1765–1774; Milford (Bucks) Pa., St. John's or Schuetz's Chh., 1769–1774; Milford, Lower Milford Chh. at Trumbauersville, 1769–1774; Nockamixon (Bucks) Pa., 1774–1779; Luth.; d. Nockamixon, Pa., 10 Nov. 1779 (suicide); will made 12 July 1779; prob. 18 Nov. 1779.

JOB RATHBONE (or Rathbun), b. Stonington, Conn., 2 Jan. 1735/6, son of the Rev. Joshua and Mary (Wightman) Rathbone; sett. Canaan, Conn.; sett. Lowville (Lewis) N.Y., ca. 1765; Rev. soldier; Bapt.

CHRISTIAN HENRY RAUCH, b. Bernberg-Anhalt, Germany, 5 July 1718; arriv. N.Y., N.Y., 21 July 1740; Germ. Ref. ministry: Oley (Berks) Pa., 1740–1742; Elizabethtown (Lanc.) Pa., 1746–1749; Lancaster (Lanc.) Pa., 1746–1749; Warwick (Lanc.) Pa., Kissel Hill Chh., 1746–1749; West Cocalico (Lanc.) Pa., Swamp or Little Cocalico Chh., 1748–1749; Mount Joy (Lanc.) Pa., Miller's Chh., 1746–1749; Jackson (Lebanon) Pa., Millback Chh., 1746–1749; Lower Salford (Montgomery) Pa., Reiff's or Skippack Chh., 1746–1749; Moravian ministry: Ord. Oley (Berks) Pa., 11 Feb. 1742; Indian missionary in Conn., 1740–1745; Shekomeko (Dutchess) N.Y., 2nd Indian Chh., 1740–1744; Bethel (Lebanon) Pa., 1743–1744; York (York) Pa., 1746–1749; Codorus (York) Pa., 1746–1749; Conewago (York) Pa., Zion's or Quickel's Chh., 1746–1748; Hellam (York) Pa., 1746–1747; Swatara (Lebanon) Pa., 1746–1749; East Cocalico (Lanc.) Pa., Chh. at Reamstown, 1748–1749; Penn (Lanc.) Pa., White Oakes Chh., 1746–1749; Lancaster (Lanc.) Pa., 1753–1754; East Coventry (Chester) Pa., Brownback's Chh., 1746–1748; Warwick (Lanc.) Pa., St. James's Chh. at Lititz, 9 Sept. 1749-20 Dec. 1753; South Lebanon (Lebanon) Pa., Hebron Chh., 1750–1753; sett. Bethabara, North Carolina, 1755–1756; Jamaica, West Indies, 1756–1763; Germ. Ref.; Morav.; d. Jamaica, West Indies, 11 Nov. 1763.

Dr. LUCAS RAUS, Cronstadt, Transylvania, 18 Oct. 1724, son of the Rev. Lucas and Justina Raus; ed. Jena, 1749; Leipsic, 1747–1749; arriv. in America, 1750; Germantown, Pa., asst., 1750–1753; Ord. New Providence, Pa., 5 Nov. 1752; sett. Oley (Berks) Pa., Christ or Hill Chh., 1750–1758; Upper Salford (Montgomery) Pa., Old Goshenhoppen Chh., 1751–1753; Franconia (Montg.) Pa., Indian Creek or Zion's Chh., 1751–1752; Bedminster (Bucks) Pa., Keller's Chh., 1751–1755; Rockhill (Bucks) Pa., Indianfield Chh., 1751–1752; Douglass (Berks) Pa., Oley Hill Chh., 1752–1756; Pike (Berks) Pa., St. John's or Hill Chh., 1754–1754; York (York) Pa., Christ Chh., 1758–1763; Latimore (Adams) Pa., Christ or Lower Bermudian Chh., 1758–1762; Hellam (York) Kreutz Creek Chh., 1760–1763; Dover (York) Pa., Salem or Strayer's Chh., 1763–1776; Springfield (York) Pa., Frieden Saal or Shuster's Chh.,

1770–1787; Conewago (York) Pa., Zion's Chh., 1770–1787; physician; Luth.; d. York, Pa., 11 July 1788, a. 64.

JACOB RAUSS, came to America, 1753; sett. Rhinebeck (Dutchess) N.Y., 1753–1759; Luth.

ISRAEL READ, A.M., b. 1718; A.B., Princeton, 1748, A.M.; Trustee, 1761–1793; Ord. Bound Brook (Somerset) N.J., 7 Mar. 1750–1793; sett. Hillsborough (Monmouth) N.J., Millstone Chh., 1759–1769; New Brunswick (Middlesex) N.J., Apr. 1768–1786; Presb.; d. Bound Brook, N.J., 28 Nov. 1793, a. 75.

JAMES REAK, sett. Mann (Bedford) Pa., Piney Creek Chh., 1774 ff.; Presb.

ABNER REEVE, A.M., b. Southold, L.I., N.Y., 21 Feb. 1707/8, son of Thomas and Bethia (Horton) Reeve; A.B., Y.C., 1731, A.M., 1735; sett. Smithtown, L.I., N.Y., Nissequag (or Nissequoque) Chh., 1735–1748; Ord. Brookhaven, L.I., N.Y., 6 Nov. 1755; sett. Brookhaven, Westhampton, Little Quogue or Moriches Chh., 1754–1764; Brookhaven, South Haven or Fire Place Chh., 1754–1763; Blooming Grove (Orange) N.Y., 1764–1768; inst. Brattleborough, Vt., 5 July 1770; sett. Brattleborough, 1768–3 Oct. 1792; Presb.; Cong.; d. Brattleborough, Vt., 16 May 1798, a. 90.

EZRA REEVE, A.B., b. Southold, L.I., N.Y., 27 Jan. 1733/4, son of the Rev. Abner and Mary Reeve; A.B., Y.C., 1757; Ord. Brookhaven, L.I., N.Y., Mt. Sinai Chh., 10 Oct. 1759–25 Oct. 1763; Wales, Mass., 13 Sept. 1765–1818; Cong.; Presb.; d. Wales, Mass., 28 Apr. 1818, a. 85.

ABRAHAM REINCKE, b. Stockholm, Sweden, 17 Apr. 1712, son of Peter and Margaret (Peterson) Reincke; ed. U. of Jena, 1738; sett. St. Petersburg, Russia, 1740–1741; London and Yorkshire, Eng., 1741–1744; arriv. N.Y., N.Y., 25 Oct. 1744; arriv. Bethlehem, 9 Nov. 1744; Ord. priest, Feb. 1745; sett. Nazareth (Northampton) Pa., Forks of the Delaware, Nov. 1745–25 June 1747; Philadelphia, Pa., June 1747–Feb. 1749, 1751–1753; Warwick (Lanc.) Pa., St. James's Chh. at Lititz, 1749–1753; Lancaster (Lanc.) Pa., Feb. 1749–Nov. 1750; Amenia Union (Dutchess) N.Y., Oblong Chh., 1753–1755; Paulin's Kill (Warren) N.J., 1753–1755; Lynn (Lehigh) Pa., Allemaengel Chh., 1755–1755; New York, N.Y., 1754–1755; Walpack (Sussex) N.J., 1753–1755; Bethel (Sullivan) N.Y., Nine Partners at Round Top, 1753–1755; Livingston Manor (Sullivan) N.Y., 1753–1755; he also served as an itinerant preacher at the following chhs. (1744–1749 and in some cases to 1755): Bridgeton, Burlington, Cape May, Cranbury, Great Egg Harbor, Lawrence, Little Egg Harbor, Maurice River, Middletown, Pennsneck, Princeton, Swedesborough, and Trenton, all in N.J.; Dover, Duck Creek, and Lewes, in Del.; and Ammasland (Del. co.), Bethlehem at Dansbury, Calkoen's Hook, Durham, Lower Salford, Manatawny, Neshaminy, and Trappe, all in Pa.; Morav.; d. Bethlehem, Pa., 7 Apr. 1760.

PETER REINHART, b. 1733; sett. Coventry (Chester) Pa., 1770-1806; Germ. Bapt.; d. Coventry, Pa., 1806.

JOHANN CONRAD REISSMAN, became a Dunkard in Germany; joined Ephrata Community, 1738; Ord. Ephrata Chloister, 1768; sett. Ephrata (Lanc.) Pa., 1738-1786; Germ. Bapt.; d. Ephrata, Pa., 20 Mar. 1786.

MATTHEW REUTZ, b. Denmark; arriv. N.Y., N.Y., 26 Nov. 1743; sett. Bethlehem, Pa., 1743-1748; Ord. 1748; sett. Graceham, Md., 1751-1751; Oldmans Creek, N.J., 1751-1753; also an itinerant preacher in the following places: Philadelphia, 1743-1747; 1743-1749: Burlington, Cranbury, Middletown, Trenton, and Princeton, in N.J., Dover, Duck Creek, and Lewes in Del., and Durham, Lower Salford, Manatawny, Neshaminy, and Trappe, in Pa.; 1745-1753: Bridgeton, Cape May, Little Egg Harbor, Maurice River, and Pennsneck in N.J., Ammasland, Calkoen's Hook, Pa., and 1743-1753: Great Egg Harbor, N.J.; 1745-1749: Swedesborough, N.J.; Morav.; d. Oldmans Creek, N.J., 7 Oct. 1753.

JAMES REYNOLDS, K.B. for N.Y., 6 May 1709; Ep.

JOSEPH RHEA, b. Ireland, ca. 1715; sett. Cumberland (Adams) Pa., Upper Marsh Creek Chh., at Gettysburg, 1770-1771; Taneytown, Md., Piney Creek Chh., 1771-11 Apr. 1776; Presb.; d. Virginia, 20 Sept. 1777, a. ca. 62.

Domine RHOADS, sett. Smithfield (Monroe) Pa., 1750-1776; Presb.

WILLIAM RHODES, b. Chichester, England; sett. Exeter, R.I.; Oyster Bay, L.I., N.Y., 1700-1724; lay preacher; Bapt.; d. Oyster Bay, L.I., N.Y., 1724.

OWEN RICE, came from Haverfordwest, Wales, to Bethlehem, Pa., 1742; Ord. deacon, 1748, preached in English at Philadelphia and Bethlehem; sett. Southampton (Bucks) Pa., Neshaminy Chh., 1742-1744; Philadelphia, Pa., 1749-1751; N.Y., N.Y., 1751-1754; Staten Island, N.Y., 1751-1752; also itinerant preacher in English at the following places: 1743-1749, Burlington, Cranbury, Lawrence, Middletown, Princeton, and Trenton, N.J., Dover, Duck Creek, and Lewes, Del., and Durham, Lower Salford, Manatawny, and Trappe, Pa.: 1745-1754, Bridgeton, Cape May, Little Egg Harbor, Maurice River, Pennsneck and Swedesborough, N.J., and Ammasland, and Calkoen's Hook, Pa.; he returned to Europe and served congregations in England and Ireland, 1754-1785; physician, surgeon, Moravian; d. Gomersal, co. York, England, 1785.

AARON RICHARDS, A.M., b. Newark, N.J., 1718, son of John, Jr. and Jane (Crane) Richards; A.B., Y.C., 1743, A.M., 1747; Ord. Rahway (Union) N.J., 15 Nov. 1748; sett. Rahway, 1748-3 May 1791; Presb.; d. Rahway, N.J., 16 May 1793, a. 75.

JOHN RICHARDS, A.M., b. Waterbury, Conn., 23 June 1726, son of Lieut. Thomas and Susanna (Turner) (Reynolds) Richards; A.B.,

Y.C., 1745, A.M.; A.M., Dart. Coll., 1782; Ord. North Guilford, Conn., 2 Nov. 1748-24 Dec. 1765; Chatham, N.Y., Christ Chh., Cong., 1771-1773; Piermont, N.H., 5 Feb. 1776-1802; Cong.; d. Weybridge, Vt., 1814, a. 88.

JOHN CHRISTIAN RICHTER, arriv. N.Y., N.Y., 12 May 1749; sett. Graceham, Md., 1755-1757; Moravian.

ARCHIBALD RIDDELL, had been imprisoned in France and in Scotland, 1680-1684, for religious principles; came to N.J., Dec. 1685; sett. Woodbridge (Middlesex) N.J., 1686-1689; Presb.

Dr. JOHN BARTHOLOMEW RIEGER, b. Oberingelheim, Palatinate, Germany, 10 Jan. 1707, son of John Adam and Anna Magdalena Rieger; matric. Heidelberg, 24 Feb. 1723/4, in philosophy; matric. Basel, 20 Apr. 1724; matric. Leyden, Holland, 22 Mar. 1744, in medicine; arriv. Philadelphia, 21 Sept. 1731; sett. Philadelphia, Pa., 1731-1734; Germantown, Pa., 1731-1734; Worcester (Montgomery) Pa., Wentz's or Skippack Chh., 1731-1734; Mill Creek (Lebanon) Pa., Tulpehocken or Trinity Chh., 1731-1734; Amwell (Hunterdon) N.J., 27 Feb. 1734/5-1739; Raritan, N.J., 1734-1739; Somerville (Somerset) N.J., 2nd Dutch Ref. Chh., 1734-1739; Lancaster (Lanc.) Pa., Apr. 1736-23 Feb. 1743/4; Brecknock (Lanc.) Pa., Muddy Creek Chh., 1739-1743; Ephrata (Lanc.) Pa., Bethany Chh., 1739-1743; returned to Holland, 1743/4, to study medicine at Leyden; ret. to America, Mar. 1745; Heidelberg (Lebanon) Pa., Schaeffer's Chh., 1746-1769; Earl (Lanc.) Pa., Zeltenreich Chh., 1747-1749, 1760-1762; Oley (Berks) Pa., dates not given, but prob. 1760-1762; physician; Germ. Ref.; d. Lancaster, Pa., 11 Mar. 1769, a. 62.

JOHN FREDERICK RIES (or Reis), sett. N.Y, N.Y., Old Swamp Chh., 1750-1751; Stone Arabia (Montgomery) N.Y., 1751-1760; Little Falls (Herkimer) N.Y., 1751-1760; Canajoharie (Montgomery) N.Y., 1751-1760; Upper Hanover (Montgomery) Pa., New Goshenhoppen Chh., 1757-1760; East Camp, N.Y., Christ Chh., 1760-1775; Wurtemburg in Hyde Park (Dutchess) N.Y., 1760-1785; Rhinebeck (Dutchess) N.Y., 1760-1785; Claverack (Columbia) N.Y., 1760-1791; Livingston (Columbia) N.Y., St. John's Chh., 1764-1791; Luth.; d. Claverack, N.Y., 1791.

JOHN JACOB RIESS (or Reis, Riesz), b. Germany, 10 Apr. 1706; arriv. Philadelphia, 24 Sept. 1742; sett. Rockhill (Bucks) Pa., Indianfield Chh., 29 Aug. 1749-Mar. 1756; Bedminster (Bucks) Pa., Tohickon Chh., 1750-1756; Lower Saucon (Northampton) Pa., 1750-1756; Franconia (Montgomery) Pa., Indian Creek Chh., 3 June 1753-11 Aug. 1766; Springfield (Bucks) Pa., Trinity Chh., 24 Apr. 1760-1763; Upper Hanover (Montgomery) Pa., New Goshenhoppen Chh., 1765-1766; Upper Salford (Montgomery) Pa., Old Goshenhoppen Chh., 1765-1766; shoemaker; Germ. Ref.; d. Rockhill, Pa., 23 Dec. 1774, a. 68 y. 7 m. 23 d. (GS).

Bishop PETER RISSER, b. Europe, 1713; arriv. in Pa., 1737; sett. Mount Joy (Lanc.) Pa., Risser's Chh., 1737–1804; Swatara (Dauphin) Pa., Stauffer's Chh., 1775–1804; Menn.; d. Mt. Joy, Pa., Feb. 1804, a. 91.

NICHOLAS RITTENHOUSE (or Cleas Rittinghuysen), b. 15 June 1666, son of the Rev. William Rittenhouse; came to Germantown, 1688; Ord. Germantown, Pa., ca. 1710; sett. Germantown, Pa., 1710–1734; Menn.; d. Germantown, Pa., 1734, a. 68.

WILLIAM RITTENHOUSE (or Rittinghuysen), b. Broich, Westphalia, 1644; made a citizen at Amsterdam, Holland, 23 June 1678; arriv. Germantown, Pa., 1688; Ord. Germantown, Pa., 1690 (or 1698), as the first Mennonite minister ordained in America; sett. Germantown, Pa., 1688–1708; built the first paper mill in America, 1690; Menn.; d. Germantown, Pa., 18 Feb. 1708, a. 64.

JOHANNES RITZEMA, b. 1710; original Trustee of Columbia, 1754; Ord. Amsterdam, Holland, 20 July 1744; came to America, 1744; N.Y., N.Y., 1st or South Dutch Chh., 1744–1784 (absent during the Rev. War); Middle Dutch Chh., 1744–1784; North Dutch Chh., 1765–1784; Harlem, N.Y., 1744–1765; Tarrytown (Westchester) N.Y., Sleepy Hollow Chh., 1744–1776; Fordham, N.Y., French Ref. Chh., 1744–1770; Montrose, Cortlandttown (Westchester) N.Y., 1764–1776; Kinderhook (Columbia) N.Y., 1778–1788; Dutch Ref.; d. N.Y., N.Y., 10 Apr. 1796.

JOHN ROAN, b. Greenshaw, Ireland, 30 Apr. 1717; arriv. in America, 3 Sept. 1739; ed. Log Coll., Pa.; lic. 27 June 1744; Ord. 16 Aug. 1745; sett. Swatara (Dauphin) Pa., Paxtang Chh., 1745–1775; Derry (Dauphin) Pa., 1745–1775; Mount Joy (Adams) Pa., Conewago Chh., 1745–1775; New Side Presb.; d. Derry, Pa., 3 Oct. 1775, a. 50 (GS).

EDWARD ROBERTS, K.B. for N.J., 10 Dec. 1705; Ep.

JOHN RODGER, sett. Newville (Cumberland) Pa., Big Spring Chh., 1772–1781; Montgomery (Franklin) Pa., Conococheague or Slate Hill Chh. at Mercersburg, 1772–1781; Associate Presb.

JOHN RODGERS, D.D., b. Boston, Mass., 5 Aug. 1727, son of Thomas and Elizabeth (Baxter) Rodgers; grad. Academy at Fagg's Manor, 1743; A.M., Princeton, 1760; A.M., U. of Pa., 1763; D.D., Edinburgh, 1768; Trustee, Princeton, 1765–1807; Vice-Chancellor, U. of the State of N.Y., 1787–1811; lic. New Castle Presbytery, 14 Oct. 1747; Ord. St. George's (New Castle) Del., 16 Mar. 1748/9–18 May 1765; sett. Appoquinimink (New Castle) Del., 1748–1765; Middletown (N.C.) Del., Forest Chh., 1749–1765; Taylor's Bridge (N.C.) Del., 1750–1765; inst. N.Y., N.Y., 1st Presb. Chh., 4 Sept. 1765–1811; N.Y., N.Y., 2nd Presb. Chh., 1767–1810; Chaplain of a N.Y. Regt., 1776–1777; Chaplain, N.Y. Legislature, 1776–1777; Moderator, Presb. General Assembly, 1789; Presb.; d. N.Y., N.Y., 7 May 1811, a. 83.

AZEL ROE, D.D., b. Setauket, L.I., N.Y., 20 Feb. 1738; A.B., Princeton, 1756; Trustee, 1778-1807; D.D., Y.C., 1800; Ord. 1761; sett. Woodbridge (Middlesex) N.J., 1763-1815; Meteucken (Mx.) N.J., 1763-1793; prisoner in "Sugar House Prison", N.Y., Rev. War; Moderator, Presb. General Assembly, 1802; Presb.; d. Woodbridge, N.J., 2 Dec. 1815.

CONRAD SEBASTIAN ROELLER, b. Germany; ed. U. of Erlangen; arriv. in Pa., 1770; sett. Upper Hanover (Montgomery) Pa., New Goshenhoppen Chh., 1771-1775; Upper Salford (Montgomery) Pa., Old Goshenhoppen Chh., 16 Feb. 1772-1799; Franconia (Montgomery) Pa., Indian Creek or Zion's Chh., 20 Apr. 1772-1795; Rockhill (Bucks) Pa., Indianfield Chh., 1772-1795; Bedminster (Bucks) Pa., Tohickon Chh., Mar. 1774-1795; Luth.; d. Indianfield, Pa., June 1799.

GODFREY ROESLER, arriv. N.Y., N.Y., 22 June 1749; missionary; escaped from the Indians at Shamokin, 1755; sett. Warwick (Lanc.) Pa., St. James's Chh. at Lititz, 1760-1762, 1774-1776; Morav.

JACOB ROGERS, arriv. America, 17 May 1752; sett. Philadelphia, Pa., 1753-1754, 1756-1762; Staten Island, N.Y., 1756-1756; Bethabara, N.C., 22 July 1758-1762; English minister at Dobb's Parish; Morav.; returned to Europe, 1 July 1762.

WILLIAM ROGERS, D.D., b. Newport, R.I., 22 July 1751, son of William and Sarah Rogers; A.B., Brown, 1769, A.M.; A.M., U. of Pa., 1773, D.D., 1790; A.M., Y.C., 1780; A.M., Princeton, 1786; Principal of the Academy at Newport, R.I., 1769-1772; lic. to preach, 1771; sett. Newport, R.I., 2nd Bapt. Chh., Aug. 1771-1772; Ord. Philadelphia, Pa., 31 May 1773; sett. Philadelphia, 1st Bapt. Chh., 1772-Mar. 1775, and as stated supply, 1781-1789; Prof. of English and Oratory, U. of Pa., 1789-1812; member, Pa. Legislature, 1816-1817; V.P., Religious Hist. Soc. of Philadelphia, 1819; Chaplain and Brigade Chaplain, 3rd. Pa. Continental Brigade, Mar. 1776-16 Jan. 1781; original member, Society of the Cincinnati, 1783; Bapt.; d. Philadelphia, Pa., 7 Apr. 1824, a. 73.

ISAAC ROLLINS, sett. Eastern Shore of Maryland, 24 Dec. 1772; Chester Circuit (Preaching stations at Marlborough, Thomas Ellis's, Woodward's, Brandywine, West Chester, Samuel Hooper's, Gorham, Uwchlan, and Coventry, all in Pa.); Meth.

Domine ROMAIN, sett. Bound Brook (Somerset) N.J., Chh. at Bridgewater, (1725)-1742; Presb.; d. Bound Brook, N.J., 1742.

DIRCK ROMEYN, D.D., b. Hackensack, N.J., 12 Jan. 1744, son of Nicholas and Rachel (Vreelandt) Romeyn; A.B., Princeton, 1765; D.D., Rutgers, 1789, Trustee, Rutgers, 1785-1804; Lector in Theology, 1792-1797; Prof. of Theology, 1797-1804; sett. Marbletown (Ulster) N.Y., May 1766-1775; Rochester (Ulster) N.Y., 1766-1775; Warwarsing (Ulster) N.Y., 1766-1775; Red Hook Landing (Dutchess) N.Y., 1773-1775; Rhinebeck Flats (Dutchess) N.Y., 1773-1775; Hackensack (Bergen) N.J., Chh. at New Barbadoes, May 1775-1784; Schraalenburg (Bergen)

N.J., 1775-1784; Dutch Ref.; d. Schraalenburg, N.J., 16 Apr. 1804, a. 60 (GS).

THOMAS ROMEYN, A.M., b. Pompton, N.J., 29 Mar. 1729, son of Nicholas and Rachel (Vreelandt) Romeyn; A.M. (hon.) Princeton, 1765; Ord. Amsterdam, Holland, 3 Sept. 1752; sett. Success, L.I., N.Y., Success Pond Chh. at North Hempstead, 1753-1760; Newtown, L.I., 1753-1760; Oyster Bay, L.I., Wolver Hollow Chh., 1753-1760; Jamaica, L.I., 1753-1760; Port Jervis (Orange) N.Y., Chh. at Deerpark, 6 Sept. 1760-1772; Lehman (Pike) Pa., Lower Wallpack Chh. at Bushkill, 1760-1772; Delaware (Pike) Pa., Chh. at Dingman's Ferry, 1760-1772; Smithfield (Monroe) Pa., Shawnee Chh. at Lower Smithfield, 1760-1772; Flatbrookville (Sussex) N.J., Middle Wallpack Chh., 1760-1772; Layton (Sussex) N.J., Wallpack Chh., 1760-1772; Wallpack (Sussex) N.J., 1760-1772; The Minisinks (Sussex) N.J., Chh. at Montague, 1760-1772; Fonda (Montgomery) N.Y., 1772-1794; Caughnawaga (Montgomery) N.Y., 1772-1794; Dutch Ref.; d. Fonda, N.Y., 22 Oct. 1794.

JOHN REINHOLD RONNER, Ord. deacon, Bethlehem, Pa., 1743; sett. Dansbury, Pa., 1748-1749; Tulpehocken, Muddy Creek, The Minisinks, Paulin's Kill (Warren) N.J., 1748-1749; Warwick, Pa., 1743-1750; St. Thomas, West Indies, 1750-1755; Bethlehem, Pa., 1755-1756; he also preached as an itinerant in the following places, 1743-1749: Dover, Duck Creek, and Lewes, Del.; Burlington, Cranbury, Lawrence, Middletown, Princeton, Swedish Settlements, and Trenton, N.J.; and Durham, Lower Salford, Manatawny, Southampton, and Upper Providence, Pa., and Philadelphia, Pa., 1743-1747; Moravian; d. Bethlehem, Pa., July 1756.

JOHN ROSBURGH, A.B. (or Rosbrugh), b. Ireland, 1722, of Scotch parents; came to America, 1735; A.B., Princeton, 1761; lic. 1764; Ord. Greenwich (Warren) N.J., 11 Dec. 1764-18 Apr. 1769; Oxford (Warren) N.J., 1764-1769; Washington Borough (Warren) N.J., Mansfield-Woodhouse Chh., 1764-1769; Knowlton (Warren) N.J., 1775-1777; Hardwick (Warren) N.J., 1764-1769; inst. Allen (Northampton) Pa., Forks West Chh., 28 Oct. 1772; sett. Allen, Pa., 1769-1777; Upper Mount Bethel (Northampton) Pa., Forks North Chh., 1769-1777; Mount Bethel (Lehigh) Pa., Hunter's Chh., 1768-1774, as stated supply; private, Continental Army, 1776; Chaplain, Rev. War., 1776-1777; Presb.; killed by the British, at Assunpink, Trenton, N.J., 2 Jan. 1777.

DAVID ROSE, A.M., b. Branford, Conn., 11 Dec. 1736, son of David and Hannah (Barker) Rose; A.B., Y.C., 1760, A.M.; lic. 28 May 1765; Ord. Brookhaven, L.I., N.Y., 4 Dec. 1765; sett. Brookhaven, Chh. at Moriches, on the South Side of L.I., 1765-1799; Brookhaven, Fireplace Chh., 1765-1799; Brookhaven, Middle Island Chh., 1766-1799; physician; Presb.; d. South Haven, L.I., N.Y., 1 Jan. 1799, a. 62.

SVEN ROSEEN, b. Torpa, West Gothland, Sweden, 1708; ed. at Upsala and Jena; theol. stud. at Upsala, and at Lindhein, 1744, a. 36;

arriv. Bethlehem, Pa., 12 Jan. 1748/9; Ord. deacon, 1748; sett. Graceham, Md., 1749-1750; Bethlehem, Pa., Brodhead Settlement at Dansbury, 1749-1750; Lynn (Lehigh) Pa., Allemaengel Chh., 1748-1750; Paulin's Kill (Warren) N.J., 1749-1750; Wallpack (Sussex) N.J., 1749-1750; and as an itinerant preacher, 1745-1750; Ammasland on Darby Creek, Pa., and Calkoen's Hook, near Chester, Pa.; and the ff. chhs. in N.J.: Bridgeton, Cape May, Great and Little Egg Harbor, Maurice River, Pennsneck, Swedesborough and Swedish Settlements; Morav.; d. Macungie, Pa., 15 Dec. 1750.

ABRAHAM ROSENCRANTZ, grad. of a German U.; came to America, 1750; sett. Canajoharie (Montgomery) N.Y., Sand Hill Chh. at Minden (D.R.), 1750-1758, 1765-1796; N.Y., N.Y., 1st Germ. Ref. Chh., 1758-1759; Schoharie (Schoharie) N.Y., D.R. Chh. at Huntersfield, 1760-1763; Stone Arabia (Montgomery) N.Y., G.R. Chh. at Palatine, 1759-1769; German Flats (Herkimer) N.Y., Luth Chh., 1763-1796; Herkimer (Herkimer) N.Y., G.R. Chh., 1765-1796; Germ. Ref., but also served in Dutch Ref. and Luth. chhs.; d. Little Falls, N.Y., 1796.

Domine ROSENCRANTZ (brother of Abraham), sett. Fort Herkimer (Herkimer) N.Y., Chh. at German Flats, 1758-1767; Dutch Ref.

AENEAS ROSS, son of the Rev. George Ross (q.v.); Ord. London, 1739; K.B. for Pa., 26 Feb. 1740/1; sett. Bristol (Bucks) Pa., Chh. of St. James the Greater, 1740-1741; Philadelphia, Pa., Christ Chh., June 1741-June 1743; Oxford (Chester) Pa., Trinity Chh., 1743-1758; Whitemarsh (Montgomery) Pa., St. Thomas's Chh., 1742-1758; New Castle (New Castle) Del., Immanuel Chh., 1758-1782; Ep.; d. New Castle, Del., ca. 1782.

GEORGE ROSS, A.M., b. Balblair, Scotland, 1679, son of David Ross; A.B., Edinburgh, 1700, A.M.; Ord. London, 1700; K.B. for N.J., 2 May 1705; arriv. Philadelphia, 23 Aug. 1705; sett. New Castle (New Castle) Del., Immanuel Chh., 1705-1708, 1713-1753; Chester (Del.) Pa., St. Paul's Chh., 1708-1714; Concord (Del.) Pa., St. John's Chh., 1708-1712; Chichester, Pa., 1708-1712; North Elk Parish (Cecil) Md., 1731-1733; Marlborough (Chester) Pa., 1715-1753, as stated supply; White Clay Creek, Del., St. James's Chh., 1714-1753; Marcus Hook (Del.) Pa., St. Martin's Chh., 1713-1724; prisoner in France, 1711; S.P.G. missionary; Ep.; d. New Castle, Del., 1753, a. 72.

JOHANNES ROTH, b. Prussia, 1726; ed. a R.C.; became a Moravian, 1748; came to America, 1756; sett. Bradford co., Pa., as an Indian missionary, 1759-1772; Ohio, 1772-1774; returned to Pa., 1774; York, Pa., twice, dates not given; Mount Joy (Lanc.) Pa., Donegal Chh., 1774-1774; Salisbury (Lehigh) Pa.; Chh. at Emaus, 1790-1791; his wife Maria was his helper in his work; Morav.; d. York, Pa., 22 July 1791.

JOHN ROTH, sett. Heidelberg (Lehigh) Pa., 1770-1770; sett. Lehigh co., Pa., 1770-1787; sett. Lynn (Lehigh) Pa., Ebenezer or Organ Chh.

and Jacob's Chh., ca. 1780-1787; Germ. Ref.; d. Lynn, Pa., as minister of Ebenezer Chh., ca. 1787.

JOHN JOSEPH ROTH, Roman Catholic theol. stud. from Siegen, Westphalia, Germany; arriv. Philadelphia, 22 Sept. 1752; Ord. deacon, 17 Aug. 1755; lic. 17 Oct. 1763; sett. Bedminster (Bucks) Pa., Tohickon Chh., Aug. 1755-15 Apr. 1758; Upper Salford (Montgomery) Pa., Old Goshenhoppen Chh., 1759-1764; Upper Milford (Lehigh) Pa., Zionsville Chh., 1761-1764; inst. Upper Saucon (Lehigh) Pa., St. Paul's, Blue or Organ Chh., 17 Oct. 1763-1764; Allentown (Lehigh) Pa., St. Paul's Chh., 17 Oct. 1763-1764; Franconia (Montgomery) Pa., Indian Creek or Zion's Chh., 1763-1764; Rockhill (Bucks) Pa., Indianfield Chh., 1763-1764; Luth.; d. Upper Saucon, Pa., 13 May 1764.

FREDERICK ROTHENBUEHLER (or Rothenbergler), b. Bern, Switzerland, 29 July 1726; ed. U. of Bern; Ord. Bern, Switzerland, 28 Feb. 1752; sett. The Hague and Amsterdam, Holland, 1759-1760; London, England, Germ. Ref. Chh., 1760-1761; came to America, 1761; sett. N.Y, N.Y., 1761-1762; Philadelphia, Pa., 1st Germ. Ref. Chh., 30 July 1762-1766; Germ. Ref.; d. Philadelphia, Pa., 7 Aug. 1766, a. 40.

LOUIS ROU, b. Holland, 1683; Ord. Terholen, Holland, 31 Aug. 1701; arriv. in America, 1710; sett. N.Y., N.Y., French Ref. Chh. of the St. Esprit, 1710-1750; New Rochelle (Westchester) N.Y., 1710-1750; Fr. Ref.; d. N.Y., N.Y., 25 Dec. 1750.

GIDEON ROUSER, sett. Amwell (Hunterdon) N.J., 1738 ff.; Germ. Bapt.

JOHN ROWLAND, b. Wales, came to America when young; ed. Log Coll.; lic. 7 Sept. 1738; Ord. as an evangelist, Reaville, N.J., 11 Oct. 1739; sett. Amwell (Hunterdon) N.J., chh. at Reaville, 1738-1742; Lawrence (Mercer) N.J., Maidenhead Chh., 1738-1742; Hopewell (Mercer) N.J., chh. at Pennington, 1738-1742; Tredyffryn (Chester) Pa., Great Valley Chh., 1741-1742; Norriton (Montgomery) Pa., 1741-1745; Charlestown (Chester) Pa., 1742-1747; Lower Providence (Montgomery) Pa., 1742-1747; New Side Presb.; d. New Providence, Pa., 1747.

JOHANNES CASPERUS RUBEL, b. Wald, Duchy of Berg, 6 Mar. 1719; matric. Marburg, 20 May 1737; came to America, 1752; sett. Philadelphia, Pa., Germ. Ref. Chh., 1751/2-1755; Red Hook (Dutchess) N.Y., 1755-1759; Rhinebeck (Dutchess) N.Y., 1755-1759; Kingsbury (Dutchess) N.Y., 1755-1759; Germantown (Columbia) N.Y., 1755-1759; sett. Brooklyn, Bushwick, Flatbush, Flatlands, and New Utrecht, all on L.I., N.Y., 1759-1783; Cortlandt Manor (Westchester) N.Y., 1768; Clarkstown, N.Y., 1770; a violent Tory; deposed 1784; Germ. Ref. and Dutch Ref.; d. 19 Mar. 1797.

ANDREW RUDMAN, Ph.M., b. Gevalia, Gestrickland, Sweden, 1668; ed. Upsala; Ord. Upsala; arriv. in Philadelphia from Gestricia (Norrland) Sweden, 30 June 1697; sett. Philadelphia, Pa., Gloria Dei

Chh., 1697-1702; Philadelphia, Christ Chh., as supply, 1707-1708; N.Y., N.Y., Holy Trinity, Luth. Chh., July 1702-Nov. 1703; Albany, N.Y., Luth. Chh., 1702-1703; Oxford (Chester) Pa., Trinity Chh., 1705-1708; Frankford, Pa., 1705-1708; Lower Providence (Montgomery) Pa., St. James's Chh. at Evansburg, 1707-1708; S.P.G. missionary; Sw. Luth.; d. Philadelphia, Pa., 17 Sept. 1708, a. 40 (GS).

CARL RUDOLPH, Prince of Wurtemberg; sett. Hanover (York) Pa., St. Michael's Chh., 1746-1747; also in N.J. and N.C.; Luth.; a disreputable man.

DANIEL RUFF, sett. Chester (Del.) Pa., Madison St. Chh., 1774-1774; Chester Circuit: for preaching stations, see under Isaac Rollins; Trenton (Mercer) N.J., Green Street Chh., 1775-1775; Meth.

CHARLES GODFREY RUNDT, arriv. Bethlehem, Pa., 10 Dec. 1751; sett. Lancaster (Lanc.) Pa., 1757-1759; Morav.

REUNÉ RUNYON, b. Piscataway, N.J., 29 Mar. 1741, son of Reuné Runyon, Esq.; called to the ministry, 10 Mar. 1771; Ord. Morristown (Morris) N.J., 18 Mar. 1772-13 Apr. 1780; Schooley's Mountain (Morris) N.J., 1772-1780; Piscataway (Middlesex) N.J., 1783-1811; Bapt.; d. Piscataway, N.J., 21 Nov. 1811.

ABRAHAM L. RUSMEYER, sett. Philadelphia, Pa., 1753-1754; Warwick (Lanc.) Pa., St. James's Chh. at Lititz, 1760-1760; Morav.

ALBRECHT LUDOLPH RUSMAYERE, had a collegiate ed.; perhaps (as Louis) it was he who sett. Newport, R.I., 1766-1783; Morav.

CHRISTIAN RUSMEYER, sett. Lancaster (Lanc.) Pa., 1756-1757, 1762-1766; Morav.

Bishop DAVID RUTH, sett. Hatfield (Montgomery) Pa., Chh. at Lansdale, 1774-1796; New Britain (Bucks) Pa., Line Lexington Chh., 1774-1796; Bishop, 1796; Menn.

THOMAS RUTTER, Ord. Philadelphia, Pa., Keithian Bapt. Chh., 12 June 1698-1707; Lower Dublin, Pa., 7th Day Bapt. Chh., 1707-1716; resided in Philadelphia, 1707-1716; resided at Pottstown, Pa., 1716-1729, where he built a forge and began the manufacture of iron, the first that was made in Pa.; Keithian Bapt.; 7th Day Bapt.; d. near Pottstown, Pa., 1729.

ISAAC RYSDYCK, b. Holland, 1720; matric. Groningen, 14 Sept. 1751; most learned theologian in the Dutch Chh. in his day; came to America, 1765; sett. Hopewell (Dutchess) N.Y., Sept. 1765-1789; New Hackensack (Dutchess) N.Y., 1765-1789; Poughkeepsie (Dutchess) N.Y., 1765-1772; Clove (Dutchess) N.Y., 1769-1789; Marbletown (Ulster) N.Y., 1765-1772; Fishkill (Dutchess) N.Y., 1772-1789; Dutch Ref.; d. New Hackensack, N.Y., 2 Nov. 1790.

RICHARD SACKETT, A.M., b. Newtown, L.I., N.Y., son of Captain Joseph and Elizabeth (Betts) Sackett; A.B., Y.C., 1709, A.M.; sett. Hopewell (Mercer) N.J., Pennington Chh., 1711-1712; Lawrence

(Mercer) N.J., Maidenhead Chh., 1711-1712; Greenwich, Conn., 1st Parish, 1714-1716; Ord. West Greenwich, Conn., 27 Nov. 1717; sett. West Greenwich, Conn., 1716-1727; Cong.; d. Greenwich, Conn., 8 May 1727.

SAMUEL SACKETT, b. Newtown, L.I., N.Y., Ord. New Brunswick Presbytery, 13 Oct. 1741; sett. Phillipstown (Putnam) N.Y., Highlands Chh., May 1742-1743; White Plains (Westchester) N.Y., May 1742-1743; Yorktown (Westchester) N.Y., Cronpond Chh., May 1742-1743, 19 May 1747-Dec. 1749, 1761-1784; Peekskill (Westchester) N.Y., Cortlandt Manor, May 1742-1743, 1747-1749; inst. Bedford (Westchester) N.Y., 12 Oct. 1743-4 Apr. 1753; Salem (in North Salem, Westchester) N.Y., 1747-1749; Hanover (Westchester) N.Y., Cortlandt Manor, 4 Apr. 1753-1 Apr. 1760; Carmel (Putnam) N.Y., Red Mills Chh., 1761-1784; Presb.; d. Yorktown, N.Y., 5 June 1784 (GS).

Provost ANDREW SANDEL, ed. Upsala; Ord. Sweden, 18 July 1701; sett. Philadelphia, Pa., Gloria Dei Chh., inst. 29 Mar. 1702-1719; Molatton (Berks) Pa., St. Gabriel's Chh., Manathanim, Douglassville, 1702-1719; Provost; Sw. Luth.; returned to Hedmore, Sweden, 25 June 1719.

Provost JOHN SANDIN, sett. Pennsneck, N.J., 1748-1748; Swedesborough, N.J., 1748-1748; Provost; Sw. Luth.; d. Swedesborough, N.J., Aug. 1748.

RICHARD SANKEY, b. Ireland, son of Jacob and Abigail Sankey; lic. 13 Oct. 1736; Ord. East Hanover (Dauphin) Pa., Hanover Chh. on Manada Creek, 31 Aug. 1738; sett. East Hanover, Pa., 1737-1760; Carlisle (Cumberland) Pa., Old Stone Chh., 1738-1755; Buffalo Creek (Prince Edward) Va., 1760-1790; Walker's Chh. (Prince Edward) Va., 1760-1790; Presb.; d. Prince Edward co., Va., 1790.

CHRISTOPHER SAUER, Jr., b. Laasphe, Wittgenstein, Germany, 26 Sept. 1721, son of Christopher and Maria Christina Sauer; came to America, 1724; Ord. deacon, May 1747; Ord. elder, 7 June 1748; Ord. Germantown, Pa., 10 June 1753-1784; Germ. Bapt.; d. Germantown, Pa., 26 Aug. 1784.

RICHARD SAUNDERLANDS, sett. Concord (Del.) Pa., St. John's Chh., ca. 1700-1700; Ep.; bur. St. John's Churchyard, Concord, Pa.

JAMES SAYRE, K.B. for N.Y., 12 Oct. 1774; Ep.

JOHN SAYRE, A.B., b. N.Y., N.Y., 4 June 1738, son of John and Esther (Stillwell) Sayre; ed. Columbia; K.B. for America, 11 Oct. 1768; sett. Newburgh (Orange) N.Y., St. George's Chh., 1767-1773; Walden (Orange) N.Y., St. Andrew's Chh., 1767-1773; Hamptonburgh (Orange) N.Y., St. David's Chh., 1767-1773; Fairfield, Conn., Ep. Chh., 1774-1779; Tory refugee to N.Y., 1779, and to New Brunswick, 1783; Ep.; d. Maugerville, N.B., 5 Aug. 1784.

JOHN MARTIN SCHAEFER (or Schaeffer), b. Germany; prob. Ord. by Andreae; arriv. in America, 1750; sett. Bedminster (Bucks) Pa.,

Tohickon Chh., June 1750–Dec. 1753; Upper Milford (Lehigh) Pa., Zionsville Chh., 1757–1758; N.Y., N.Y., (Old Swamp Chh., Luth.), 1758–1761; Waldoborough, Maine, 1761–1794; physician; Luth.; d. Waldoborough, Me., 1794.

PETER SCHAEFFER, A.M., b. Finland; A.M., U. of Abo; sett. Sweden; Halle; came to Pa., 1699; missionary to the Indians in the Conestoga; mystic; schoolmaster at Wicacoa, Pa., 1700; Pennsneck, N.J.; returned to Europe; Pietist; d. Gefle, Finland.

GIDEON SCHAETS, b. Leerdam, Holland, 1607; schoolmaster at Beest and candidate in theology; Ord. by the Classis at Amsterdam, Holland, 1652; called as minister to Rensselaerwyck, 6 May 1652; came to New Netherlands in the ship "Flower of Guelder," 1652; missionary to the Indians; teacher of the catechism and schoolmaster, 1652–1657; sett. Albany, N.Y. (then called Fort Orange) and Beverwyck, N.Y., 1652–1694; Schenectady, N.Y., 1662–1680; received the Rev. Nicholas Van Rensselaer as colleague, 1675; Dutch Ref.; d. Albany, N.Y., 27 Feb. 1694.

BEN SCHANTZ, Menn.

JOHN HELFRICH SCHAUM, b. Giessen, Hesse-Darmstadt, Germany, son of John Philip H. Schaum; ed. Halle; arriv. Philadelphia, 26 Jan. 1744/5; arriv. York, Pa., 17 May 1748; Ord. Lancaster, Pa., 4 June 1749; sett. Cohansey and Somerset, N.J., 1746–1747; Raritan (Somerset) N.J., 1747–1748; York (York) Pa., Christ Chh., 17 May 1748–Apr. 1755; Latimore (Adams) Pa., Christ Chh. or Lower Bermudian Chh., 1748–1755; Hanover (York) Pa., St. Michael's Chh., 1748–1752; Frederick, Md., 1752–1755; Bedminster (Bucks) Pa., Keller's Chh., Apr. 1755–1759; Upper Dublin, Pa., Puff's Chh., 1758–1762; New Hanover (Montgomery) Pa., Falkner's Swamp Chh., 1759–1762; Douglass (Berks) Pa., Oley Hill Chh., 1759–1762; Oley (Berks) Pa., Christ or Hill Chh., 1759–1778; Pike (Berks) Pa., St. John's or Hill Chh., 1759–1778; Upper Providence (Montgomery) Pa., Augustus Chh. at Trappe, 1759–1778; Amity (Berks) Pa., St. Paul's Chh., 1761–1767; Richmond (Berks) Pa., Zion or Moselem Chh., 1761–1778; North Whitehall (Lehigh) Pa., Schlosser's Chh., 1762–1769; Rockland (Berks) Pa., Bieber Creek Chh., 1759–1778; Luth.; d. Rockland, Pa., 26 Jan. 1778.

JOHN JOSEPH SCHEBOSH (Running Water), b. Skippack (Montgomery) Pa., 27 May 1721; Indian missionary with David Zeisberger, 1742–1788; sett. Nain (Lehigh) Pa., Moravian Indian Chh., 1760–1765; his real name was John Joseph Bull (Running Water); Morav.; d. New Salem, Ohio, 4 Sept. 1788.

HERMAN JACOB SHELLHARD, sett. Weisenberg (Lehigh) Pa., Weisenberg Chh., 1770–1780; Luth.

WILLIAM SCHENCK, A.B., b. near Marlborough (Monmouth) N.J., 13 Oct. 1740; A.B., Princeton, 1767; sett. Allentown (Monmouth) N.J., Presb. Chh., 1771–1777; Cranbury (Middlesex) N.J., Presb. Chh.,

1771-1777; Northampton (Bucks) Pa., Dutch Ref. Chh., 3 Mar. 1777-1780; Southampton (Bucks) Pa., Dutch Ref. Chh., 3 Mar. 1777-1780; Pilesgrove, N.J., Presb. Chh., 3 May 1780-1786; Ballston, N.Y., Presb. Chh., 1786-1793; Huntington, L.I., N.Y., Presb. Chh., 1793-1817; Franklin co., Ohio, 1817-1827; Chaplain, Rev. War; Dutch Ref.; Presb.; d. Franklin co., Ohio, 1 Sept. 1827.

JACOB FREDERICK SCHERTLEIN, A.M., b. Hornberg, Baden, Germany; A.M., Tuebingen, 1717; sett. Zell and Altbach, near Esslingen, Wurtemberg, 1733-1748; arriv. Philadelphia, 27 Sept. 1752; sett. South Whitehall (Lehigh) Pa., Jordan Chh., 1752-1767; Lower Macungie (Lehigh) Pa., Holy Trinity or Zion Chh., 1753-1765; Bedminster (Bucks) Pa., Tohickon Chh., 1754-1755; Heidelberg (Lehigh) Pa., Heidelberg Chh., 1754-1755; Weisenberg (Lehigh) Pa., Ziegel Chh., 1754-1763; Upper Milford (Lehigh) Pa., Zionsville Chh., 1758-1760; Salisbury (Lehigh) Pa., 1764-1765; Luth.; d. (South Whitehall) Pa., Nov. 1768.

MICHAEL SCHLATTER, b. St. Gall, Switzerland, 14 July 1716, son of Paulus and Magdalena (Zollikofer) Schlatter; ed. St. Gall; matric. Leyden, 27 Dec. 1736, and Helmstedt, Brunswick, Germany; Ord. St. Gall, Switzerland, 10 Apr. 1739; Rector, Wigoldingen, Switzerland, 1744-1745; Linzebuehl near St. Gall, 19 Aug. 1745-Jan. 1746; agent to the German chhs. in Pa., 1746; arriv. Boston, Mass., 1 Aug. 1746; arriv. Philadelphia, 6 Sept. 1746; sett. Lancaster, Pa., 1746-1746; Northampton (Bucks) Pa., Dutch Ref. Chh., 1746-1750 and Neshaminy Germ. Ref. Chh., 1748-1750; Southampton (Bucks) Pa., Dutch Ref. Chh. at Churchville, 1746-1752 and North and Southampton Germ. Ref. Chh., 1748-1750; Upper Providence (Montgomery) Pa., St. Luke's Chh. at Trappe, 1746-1746; Penn (Lanc.) Pa., Chh. at Unionville, 1747-1747; Frederick, Md., 1747-1748; Union (Adams) Pa., 1747-1747; Lebanon (Hunterdon) N.J., Rockaway Chh. at Clinton, 1747-1750; Philadelphia, Pa., 1747-1751, 1752-1757; Germantown, Pa., 1747-1751; Whitpain (Montgomery) Pa., Boehm's Chh., 1749-1756; Reading (Berks) Pa., 1754-1754; Whitemarsh (Montgomery) Pa., St. Peter's Chh., Barren Hill, 1759-1777; went to Holland, 5 Feb. 1751-12 May 1752; to Europe, 28 Nov. 1753-28 Sept. 1754; Supt. of Charity Schools in the colonies, 1754-1757; Chaplain, appointed 25 Mar. 1757, at Louisburg and Fort Duquesne, 1757-1759; Chaplain, 2nd Pa. Battalion, 1764; Germ. Ref.; d. Philadelphia, Pa., 31 Oct. 1790.

JOHN FREDERICK SCHLEGEL, arriv. N.Y., N.Y., 12 May 1749; sett. Bethel (Lebanon) Pa., 1756-1763; York (York) Pa., 1757-1758; Bethlehem (Northampton) Pa., Sept. 1784-Apr. 1785; Morav.

Domine SCHMELZER, sett. Swatara (Lebanon) Pa., Zion's Chh. at Jonestown, time not given, perhaps some time between 1734 and 1764; Luth.

JOHN JACOB SCHMICK, b. 1714; ed. at Jena; Ord. in Europe; arriv. N.Y., N.Y., 24 Sept. 1751; sett. Shamokin Indian Chh., at Sunbury (Northumberland) Pa., 1755-1756; Indian missionary at New Gnadenhuetten, Ohio, 1756-1756; Nain (Lehigh) Pa., Indian Chh., 1760-1765; Hope (Warren) N.J., 1771-1772; Morav.; d. 1778.

FREDERICK SCHMIDT, sett. Newport, R.I., 1763-1763; Oldmans Creek (Gloucester) N.J., chhs. at Pilesgrove and Woolwich, 1769-1783; Morav.

JOHN SCHMIDT, sett. Mount Joy (Lanc.) Pa., Donegal Chh., 1752-1753; Morav.

JOHN FREDERICK SCHMIDT, D.D., b. Frohse, Aschersleben, Halberstadt, Germany, 9 Jan. 1746; matric. Halle, 1765; D.D., U. of Pa.; Ord. Wernigerode, Germany, 1768; arriv. Philadelphia, 2 Apr. 1769; sett. Germantown, Pa., St. Michael's Chh., 1769-1786; Upper Dublin, Pa., Puff's Chh., 1769-1785; Whitemarsh (Montgomery) Pa., St. Peter's Chh., Barren Hill, June 1769-1785; Frankford, Pa., 1769-1786; Whitpain (Montgomery) Pa., St. John's Chh. at Center Square, 1769-1786; Lower Gwynedd (Montgomery) Pa., St. Peter's Chh. at North Wales, 1775-1785; Philadelphia, Pa., St. Michael's and Zion's Chhs., 1785-1812; Luth.; d. Philadelphia, Pa., 16 May 1812, a. 66.

JOHN GEORGE SCHMIDT, sett. New Hanover (Montgomery) Pa., Falkner's Swamp Chh., 1736-1742; South Whitehall (Lehigh) Pa., Jordan Chh., 1736-1739; Tulpehocken (Berks) Pa., Little Tulpehocken Chh., 1739-1740; Oley Hills (Berks) Pa., Hill Chh. at Colebrookdale, 1736-1741; Pike (Berks) Pa., St. John's Chh., 1739-1740; the New Hanover and Hill Chh. at Oley Hills had the same minister for the first 125 years; Luth.

MELCHIOR SCHMIDT, arriv. N.Y., N.Y., 12 May 1749; sett. Lynn (Lehigh) Pa., Allemaengel Chh., 1755-1756; Morav.

GEORGE SCHNEIDER, came from Zauchtenthal, Moravia; sett. Lynn (Lehigh) Pa., Allemaengel Chh., 1742-1742; Salisbury (Lehigh) Pa., Chh. at Emaus, 1755-1756; carpenter; his wife Gertrude was also ordained; Morav.; d. Bethlehem, Pa., Oct. 1773.

JOHN SCHNEIDER, arriv. N.Y., N.Y., 12 May 1749; sett. Oley (Berks) Pa., 1753-1755; this chh. was broken up by the Indian Wars; Morav.

THEODORE SCHNEIDER, S.J., b. Geinsheim, Speyer, Germany, 7 Apr. 1703; Prof. of Philosophy and Theology in Liege, Belgium; arriv. in Pa., 1741; sett. Tulpehocken (Berks) Pa., 1741-1764; Allentown (Lehigh) Pa., 1741-1764; Maxatawny (Berks) Pa., 1741-1764; Lancaster (Lanc.) Pa., St. John Nepomucene's Chh., 1741-1764; Philadelphia, Pa., St. Joseph's Chh., 1741-1764; Washington (Berks) Pa., St. Paul's Chapel at Bally, 1742-1743, and Chh. of the Blessed Sacrament, 1734-1764; Haycock (Bucks) Pa., St. John's Chh., 1743-1764; Alloway (Salem) N.J., at Glass House, 1743-1758; Bound Brook (Somerset) N.J., 1743-1758; Frankford, Pa., 1744-1764; Concord (Chester) Pa., Chh. at Ivy Mills, 1757-1764; physician; R.C.; d. Washington, Pa., 10 July 1764, a. 62.

LEONARD SCHNELL, sett. Bethlehem, Pa., 25 June 1742-1748; was at Germantown, Va., 22 Nov. 1743; and took a missionary tour afoot in Georgia, 1743; sett. Lancaster, Pa., 1748-1748; Warwick (Lanc.) Pa., St. James's Chh. at Lititz, 1747-1748; Salisbury (Lehigh) Pa., Chh. at Emaus, 1742-1747; Lynn (Lehigh) Pa., Allemaengel Chh., 1742-1743; Ord. Priest, 1748; left the Moravian Chh., 1751; became a Lutheran; sett. "Maguntsche," i.e. Macungie, prob. sett. Lower Macungie (Lehigh) Pa., Luth. Holy Trinity or Zion Chh., perhaps, 1748-1749; he also preached at Muddy Creek, Heidelberg, Saucon, Tulpehocken, Lebanon, Donegal, and beyond the Susquehannah; Morav.; Luth.

CASPER LUDWIG SCHNORR (or Schnoor), prob. b. Ludinghusan's monastery, near Munster, Westphalia; matric. Marburg, 12 July 1735; minister at Zweibruecken, Germany; appeared in Pa., 10 Mar. 1744; sett. Lancaster (Lanc.) Pa., Germ. Ref. Chh., Nov. 1744-Mar. 1746; Tulpehocken, 1744-1746; Germantown (Columbia) N.Y., Dutch Ref. Chh., 1746-1748; Catskill (Greene) N.Y., Dutch Ref. Chh., 1747-1748; Rhinebeck (Dutchess) N.Y., Germ. Ref., 1746-1748; Kingsbury (Dutchess) N.Y., Dutch Ref., 1746-1748; Dutch Ref. and Germ. Ref.; "an ecclesiastical vagabond!"; last mentioned, 16 June 1750.

HENRICUS SCHOONMAKER, b. Rochester (Ulster) N.Y., 18 July 1739; Ord. in America, 1763; sett. Poughkeepsie (Dutchess) N.Y., 1763-1774; Fishkill (Dutchess) N.Y., 1763-1774; Passaic (Passaic) N.J., Dutch Ref. Chh. at Acquackanonk, 1774-1816; Bellville, N.J., 1789-1794; Paterson, N.J., 1799-1816; Dutch Ref.; d. Jamaica, L.I., N.Y., 19 Jan. 1820, a. 80.

MARTINUS SCHOONMAKER, b. Rochester (Ulster) N.Y., 1737; read the classics under Goetschius, 1753-1756; studied theology under Marinus; Ord. in America, 1765; sett. the following chhs., all except Harlem, on L.I., N.Y.: Gravesend, 1765-1824; Harlem, 1765-1784; Flatbush, 1784-1824; Brooklyn, 1784-1824; New Utrecht, 1784-1824; Flatlands, 1784-1824; Bushwick, 1784-1824; Dutch Ref.; d. ca. 1824.

LUDOLPH HEINRICH SCHRENCK, came from Lueneberg, Germany, Mar. 1749; Ord. Upper Saucon (Lehigh) Pa., 5 Nov. 1752; sett. Upper Saucon, Pa., St. Paul's, Blue or Organ Chh., 1749-1754; Lower Milford (Lehigh) Pa., Upper Milford Chh., 1749-1753; Easton (Northampton) Pa., St. John's Chh., 1749-1754; Williams (Northampton) Pa., at Cedarville, 1749-1756; New Germantown, N.J., Zion Chh., Tewksbury, 1753-1756; Pluckemin (Somerset) N.J., at Bedminster, 1753-1756; Fairmount, Fox Hill Chh. at Tewksbury, N.J., 1753-1756; Whitehouse (Hunterdon) N.J., at Leslyland, 1753-1756; Bedminster (Somerset) N.J., St. Paul's Chh., 1753-1756; Raritan (Somerset) N.J., 1753-1756; Potterstown (Hunterdon) N.J., at Rockaway, 1753-1756; German Valley (Morris) N.J., at Washington, 1753-1756; Luth.; went to Ireland.

DANIEL SCHROEDER, sett. Whitemarsh (Montgomery) Pa., St. Peter's Chh., Barren Hill, ca. 1760; Luth.

MATTHEW SCHROPP, came from Kaufbeuren, Swabia; arriv. N.Y., N.Y., 26 Nov. 1743; Ord. deacon, 1748; sett. Nazareth, 25 June 1747 ff.; Bethabara, North Carolina, 1766-1767; glover; Morav.; d. Bethabara, N.C., 1767.

CHRISTOPHER SCHULTZ, b. Harpersdorf, Silesia, 26 Mar. 1718, son of Melchior and Susanna (Kriebel) Scholtze; ed. by the Rev. George Weiss (q.v.); sett. Lower Salford (Montgomery) Pa., Schwenkfelders Chh., 1762-1789; Schwenkfelder; d. Washington, Pa., 9 May 1789.

CHRISTOPHER EMANUEL SCHULZE, b. Probstzell, Saxony, 25 Dec. 1740, son of John Andrew and Amelia Schultze; ed. Frederick Coll., Halle; Ord. Wernigerode, Germany, 1765; arriv. Philadelphia, 24 Oct. 1765; sett. Philadelphia, Pa., St. Michael's Chh., 1765-1770, and Zion's Chh., 1769-1770; Heidelberg (Lebanon) Pa., chh. at Schaeffertown, 1765-1809; Strasburg (Lanc.) Pa., St. Michael's or Beaver Creek Chh., 1767-1769; Marion (Berks) Pa., Zion or Rieth's Chh. (the original Old Tulpehocken Chh.), Dec. 1770-1809, and Christ Chh. at Stouchsburg (Old Tulpehocken Chh.), 1770-1809; Mill Creek (Lebanon) Pa., Reed's or Old Tulpehocken Chh. (i.e. 3 divisions of the original Old Tulpehocken Chh.), 1770-1809; Tulpehocken (Berks) Pa., Christ or Rehrersburg Chh., 1770-1809; son-in-law of Dr. Muhlenberg, and father of the Rev. John Andrew Schultze who was also Governor of Pa.; Luth.; d. Marion, Pa., 9 Mar. 1809.

FREDERICK SCHULZE, b. Koenigsberg, Prussia; ed. at Halle; Ord. Wernigerode, Germany, 11 July 1751; arriv. Philadelphia, 1 Dec. 1751; sett. New Hanover (Montgomery) Pa., Falkner's Swamp Chh., as assistant, 1752-1754; Upper Hanover (Montgomery) Pa., New Goshenhoppen Chh., 1752-1756; Rockland (Bucks) Pa., Indianfield Chh., 1752-1763; Upper Salford (Montg.) Pa., Old Goshenhoppen Chh., 1753-1759; Franconia (Montg.) Pa., Indian Creek or Zion's Chh., 1752-1763; Lunenberg, Nova Scotia, 1772-1782; physician; Luth.; d. 1809.

JOHANN CHRISTIAN SCHULTZE, b. Schainbach, Wertemberg, Germany, 11 June 1701, son of the Rev. John Valentine and Anna Juliana Schultze; arriv. in Pa., 25 Sept. 1732; sett. New Hanover (Montgomery) Pa., Falkner's Swamp Chh., 1732-1733; Upper Providence (Montgomery) Pa., Augustus Chh. at Trappe, 1732-1733; Lancaster (Lanc.) Pa., 1733-1733; Brecknock (Lanc.) Pa., Muddy Creek Chh., 1733-1733; Philadelphia, Pa., St. Michael's Chh., 1733-1734; became blind; Luth.; returned to Germany, 1734.

DANIEL SCHUMACHER, sett. Nova Scotia, 1751-1754; Exeter (Berks) Pa., Schwartzwald Chh., 1754-1755; Muhlenberg (Berks) Pa., Alsace Chh., 1754-1755; Reading (Berks) Pa., Trinity Chh., 1754-1755; Albany (Berks) Pa., Allemaengel Chh., 1755-1769, and 2nd, White, or Bethel Chh., 1769-1770; Greenwich (Berks) Pa., Bethel Chh., 1755-1759, 1759-1769; Heidelberg (Lehigh) Pa., Heidelberg Chh., 1755-1768; Lynn (Lehigh) Pa., Jerusalem Chh. at Allemaengel, 1755-1770; Weisenberg (Lehigh) Pa., Ziegel Chh., 1755-1769, and Weisenberg Chh., 11 Dec.

1757–1769; Windsor (Berks) Pa., Lebanon Chh. at the Blue Mountains, now St. Paul's Chh., 1755–1765; Upper Tulpehocken (Berks) Pa., Blue Mountain or North Kill Chh., 1755–1769; Whitehall (Lehigh) Pa., Egypt Chh., 1757–1760; Maxatawny (Berks) Pa., chh. at Bower's, 1759–1769; Salisbury (Lehigh) Pa., New Jerusalem Chh., East Salisbury, 1759–1768, and Jerusalem Chh., West Salisbury, 1766–1769; Perry (Berks) Pa., Zion's Chh., 1763–1765; Upper Bern (Berks) Pa., St. Michael's Chh., 1770–1770; Luth.; d. Weisenberg, Pa., ca. 1769.

JACOB SCHUMACHER, b. Palatinate, 31 Mar. 1708; came to America, 1737; Ord. Skippack (Montgomery) Pa., 1746–1793; Menn.; d. Skippack, Pa., 28 June 1793.

JOHANNES SCHUNEMAN, b. East Camp, N.Y., 18 Aug. 1712, son of Capt.Hermann and Elizabeth (Muller) Schuneman; Ord. Amsterdam, Holland, 9 Jan. 1753; sett. Shawangunk (Ulster) N.Y., Chh. at Bruynswick, 1753–1754; New Paltz (Ulster) N.Y., 1753–1754; Catskill (Greene) N.Y., 1753–1794; Coxsackie (Greene) N.Y., 1753–1794; Leeds (Greene) N.Y., Old Catskill Chh., 1753–1794; Kaatsbaan (Ulster) N.Y., 1762–1775; Dutch Ref.; d. Coxsackie, N.Y., 16 May 1794, a. 81.

JOHANNES SCHUYLER, Ord. Schoharie (Schoharie) N.Y., 18 Apr. 1738; sett. Schoharie, N.Y., 1736–1755, 1766–1769; Hackensack (Bergen) N.J., 2nd Chh., 1755–1766; Schraalenburg (Bergen) N.J., 2nd or Du Mont Chh., 1755–1766; Cobleskill (Schoharie) N.Y., 1766–1769; Beaverdam (Albany) N.Y., 1767–1777; Middleburg (Schoharie) N.Y., Upper Schoharie Chh.,1736–1775;preached occasionally at StoneArabia, N.Y.; Dutch Ref.; d. (Schoharie, N.Y.), 1779.

JOHANNES SCHWARZBACH, b. 8 Mar. 1719; sett. Elizabeth (Lancaster) Pa., Emmanuel Chh., 1775–1776; Upper Hanover (Montgomery) Pa., New Goshenhoppen Chh., 1775–1776; Madison (Madison) Va., Old Hebron Chh., 1775–1776; Luth.; d. Bensalem, Pa., 31 Aug. 1800.

JOHANNES SCHWEISHAUPT (Schweisshaupt or Schweitzhaupt), arriv. N.Y., N.Y., 12 May 1749; sett. Salisbury (Lehigh) Pa., Chh. at Emaus, 1758–1760; Mount Joy (Lanc.) Pa., Donegal Chh., 1763–1774; Graceham, Md., 1775–1784; York, Pa.; Moravian; his wife, Magdalena, was also ordained.

JOHN WILLIAM SAMUEL SCHWERDTFEGER, b. near Neustadt on the Aisel, Mittelfranken, Bavaria, 1722; an orphan; stud. theol. and law at Erlangen U.; came to Md., 1753/4; Ord. York (York) Pa., Christ Chh., 1755–1756; Brecknock (Lanc.) Pa., Muddy Creek Chh., 1758–1763; Earl (Lanc.) Pa., Chh. at New Holland, 1758–1763; Ephrata (Lanc.) Pa., Bergstrasse Chh., 1758–1763; Frederick, Md., 1763–1768; Antietam, Md., 1763–1768; Brunswick (Rensselaer) N.Y., Gilead Chh., 1768–1788; Luth.; d. 1788.

SAMUEL SEABURY, A.M., b. Groton, Conn., 8 July 1706, son of Dea. John and Elizabeth (Alden) Seabury; A.B., H.C., 1724, A.M.;

preached in Salem, Conn., 1727-1727; North Yarmouth, Me., 1729-1729; became an Ep.; appointed S.P.G. Missionary at New London, Conn., 21 Aug. 1730; K.B. for N.E., 20 Oct. 1730; Ord. London, 1731; sett. New London, Conn., St. James's Chh. (org. 10 Apr. 1732), Mar. 1730/1-1743; Hebron, Conn., 1739; Hempstead, L.I., N.Y., St. George's Chh., Aug. 1743-1764; Huntington, L.I., N.Y., St. John's Chh., 1750-1764; Ep.; d. Hempstead, L.I., N.Y., 15 June 1764, a. 58 (GS).

Bishop SAMUEL SEABURY, D.D., b. Ledyard, Conn., 30 Nov. 1729, son of the Rev. Samuel and Abigail (Mumford) Seabury; A.B., Y.C., 1748, A.M.; M.D.; A.M., Columbia, 1761; D.D., Oxford, 1777; Ord. by Bsp. of Carlisle, 23 Dec. 1753; K.B. for N.J., 16 Jan. 1754; catechist, Huntington, L.I., N.Y., 1748-1752; sett. Burlington (Burlington) N.J., St. Anne's, now St. Mary's Chh., 25 May 1754-1757; New Brunswick (Middlesex) N.J., Christ Chh., 25 May 1754-13 Jan. 1757; Jamaica, L.I., N.Y., Grace Chh., 12 Jan. 1757-1765; Newtown, L.I., N.Y., 1757-1765; Flushing, L.I., N.Y., St. George's Chh., 1757-1765; Westchester (Westchester) N.Y., St. Peter's Chh., 3 Dec. 1766-1776; Eastchester (Westchester) N.Y., St. Paul's Chh., 1766-1776; Chaplain, British Army, 1776; Staten Island, N.Y., St. Andrew's Chh., 1778-1782; New London, Conn., St. James's Chh., 1785-1796; chosen Bsp. of Conn., 25 Mar. 1783; consecrated at Aberdeen, Scotland, 14 Nov. 1784; Bishop of R.I., 1790-1796; Ep.; d. New London, Conn., 25 Feb. 1796, a. 68 (GS).

JOHANN GOTTFRIED SEELIG, b. Lemgo, Lippe-Detmold, Germany, 1668; came to Pa., 1694; sett. Pietistic Community at Wissahickon, Pa., 1709-1710; bookbinder, teacher; preacher; resided at Roxborough; Pietist; d. Roxborough, Pa., 26 Apr. 1745, a. 77.

Bishop NATHANIEL SEIDEL, b. Laubau, Prussian Silesia, 1718; came to Bethlehem, Pa., 15 June 1742; Indian missionary, 1742-1758; Ord. priest, 1748; Ord. Bishop, 12 May 1758; arriv. Bethlehem, second visit, 21 Oct. 1761; successor to Bishop Spangenberg at Bethlehem, Pa., 1762-1782; Trustee of the Moravian Estates in North America; Moravian; d. Bethlehem, Pa., 12 May 1782.

ANTON SEIFFERT, b. Thrulichen, Bohemia; went to Herrnhut, then to Georgia; arriv. Savannah, Ga., 22 Mar. 1734/5; Ord. Savannah, Ga., 28 Feb. 1735/6; sett. Savannah, Ga., 1736-1739; Bethlehem, Pa., 25 June 1742-1745; returned to Europe, 8 Apr. 1745; served chhs. in England, Ireland, and Holland; first person ord. by a Moravian Bishop in America; Moravian; d. Zeist, Holland, 19 June 1785.

HENRICUS SELYNS, b. Amsterdam, Holland, 1636, son of Jan and Agneta (Kock) Selyns; U. of Utrecht, 1654; matric. Leyden, 19 Mar. 1657, a. 21, in theology; lic. 2 Oct. 1657; Ord. Amsterdam, 16 Feb. 1660; came to America, 1660; inducted, Brooklyn, N.Y., 3 Sept. 1660-July 1664; sett. Bushwyck, N.Y., 7 Sept. 1660-1664; Gravesend, N.Y., 1660-1664; N.Y., N.Y., St. Mark's in the Bowery, 1660-1664; Staten Island, N.Y., Dutch Ref. Chh., 1660-1664, French Ref. Chh.,

South Side, 1660-1664, Fr. Ref. Chh., Fresh Kills, 1660-1664; Bergen (Bergen) N.J., supply, 1660-1664; Harlem, N.Y., supply, 1660-1664; returned to Holland, where he was a Chaplain in the Dutch Army, 1675; sett. Waverveen, Holland, 1666-1682; returned to N.Y., 1682; sett. N.Y., N.Y., 1st Dutch Ref. or South Dutch Chh., 1682-1701; an accomplished scholar; Dutch Ref.; d. N.Y., N.Y., Sept. 1701, a. 64.

GOTTLOB SENSEMANN, b. 9 Oct. 1745, son of the Rev. Henry Joachim and Anna Catherine (Ludwig) Sensemann; Indian missionary in the Susquehannah Valley and in western New York, 1768-1781; taken captive to Schenectady, 1781; sett. New Salem, Ohio, 17 May 1785-9 Nov. 1790; Moravian; d. Fairfield, Canada, 4 Jan. 1800.

HENRY JOACHIM SENSEMANN, came from Hesse-Cassel; at Bethlehem, Pa., 1743; Ord. deacon, 1749; Indian missionary, 1743-1755; sett. Gnadenhuetten, Indian Chh., 1775-1775; Nain (Lehigh) Pa., Indian Chh., 1760-1765; missionary at Jamaica, West Indies, 1766-1774; baker and bellringer; Moravian; d. Carmel, Jamaica, 1774.

JOHN CHRISTIAN SEYFERT, sett. Lower Milford, Pa., Great Swamp Chh., 1739-1741; Germ. Ref.; liv. 1747.

Captain ISRAEL SEYMOUR, b. New Castle co., Del.; Ord. Ephrata, Pa., 1746; sett. French Creek (Chester) Pa., 1746-1747; Broad River Bapt. Chh., in St. Mark's Parish (Craven) S.C., 1757-1759; sea captain; 7th Day Bapt.; Germ. Bapt.; d. S.C. after 1783.

JOHN SHARPE, D.D., matric. Edinburgh, 1694, A.M., D.D., 1694; missionary to the Leeward Islands, West Indies, 27 Feb. 1700/1; N.Y., N.Y., Chaplain in the Fort, 1704-1717; Chaplain to Lord Cornbury, Governor of the Jerseys, 1702-1717; preached at Burlington, N.J., 1704; Maidenhead, N.J., 1704; Hopewell (Mercer) N.J., 1704-1705; Perth Amboy, N.J., 1704; Elizabethtown, N.J., 1704; Staten Island, N.Y., 1704; Cheesequake (Middlesex) N.J., 1704; K.B. for N.Y., 1710; Woodbridge, N.J., 1704; Trenton, N.J., 1704; returned to London, 1717; Ep.

CHRISTIAN SHAUB, sett. Strasburg (Lanc.) Pa.; assistant to Bishop Jacob Neff, in the New Providence district; dates not given; Menn.

JOSEPH SHAW, b. Little Ryder, near St. James, London; designed for the Chh. of England; came to America in the ship "Catharine"; arriv. Bethlehem, Pa., 21 June 1742; sett. Shekomeko (Dutchess) N.Y., teacher among the Indians, 1742-1745; Wallpack (Sussex) N.J., 1745-1747; Paulin's Kill (Warren) N.J., 1745-1747; Bethlehem (Northampton) Pa., Brodhead Settlement at Dansbury, 1745-1747; Ord. Aug. 1747; started for St. Thomas, West Indies, 1747; Moravian; d. at sea en route to St. Thomas, West Indies, Oct. 1747.

JOHN SHENK, sett. Heidelberg (York) Pa., Bairs Chh., 1775 ff.; was already a minister on 14 May 1775, as shown by a deed of that date at Manheim, York co., Pa.; Menn.

SAMUEL SHEPARD, A.B., bapt. Rowley, Mass., 25 Aug. 1667, son of the Rev. Samuel and Dorothy (Flint) Shepard; A.B., H.C., 1685; sett. Woodbridge (Middlesex) N.J., Oct. 1695–1703; J.P., N.J., 1706; Cong.; d. Woodbridge, N.J., 1722/3, a. 55 (inventory, 17 Mar. 1722/3).

DAVID SHEPPARD, sett. Dividing Creek (Cumberland) N.J., 1764 ff.; Bapt.

JOB SHEPPARD, b. 1707; called to the ministry, 1742; Ord. 1750; sett. Salem (Salem) N.J., Bapt. Chh., 17 May 1755–1757; Bapt.; d. Salem, N.J., 2 Mar. 1757, a. 50.

Bishop EWALD GUSTAVUS SHEWKIRK, b. Stettin, Prussia, 28 Feb. 1725; came to America, 1774; sett. N.Y., N.Y., Moravian Chh., 1775–1776; Ord. Bishop, 1785; missionary Bishop to the West Indies; strong Tory in the Rev. War; Moravian; d. Herrnhut, Saxony, 1805.

PETER SHIRK, Ord. East Earl (Lanc.) Pa., 1750; sett. East Earl, Pa., Chh. at Weaverland, 1750–1770; Menn.; d. East Earl, Pa., Feb. 1770; will made 7 Feb. 1770; proved 12 Mar. 1770.

JOSEPH SHOWALTER, Ord. before 1773; sett. East Vincent (Chester) Pa., 1773–1802; East Coventry (Chester) Pa., 1773–1802; Phoenixville (Chester) Pa., 1773–1802; bought land in Charlestown township, Chester co., 1771; Menn.; d. Chester co. Pa., 1802 (will proved that year).

THOMAS SIMMONS, b. England; Ord. Philadelphia, Pa.; sett. Hopewell (Mercer) N.J., ca. 1715–1725; Charleston, S.C., Bapt. Chh., 20 Mar. 1725–1749; Bapt.; d. Charleston, S.C., 31 Jan. 1749.

JOHN SIMONTON, b. Ireland; Ord. Tredyffryn (Chester) Pa., 16 Apr. 1761; sett. Tredyffryn, Pa., Great Valley Chh., 1761–1791; Presb.; d. Tredyffryn, Pa., Oct. 1791.

DAVID SIMPSON, minister at Killean, Scotland; imprisoned; liberated, 17 Mar. 1685; came to New Jersey; not known to have been settled here; Presb.; d. New Jersey.

MALIGUS SIMS, sett. Bensalem (Bucks) Pa., Dutch Ref. Chh., Apr. 1719 ff.; Dutch Ref.

DUGALD SIMSON, b. Scotland; sett. Brookhaven, L.I., N.Y., Setauket Chh., 1685–1691; Presb.; returned to Scotland, 1691, where he was a member of the Lochmaben Presbytery.

MATTHEW SITTENSPERGER (changed his name to Manners), b. Germany; sett. Lancaster (Lanc.) Pa., St. John Nepomucene's Chh., 1748–1752; Conewago (Adams) Pa., Sacred Heart Chh., 1758–1758; Mill Creek (New Castle) Del., St. Mary's Chapel at Coffee Run, Jan. 1772–1786, and St. John's Chh., at Mt. Cuba or Cuba Rock, Jan. 1772–1786; R.C.

ISAAC SKILLMAN, D.D., b. New Jersey, 1740; A.B., Princeton, 1766, A.M.; A.M., Brown, 1774, D.D., 1798; Ord. N.Y., N.Y., 1st Bapt. Chh., 1773; sett. Boston, Mass., 2nd Bapt. Chh., Sept. 1773–7 Oct.

1787; Salem (Salem) N.J., 1790-1799; Bapt.; d. Salem, N.J., 8 June 1799, a. 59.

WILLIAM SKINNER, b. Scotland, ca. 1687; Ord. London, Autumn of 1722; fought in the battle of Preston-Pans, Scotland, 1715; K.B. to Philadelphia, Pa., 10 June 1718; schoolmaster at Philadelphia, 1718-1722; occasional preacher at Freehold (Mercer) N.J., St. Peter's Chh., 1718-1733; sett. Perth Amboy (Middlesex) N.J., St. Peter's Chh., 22 Nov. 1722-1758; S.P.G. missionary; Piscataway (Middlesex) N.J., St. James's Chh. 1722-1758; Shrewsbury (Monmouth) N.J., Christ Chh., 1722-1725; Woodbridge (Middlesex) N.J., Trinity Chh., 1722-1752; New Brunswick (Middlesex) N.J., Christ Chh., 1742-1749; Spotswood (Middlesex) N.J., St. Peter's Chh. at East Brunswick, 1756-1758; Mr. Skinner built the chh. at Spotswood; a Rev. William Macgregor Skinner, perhaps a descendant, was matriculated in the Lyon Register of Arms, 1810; Ep.; d. Perth Amboy, N.J., 1758, a. 70.

JOHN SLEMONS, A.M., b. Chester co., Pa., 1735, of Irish parentage; A.B., Princeton, 1760, A.M.; lic. 1762-1763; Ord. Highland (Adams) Pa., 23 May 1765; sett. Highland, Pa., Lower Marsh Creek Chh., 1764-1774; Taneytown (Carroll) Md., 1764-1770; Lower Chanceford (York) Pa., 1774-1799; Slate Ridge, Pa., 1781-Sept. 1791; Presb.; bur. Piney Creek, Md., June 1814, a. 79.

JOHN SMART, arriv. in America, 1761; preached for a time here, then returned to Scotland; Associate Presb.

CALEB SMITH, A.M., b. Brookhaven, L.I., N.Y., 29 Dec. 1723, son of Major William Henry and Hannah (Sears) Smith; A.B., Y.C., 1743, A.M.; Trustee, Princeton, 1750-1762; Pres., pro temp.; Ord. Orange (Essex) N.J., 30 Nov. 1748; sett. Orange, at Newark Mountain, N.J., 1748-1762; first Tutor of Princeton Coll., 1746; Presb.; d. Newark, N.J., 22 Oct. 1762, a. 39 (GS).

DAVID SMITH, b. Cape May, N.J., 1730; Ord. Cape May (Cape May) N.J., Mar. 1776; sett. Cape May, N.J., 1776-1784; Bapt.; d. Cape May, N.J., Feb. 1784, a. 54.

DELIVERANCE SMITH, A.M., (prob. b. Roxbury, Conn.), A.B., Y.C., 1749, A.M.; lic. 28 May 1751; sett. Pleasant Valley (Dutchess) N.Y., Pittsburgh Chh. at Washington Hollow, 1747-1765; Ord. Hillsdale (Columbia) N.Y., 11 Dec. 1765; sett. Hillsdale, N.Y., 1765 ff.; Presb.; d. Woodbury, Conn., Sept. 1785.

JOHN SMITH, A.M., b. Newport Pagnel, Bucks, England, 5 May 1702, son of Thomas and Susanna (Odell) Smith; came to N.Y., N.Y., 1715; A.B., Y.C., 1727, A.M.; Ord. Rye (Westchester) N.Y., 15 May 1729; sett. Rye, N.Y., 1729-1771; White Plains, N.Y., 1729-1771; Sing Sing, N.Y., 1763-1771; physician; Presb.; d. Rye, N.Y., 26 Feb. 1771, a. 69.

JOHN SMITH (A.B., Princeton, 1770), sett. Bart (Lanc.) Pa., Middle Octoraro Chh., 1772-1794; Mt. Nebo (Lanc.) Pa., near Pequea, 1772-1794; Associate Ref. Presb.; d. (1820).

JOSEPH SMITH, A.B., b. Hadley, 1674, son of Lieut. Dea. Philip and Rebecca (Foote) Smith; A.B., H.C., 1695; sett. Brookfield, Mass., 1702-1705; Ord. Fairfield (Cumberland) N.J., Chh. at Cohansey, 10 May 1709; sett. Cohansey, N.J., 1708-1713; inst. Middletown, Conn., 2nd Chh. at Cromwell, 5 Jan. 1714/5, as the first minister; sett. Cromwell, Conn., 1715-1736; Cong.; Presb.; d. Middletown, Conn., 8 Sept. 1736.

JOSEPH SMITH, A.B., b. Nottingham, Pa., 1736; A.B., Princeton, 1764; lic. 5 Aug. 1767; Ord. Lower Brandywine (New Castle) Del., 19 Apr. 1769; sett. Lower Brandywine, 1769-22 Aug. 1772; Brandywine, 1769- Apr. 1778; Wilmington, Del., 2nd Presb. Chh., 27 Oct. 1774-29 Apr. 1778; Buffalo (Washington) Pa., and Cross Creek (Washington) Pa., 21 June 1779-1792; fdr. Jefferson Coll., 1791; Presb.; d. Buffalo, Washington co., Pa., 19 Apr. 1792.

ROBERT SMITH, D.D., b. Londonderry, Ireland, 1723; came to America, 1730; ed. Fagg's Manor Academy; A.M. (hon.) Princeton, 1760; D.D., 1786; Trustee, 1772-1793; lic. 27 Dec. 1749; called to Pequea, 1 Oct. 1750; Ord. Pequea, Pa., 25 Mar. 1750/1; sett. Salisbury (Lanc.) Pa., Pequea Chh., 1751-1793; Leacock (Lanc.) Pa., 1751-9 Oct. 1759; East Earl (Lanc.) Pa., Cedar Grove Chh., 1775-1785; Principal, Dr. Robert Smith's Academy, Pequea, Pa.; New Side Presb.; Moderator of the General Assembly, 1790; d. Rockville, Chester co., Pa., 15 Apr. 1793, a. 71.

SAMPSON SMITH, came from Ireland; member, Donegal Presbytery, 3 Apr. 1753; Ord. 1752; sett. Chestnut Level (Lanc.) Pa., chh. at Drumore, 1752-1771; Hopewell (York) Pa., Shrewsbury Chh., 1761-1771; missionary at the South Branch of the Potomac River, Va., 1772-1774; suspended, 1774; teacher; Presb.; killed by lightning; time not given.

SIMON SMITH (prob. b. 1669, son of Simon Smith of Corscombe, Devon, matric. Magdalen Hall, Oxford, 30 Mar. 1688, a. 19); N.Y., N.Y., Chaplain in the Fort, 1699 ff.; K.B. for Jamaica, 7 Jan. 1694; Ep.

THOMAS SMITH, A.M., A.B., Princeton, 1758, A.M.; inst. Cranbury (Middlesex) N.J., 1762-1789; Penns Neck (Mercer) N.J., near Princeton, 1762-1789; St. George's (New Castle) Del., 1769-1774; Presb.; d. Cranbury, N.J., 23 Dec. 1789.

TITUS SMITH, A.B., b. South Hadley, Mass., 4 June 1734, son of Dea. John and Elizabeth (Smith) Smith; A.B., Y.C., 1764; Ord. N.Y. State, 24 Apr. 1765, as an Indian missionary; preached occasionally; became a Sandemanian, 1772; re-Ord. in Boston; Cong.; Sandemanian; d. Halifax, Nova Scotia, 15 Sept. 1807, a. 73.

President WILLIAM SMITH, D.D., b. Aberdeen, Scotland, 7 Sept. 1727; A.B., Aberdeen, 1747, A.M., D.D., 1759; D.D., Oxford, 27 Mar. 1759; D.D., Trinity Coll., Dublin, Ireland; Ord. London, by Bsp. of Carlisle, Dec. 1753; K.B. for Pa., 16 Jan. 1754; Pres., U. of Pa., May

1754–Nov. 1779, 1789–1803; Pres., Washington Coll., Md., 1782–1786; sett. Oxford (Chester) Pa., Trinity Chh., 1766–1777; Whitemarsh (Montgomery) Pa., St. Thomas's Chh., 1766–1779, 1784–1796; Lower Dublin, Pa., All Saints Chh., 1772–1779; Rector, Chester Parish, Chestertown (Kent) Md., 1779–1782; St. Paul's Chh. (Kent) Md., 1783–1785; elected 1st Bishop of Maryland, 1783, but was not consecrated; Ep.; d. Philadelphia, Pa., 14 May 1803, a. 76.

GEORGE SOELLE, had a collegiate ed.; arriv. N.Y., N.Y., 9 Sept. 1753; sett. York (York) Pa., 1756–1757; Staten Island, N.Y., 1761–1762; Amelia (Orangeburg) N.C., 1773–1773; Moravian.

HANS PETER SOMEY, an exiled Palatinate minister; arriv. Philadelphia, 28 Sept. 1733; sett. West Earl (Lanc.) Pa., Groffdale Chh., 1733 ff.; Menn.

PETER NICHOLAS SOMMER (or Sommers), b. Hamburg, Germany, 9 Jan. 1709; Ord. 1742; left Germany, 24 Oct. 1742; arriv. N.Y., N.Y., 21 Apr. 1743; sett. Schoharie (Schoharie) N.Y., 25 May 1743–1795; Canajoharie (Montgomery) N.Y., 1743–1751; Little Falls (Herkimer) N.Y., 1743–1751; Stone Arabia (Montgomery) N.Y., 1743–1751; Knox (Albany) N.Y., Zion's Chh., 1745–1795; Helderberg (Albany) N.Y., Dutch Ref. Chh. at Guilderland, 1745 ff.; Albany, N.Y., 1751–1791; Claverack (Columbia) N.Y., St. Thomas's Chh., 1751–1760; Cobleskill (Schoharie) N.Y., 1758–1768; Seward (Schoharie) N.Y., St. Peter's Chh. at New Rhinebeck, now Lawtersville, 1760–1775; Beaverdam (Albany) N.Y., Dutch Ref. Chh., 1765–1767; Hoosick (Rensselaer) N.Y., ca. 1767; Palatine Bridge (Montgomery) N.Y., 1770 ff.; Sharon (Schoharie) N.Y., St. John's Chh., 1775–1795; blind after 1768; retired to Sharon (Schoharie) N.Y., 1788; Luth.; d. Sharon, N.Y., 27 Oct. 1795, a. 86.

JACOB SONDAY, b. Germany, 1700; came to America, 1735; Ord. 1763; sett. Cocalico (Lanc.) Pa., Conestoga Chh., 1763–1770; Germ. Bapt.

JOHN SPALLER, sett. Rhinebeck (Dutchess) N.Y., 1709–1709; Luth.

Bishop AUGUSTUS GOTTLIEB SPANGENBERG, A.M., b. Klettenberg, Hohenstein, Saxony, 15 July 1704, son of the Lutheran minister of that place; A.B., Jena, A.M.; Prof. at Jena; Prof. at Halle, Saxony; became a Moravian, 1733; arriv. Savannah, Ga., 22 Mar. 1734/5; sett. Savannah, Ga., 1738–1739; Pa., Apr. 1736–1738; returned to Europe, 1739; sett. Oley (Berks) Pa., 1742–1744; Bethlehem, Pa., 1744–1748; 1751–1762; Bishop of the Moravians in America, 1745–1751, 1754–1762; consecrated Bishop at Herrnhag, 15 June 1744; Vicar General in America, 1744–1748; returned to America, 10 Dec. 1751; left for Europe, 1 July 1762; Moravian; d. Berthelsdorf, Germany, 18 Sept. 1792, a. 88.

ELIHU SPENCER, D.D., b. Millington Parish, East Haddam, Conn., 21 Feb. 1721/2, son of Dea. Isaac and Mary (Selden) Spencer;

A.B., Y.C., 1746, A.M.; D.D., U. of Pa., 1782; Trustee of Princeton, 1752-1784; Ord. Boston, Mass., 14 Sept. 1748, as a missionary to the Oneidas; inst. Elizabethtown (Union) N.J., 1st Chh., Cong.-Presb., 7 Feb. 1749/50-1756; Jamaica, L.I., N.Y., 1756-1758; Shrewsbury (Monmouth) N.J., Nov. 1759-1764; Middletown (Monmouth) N.J., Chh. at Middletown Point, 1759-1764; Shark River (Monmouth) N.J., 1759-1764; Perth Amboy (Middlesex) N.J., 1759-1764; St. George's (New Castle) Del., inst. 17 Apr. 1766; sett. St. George's, Del., 1764-1769; Middletown (New Castle) Del., Forest Chh., 1764-19 Oct. 1769; Appoquinimink (New Castle) Del., 1764-1767; inst. Trenton (Mercer) N.J., 1st Presb. Chh., 18 Nov. 1769-1784; Hopewell, N.J., Ewing Chh., 1769-1784; Lawrenceville, N.J., Maidenhead Chh., 1769-1784; Chaplain, 1758, 1777; Presb.; d. Trenton, N.J., 27 Dec. 1784, a. 63 (GS).

GEORGE SPENCER, Ord. London, 1767; lic. 19 Jan. 1767, for New Jersey; S.P.G., 19 Dec. 1766; K.B. for N.J., 23 Jan. 1767; sett. Spotswood (Middlesex) N.J., St. Peter's Chh. at East Brunswick, 1767-1767; Freehold (Monmouth) N.J., St. Peter's Chh., 1767-1767; recalled; disreputable; went to North Carolina; Ep.

SAMUEL SPRING, D.D., b. Northbridge, Mass., 27 Feb. 1745/6, son of Col. and Dea. John and Sarah (Read) Spring; A.B., Princeton, 1771, A.M.; A.M., Dartmouth, 1789, D.D., Williams, 1806; Chaplain, Canadian Expedition, 1775-1776; sett. Newburyport, Mass., 1780-1819; Cong.; d. Newburyport, Mass., 4 Mar. 1819.

JAMES SPROAT, D.D., b. Middleborough, Mass., 11 Apr. 1722, son of Lieut. Ebenezer and Experience Sproat; A.B., Y.C., 1741, A.M., 1757; D.D., Princeton, 1780; Ord. Guilford, Conn., 4th Cong. Chh., 23 Aug. 1743-18 Oct. 1767; inst. Philadelphia, Pa., 2nd Presb. Chh., 30 Mar. 1769-1793; New Side Presb.; Cong.; Presb.; d. Philadelphia, Pa., 18 Oct. 1793, a. 71 (GS). (Died of yellow fever.)

JOHN CHRISTIAN STAHLSCHMIDT, b. Freudenberg, Nassau-Siegen, Germany, 3 Mar. 1740, son of Landhauptman Stahlschmidt; sailor; arriv. Batavia, West Indies, 3 June 1760; to Canton, China, and on to Amsterdam, June 1761; to Bengal, India, 1764/5; home July 1765; arriv. Philadelphia, Aug. 1770; sett. Frankford, Pa., 1773-1774; Tulpehocken, Pa., 1774; Conewago (York) Pa., Quickel's or Zion's Chh., 1775-1779; also at Freyen, Bleymayer's, Schierster's, and three other congregations near York, Pa.; returned to Germany; Germ. Ref.; d. Muelheim, Germany, 1 June 1826, a. 86.

JACOB STALL, b. 1730; sett. Cocalico (Lanc.) Pa., Conestoga Chh., 1772-1822; Tunker or Germ. Bapt.; d. (Cocalico) Pa., 1822, a. 92 y.

THOMAS STANDARD, A.M., (M.D.), b. Taunton, co. Somerset, England; K.B. for Va., 7 May 1723; S.P.G. missionary at Brookhaven, L.I., N.Y., Caroline Chh., Setauket, arriv. 5 Oct. 1725; sett. 1725-1725; Yonkers (Westchester) N.Y., St. John's Chh., 1726-1760; Westchester (Westchester) N.Y., St. Peter's Chh., 8 July 1727-1760; East

Chester (Westchester) N.Y., St. Paul's Chh., 1727-1760; physician; Ep.; d. Westchester, N.Y., before 1 Aug. 1760.

WILLIAM STANDFORTH (perhaps pensioner, Trinity Coll., Dublin, 4 June 1760); K.B. to N.Y., 22 July 1775; Ep.

CASPAR MICHAEL STAPEL, Ph.D., M.D., b. Germany, 1721; Herborn Seminary; a former Lutheran minister at Mecklenburg, Germany; arriv. in America, 1761; sett. Amwell (Hunterdon) N.J., 12 July 1762-1766; Lebanon (Hunterdon) N.J., Rockaway Chh. at Clinton, 1762-1766; Fairmount (Hunterdon) Fox Hill Chh. at Tewksbury, 1762-1766; Alexandria (Hunterdon) N.J., 1763-1766; physician; Germ. Ref.; d. Amwell, N.J., 17 Mar. 1766.

JOHN STEEL, b. Ireland, 1716; came from the Londonderry Presbytery; sett. New London (Chester) Pa., Old Side Chh., 1744-1752; Montgomery (Franklin) Pa., Hill Chh. at Mercersburg, 1752-1755; broken up by the Indian Wars; Antrim (Franklin) Pa., Old Red. Chh., 1754-1755; Carlisle (Cumberland) Pa., Old School Chh., inst. June 1759-1779; Silver Spring (Cumberland) Pa., Chh. at Lower Pennsborough, June 1759-1779; Captain, 1755, in the Indian Wars; Old Side Presb.; d. Carlisle, Pa., Aug. 1779.

JOHN CONRAD STEINER, Senior, b. Winterthur, Switzerland, 1 Jan. 1707, son of the Hon. Jacob and Ursula (Sutzer) Steiner; vicar, Mettmenstetten, Switzerland, 1726-1728, 1733-1735; minister, St. Peterzell, 1735-1747; also sett. at St. Gall, Hemburg, and St. George, near Winterthur; arriv. Philadelphia, 25 Sept. 1749; sett. Philadelphia, Pa., 1749-1751, 1759-1762; Germantown, Pa., 1749-1756; Whitpain (Montgomery) Pa., Boehm's Chh., 1752-1756; Reading (Berks) Pa., 1756-1757; Union (Adams) Pa., 1756-1759; Conewago (York) Pa., Zion's or Quickel's Chh., 1756-1759; Winchester (Frederick) Va., 1756-1759; and the following six chhs. in Md.: 1756-1759: Antietam (Washington) Md., Frederick, Md., Glade (Garrett) Md., near Oakland, Middletown (Frederick) Md., Zion or Kittatinny Mountain Chh., Pipe Creek (Frederick) Md., and Turkey, Md.; Germ. Ref.; d. Philadelphia, Pa., 6 July 1762, a. 55 years (GS).

JOHN CONRAD STEINER, Jr., b. Peterzell, Switzerland, 8 May 1737, son of the Rev. John Conrad and Regula (Hegner) Steiner; Ord. Lancaster, Pa., 17 June 1772; sett. Salisbury (Lehigh) Pa., Jerusalem Chh., 1770-1771; Albany (Berks) Pa., Frieden's Chh., 1771-1774; Greenwich (Berks) Pa., Dunkel Chh., 1771-1775; Oley (Berks) Pa., 1771-1774; Heidelberg (Lehigh) Pa., 1771-1772; Lowhill (Lehigh) Pa., 1771-1772; Lynn (Lehigh) Pa., Ebenezer or Organ Chh., 1771-1774; Jacob's Chh., 1771-1774, Tresbacker Chh., 1771-1776; Lehigh (Northampton) Pa., Driesbach Chh., 1771-1781; Moore (Northampton) Pa., Union Chh., 1771-1781, Emmanuel Chh., 1774-1781; Allen & Lehigh (Northampton) Pa., 1774-1781; Germ. Ref.; d. Allentown, Pa., 14 Nov. 1781.

FERDINAND STEINMEYER, S.J. (also called Ferdinand Farmer), b. Swabia, Germany, 13 Oct. 1720; adm. S.J., at Landsberg, 26 Sept. 1743; arriv. in America, 20 June 1752; Trustee, U. of Pa., 1779; sett. Lancaster (Lanc.) Pa., 1752-1758; in Berks co., Pa., 1757; Philadelphia, Pa., St. Joseph's Chh., 1758-1786; Concord (Chester) Pa., at Ivy Mills, 1759-1786; Alloway (Salem) N.J., at Glass House, 1759-1786; Bound Brook (Somerset) N.J., 1759-1786; Macopin (Passaic) N.J., at Echo Lake, 1759-1786; he was the priest who visited Roman Catholic families in a house in N.Y., N.Y., just prior to 1775; R.C.; d. Philadelphia, Pa., 17 Aug. 1786.

BENJAMIN STELLE, b. New Rochelle, N.Y., 1683, son of Poncet Stelle, a Huguenot; Ord. Piscataway Chh., at Stelton, 1739; sett. Piscataway (Middlesex) N.J., 1739-1759; other authorities give 1794-1759; magistrate; Bapt.; d. Piscataway, N.J., Jan. 1759, a. 75.

ISAAC STELLE, b. Piscataway, N.J., 6 Feb. 1718/9, son of the Rev. Benjamin Stelle; Ord. Piscataway (Middlesex) N.J., Chh. at Stelton, 1752; sett. Piscataway, N.J., 1752-1781; Bapt.; d. Piscataway, N.J., 9 Oct. 1781, a. 62.

JOHN STEPHENS, b. Staten Island, N.Y.; Ord. Oyster Bay, L.I., N.Y., 1st Bapt. Chh., 1747; sett. Horseneck Chh., Greenwich, Conn., 1747-1750; sett. N.Y., N.Y., 1st Bapt. Chh., 1747-1750; sett. Ashby River, South Carolina, 22 June 1750-1769; left because of drunkenness; Bapt.; d. Black River, S.C., 1785.

ANDREW STERLING, Ord. Sadsbury (Chester) Pa., 2nd or Upper Octoraro Chh., 1747; sett. Sadsbury, Pa., 1747-24 Apr. 1765; East Fallowfield (Chester) Pa., Doe Run Chh., 1747-1765; Presb.; New Side; d. Sadsbury, Pa., Oct. 1765.

HUGH STEVENSON, came from Ireland to America, 1726; lic. 13 Sept. 1726; sett. New Castle (New Castle) Del., 1727-1728; Nottingham (Chester) Pa., 1727-1728; Lewes (Sussex) Del., 1727-1728; Ord. Snow Hill (Worcester) Md., 1728 (before June 1729); sett. Snow Hill, Md., 1728-1733; Potomac Chh. (Northumberland) Va., 1733-1733; teacher at Philadelphia, Pa., 1739-1744; Presb.; d. Philadelphia, Pa., May 1744.

SAMUEL STILLMAN, D.D., b. Philadelphia, Pa., 27 Feb. 1737; A.M. (hon.) U. of Pa., 1761; A.M. (hon.) H.C., 1761; A.M., Brown, 1769, D.D., 1788; Trustee and Fellow, Brown U., 1764-1807; Ord. Charleston, S.C., 26 Feb. 1759; sett. James Island, S.C., 1759-1761; Bordentown (Burlington) N.J., 1762-1763; Boston, 2nd Bapt. Chh., 1764-1764; inst. Boston, 1st Bapt. Chh., 9 Jan. 1765-1807; member, Am. Phil. Soc., 1768; Artillery Election Sermon, 1770; Election Sermon, 1779; Bapt.; d. Boston, Mass., 12 Mar. 1807, a. 70.

JOHN CASPAR STOEVER, Senior, b. Frankenberg, Hesse, 1685, son of Dietrich and Magdalena (Eberwein) Stoever; arriv. in Pa., 11 Sept. 1728; sett. Philadelphia, Pa., St. Michael's Chh., Sept. 1728-1733;

Madison (Madison) Va., Old Hebron Chh., at White Oak Run, 1728–1733; Winchester (Frederick) Va., Strasburg Chh., 1728–1734; Woodstock (Shenandoah) Va., 1730–1734; Frederick, Md., 1730–1734; Mill Creek (Lebanon) Pa., Reed's or Old Tulpehocken Chh., 1729–1729; Elizabeth (Lancaster) Pa., Emmanuel Chh., 1730–1734; Wissahickon, Pa., 1730; Oley (Berks) Pa., Christ or Hill Chh., 1731–1734; Marion (Berks) Pa., Zion's or Rieth's Chh., the original Old Tulpehocken Chh., 1733–1734; he originated or preached to the following Lutheran churches: Oley, Colebrookdale, Hosensack, Melancthon, Manatawny, Coventry, Chestnut Hill, Moselem, Elizabeth, French Creek, Codorus, South Mountain, North Kill, Monocacy, Quittopehilla, Swatara, Conestoga, Shepherdstown, Opequon, Fredericksburg, and others; went to Germany in 1734 to obtain funds, and resided there, 1734–1738; Luth.; d. at sea en route to Virginia, 1738/9.

JOHN CASPAR STOEVER, Jr., b. Luedorff, Unter Pfaltz, Germany, 21 Dec. 1707, son of the Rev. John Caspar and Gertrude Stoever; arriv. Philadelphia, 11 Sept. 1728; Ord. in Montgomery co., Pa., 8 Apr. 1733; he organized or ministered to the following 39 Lutheran churches in Pa.: *Berks co.:* Douglass, Oley Hill Chh., Colebrookdale, 1730–1742; Marion, Zion's or Rieth's Chh., the original Old Tulpehocken Chh., at Stouchsburg, 1735–1742; Maxatawny, at Bower's, 1730–1742; Oley, Christ or Hill Chh., 1736–1740; Penn, St. John's or North Kill at Bernville, 1730–1745; Pike, St. John's or Hill Chh., Manatawny, 1730–1742; Richmond, Zion or Moselem Chh., 1742–1742; *Chester co.:* East Coventry, 1730–1742; East Nantmeal, 1730–1742; East Vincent, Schuylkill Valley, 1730–1742; Nantmeal, French Creek Chh., 1730–1742; *Lancaster co.:* Earl, Chh. at New Holland, May 1730–1746, 1755–1758; Brecknock (East Cocalico), Muddy Creek Chh., 1746–1749, 1755–1758; Elizabeth, Emmanuel Chh., 1731–1754; Lancaster, Holy Trinity Chh., called 7 Nov. 1736, sett. 1729–1740; Upper Leacock, 1730–1742; Strasburg, St. Michael's or Beaver Creek Chh., 1730–1746; Warwick, 1777–1779; *Lebanon co.:* Bethel, St. John's Chh., 1774–1779; Conestoga, 1730–1779; Jonestown, Zion's Chh., 1764–1779; Lebanon, Salem or Kruppe Chh., 1731–1765; Mill Creek, Reed's or Old Tulpehocken Chh., 1735–1742; North Annville, Berg Chh. or Hill Chh., 1733–1779; Swatara, 1731–1734; *Lehigh co.:* Lower Macungie, Holy Trinity or Zion Chh., 1745–1745; Lower Milford, Upper Milford or Hosensack Chh., 1743–1743; South Whitehall, Jordan Chh., 1734–1736; *Northampton co.:* Williams, Chh. at Cedarville, 1730–1736; *Montgomery co.:* New Hanover, Falkner's Swamp Chh., 1734–1735; Perkiomen, 1730–1742; Upper Providence, Augustus Chh. at Trappe, 1733–1742; Worcester, Skippack Chh., 1730 ff.; *Philadelphia co.:* Chestnut Hill, 1730–1742; Germantown, 1730–1735; Philadelphia, St. Michael's Chh., 1734–1735; Wissahickon, 1730–1742; *York co.:* York, Christ Chh., 1733–1743; Hanover, St. Michael's, 1732–1738; Schiefenthal (?), 1730–1742; and Spotsylvania, Virginia, 1739 ff.; Luth.; 42 churches in all; d. North Annville, Pa., 13 May 1779, a. 71 years.

CHRISTIAN STOLTZFUS, b. 1748; sett. Maiden Creek Congregation, near Leesport and Shillington (Berks) Pa., 1775-1832; Amish; d. Maiden Creek, Pa., 1832.

JOHN STORRS, A.M., b. Mansfield, Conn., 1 Dec. 1735, son of John and Esther (Gurley) Storrs; A.B., Y.C., 1756, A.M., Tutor, 1761-1762; A.M., Dartmouth, 1792; Ord. Southold, L.I., N.Y., 1st Chh., 15 Aug. 1763-1776, June 1782-13 Apr. 1787; Chaplain in the Regt. of Col. Fisher Gay, 1776-1778; 1787-1796; Cong.; d. Mansfield, Conn., 9 Oct. 1799, a. 63.

Dr. HENRY WILLIAM STOY, b. Herborn, Westphalia, Germany, 14 Mar. 1726, son of John George Stoy; ed. in theology, U. of Herborn, 1761; in medicine, 1763; lic. 15 Sept. 1749; studied medicine at Leyden, 1763-1767; Ord. Amsterdam, Holland, 14 Mar. 1752; arriv. Philadelphia, 28 July 1752; sett. Center (Berks) Pa., 1752-1755; Tulpehocken (Berks) Pa., Host Chh., 1752-1755; Jackson (Lebanon) Pa., Millbach Chh., 1752-1755; Mill Creek (Lebanon) Tulpehocken or Trinity Chh., 1752-1755; Tolpehil (Lebanon) Pa., 1752-1755; Mount Joy (Lancaster) Pa., Chh. at Miller's, 1752-1763; Germantown, Pa., 1756-1757; Lancaster, Pa., Oct. 1758-Jan. 1763; Philadelphia, Pa., 1756-1758; Pequea (Lanc.) Pa., 1758-1763; Lebanon (Lebanon) Tabor Chh., 1760-1763; Lebanon (Lebanon) Pa., Chh. at Steitztown, 1763-1814; he withdrew from the Coetus, 1772; elected to the Pa. legislature, 1784; physician; Germ. Ref.; d. Jonestown, Pa., 14 Sept. 1801 (GS) a. 75 years 6 months.

PIERRE STOUPPE, A.M., b. France, 1690; A.B., Geneva, Switzerland, A.M.; sett. Charleston, S.C., Huguenot Chh., 1722-1723; Ord. London, England, as an Ep., 25 Dec. 1723; K.B. for N.Y., 15 Feb. 1723/4; sett. New Rochelle (Westchester) N.Y., Trinity Chh., Episcopal, 20 July 1724-1760; French Ref.; Ep.; d. New Rochelle, N.Y., July 1760.

JOHN STRAIN, A.B., b. ca. 1731; A.B., Princeton, 1757; lic. 1759; Ord. 29 May 1759; sett. Lower Chanceford (York) Pa., 17 Dec. 1760- inst. 17 Nov. 1762-1774; Peach Bottom (York) Pa., Slate Ridge Chh., 1760-1774; Presb.; d. Peach Bottom, co. York, Pa., 12 Apr. 1774, a. 43 (GS).

JOHN WILLIAM STRAUB, b. Europe, 1688; not ordained; schoolteacher at Gronau, Palatinate; arriv. Philadelphia, 21 Sept. 1732, ae. 44 years, in the "Pink Plaisance"; sett. Salisbury (Lehigh) Pa., Jerusalem Chh., 1741-1743; Worcester (Montgomery) Pa., Wentz's or Skippack Chh., 1741-1744 (Good gives 1739-1741, and also places him at Franconia, Indian Creek Chh., 20 Oct. 1746); Germ. Ref.

CHRISTIAN STREIT, 'A.M., b. New Jersey, of Swiss parents, 7 June 1749; ed. Halle; A.M., U. of Pa., 1768; lic. 1769; Ord. Reading, Pa., Oct. 1770; sett. Easton (Northampton) Pa., St. John's Chh., 1769-1779; Lehigh (Northampton) Pa., St. Paul's Chh. at Cherryville, 1769-1779; Upper Saucon (Lehigh) Pa., St. Paul's, Blue or Organ Chh., 1769-1778; Williams (Northampton) Pa., Chh. at Cedarville, 1770-1783; Moore (Northampton) Pa., 1772-1779; Greenwich (Warren) N.J., St. James's

Chh., 1773-1777; Charleston, South Carolina, St. John's Chh., 1779-1782; New Hanover (Montgomery) Pa., Falkner's Swamp Chh., 1783-1785; Winchester, Virginia, Strasburg Chh., 19 July 1785-1812; Chaplain, Rev. War, 8th Va., Regt., 1776-1777; Luth.; d. Winchester, Va., 10 Mar. 1812.

WILLIAM STRINGER, pens. Trinity Coll., Dublin, 1 Nov. 1767-1770; K.B. for Philadelphia, 12 Mar. 1773; sett. Philadelphia, Pa., St. Paul's Chh., 1773-Oct. 1777; resigned; Ep.

ALEXANDER STUART, A.M., K.B. for N.Y., 17 Apr. 1703; appointed to St. Matthew's Chh., Bedford (Westchester) N.Y., 1704; perhaps never sett. there; Ep.

JOHN STUART, D.D., b. Harrisburg, Pa., 24 Feb. 1740, son of Andrew Stuart; A.B., U. of Pa., 1763, A.M., 1770, D.D., 1779; A.M. (hon.) Columbia, 1773; Ord. London, 1770; K.B. for N.Y., 3 Sept. 1770; sett. Fort Hunter, N.Y., Queen Anne's Chapel, 1770-1778; Tory prisoner at Schenectady, N.Y., 1778-1780; sett. Kingston, Canada, 1780-1811; Montreal, Canada, 1780-1785; Ep.; Kingston, Upper Canada, 15 Aug. 1811, a. 75.

ROBERT STURGEON, came from Ireland or Scotland; sett. Watertown, Mass., Independent Chh., 1721-1 May 1722; Wilton, Conn., 1st Cong. Chh., 20 July 1726-1732; Bedford (Westchester) N.Y., 1st Presb. Chh., 1732-1743; member of N.Y. Presbytery, 1745; not mentioned after 1750; Presb.

WILLIAM STURGEON, A.M., b. 1722, son of the Rev. Robert Sturgeon; A.B., Y.C., 1745, A.M.; Ord. London, May 1747; appointed, 30 May 1747, S.P.G. missionary and school-master, 1747-1766; K.B. for Pa., 1 Dec. 1747; sett. Philadelphia, Pa., assistant (United Chhs.), Christ Chh., 1757-1766; St. Peter's, 1757-31 July 1766; Ep.; d. Philadelphia, Pa., 3 Nov. 1770.

ABNER SUTTON, b. Basking Ridge, N.J., 8 May 1741; Ord. Mount Bethel (Warren) N.J., Bapt. Chh., Jan. 1775-1791; Bapt.; d. Mt. Bethel, N.J., Mar. 1791.

DAVID SUTTON, b. Basking Ridge, N.J.; sett. Baptisttown, Kingwood (Hunterdon) N.J., 26 Mar. 1764-3 Aug. 1783, resigned; Flemington (Hunterdon) N.J., 1766-1783; Bapt.

ISAAC SUTTON, lic. 8 Nov. 1770; sett. Uniontown (Fayette) Pa., Great Bethel Chh., 1770-1773; Robinson (Washington) Pa., Laurel Hill Chh., 1775 ff.; Bapt.

JAMES SUTTON, sett. Tuckahoe (Cape May) N.J., 1771-1772; Cowmarsh, Del., 1771-1772; Amwell (Washington) Pa., Chh. at Ten Mile, 1773-1775; Uniontown (Fayette) Pa., Redstone Settlement, at Goshen, 1773-1775; Bapt.

JOHN SUTTON, b. Basking Ridge, N.J., 12 Feb. 1733; ed. at Hopewell; Ord. Scotch Plains, N.J., 1763; sett. Salem (Salem) N.J., 1761-1766; Cape May, N.J., 1 Apr. 1764-6 May 1766; Pencader Hundred

(New Castle) Del., Welsh Tract Bapt. Chh., 3 Nov. 1770–1777; Kenton Hundred (Kent) Del., Old Dutch or Bryn Zion Chh., 1770–1777; Simpson's Creek, Va., 1777–1788; went to Kentucky, 1788; Bapt.; d. Kentucky, ca. 1800.

Bishop ABRAHAM SWARTZ, Ord. minister, 1738; Ord. Bishop, 1756; sett. Bedminster (Bucks) Pa., Deep Run Chh., 1738–1778, as the first minister; Hilltown (Bucks) Pa., Perkasie or Blooming Grove Chh., 1753–1778; Menn.; became blind.

SAMUEL SWEAZEY, sett. Chester (Morris) N.J., Cong. Chh., 1750–1770; removed to Mississippi; Cong.

JOB SWIFT, D.D., b. Sandwich, Mass., 17 June 1743, son of Josiah and Abigail Swift; A.B., Y.C., 1765, A.M.; A.M. (hon.) Dartmouth, 1790, Trustee, 1788–1801; S.T.D., Williams, 1803, Trustee, 1794–1802; Ord. Richmond (Berkshire co.) Mass., 14 Oct. 1767–27 Dec. 1774; Amenia (Dutchess) N.Y., Smithfield Chh., 1775–1783; Manchester, Vt., 1783–1786; inst. Bennington, Vt., 31 May 1786–7 June 1801; Chaplain, Rev. War; d. Enosburg, Vt., 20 Oct. 1804, a. 60.

JOHN DANIEL SYDRICK, b. 1727; arriv. N.Y., N.Y., 1st time, 22 June 1749; 2nd time, 15 Apr. 1754; sett. Philadelphia, Pa., 1774–1784; Graceham, Md.; Hope (Warren) N.J., 1774–1775; Moravian; d. 1790.

TIMOTHY SYMMES, A.M., b. Scituate, Mass., 27 May 1714, son of Timothy and Elizabeth (Collamore) (Rose) Symmes; A.B., H.C., 1733, A.M.; Ord. Millington in East Haddam, Conn., 2 Dec. 1736–1743; sett. Riverhead, L.I., N.Y., Chh. at Lower Aquebogue, 1740–1744; in West Jersey, 1744–1746; Springfield (Union) N.J., inst. 16 Oct. 1746–26 Dec. 1750; New Providence (Union) N.J., Turkey Christian Chh., 1746–1750; Ipswich, Mass., 1st Parish, 1752–1756; Cong.; Presb.; d. Ipswich, Mass., 6 Apr. 1756, a. 41.

JOHN TALBOT, A.M., bapt. Wymondham, Norfolk co., England, 6 Nov. 1645, son of Thomas and Jane (Mede) Talbot; sizar, Christ's Coll., Cambridge, 17 Feb. 1659/60; A.B., 1663/4; Fellow of Peterhouse, 1664; A.M., 1671; Rector, Icklingham St. James, co. Suffolk, 1673–1689; sett. over a chh. in Virginia, ca. 1690–1695; Rector of Fretheme, co. Gloucester, England, 1695–1701; Chaplain, H.M.S. "Centurion", 1702; came again to America, 24 Apr. 1702; 1st resident S.P.G. missionary in N.J., 1702–1704; sett. Albany, N.Y., 1704–1704; Burlington, N.J., St. Mary's Chh., 1704–1705, 1706–1724; Woodbridge, N.J., 1704–1705, 1707–1709; Perth Amboy, N.J., 1704–1704; Hopewell, N.J., 1705–1723; Elizabeth, N.J., 1707–1709; Bristol (Bucks) Pa., Chh. of St. James the Greater, 1712–1727; Philadelphia, Pa., Christ Chh., 1715–1715 supply, June 1724–1727, stated supply; non-juror, consecrated Bishop with Dr. Robert Welton; Ep.; d. Burlington, N.J., 29 Nov. 1727.

BENJAMIN TALLMADGE, A.M., b. New Haven, Conn., 31 Dec. 1725, son of Capt. James and Hannah (Harrison) Tallmadge; A.B., Y.C., 1747, A.M.; Ord. Setauket Chh., Brookhaven, L.I., N.Y., 23 Oct. 1754;

sett. Setauket, 1752–15 June 1785; Presb.; d. Setauket, L.I., N.Y., 5 Feb. 1785, a. 61.

JACOB TANNER, son of Michael Danner or Donner; sett. Codorus (York) Pa., 1758–1770; Monocacy (Frederick) Md., 1770–1789; Germ. Bapt.; living 1789.

JOSEPH TATE, b. 1711, Ord. East Donegal (Lancaster) Pa., 23 Nov. 1748; sett. Cumberland (Adams) Pa., Marsh Creek Chh. at Gettysburg, 1748–1754; Silver Spring (Cumberland) Pa., Chh. at Lower Pennsborough, 1748–1758; East Donegal, Pa., 1748–1770; Highland (Adams) Pa., 1748–1768; sett. Wilmington (New Hanover) North Carolina, 1770–1774; visited Fairforest, S.C., 1754; kept a classical school at Wilmington; Old Side Presb.; d. Wilmington, N.C., 11 Oct. 1774, a. 63.

DANIEL TAYLOR, A.M., b. Saybrook, Conn., 15 Jan. 1684, son of Justice Daniel Taylor; A.B., Y.C., 1707, A.M.; sett. Smithtown, L.I., N.Y., Chh. at Nissequag (Nissequoque), 1713–1717; Orange (Essex) N.J., at Newark Mountain, 1721–1748; Presb.; d. Orange, N.J., 8 Jan. 1747/8, a. 64 (GS).

JOHN TAYLOR, A.B., b. New Haven, Conn., 5 Oct. 1678, son of the Rev. Joseph Taylor; A.B., H.C., 1699; sett. Southampton, L.I., N.Y., 1700–1701; Cong.; Presb.; d. Southampton, L.I., N.Y., 10 Aug. 1701, a. 23 (GS).

JOSEPH TAYLOR, A.M., b. Cambridge, Mass., 1651, son of John and Katherine Taylor; A.B., H.C., 1669, A.M.; sett. New Haven, Conn., 1674–1679; Ord. Southampton, L.I., N.Y., Mar. 1680; sett. Southampton, L.I., N.Y., 1679–1682; Cong.; d. Southampton, L.I., N.Y., 14 Apr. 1682, a. 31 (GS).

DAVID TELFAIR, b. 1720; arriv. in America, 1766; settlement not known; Associate Presb.; d. 11 Apr. 1789, a. 69.

JOHN CONRAD TEMPLEMAN, bapt. Weinheim, Palatinate, 22 Mar. 1692, son of Henry and Anna Maria (Linck) Templeman; tailor at Heidelberg, Germany; came to America, between 1721 and 1725; resided in the Conestoga valley, 1725, and in the Lebanon valley, 1735; Ord. Lancaster (Lanc.) Pa., 21 Sept. 1752; Ephrata (Lanc.) Pa., Bethany Chh., 1725–1727; sett. Conestoga (Lanc.) Pa., 1727–1760; Penn (Lanc.) Pa., White Oaks Chh., 1727–1752; Mount Joy (Lanc.) Pa., Miller's Chh., 1727–1760; Upper Leacock (Lanc.) Pa., Hellers' Hill, Conestoga or Salem Chh., 1727–1760; Swatara (Lebanon) Pa., 1727–1760; also Little Swatara Chh., 1754–1760; Brecknock (Lanc.) Pa., Muddy Creek Chh., 1734–1739, Dec. 1745–1748; North Annville (Leb.) Pa., Hill or Quittopehilla Chh., 1735–1760; Jonestown (Leb.) Pa., 1745–1760; Elizabethtown (Lanc.) Pa., 1750–1760; Lebanon (Leb.) Pa., Tabor Chh., 1750–1760; Rapho (Lanc.) Pa., 1753–1760; North Lebanon (Leb.) Pa., St. Jacob's or Kimmerling Chh., 1754–1761; Earl (Lanc.) Pa., Zeltenreich Chh., 1756–1760; (Good adds: Heidelberg, Pa., Muehlbach Chh., 1751–1754;

and West Cocalico (Lanc.) Pa., Swamp or Little Cocalico Chh., 1755–1760); became blind, 1757; Germ. Ref.; d. Lebanon, Pa., 1761.

GILBERT TENNENT, D.D., b. co. Armagh, Ireland, 5 Feb. 1702/3, son of the Rev. William (I) and Catharine (Kennedy) Tennent; came to America, a. 14 years, ca. 1716; A.M. (hon.) Y.C., 1725; D.D.; lic. Philadelphia, May 1725; Ord. New Brunswick, N.J., 1726–1743; sett. New Castle, Del., 1st Chh., 1726–1727; Philadelphia, Pa., 2nd Presb. or Whitefield Soc., May 1743–1764; Trustee of Princeton, 1746–1764; went abroad in 1753 to solicit funds for Princeton; in 1740, he went on a preaching tour to Boston; Old Side Presb.; d. Philadelphia, Pa., 10 Feb. 1764, a. 62 (GS).

JOHN TENNENT, b. co. Antrim, Ireland, 12 Nov. 1707, son of the Rev. William (I) and Catharine (Kennedy) Tennent; came to America, a. 12 years; ed. Log Coll.; lic. by the New Castle Presbytery, 18 Sept. 1729; Ord. Freehold, N.J., Tennent Chh., 19 Nov. 1730–23 Apr. 1732; Presb.; d. Freehold, N.J., 23 Apr. 1732, a. 25 (GS).

WILLIAM (I) TENNENT, b. Ireland, 1673, a distant relation to the Laird of Dundas and the Earl of Panmure; grad. U. of Edinburgh, 11 July 1693; Ord. Ep., by the Bishop of Down, 22 Sept. 1706; arriv. Philadelphia, 6 Sept. 1718; became a Presb., 17 Sept. 1718; received by the Synod of Philadelphia, 17 Sept. 1718; sett. East Chester (Westchester) N.Y., 22 Nov. 1718–May 1720; Bedford (Westchester) N.Y., 3 May 1720–Aug. 1721; Bensalem (Bucks) Pa., 1721–1726; Smithfield (Monroe) Pa., 1721–1726; Warwick (Bucks) Pa., 1726–1742; founder of the Log Coll.; Ep.; Presb.; d. Warwick, Pa., 6 May 1746, a. 73 (GS).

WILLIAM (II) TENNENT, b. co. Antrim, Ireland, 3 June 1705, son of the Rev. William (I) and Catharine (Kennedy) Tennent; came to America, ae. 13, in 1718; Ord. Freehold (Monmouth) N.J., Tennent Chh., 25 Oct. 1753; sett. Freehold, N.J., 1732–1777; sett. Kingston (Franklin) N.J., 1750–1750; Presb.; d. Freehold, N.J., 8 Mar. 1777, a. 72 (GS).

WILLIAM MACKY TENNENT, D.D., b. New Castle co., Del., 1 Jan. 1744, son of the Rev. Charles and Martha (Macky) Tennent; A.B., Princeton, 1763, Trustee, 1785–1808; D.D., Y.C., 1794; lic. 17 June 1772; Ord. Greenfield, Conn., 17 June 1772–Dec. 1781; sett. Abington (Montgomery) Pa., 1781–1810; Chaplain, Conn. Regt., Rev. War, 1776; moderator, General Assembly of the Presb. Chh., 1797; Presb.; d. Abington, Pa., 2 Dec. 1810, a. 66.

PETER TESSCHENMAEKER, ed. Leyden, 1669, Groningen, 1671, and Utrecht, 1671–1673; Ord. South River (Middlesex) N.J., 9 Oct. 1679 (first Dutch Reformed minister ordained in America); sett. Kingston (Ulster) N.Y., Chh. at Esopus, 1675–1676, Apr. 1678–Sept. 1678; Guiana, South America, 1676–1678; New Castle (New Castle) Del., 1st Chh., 1679–1682; Staten Island, N.Y., Dutch Ref. Chh. at Port Richmond, 1680–1682, Fr. Ref. Chh. at Fresh Kills, 1682–1683, Fr. Ref. Chh. at South Side, 1682–1683; Schenectady, N.Y., 1682–1690/1; Hackensack (Bergen) N.J., Chh. at New Barbadoes, 1686–1687; Dutch Ref.; massacred by the Indians at Schenectady, N.Y., 8 Feb. 1690/1.

Dominie TETARD (Tetrard?), sett. Fordham, N.Y. (formerly West Farms, now part of the City of N.Y.), 1712–1744; French Ref.

JEAN PIERRE TETRARD, b. Switzerland, 1722 (poss. a son or relative of the preceding), sett. Charleston, S.C., Huguenot Chh., 1753–1764; N.Y., N.Y., Chh. of the Saint Esprit, 1764–1767; New Rochelle (Westchester) N.Y., Fr. Ref. Chh., 1764–1775; Fordham, N.Y., 1764–1775; Fr. Ref.; d. N.Y. state, 1787.

DANIEL THANE, A.M., b. Scotland; ed. Aberdeen; A.B., Princeton, 1748; A.M.; Ord. Connecticut Farms (Union) N.J., 29 Aug. 1750–1756; inst. New Castle (New Castle) Del., 1st Chh., 1 May 1757–1763; White Clay Creek, Del., New Side Chh., 1757–1763; Christiana Bridge (New Castle) Del., 1753–1763; New Windsor (Orange) N.Y., 1763–1764; Presb.; d. Del., 1764.

DANIEL THAXTER, sett. Wallpack (Sussex) N.J., Old Shapanack Chh., 1772–1785; Presb.

JOHN THOMAS, b. Radnor, Wales, 9 Dec. 1703, son of the Rev. William Thomas; called to the ministry, 1749; Ord. 1751; sett. Montgomery (Montgomery) Pa., 1749–1783; Hilltown (Bucks) Pa., Upper Perkasie Chh., 1749–1783, and Lower Chh., 1749–1783; New Britain (Bucks) Pa., Perkasie Chh., 1754–1783; Bapt.; d. Montgomery, Pa., 1790.

JOHN THOMAS, K.B. for Pa., 5 July 1700; sett. Philadelphia, Pa., Christ Chh., assistant and school-master, 1700–1704; Oxford, Pa., Trinity Chh., assistant and school-master, 1702–1704; inst. Hempstead, L.I., N.Y., St. George's Chh., 26 Dec. 1704–1724; S.P.G. missionary; Ep.; d. Hempstead, L.I., N.Y., 1724.

JOSEPH THOMAS, sett. New Britain (Bucks) Pa., 1749–1766; Ord. 1766; Bapt.

OWEN THOMAS, b. Gwrgodllys, Cilmanllwyd, Pembroke, Wales, 1692; came to America, 1707; sett. Pencader Hundred (New Castle) Del., Welsh Tract Chh., 1740–27 May 1748; Newlin (Chester) Pa., Hephzibah Chh., 1748–1759; Yellow Springs (Frederick) Md., 1748–1760; Vincent (Chester) Pa., 1748–1760; Bapt.; d. Vincent, Pa., 12 Nov. 1760, a. 68 (GS).

WILLIAM THOMAS, b. Llanwenarth, Monmouthshire, Wales, 1678; arriv. in America, 14 Feb. 1712; sett. Montgomery (Montgomery) Pa., 1722–1757; Hilltown (Bucks) Pa., Lower Chh., 1737–1757, and Perkasie Chh., 1737–1757; New Britain (Bucks) Pa., Upper Perkasie Chh., 1754–1757; Bapt.; lay preacher; d. Montgomery, Pa., 1757.

THOMAS THOMPSON, A.M., b. Gilling, Richmond, co. York, England, 1708, son of William Thompson; adm. pens. Christ's Coll., Camb., 29 Feb. 1727/8, A.B., 1731/2, A.M., 1735, Fellow, 1738–1745; Senior Dean, 1744; lic. by Bsp. of London, 25 Mar. 1744/5; K.B., N.J.,

2 Apr. 1745; sailed, 8 May 1745; arriv. N.Y., N.Y., 29 Sept. 1745; sett. Shrewsbury, N.J., Christ Chh., 1745–Sept. 1751; Middletown, N.J., Christ Chh., 1745–1751; Freehold, N.J., St. Peter's Chh., 1745–1751; Allentown, N.J., Christ Chh., 1745–1751; left N.J., 25 Nov. 1751; sett. Sierre Leone, West Africa, 1751–1756; vicar, Reculver, Kent, England, 1756–1761; vicar, Elham, England, 1761–1763; in 1758, he published a short account of his missionary travels; Ep.; d. Elham, England, 5 June 1773.

JOHN THOMSON, b. Scotland, 1690, came from co. Down, Ireland, to N.Y., N.Y., 1715; Ord. Lewes (Sussex) Del., Apr. 1717–1729; Bart (Lanc.) Pa., Middle Octoraro Chh., 1730–1732; Chestnut Level (Lanc.) Pa., Drumore Chh., 1732–31 July 1744; North Middleton, Pa., Meeting House Springs Chh., 1735–1735; Opequon Creek (Frederick) Va., 1739–1739; Cub Creek (Charlotte) Va., Round Oak Chh., 1744–1753; Buffalo (Prince Edward) Va., 1744–1753; made missionary visits to North Carolina, 1744, 1751, 1753; Moderator of the Presb. Chh. of America, 1722; Presb.; d. Centre, North Carolina, 1753.

SAMUEL THOMSON, Ord. Pennsborough, Pa., 14 Nov. 1739; sett. Guilford (Franklin) Pa., Falling Springs Chh. at Chambersburg, 1737–1739; Silver Spring (Cumberland) Pa., Lower Pennsborough Chh., 1739–1745; North Middleton (Cumberland) Pa., Meeting House Springs Chh., Upper Pennsborough, 1739–1749; Straban (Adams) Pa., Hunterstown Chh., 1749–1787; Presb.; d. Hunterstown, Pa., 29 Apr. 1787.

THOMAS THOMSON, Ord. (Bsp. of Litchfield) 15 Nov. 1730; K.B., 1 Sept. 1743; sett. St. Bartholomew's Parish (Colleton) S.C., 1734–1744; St. George's Parish, Dorchester (Dorchester) S.C., 1744–1746; returned to England; K.B. again for N.J., 20 July 1748; sett. St. John's Parish (Colleton) S.C., Sept. 1748–1750; Salem (Salem) N.J., St. John's Chh., 1750–1750; Chester (Del.) Pa., St. Paul's Chh., 1750–1758; Concord (Del.) Pa., St. John's Chh., 1750–1756; Antrim Parish (Halifax) Va., 1762–1763, an aged man; Ep.

WILLIAM THOMSON, D.D., b. Pa., 22 May 1735, son of the Rev. Samuel Thomson (a Presb. clergyman) of Carlisle, Pa.; D.D., Washington Coll., 1785; Ord. deacon (Bsp. of London) 1759; lic. 23 Dec. 1759, K.B. for Pa., 16 Jan. 1760; S.P.G. missionary, 1760–1769; sett. Carlisle (Cumberland) Pa., St. John's Chh., 1760–1769; Huntington (Adams) Pa., Chh. at York Springs, 1760–1769; York (York) Pa., St. John's Chh., 1760–1769; Trenton (Mercer) N.J., St. Michael's Chh., 1 Apr. 1769–12 Apr. 1773; resigned; Lawrence (Mercer) N.J., Maidenhead Chh., 1769–1773; Allentown (Monmouth) N.J., Christ Chh., 1769–1773; North Elk (Cecil) Md., St. Mary Anne's Parish, 1773–1779; North Sassafras Parish (Cecil) Md., 1779–1785; Augustine Parish (Cecil) Md., 1780–1785; Ep.; d. North Sassafras Parish (Cecil) Md., 1785, a. 50.

DANIEL THORN, b. Delaware; Ord. by the Donegal Presbytery, between May 1746 and May 1747; sett. Chestnut Level (Lanc.) Pa., Chh. at Drumore, 1746–1750; Presb.; d. Chestnut Level, Pa., 1750.

Colonial Clergy of the Middle Colonies

SYDENHAM THORN, K.B. for Pa., 12 Sept. 1774; sett. Philadelphia, Pa., St. Paul's Chh., 1774-1781; Milford (Kent) Del., Christ Chh., 1774-1781; Mispillion (Kent) Del., Christ Chh., 1774-1781; Ep.

AMANDEUS PAUL THRANE, b. Aalborg, Jutland, Denmark, 1716; theol. student at Lindheim, 1744, a. 25; cantor and asst. minister at Aalborg, before 1744; arriv. N.Y., N.Y., 19 Oct. 1761; sett. Bethlehem, Pa., as head pastor, 1761-1776; Moravian; d. Bethlehem, Pa., 19 Apr. 1776.

WILLIAM THROOP, A.M., b. Bristol, R.I., 22 Aug. 1720, son of William and Abigail Throop; A.B., Y.C., 1743, A.M.; A.M., Princeton, 1755; Ord. Mansfield, Conn., 2nd or North Chh. at Storrs, 11 Oct. 1744, as the first minister; sett. Storrs, Conn., 1744-15 Jan. 1746/7; inst. Southold, L.I., N.Y., 21 Sept. 1748-1756; Cong.; Presb.; d. Southold, L.I., N.Y., 29 Sept. 1756, a. 36.

JACOB TILL, arriv. N.Y., N.Y., 19 Sept. 1753; sett. Warwick (Lanc.) Pa., St. James's Chh. at Lititz, 1759-1760; Moravian.

WILLIAM TILLINGHAST, A.M., A.M. (hon.) Brown, 1774; sett. Pa.; Bapt.

JOHN TITTLE, K.B. for N.Y., 24 Sept. 1729; Ep.

LARS TOLLSTADIUS, sett. Philadelphia, Pa., Gloria Dei Chh., 1702-1702; Swedesborough (Gloucester) N.J., Trinity Chh., on Raccoon Creek, 1703-1706; Pennsneck (Salem) N.J., St. George's Chh., 1703-1706; Sw. Luth.; drowned, 9 May 1706.

ICHABOD TOMPKINS, b. Morristown, N.J.; Ruling Elder at Morristown, 19 Aug. 1752; lic. 28 Dec. 1757; Ord. Morristown (Morris) N.J., 6 Nov. 1759; sett. Morristown, N.J., 1759-1761; Bapt.; d. Morristown, N.J., 8 Jan. 1761.

EPENETUS TOWNSEND, A.M., b. Cedar Swamp, L.I., N.Y., Apr. 1742, son of Micajah and Elizabeth (Platt) Townsend; A.B., Columbia, 1759, A.M.; Ord. London, 1767; K.B. for N.Y., 7 Jan. 1768; arriv. N.Y., N.Y., 22 Apr. 1768; sett. North Salem (Westchester) N.Y., St. James's Chh., 29 May 1768-1779; South Salem (Westchester) N.Y., St. John's Chh., 1768-1779; Chaplain of a Tory Regt., 1779; Ep.; d. off Halifax, Nova Scotia, 1779.

PETER TRANBERG, sett. Pennsneck (Salem) N.J., St. George's Chh., 1726-1741; Swedesborough (Gloucester) N.J., Trinity Chh. in Raccoon Creek, 1726-1741; Chester (Del.) Pa., Chh. at Upland, 1742-1748; Wilmington (New Castle) Del., Old Swedes Chh., 1742-1748; preached in German, Swedish and English; Sw. Luth.; d. Pennsneck, N.J., 8 Nov. 1748.

AGUR TREADWELL, A.M., b. Stratford, Conn., 16 Dec. 1734, son of Lieut. Hezekiah and Mehitable (Minor) Treadwell; A.B., Y.C., 1760, A.M.; A.B., Columbia, 1761; became an Ep., Aug. 1760; Ord. Apr. 1762; lic. 30 Apr. 1762; K.B. for N.J., 7 May 1762; sett. Trenton (Mercer) N.J., St. Michael's Chh., 4 Apr. 1763-1765; Lawrence (Mercer) N.J., Maidenhead Chh., 1763-1765; Allentown (Monmouth) N.J., Christ Chh., 1763-1765; S.P.G. missionary, 1763-1765; Ep.; d. Trenton, N.J., 19 Aug. 1765, a. 31.

JOSEPH TREAT, A.M., b. Abington, Pa., son of the Rev. Dr. Richard and Rebecca Treat; A.B., Princeton, 1757, A.M., Tutor, 1758-1760; lic. 1760; sett. N.Y., N.Y., 1st Presb. Chh., 1762-1784; Greenwich (Warren) N.J., 1776-1776, 1784-1797; Chaplain, Continental Army; Presb.; d. Greenwich, N.J., 1797.

RICHARD TREAT, D.D., b. Milford, Conn., 25 Sept. 1708, son of Capt. Joseph Treat; A.B., Y.C., 1725, A.M., D.D., 1776; Trustee, Princeton, 1748-1778; Ord. Abington (Montgomery) Pa., 30 Dec. 1731-1778; sett. Norriton (Montgomery) Pa., 1731-1741, 1763-1772; Tinicum (Bucks) Pa., 1741-1768; Presb.; d. Abington, Pa., 20 Nov. 1778, a. 70.

Bishop HANS TSCHANTZ, minister and Bishop in Europe; came to America, 1711; sett. Strasburg (Lanc.) Pa., 1717-1742; West Lampeter (Lanc.) Pa., Willow Street Chh., 1719-1742; Menn.; d. West Lampeter, Pa., after 1742.

NATHAN TUCKER, A.B., b. Milton, Mass.; A.B., H.C., 1744; Ord. (N.Y. Presbytery) 9 Apr. 1747; Presb.; d. Stratford, Conn., Dec. 1747.

SAMUEL TUDOR, A.M., b. Windsor, Conn., 8 Mar. 1704/5, son of Samuel and Abigail (Filley) Tudor; A.B., Y.C., 1728, A.M.; sett. Goshen (Orange) N.Y., 1733-1735; Ord. Windsor, Conn., Jan. 1740-1757; Cong.; Presb.; d. Windsor, Conn., 21 Sept. 1757, a. 53.

JAMES TUTTLE, A.M., A.B., Princeton, 1764, A.M.; Ord. Hanover (Morris) N.J., Parsippany Chh., Apr. 1768-1770; sett. Rockaway (Morris) N.J., Pequannock Chh., 1768-1771; Presb.; d. Rockaway, N.J., Apr. 1771.

MOSES TUTTLE, A.M., b. New Haven, Conn., 25 June 1715, son of John and Hannah (Humiston) Tuttle; A.B., Y.C., 1745, A.M.; Ord. Granville, Mass., Jan. 1746/7-1754; sett. Laurel (Sussex) Del., 1756-Sept. 1762; sett. New Jersey, May 1764-May 1769; Cong.; New Side Presb.; d. Southold, L.I., N.Y., 21 Nov. 1785, a. 70.

ERIC UNANDER, sett. Swedesborough (Gloucester) N.J., Trinity Chh. on Raccoon Creek, 1749-1755; Pennsneck (Salem) N.J., St. George's Chh., 1749-1756; Marcus Hook (Del.) Pa., St. Matin's Chh., 1749-1756; Wilmington, Del., Old Swedes Chh., 1755-1759; Chester (Del.) Pa., Chh. at Upland, 1755-1759; left for Sweden, July 1760; Sw. Luth.

PETER UNDERHILL, b. Oyster Bay, L.I., N.Y., 24 Jan. 1737, son of Peter and Penelope (Alling) Underhill; sett. Oyster Bay, L.I., N.Y., Separatist Bapt. Chh., 1759-1789, and 1st Bapt. Chh., 1789-1806, during which time he was asst. to Dr. Benjamin Coles, 1783-1806, who had formerly been the minister of the Baptist Chh. at Hopewell, N.J. (1774-1781), q.v.; blacksmith and preacher; Bapt.; d. Oyster Bay, L.I., N.Y., 24 June 1806.

Bishop MARTIN URNER, b. Alsace, France, 1695, son of Ulrich Urner, of Swiss descent; came to Pa., 1708; resided in Lancaster co., Pa., 1712; Ord. Coventry (Chester) Pa., 1729; sett. Coventry, Pa., 1722-1755; Germ. Bapt.; d. Coventry, Pa., 1755.

Bishop MARTIN URNER II, b. New Hanover, Pa., 1725, son of Jacob Urner; Ord. Bishop, Coventry (Chester) Pa., 1756; sett. Coventry, Pa., 1756-1799; Germ. Bapt.; d. Coventry, Pa., 1799.

WILLIAM URQUHART, b. Scotland; K.B. for N.Y., 29 Jan. 1703/4; Jamaica, L.I., N.Y., Grace Chh., induct. 27 July 1704-1708; sett. Flushing, L.I., N.Y., St. George's Chh., 1705-1707; Ep.; d. Jamaica, L.I., N.Y., 1709.

JOHN URY, sett. N.Y., 1741, as a school-teacher; was accused of fomenting a plot and of being a Roman Catholic—both were incorrect, but he was declared guilty and hanged; a non-juring Ep. clergyman; hanged, N.Y., 15 Aug. 1741.

ARTHUR USSHER, A.M., b. co. Waterford, Ireland, 1705, son of James Ussher, gent.; pens. Trinity Coll., Dublin, 9 June 1724, a. 19 yrs.; scholar, 1727, A.B., 1728, A.M., 1734; K.B., 10 Feb. 1736/7; S.P.G. missionary; sett. Dover (Kent) Del., Christ Chh., 1737-1743; Milford (Kent) Del., Christ Chh., 1740-1743; Mispillion (Kent) Del., Christ Chh., 1740-1743; Smyrna (Kent) Del., St. Peter's Chh., 1740-1743; Broadkill (Sussex) Del., St. John Baptist Chh., 1744-1752; Cedar Creek Hundred, Del., St. Matthew's Chh., 1744-1752; Dagsborough (Sussex) Del., Prince George's Chapel, 1744-1752; Indian River (Sussex) Del., St. George's Chapel, 1744-1752; Lewes (Sussex) Del., St. Peter's Chh., 1744-1752; Newtown (Del.) Pa., St. David's Chh. at Radnor, 1749-1753; resigned, 1753; Ep.

RICHARD UTLEY, b. Yorkshire, England, 22 Feb. 1722; became a Moravian, 1742; arriv. Staten Island, N.Y., 26 Nov. 1743; Ord. deacon, Philadelphia, Pa., 14 Aug. 1746; sett. N.Y., N.Y., 1743-1748; Lancaster (Lanc.) Pa., 1748-1748; Oley (Berks) Pa., 1749-1750; Graceham (Frederick) Md., 1752-1755, 1770-1771; Staten Island, N.Y., 1755-1755; Newport, R.I., 1758-1758; Philadelphia, Pa., 1762-1772; Bethabara, North Carolina, at Wacovia, 1766-1770; Salem, N.C., 1772-1775; also an itinerant preacher at the following places between the years 1743-1749; Dover, Duck Creek and Lewes, Del., Burlington, Cranbury, Lawrence, Middletown, Princeton, Swedish Settlements, and Trenton, N.J.; and Durham (Bucks), Lower Salford (Montgomery), Manatawny (Berks), Southampton (Bucks), and Upper Providence (Montgomery), all in Pa.; Moravian; d. Salem, N.C., 9 Oct. 1775.

FRANCIS VAILLANT DU GUESLIS, sett. Victor (Ontario) N.Y., Mission of the Conception to the Senecas, 1678-1709; R.C.

JACOB VAN ARSDALEN, A.M., A.B., Princeton, 1765, A.M., Trustee, 1793-1802; sett. Kingston (Franklin) N.J., 19 June 1771-13 Dec. 1775; Springfield (Union) N.J., 1775-1801; Presb.; d. Springfield, N.J., 1803.

JOHN HERMAN VAN BASTEN, arriv. on the "St. Andrew Galley," 26 Sept. 1737; preached as a candidate in theology, at Poughkeepsie, N.Y., 1739–1739; sett. Jamaica, L.I., N.Y., 1739–1740; Success, L.I., N.Y., Success Pond Chh. at North Hempstead, 1739–1740; Oyster Bay, L.I., N.Y., Chh. at Wolver Hollow, 1739–1740; Newtown, L.I., N.Y., 1739–1740; Dutch Ref.

ELIAS VAN BUNSCHOOTEN, A.B., b. New Hackensack, N.Y., 26 Oct. 1738, son of Teunis Van Bunschooten; A.B., Princeton, 1768; Trustee of Rutgers Coll., 1787–1815; Ord. 1773; sett. Schagticoke (Rensselaer) N.Y., 1773–1785; Minisink (Sullivan) N.Y., 28 Aug. 1785–1799; Mahakemack (i.e. Port Jervis) (Orange) N.Y., 28 Aug. 1785–1799; Wallpack (Sussex) N.J., 28 Aug. 1785–1799; Westtown (Orange) N.Y., 1788–1799; Clove (Dutchess) N.Y., 1788–1812; Dutch Ref.; d. New Brunswick, N.J., 10 Jan. 1815, a. 76(GS).

JACOB VAN BUSKIRK, b. Hackensack, N.J., 11 Feb. 1739, son of Captain Jacob Van Buskirk; ed. Halle; studied under Weyberg and Muhlenberg, 1759–1762; Ord. New Hanover, Pa., 12 Oct. 1763, sett. New Hanover (Montgomery) Falkner's Swamp Chh., 1762–1765; Germantown, Pa., asst., 1765–1769; Douglass (Berks) Pa., Oley Hill Chh., 1762–1765; Upper Providence(Montgomery) Pa., Augustus Chh. at Trappe, 1763–1765; Pikeland (Chester) Pa., Zion Chh., 1763–1765; Upper Dublin, Pa., Puff's Chh., 1765–1769, 1793–1800; Whitemarsh (Montgomery) Pa., St. Peter's Chh., Barren Hill, 1765–1769; Allentown (Lehigh) Pa., St. Paul's Chh., 1769–1778; Germantown, Pa., St. Michael's Chh., 1765–1786; Lower Macungie (Lehigh) Pa., 9 July 1769–18 Feb. 1800; Upper Milford (Lehigh) Pa., Zionsville Chh., 1769–1793; 1795–1800; Whitehall (Lehigh) Pa., Egypt Chh., 1769–1770; Salisbury (Lehigh) Pa., 1769–1793, 1795–1800; Upper Saucon (Lehigh) Pa., St. Paul's, Blue, or Organ Chh., 1769–1793, 1797–1800; Lower Saucon (Northampton) Pa., 1769–1793, 1795–1800; Whitpain (Montgomery) Pa., St. John's Chh. at Centre Square, 1793–1800; Gwynedd (Montgomery) Pa., 1793–1800; North Wales (Montgomery) Pa., 1783–1797; Luth.; d. North Wales, Pa., 5 Aug. 1800.

LAURENTIUS VANDENBOSCH (or Lawrence Van den Bosch), arriv. Boston, Mass., 1685; sett. Boston, Mass., French Protestant Chh., 1685–1686; Kingston (Ulster) N.Y., Dutch Ref. Chh. at Esopus, 20 June 1686–Oct. 1689; Staten Island, N.Y., French Ref. Chh., South Side, 1686–1687; North Sassafras Parish (Cecil) Md., 1692–1696; Shrewsbury Parish (Kent) Md., 1692–1696; St. Paul's Parish (Kent) Md., 1693–1696; Huguenot; Dutch Ref.; Ep.; d. St. Paul's Parish (Kent) Md., 1696.

BENJAMIN VANDERLINDE, b. Pollifly, near Hackensack, N.J., 1719; studied under Dorsius and Goetschius; Ord. N.J., 1748; sett. Paramus (Bergen) N.J., 27 Sept. 1748; Ponds (Bergen) N.J., 1748–1789; Saddle River (Bergen) N.J., 1784–1789; Dutch Ref.; d. N.J., 1789.

JOHN BERNHARD VAN DIEREN, b. Koenigsberg, Germany; came from London to N.Y., N.Y.; Ord. New Hanover (Montgomery) Pa., 1717, by the Rev. Gerhard Henkel; sett. Schoharie (Schoharie) N.Y., Luth. Chh. at Huntersfield, 1717-1724; sett. N.J.: Luth.

PETRUS HENRICUS VAN DRIESSEN, called Coevordiensis, brother of Johannes Van Driessen; matric. Groningen, 2 Nov. 1705; came to America, 1712; sett. Albany, N.Y., 1712-1738; Kinderhook (Columbia) N.Y., 1712-1727; Linlithgo (Columbia) N.Y., 13 Jan. 1722-1737; Fishkill (Dutchess) N.Y., 1727-1731; also an Indian missionary; Dutch Ref.; d. Jan. 1738.

JOHANNES VAN DRIESSEN, b. 1697; matric. Groningen, 13 May 1717; Ord. New Haven, Conn., (as a Congregationalist); sett. Claverack (Columbia) N.Y., 1 Aug. 1727-1728; Kinderhook (Columbia) N.Y., 1727-1735; Livingston Manor (Sullivan) N.Y., 1727-1728; New Paltz (Ulster) N.Y., 1727-1736, 1751-1751; Poughkeepsie (Dutchess) N.Y., 1727-1735, 1751-1751; Linlithgo (Columbia) N.Y., 1727-1738; Germantown (Columbia) N.Y., 1728-1735; Kingsbury (Dutchess) N.Y., 1728-1735; Passaic (Passaic) N.J., Acquackanonk Chh., 1735-1748; Pompton Plains (Morris) N.J., 1735-1748; Paramus (Bergen) N.J., 1731-1732, 1735-1748; Ponds (Bergen) N.J., at Oakland, 1735-1738; silenced 1748; Dutch Ref.

LAURENTIUS VAN GAASBEECK, grad. Leyden U., 25 May 1674; arriv. N.Y., N.Y., 21 Aug. 1678; Ord. Amsterdam, Holland, 7 Mar. 1678; sett. Kingston (Ulster) N.Y., 15 Sept. 1678-1680; Hurley (Ulster) N.Y., 1678-1680; Marbletown (Ulster) N.Y., 1678-1680; physician; Dutch Ref.; d. N.Y., N.Y., Feb. 1680.

JOHANNES MARTINUS VAN HARLINGEN, b. near Millstone, N.J., 1724, son of Johannes Martinus and Maria (Bussing) Van Harlingen; ed. Princeton; Trustee of Rutgers Coll., 1770; Ord. Amsterdam, Holland, 4 May 1761; sett. Harlingen (Somerset) N.J., Chh. at Montgomery, 1762-1795; Neshanic (Somerset) N.J., Chh. at Hillsborough, 1762-1795; Hillsborough (Somerset) N.J., Chh. at Millstone, 1766-1774; Conewago (Adams) Pa., Chh. at Hunterstown, 1769-1769, 1772-1772; Dutch Ref.; d. Harlingen, N.J., 23 Dec. 1795, a. 71 (GS).

PETER PETERSON VAN HORN, b. Middletown (Bucks) Pa., 24 Aug. 1719, son of Peter Van Horn; Ord. Pennypack Bapt. Chh., Lower Dublin, Pa., 18 June 1747; sett. Lower Dublin, Pa., 1747-1762; Pemberton (Burlington) N.J., Chh. at New Mills, 23 June 1764-2 Apr. 1768; Cape May (Cape May) N.J., 7 Apr. 1770-1775; Dividing Creek (Cumberland) N.J., 1779-1783; Salem (Salem) N.J., 1789 ff.; Bapt.

WILLIAM VAN HORN, A.M., b. Pennypack, Lower Dublin, Pa., 8 July 1747, son of the Rev. Peter Peterson Van Horn; A.M. (hon.) Brown, 1774; Ord. Southampton (Bucks) Pa., 29 May 1772-1785; Scotch Plains, N.J., 1785-1807; Chaplain, Rev. War, 1 Jan. 1778, 1780; Bapt.; d. Pittsburgh, Pa., 31 Oct. 1807, a. 60.

EGGO TONKENS VAN HOVENBERGH, ed. Groningen, 1732; sett. Surinam, South America, 1743–1759; came to N.Y., N.Y., 1750; sett. Claverack (Columbia) N.Y., 1750–1756; Livingston Manor (Sullivan) N.Y., 1750–1756; Linlithgo (Columbia) N.Y., 1750–1756; Rhinebeck Flats (Dutchess) N.Y., 1756–1764; not sett. but preached 1764–1767; Dutch Ref.

RYNIER VAN NEST, b. near North Branch, N.J., 8 Feb. 1739, son of Peter and Margaret (Arianson) Van Nest; studied under Hardenbergh; Trustee of Rutgers, 1786; Ord. 1773; sett. New Paltz (Ulster) N.Y., 2nd or Wallkill Chh., 1774–1778; Shawangunk (Ulster) N.Y., at Bruynswick, 1774–1785; Pawagtenog, N.Y., 1774–1778; Middleburgh (Schoharie) N.Y., at Upper Schoharie, 1774–1780; Schoharie (Schoharie) N.Y., supply, 1780–1785, 1797–1803; Rochester (Ulster) N.Y., 1776–1781; Jamaica, Newtown, Oyster Bay and Success, all on L.I., N.Y., 1785–1797; Dutch Ref.; d. N.Y., 9 July 1813.

WILHELMUS VAN NIEUWENHUYSEN, ed. U. of Leyden, 1661; Ord. Amsterdam, Holland, 16 Mar. 1671; came to America, 1671; sett. N.Y., N.Y., 1st or South Dutch Ref. Chh., 1671–1681; Dutch Ref.; d. N.Y., N.Y., 17 Feb. 1681.

JACOBUS VAN NIST, Ord. America, 1758; sett. Poughkeepsie (Dutchess) N.Y., 1758–1761; Fishkill (Dutchess) N.Y., 1758–1761; Dutch Ref.; d. Fishkill, N.Y., 1761 (GS).

NICHOLAS VAN RENSSELAER, b. Netherlands, 1647, son of the first patroon; matric. Leyden, 1670; Ord. England, deacon, 1665; came to America, 1675; sett. Albany, N.Y., 1675–1677; deposed; Dutch Ref.; d. Albany, N.Y., Nov. 1678.

CORNELIUS VAN SANTVOORD, b. 1688; matric. Leyden, 25 Feb. 1707; arriv. in America, 1718; sett. Staten Island, N.Y., Dutch Ref. Chh. at Port Richmond, 1718–1742, and Richmond Union Dutch Ref. Chh., 1718–1742; inst. Northampton (Bucks) Pa., 30 May 1730–1737; Southampton (Bucks) Pa., Neshaminy Chh., at Churchville, 30 May 1730–1737; Bellville (Essex) N.J., Dutch Ref. Chh. at Second River, 1730–1732; Schenectady, N.Y., 1742–1752; preached in French and Dutch; Dutch Ref.; d. Schenectady, N.Y., 1752.

CORNELIUS VAN SCHIE, b. 1703; matric. Leyden, 1 Aug. 1721; Ord. Amsterdam, Holland, 4 June 1731; came to America, 1731; inst. Fishkill (Dutchess) N.Y., 4 Oct. 1731–1738; Poughkeepsie (Dutchess) N.Y., 1731–1733; Rhinebeck Flats (Dutchess) N.Y., 1731–1733; Claverack (Columbia) N.Y., 1732–1743; Albany, N.Y., 1733–1744; Kinderhook (Columbia) N.Y., 1735–1735; Catskill (Greene) N.Y., 1736–1738; Dutch Ref.; d. Albany, N.Y., 15 Aug. 1744.

ULPANIUS VAN SINDERIN, b. in the Netherlands, 12 Dec. 1708; came to America, 1746; inst. Long Island circuit, 11 Jan. 1746; sett. Brooklyn, Bushwick, Flatlands, Flatbush, and New Utrecht, all on L.I., N.Y., 1746–1784, and Gravesend, 1747–1765; emeritus, 1784; Dutch Ref.; d. 23 July 1796.

PAULUS VAN VLECK (or Van Vlecq), b. Holland, a nephew of Jacob Phoenix of N.Y.; schoolmaster at Kinderhook (Columbia) N.Y., 1702; in N.Y., 1709; Chaplain to the N.Y. Dutch Troops, Fr. and Ind. War, 1709-1710; Ord. July 1710 by the Rev. Bernard Freeman; Bensalem (Bucks) Pa., 1710-1713, 1st minister, of this Dutch Ref. Chh.; Southampton (Bucks) Pa., Neshaminy Dutch Ref. Chh. at Churchville, 1st minister; installed 20 May 1710-1712; Northampton (Bucks) Pa., D.R. Chh., 1st minister, 1710-1712; Norriton (Montgomery) Pa., Presb. Chh., 1710-1715, 1st minister; Germantown, Pa., D.R. Chh., 1710-1713, 1st minister; Whitemarsh (Montgomery) Pa., 1st minister, St. Peter's Germ. Ref. Chh., Barren Hill, 1710-1712; adm. to the Presbytery of Philadelphia, 21 Sept. 1710; Six Mile Run (Somerset) N.J., D.R. Chh. at Franklin, 1710-1712, 1st minister; Dutch Ref.; Presb.; left America, 21 Sept. 1715.

STEPHEN VAN VOORHEES, A.M. (or Van Voorhis), A.B., Princeton, 1765, A.M.; Ord. 1772; sett. Poughkeepsie (Dutchess) N.Y., 1773-1776; Dover (Dutchess) N.Y., 1774-1774; Red Hook Landing (Dutchess) N.Y., 1776-1780; Rhinebeck Flats (Dutchess) N.Y., 2 June 1776-Dec. 1785; Tarrytown (Westchester) N.Y., 1785-1788; Cortlandttown (Westchester) N.Y., 1785-1788; Kingston (Franklin) N.J., Presbyterian Chh., 1793-1796; Assunpinck (Mercer) N.J., near Trenton, 1793-1796; Dutch Ref.; d. N.J., 23 Nov. 1796.

CASPARUS VAN ZUUREN, b. 1648; matric. Leyden, 7 Sept. 1668; Ord. Amsterdam, Holland, 15 Mar. 1677; came to America, 1677; sett. Flatbush, L.I., N.Y., at Midwout, 1677-1685; sett. New Utrecht, Bushwick, Brooklyn, and Flatlands, L.I., N.Y., 1677-1685; Gravesend, L.I., N.Y., 1677-1685; Staten Island, N.Y., D.R. Chh. at Port Richmond, 1680-1685; returned to Holland, 17 May 1685; sett. Gonderach, Holland, 1685-1704; Dutch Ref.

JOHN VARDILL, A.M., b. 1752; A.B., Columbia, 1766, A.M., Fellow and Prof. of Natural Law, 1773-1778; Regius Prof. of Divinity, 1778; A.M., Oxford, 23 June 1774; K.B., N.Y., 26 Apr. 1774; rector, Skirbeck, co. Lincoln, and Fishtoft, co. Lincoln, England, 1780-1811; Ep.; d. Skirbeck, England, 16 Jan. 1811, a. 59.

RUDOLPHUS VARICK, matric. Utrecht, 1666; in the East Indies, 1673-1678; sett. Hem, Holland, 1679-1686; arriv. America, July 1686; sett. L.I., N.Y., 1679-1694, in the following chhs.; Brooklyn, Bushwick, Flatbush, Flatlands, Gravesend and New Utrecht; Staten Island, N.Y., Port Richmond Chh., 1686-1694; New Castle (New Castle) Del., 1st Chh., 1687-1687; Hackensack (Bergen) N.J., D.R. Chh. at New Barbadoes, 1687-1689; Dutch Ref.; d. L.I., N.Y., Aug. 1694.

PETRUS VAS, b. ca. 1656, candidate in theol., 4 May 1699; arriv. Kingston (Ulster) N.Y., 19 Dec. 1710; sett. Kingston, N.Y., Chh. at Esopus, Dec. 1710-1752; Rhinebeck Flats (Dutchess) N.Y., 1731-1742, 1st minister; supply, Staten Island, N.Y., at Port Richmond, 1710-1718, and at Richmond, 1714-1718; Dutch Ref.; d. Kingston, N.Y., 1752, a. 96.

EDWARD VAUGHAN, son of the Rector of Wolver-Newton, Llandaff, Wales; Ord. ca. 1709; K.B. for N.J., 12 Apr. 1709; S.P.G. missionary, N.J.; sett. Elizabethtown (Middlesex) N.J., St. John's Chh., 1709-1747; Woodbridge (Middlesex) N.J., Trinity Chh., 1711-1722, every 2 weeks; Perth Amboy (Middlesex) N.J., St. Peter's Chh., 1709-1711, 1714-1721, every 4th Sunday; Piscataway (Middlesex) N.J., St. James's Chh., preached occasionally, 1711-1722, sett. 1718-1747; Newark (Essex) N.J., Trinity Chh., occasional preacher, 1731-1743; portrait in *Proceedings of the American Antiquarian Society*, 50: 310; Ep.; d. Elizabethtown, N.J., 1747.

SAMUEL VERBRYCK, b. 18 Apr. 1721; Ord. in America, 1749; Trustee, Rutgers Coll.; sett. Tappan (Rockland) N.Y., 1750-1784; Clarkstown (Rockland) N.Y., 1750-1784; Dutch Ref.; d. Tappan, N.Y., 31 Jan. 1784, a. 62 (GS).

Commissary WILLIAM VESEY, A.M., b. Braintree (now Quincy) Mass., 10 Aug. 1674, bapt. 1st Chh. in Braintree, 6 Sept. 1674, son of Ensign William and Mary Veazie; A.B., H.C., 1693; A.M., Merton Coll., Oxford, 8 July 1697; Ord. London, England, 2 Aug. 1697; N.Y., N.Y., inst. Trinity Chh., 6 Feb. 1696/7; induct., 25 Dec. 1697; sett. 2 Nov. 1696-1746; Bishop's Commissary for N.Y., 1712-1746; he was the 1st minister of the 1st Ep. Chh. in N.Y., N.Y.; as Bishop's Commissary he had much to do with the founding of Ep. Chhs. in the state of N.Y.; he began with one; he ended with twenty-two; K.B. for N.Y., 22 Jan. 1714/5; Brooklyn, N.Y., 1702-1705; Ep.; d. N.Y., N.Y., 11 July 1746, a. 71.

JOHN VICARY, lic. for Pa., 1719; sett. Philadelphia, Pa., Christ Chh., 4 Sept. 1719-1723; Ep.; d. Philadelphia, Pa., bef. 12 Apr. 1723.

JOHN FREDERICK VIGERA, sett. New Hanover (Montgomery) Pa., Falkner's Swamp Chh., 1744-1745, as asst. minister; stated supply, Lower Milford (Lehigh) Pa., Upper Milford Chh., 1749-1749; schoolmaster; Luth.

LUDWIG FERDINAND VOCK (or Lewis Ferdinand Vock), b. abroad, 15 Nov. 1690; arriv. Philadelphia, Dec. 1749; sett. Lancaster (Lanc.) Pa., Jan. 1750/1-Jan. 1751/2; Ephrata (Lanc.) Pa., Bethany Chh., 1750-1751; Germ. Ref.; d. soon after Jan. 1751/2.

JOHN LEWIS VOIGHT, b. Mansfield, Saxony, 9 Nov. 1731; teacher at the Orphan House at Halle; Ord. Wernigerode, Germany, 1763; arriv. Philadelphia, 1 Apr. 1764; sett. Whitemarsh (Montgomery) Pa., St. Peter's Chh., Barren Hill, 1764-1765; Germantown, Pa., St. Michael's Chh., 1764-1765; Upper Providence (Montgomery) Pa., Augustus Chh. at Trappe, 1765-1800; New Hanover (Montgomery) Pa., Falkner's Swamp Chh., 1765-1800; Douglass (Berks) Pa., Oley Hill Chh., 1765-1800; Amity (Berks) Pa., St. Paul's Chh., 1767-1800; Pikeland (Chester)

Pa., St. Peter's Chh., 1770-1800, and Zion's Chh., 1770-1800; Pottstown (Montgomery) Pa., Emanuel Chh., 1772-1800; Luth.; d. Vincent, Pa., 28 Dec. 1800, a. 69 (GS).

VON KOCKERTHAL, see Kockerthal.

VON ZINZENDORF, see Zinzendorf.

BARENT VROOMAN, b. Schenectady, N.Y., 24 Dec. 1725, son of Walter Vrooman; ed. U. of Utrecht, 1750-1752; Ord. Amsterdam, Holland, 3 July 1752; sett. New Paltz (Ulster) N.Y., 2nd Chh., 1753-1754; Shawangunk (Ulster) N.Y., at Bruynswick, 1753-1754; Pawagtenog, N.Y., 1753-1754; Montgomery (Orange) N.Y., Wallkill Chh., 1753-1754; Schenectady, N.Y., 1 Nov. 1754-1783; Fonda (Montgomery) N.Y., 1758-1772; Trustee, Rutgers; Dutch Ref.; d. Schenectady, N.Y., 15, Nov. 1783.

CASPAR WACK, b. Philadelphia, Pa., 15 Aug. 1752, son of Elder John George and Elizabeth (Schuyler) Wack; studied under Dr. Weyberg; Ord. Lancaster (Lanc.) Pa., 17 June 1772; sett. Lancaster, Pa., 1770-1771; Bedminster (Bucks) Pa., Tohickon Chh., 23 Nov. 1771-26 Aug. 1781; Milford (Bucks) Pa., Lower Milford Chh. at Trumbaursville, 1771-1773; Lower Milford (Lehigh) Pa., 1773-1773, 1780-1781; Lower Saucon (Northampton) Pa., 1773-1782, 1782-1785; Rockhill (Bucks) Pa., Indianfield Chh., 1773-1782; Franconia (Montgomery) Pa., Indian Creek Chh., 1773-1780; Nockamixon (Bucks) Pa., 1773-1785; Springfield (Bucks) Trinity Chh., 1773-1782, 1782-1785; Fox Hill (Hunterdon) N.J., 1785-1809; German Valley (Morris) N.J., 1785-1809; Knowlton (Warren) N.J., 1785-1790; Lebanon (Hunterdon) N.J., 1785-1809; Stillwater (Sussex) N.J., 1785-1809; Germantown, Pa., 1809-1821; Whitemarsh (Montgomery) Pa., 1809-1823; he was the first minister to be born, educated, licensed, and ordained by the German Reformed Church in America; Germ. Ref.; d. Upper Providence, Pa., at Trappe, 17 July 1839, a. 87.

Dr. JOHN WADE, b. England; arriv. Bethlehem, Pa., 12 Jan. 1746/7; Ord. deacon, 1746; sett. Staten Island, N.Y., 1749-1750; at N.Y., N.Y., 1746-1748; said to have been an itinerant preacher at Burlington, Maurice River, Pennsneck, Pilesgrove, Raccoon and Trenton, N.J.; Wilmington, Del.; and Great Swamp, North Wales, Neshaminy, Darby and Chester, Pa., but no evidence has been presented; Moravian.

NATHANIEL WADE (H.C., 1673, non-grad.); Ord. Woodbridge, N.J., before 1708; sett. Woodbridge, N.J., 1708-1711; physician; Presb.

ANTHONY WAGNER, came from Mulhouse, Alsace, France; arriv. N.Y., N.Y., 26 Nov. 1743; Ord. deacon, 1753; preached until 1779; sett. Heidelberg (Berks) Pa., Jan. 1744-1745; Macungie, Pa., 1745-1747; Salisbury (Lehigh) Pa., Chh. at Emaus, 1747-1750, 1763-1766; Mill Creek (Lebanon) Pa., Muehlbach Chh., 1747-1754; Mount Joy (Lanc.) Pa., Donegal Chh., 1754-1763; wife Elizabeth was also ordained; Moravian; d. Emaus, Pa., Dec. 1786.

Colonial Clergy of the Middle Colonies

DANIEL WAGNER, b. Eibelshausen, near Dillenburg, Nassau, Germany, 11 Jan. 1750; arriv. Chester, Pa., 1752; studied Latin, Greek, and Hebrew, at N.Y., N.Y., under the Rev. Dr. Gross, 1768-1769; Ord. Lancaster, Pa., 17 June 1772; sett. Hellam (York) Pa., Kreutz Creek Chh., 1771-1786; York (York) Pa., May 1774-1786, Oct. 1793-Oct. 1802; Lower Windsor (York) Pa., 1774-1786; Tulpehocken, Pa., 1786-1793; Frederick, Md., Oct. 1802-Oct. 1810; Germ. Ref.; d. York, Pa., 17 Dec. 1810.

TOBIAS WAGNER, came of a distinguished Lutheran family; had been sett. at Hockheim, Wurtemberg, Germany, 1733-1742; arriv. in Pa., by way of Waldoborough, Maine, where he had visited the Lutheran chh., 1743; sett. Richmond (Berks) Pa., Zion or Moselem Chh., 1743-1759; Marion (Berks) Pa., Zion's or Rieth's Chh., original Old Tulpehocken Chh., at Stouchsburg, 1743-1747, and Christ Chh., at Stouchsburg, the Old Tulpehocken Chh., 25 Oct. 1743-30 Apr. 1746; Mill Creek (Lebanon) Pa., Reed's or Old Tulpehocken Chh., 1743-1747; Penn (Berks) Pa., St. John's or North Kill Chh., at Bernville, 1744-1746; Bern (Berks) Pa., 1745-1750; Brecknock (Lanc.) Pa., Muddy Creek Chh., 1749-1755; Earl (Lanc.) Pa., Chh. at New Holland, 1749-1755; Rockland (Berks) Pa., Bieber Creek Chh., 1749-1759; Lancaster, Holy Trinity Chh., 1751-1753; Strasburg (Lanc.) Pa., St. Michael's Chh., 1751-1753; Reading (Berks) Pa., Trinity Chh., 1751-1752; Muhlenberg (Berks) Pa., Alsace Chh., 1748-1752; Lynn (Lehigh) Jerusalem Chh. at Allemaengel, 1749-1755; Luth.; returned to Germany, 1759; d. Germany, 1775.

WILLIAM WAIT, from Rhode Island; sett. Cambridge (Washington) N.Y., 1772-1780; Bapt.

JABEZ WAKEMAN, A.B., b. Fairfield, Conn., 1678, son of the Rev. Samuel and Hannah (Goodyear) Wakeman; A.B., H.C., 1697; sett. Newark, N.J., 16 Nov. 1699-1704; Presb.; d. Newark, N.J., 8 Oct. 1704, a. 26 (GS).

SAMUEL WALDO, b. Conn., 1730; Ord. Dover (Dutchess) N.Y., Oblong Bapt. Chh., 4 Jan. 1758-1792; Bapt.; d. Dover, N.Y., 1792, a. 62.

JOHN WALDSCHMIDT, b. Dillenburg, Nassau, Germany, 6 Aug. 1724, son of John Henry Waldschmidt; ed. Herborn; Ord. Amsterdam, Holland, 14 Mar. 1752; arriv. N.Y., N.Y., 27 July 1752; sett. over the following chhs. in Lancaster co., Pa.: Brecknock, Muddy Creek Chh., 22 Oct. 1752-28 Oct. 1754; Earl, Zeltenreich Chh., 1752-1756; Elizabethtown, 1752-1756*; Ephrata, Bethany Chh., 1752-1762; Lancaster, 1763-1764*; Penn, White Oaks Chh., 1752-1761, and the Unionville Chh., 1752-1786; and West Cocalico, Swamp or Little Cocalico Chh., 1752-1786; in Berks co.: Bern, Bern Chh., 1766-1770 (*1763-1770); Brecknock, 1770-1786; Epler, 1769-1771; Exeter, Schwartzwald Chh., 1770-1770; Heidelberg, Hain's or Cacusi Chh., 1763-1786; Muhlenberg, Alsace Chh., 1770-1770; Oley, 1766-1770; Reading, 1757-1758, 1770-1770; Tulpehocken, Host Chh., 1756-1758; and Upper Bern,

St. Michael's Chh., 1770–1770; inst., Mill Creek (Lebanon) Pa., Tulpehocken or Trinity Chh., 10 July 1756–1758; Heidelberg (Lehigh) Pa., 1757–1770* (*Good, 511; Dubbs, 416); Germ. Ref.; d. Cocalico, Pa. Swamp Chh., 14 Sept. 1786, a. 62.

ELEAZER WALES, A.M., b. Windham, Conn., son of Deacon Nathaniel Wales; A.B., Y.C., 1727, A.M.; sett. Allen (Northampton) Pa., 1731–1734; Allentown (Monmouth) N.J., 1731–Sept. 1734; Cranbury (Middlesex) N.J., 1731–1734; Crosswicks (Burlington) N.J., 1731–Sept. 1734; Millstone (Somerset) N.J., Sept. 1735–1750; Kingston (Sussex) N.J., at Franklin, 1735–1750; Smithfield (Monroe) Pa., 1750–1750; Presb.; d. Millstone, N.J., between 16 May and 8 Aug. 1750.

ROBERT WALKER (poss. matric. Edinburgh, 1695); K.B. for Md., 8 Apr. 1707; school-teacher, 1707–1714/5; K.B. Barbadoes, 10 Mar. 1714/5; S.P.G. missionary in N.J., 1715–1720; sett. Hopewell (Mercer) N.J., Oct. 1715–1720; Lawrence (Mercer) N.J., Maidenhead Chh., 1715–1718; Burlington, N.J., St. Anne's, now St. Mary's Chh., 1714–1717; and prob. Bristol (Bucks) Pa., St. James the Greater Chh., 1714–1717; Ep.; living at Hopewell, N.J., 29 Mar. 1720.

ZACHARIAH WALKER, b. Boston, 15 Sept. 1637, son of Robert and Sarah Walker; bapt. Boston, 1st Chh., 1 Oct. 1637; H.C., 1653–1655, non-grad.; sett. Jamaica, L.I., N.Y., 1662–1668; Ord. Woodbury, Conn., 2nd Chh. in Stratford, 5 May 1670, as the first minister; sett. Woodbury, Conn., 1668–1700; Cong.; d. Woodbury, Conn., 20 Jan. 1699/1700.

JOHN WALTON, A.B., b. New London, Conn., son of John Walton; A.B., Y.C., 1720; sett. Allentown (Monmouth) N.J., May 1721–Oct. 1723; Cranbury, N.J., 1721–1723; Rye (Westchester) N.Y., 1723–1728; White Plains (Westchester) N.Y., 1723–1728; physician at Rhode Island, 1728–1730; deputy to the General Assembly from Gloucester, R.I., 1743; Presb.; Bapt.; d. 1764.

JOHN WALTON, Jr., b. Providence, R.I., Nov. 1735, son of the Rev. John and Susanna Walton; lic. Morristown, N.J., 26 Feb. 1766; Ord. Morristown (Morris) N.J., 17 July 1767; sett. Morristown, 1765–1770; Presb.; d. Morristown, N.J., 7 Oct. 1770, a. 35.

WILLIAM WAPPELER, S.J., b. Neuen Sigmaringen, Westphalia, Germany, 22 Jan. 1711; S.J., 1738; arriv. in Pa., 1741; sett. Conewago (Adams) Pa., Sacred Heart Chh., 1741–1748; Lancaster, Pa., St. John Nepomucene's Chh., 1741–1748; Washington (Berks) Pa., St. Paul's Chapel at Bally, 1742–1748; returned to Europe, 1748; R.C.

EDMUND WARD, A.M., b. Guilford, Conn., 22 Sept. 1706, son of Captain Andrew, Jr. and Deborah (Joy) Ward; A.B., Y.C., 1727, A.M.; sett. Rye (Westchester) N.Y., Presb. Chh., 1728–1729; White Plains (Westchester) N.Y., Presb. Chh., 1728–1729; Ord. Guilford, Conn. (Cong.), 21 Sept. 1730; sett. Guilford, Conn. 4th Society, Oct. 1729–1731; became an Ep.; Representative to the General Court, 1759–1761; Cong.; Presb.; Ep.; d. Guilford, Conn., 15 Nov. 1779, a. 73.

WILLIAM WOODROP (prob. son of John Woodrop, gent., of Yarmouth, co. Norfolk, England; matric. Corpus Christi Coll., Camb., Easter, 1660; adm. Gray's Inn, 28 Jan. 1660/1); a non-conformist clergyman driven from his church in England, 1662; Jamaica, L.I., N.Y., 1675-1676; preached at Lancaster, Mass.; doubtless the Mr. Wardrope, who preached at Norriton (Montgomery) Pa., ca. 1685; returned to England, 12 July 1687; Cong.; Presb.

HENRY BURCHES GABRIEL WARTMANN, arriv. in America, 1753; sett. Reading (Berks) Pa., Trinity Chh., 1753-1753; Lancaster, Pa., Trinity Chh., 1753-Mar. 1753; Muhlenberg (Berks) Pa., Alsace Chh., 1753-1753; Savannah, Ga., 1760-1761; Charleston, S.C., St. John's Chh., 1761-1763; Luth.

HEZEKIAH WATKINS, A.M., bapt. Stratford, Conn., 3 Apr. 1709; A.B., Y.C., 1737, A.M.; Ord. by the Bsp. of London, 1742; K.B. for N.Y., 11 Oct. 1744; Hamptonburgh (Orange) N.Y., St. David's Chh. on the Otterkill, 1744-1765; Wallkill (Ulster) N.Y., 1744-1753; New Windsor (Orange) N.Y., 1744-1753; Milemantown (Ulster) N.Y., 1744-1753; Newburgh (Orange) N.Y., St. George's Chh., 1745-1765; Walden (Orange) N.Y., St. Andrew's Chh., 19 July 1747-1765; Ep.; d. Newburgh, N.Y., 10 Apr. 1765, a. 57.

JAMES WATT, A.M., b. 12 Mar. 1743; A.B., Princeton, 1763, A.M.; Ord. Greenwich, N.J., Apr. 1770; sett. Cape May, N.J., Chh. at Cold Spring, inst. 12 May 1770-1778; Presb.; d. Cape May, N.J., 19 Nov. 1789.

WILLIAM WATTERS, b. Baltimore, Md., 16 Oct. 1751; sett. Trenton (Mercer) N.J., Green Street Chh., 1773-1774; Baltimore Conference, 1773-1833; Chester Circuit, Chester co., Pa., 1774 (for the preaching stations on this circuit, see Isaac Rollins); Frederick, Md., 1775-1775; Meth.; d. 1833.

JOHN WATTS, b. Lydd, Kent, England, 3 Nov. 1661, son of Henry and Elizabeth Watts; came to America, 1686; called to the ministry, 1688; sett. Lower Dublin, Pa., Pennypack Bapt. Chh., 1688-1702; Philadelphia, Pa., 1st Bapt. Chh., 1698-1702; Bapt.; d. Lower Dublin, Pa., 27 Aug. 1702, of small pox.

JOSEPH WEBB, Jr., A.M., b. Fairfield, Conn., 21 Sept. 1693, son of the Rev. Joseph and Elizabeth (Nichols) Webb; A.B., Y.C., 1715, A.M.; Ord. Newark, N.J., 22 Oct. 1719; sett. Newark, N.J., 1718-1736; Presb.; returned to New Haven; drowned in the Connecticut River, near Saybrook, 20 Oct. 1741.

Captain THOMAS WEBB, b. England, 1724; came to America, ca. 1766; sett. N.Y., N.Y., John Street Chh., 1766-1771; Pemberton (Burlington) N.J., at New Mills, 1770-1771; visited England, 1771-1773, 1774-1782; Philadelphia and New York Conferences; sett. Bristol, England, 1783-1796; lost an eye at the siege of Louisburg; Captain in the British Army; fought under General Wolfe at Quebec, 1758; Meth.; d. Bristol, England, 10 Dec. 1796, a. 72.

JOHN WILLIAM WEBER, b. Wittgenstein, Germany, 5 Mar. 1735; school-teacher at Wittgenstein, 23 Apr. 1764; arriv. Philadelphia, 20 Sept. 1764; Ord. Lancaster, Pa., 17 June 1772; sett. Wind Gap (Monroe) Pa., 1771–1776; in 1776, he was preaching in Plainfield (Northampton) Pa., Greenwich (Berks) Pa., Hamilton (Monroe) Pa., Easton, Pa., and other places; he was the first minister of any denomination to settle in Pittsburgh; sett. Pittsburgh, Pa., Sept. 1782–1814; and in Westmoreland co., at Bush Creek, Hempfield, Mt. Pleasant, Heralds, etc.; Germ. Ref.; d. Hempfield, Westmoreland co., Pa., July 1816, a. 82.

RICHARD WEBSTER, sett. Eastern Shore, Maryland, 24 Dec. 1772; Chester (Del.) Pa., Madison Street Chh., 1775–1775; Goshen (Chester) Pa., at West Whiteland, 1775–1775; Uwchlan (Chester) Pa., Benson's Chapel, 1775–1775; Chester Circuit, Chester co., Pa., 1775–1775 (see Isaac Rollins); Meth.

JOHANNES WEEKSTEEN, b. ca. 1643; matric. Leyden, for theology, 27 Feb. 1674, a. 30; Ord. Amsterdam, Holland, 5 May 1681; arriv. Kingston, 11 Sept. 1681; sett. Kingston (Ulster) N.Y., Chh. at Esopus, 1681–1687; Dutch Ref.; d. Kingston, N.Y., 17 Mar. 1687.

Colonel JOHANN CONRAD WEISER, J.P., b. Astaet, Hermberg, Wurtemberg, Germany, 2 Nov. 1696, son of Johann Conrad and Anna Magdalena (Uebelen) Weiser; arriv. N.Y., N.Y., 13 June 1710; Ord. Ephrata (Lancaster) Pa., German Bapt. Chloister, as German Bapt. priest, Aug. 1740, as "Brother Enoch"; sett. Ephrata, Pa., 1735–1741; resigned, 3 Sept. 1743; teacher at Tulpehocken German Ref. Chh., 1735–1735; appointed Justice of the Peace, 1741; Colonel, 1755; Commanded the 2nd Battalion, Pa., Regt., in the French and Indian Wars; Germ. Ref.; Germ. Bapt.; Luth.; d. Heidelberg, Pa., 13 July 1760.

GEORGE WEISS, b. Harpersdorf, Lower Silesia, Germany, 1687, son of the Rev. Caspar Weiss; was at Herrnhut, Saxony, 5 May 1726; arrived in America, 9 Dec. 1735; sett. Lower Salford (Montgomery) Pa., 9 Dec. 1735–10 Mar. 1740, as the first minister of the Schwenkfelders in America; with his father, he compiled the "Weiss Hymn-Book of the Schwenkfelders"; d. Lower Salford, Pa., 10 Mar. 1740, a. 53 (GS).

GEORGE MICHAEL WEISS, bapt. Eppingen, Neckar Valley, Germany, 23 Jan. 1700, son of John Michael and Maria (Frank) Weiss; matric. Heidelberg, 18 Oct. 1718, in philosophy; Ord. Heidelberg, 1725; arriv. on the "William and Sarah", at Philadelphia, 18 Sept. 1727; sett. Philadelphia, Pa., organized, 24 Sept. 1727–1732; Germantown, 1727–1731; Lower Salford (Montgomery) Pa., Reiff's or Skippack Chh., 1727–1729; Conestoga (Lancaster) Pa., 1727–1729; Lower Milford (Lehigh) Pa., Great Swamp Chh., 1727–1730, 1746–1761; Mill Creek (Lebanon) Pa., Tulpehocken or Trinity Chh., 1727–1729; North Annville (Lebanon) Pa., Hill Chh. or Quittopehilla, 1727–1729; Upper Salford (Montgomery) Pa., Old Goshenhoppen Chh., 1727–1730, 1746–1761; Upper Hanover (Montgomery) Pa., New Goshenhoppen Chh., 1727–1731, 1746–1761; Worcester (Montgomery) Pa., Wentz's or Skippack Chh.,

1727-1729; Ephrata (Lanc.) Pa., Bethany Chh., 1728-1729; Schoharie (Schoharie) N.Y., Dutch Ref. Chh. at Huntersville, 1731-1732; Huntersville (Schoharie) N.Y., Germ. Ref. Chh. at Barton Hill, 1731-1732; Leeds (Greene) N.Y., Old Catskill Dutch Ref. Chh., 1731-1736; Catskill (Greene) N.Y., D.R. Chh., 8 Feb. 1732-1735, 1744-1744; Coxsackie (Greene) N.Y., Dutch Ref. Chh., 1732-1735; East Camp, N.Y., 1732-1736; Burnetsfield (Herkimer) N.Y., D.R. Chh., at German Flats, 1736-1742; Rhinebeck (Dutchess) N.Y., Germ. Ref. Chh., 17 Sept. 1742-29 July 1746; Rhinebeck Flats (Dutchess) N.Y., D.R. Chh., 1746-1746; Muhlenberg (Berks) Pa., Alsace Chh., 1746-1761; Oley (Berks) Pa., 1746-1761; Exeter (Berks) Pa., Schwartzwald Chh., 1754-1761; Lower Heidelberg (Berks) Pa., St. John's Chh., 1754-1761; Reading (Berks) Pa., 1760-1761; in 1730-1731, he returned to Germany to collect money to aid the Germ. Ref. Chhs. in the American colonies; he was the first German Reformed Chh. minister in the colonies, and was a pioneer and founder of that church in America; unfortunately he left no issue, to cause his name to be remembered; d. New Goshenhoppen, Pa., Aug. 1761.

LEWIS WILLIAM WEISS, Esq., b. Berlin, Germany, 1718; ed. Moravian Theol. Sem. at Lindheim, 1744, a. 26; Ord. Germany, 1746; arriv. N.Y., N.Y., 12 Aug. 1755; sett. Philadelphia, Pa., 1755-1755; conveyancer, lawyer, and Justice at Philadelphia; Morav.

TIMOTHY WELLS, b. 1720; Ord. Riverhead, Upper Aquebogue, L.I., N.Y., 21 Oct. 1759-1783; Cong.; d. Cutchogue, L.I., N.Y., 15 Jan. 1783, a. 63.

RICHARD WELTON, D.D. (or Robert), Ord. 1722; minister at St. Mary's Whitechapel, London, 1722-1724; sett. Philadelphia, Pa., Christ Chh., 27 July 1724-Jan. 1726; he was consecrated Bishop by an English non-juring Bishop, 1723, and was commanded to return to London at once when it was discovered; Ep.; d. Lisbon, Portugal, ca. 31 Aug. 1726.

JOHN AEMILIUS WERNICK (or John Emil Werring), came to America, 1752; sett. Stone Arabia (Montgomery) N.Y., Chh. at Palatine, 1752-1752; Germ. Ref.

EILARDUS WESTERLO, D.D., b. Cantes, Groningen, Holland, Oct. 1738, son of the Rev. Isaac and — (Reiners) Westerlo, of Groningen; matric. Groningen, 11 Oct. 1754, in theol.; Ord. 1760; came to America ca. 1760; sett. Albany, N.Y., Dutch Ref. Chh., Mar. 1760-1790; Schaghticoke (Rensselaer) N.Y., at Reynolds, 1760-1763; Kaatsbaan (Ulster) N.Y., 1762-1775; first Dutch Ref. minister at Albany to preach in English; Dutch Ref.; d. Albany, N.Y., 26 Dec. 1790 (GS).

JAMES WETMORE, A.M., b. Middletown, Conn., 25 Dec. 1695, son of Izrahiah and Rachel (Stow) Wetmore; A.B., Y.C., 1714, A.M.; Ord. North Haven, Conn. (Cong. Chh.) Nov. 1718-1722; became an Ep.; Ord. London, England, 25 July 1723; K.B. for N.Y., 5 Aug. 1723; S.P.G. missionary, N.Y., 1723-1726; sett. N.Y., N.Y., Trinity Chh., asst.,

1723–1726; Setauket, L.I., N.Y., Caroline Chh., 1723–1725; Westchester (Westchester) N.Y., St. Peter's Chh., 1726–1726; Rye (Westchester) N.Y., Christ Chh., 1726–1760; Bedford (Westchester) N.Y., St. Matthew's Chh., 1726–1760; Peekskill (Westchester) N.Y., St. Peter's Chh. in the Manor of Cortlandt, 1744–1760; Ep.; d. Rye, N.Y., 15 May 1760, a. 64.

CASPARUS DIEDERUS WEYBERG, D.D. (or Caspar Dietrick), b. Westofen, Westphalia, Germany, 4 Oct. 1734; matric. U. of Duisburg, 15 Oct. 1756; Ord. abroad; arriv. Philadelphia, 1762 or 1763; A.M., U. of Pa., 1780; D.D., Princeton, 1788; sett. Easton (Northampton) Pa., 7 Mar. 1763–8 Oct. 1763, as the 1st minister; Philadelphia, Pa., 1st Germ. Ref. Chh., 13 Nov. 1763–1790; Philadelphia, Pa., 2nd Germ. Ref. Chh., 1763–1790; Greenwich (Berks) Pa., Dunkel Chh., 1763–1763; Greenwich (Warren) N.J., 1763–1763; Plainfield (Northampton) Pa., St. Peter's Chh., 1763–1763; Dryland (Northampton) Pa., 1763–1763; Lehigh (Northampton) Pa., Driesbach Chh., 1763–1763; Chaplain, Rev. Army; Germ. Ref.; d. Philadelphia, Pa., 21 Aug. 1790, a. 56 (GS).

PHILIP WEYBERG, an original Trustee of Rutgers Coll., 1770; sett. in Pa., ca. 1770; names of churches served not found; Germ. Ref.

JOHN ALBERT WEYGANDT (or Weygand) b. Hanau, Hessen, Germany; ed. at Halle; arriv. Philadelphia, 7 Sept. 1748; Ord. Raritan, N.J., 2 Dec. 1750; sett. Raritan (Somerset) N.J., 1748–1753; New Germantown (Hunterdon) N.J., Zion Chh., Tewksbury, 1748–1753; German Valley (Morris) N.J., Chh. at Washington, 1748–1753; Bedminster (Somerset) N.J., St. Paul's Chh., 1748–1753; Pluckemin (Somerset) N.J., at Bedminster, 1748–1753; Fox Hill (Hunterdon) N.J., Germ. Ref. Chh., 1748–1752; Fairmount (Hunterdon) N.J., Fox Hill Luth. Chh., at Tewksbury, 1748–1753; Potterstown (Hunterdon) N.J., Rockaway Chh., 1748–1753; Whitehouse (Hunterdon) N.J., Chh. at Leslyland, 1748–1753; Reading (Berks) Pa., Trinity Chh., 1748–1750; Muhlenberg (Berks) Pa., Alsace Chh., 1748–1750; New Hanover (Montgomery) Pa., Falkner's Swamp Chh., 1748–1748; N.Y., N.Y., Holy Trinity Chh., 1750–1762; Hackensack (Bergen) N.J., Lutheran Chh., 1753–1767; retired, 1767; Luth.; d. bef. May 1770.

ROBERT WEYMAN, b. Wales, 1694, son of William Weyman, of Pembrokeshire, Wales; matric. Jesus Coll., Oxford, 3 Mar. 1713/4, a. 19; K.B. for Pa., 1 Oct. 1719; S.P.G. missionary, 1719–1728, at Trenton, N.J., Perkiomen (Montgomery) Pa., and Tredyffryn (Chester) Pa.; sett. Bristol (Bucks) Pa., Chh. of St. James the Greater, 1719–1728, 1730–1737; Caernarvon (Lanc.) Pa., Bangor Chh., 1719–1728; Frankford (Philadelphia) Pa., 1719–1728; Newtown (Del.) Pa., St. David's Chh. at Radnor, Dec. 1719–1730; Oxford (Chester) Pa., Trinity Chh., 1719–1728/9; Whitmarsh (Montgomery) Pa., St. Thomas's Chh., 1719–1730; St. George's Parish (Harford) Md., Spesutia Chh., 1722–1724; Lower Providence (Montgomery) Pa., St. James's Chh. at Evansburg, 1723–

1730; Burlington, N.J., St. Anne's Chh., now St. Mary's Chh., 1730-1737; Ep.; d. Burlington, N.J., 28 Nov. 1737.

JACOB WEYMER, b. Germany, 1734; came to Pa., 1751, and was a school-teacher, catechist and preacher, 1751-1768; Ord. 1770; sett. Albany (Berks) Pa., Frieden's Chh., 1770-1770; Heidelberg (Lehigh) Pa., 1770-1770; Greenwich (Berks) Pa., Dunkel Chh., 1770-1770; Lowhill (Lehigh) Pa., 1770-1770; Lynn (Lehigh) Pa., Ebenezer or Organ Chh., 1770-1770, Jacob's Chh., 1770-1770, Tresbacker's Chh., 1770-1770; Washington (Franklin) Pa., Salem or Besore's Chh. near Waynesborough, Pa., 1773-1786; Chambersburg (Franklin) Pa., 1784-1790; Cavetown (Washington) Md., Baird's Chh., 1770-1790; Funkstown (Washington) Md., 1770-1790; Hagerstown, then called Elizabethtown (Washington) Md., Sept. 1770-1790; Mechanicstown (Frederick) Md., Apple's Chh., 1770-1790; Troxel's Chh., Md., 1771-1790; Conococheague (Washington) Md., St. Paul's Chh., near Clear Spring, Sept. 1770-1790; Germ. Ref.; d. Hagerstown, Md., 12 May 1790, a. 66.

NATHANIEL WHITAKER, A.B., b. L.I., N.Y., 22 Feb. 1732; A.B., Princeton, 1752; supply, Woodbridge, N.J., 1756-1761; inst. Chelsea, Norwich, Conn., 25 Feb. 1761-1769; inst. Salem, Mass., 3rd Chh., 28 July 1769-26 Feb. 1784; inst. Norridgewock, Me., 10 Sept. 1784; Presb.; accompanied Samson Occum to England to secure funds for the Indian Charity School which later became Dartmouth Coll.; d. Va., 21 Jan. 1795.

EBENEZER WHITE, A.M., b. Weymouth, Mass., 17 Feb. 1671/2, son of Captain Ebenezer and Hannah (Phillips) White; A.B., H.C., 1692, A.M.; Ord. Bridgehampton, L.I., N.Y., 9 Oct. 1695-1748; Cong.; Presb.; d. Bridgehampton, L.I., N.Y., 4 Feb. 1756, a. 84.

SYLVANUS WHITE, A.M., b. Bridgehampton, L.I., N.Y., 16 Dec. 1702, son of the Rev. Ebenezer and Hannah (Pierson) White; A.B., H.C., 1722, A.M.; Ord. Southampton, L.I., N.Y., 17 Nov. 1727-1782; Cong.; Presb.; d. Southampton, L.I., N.Y., 22 Oct. 1782, a. 79.

Bishop WILLIAM WHITE, D.D., b. Philadelphia, Pa., 24 Mar. 1747/8, son of Colonel Thomas and Esther (Hewlings) (Newman) White; A.B., U. of Pa., 1765, A.M., D.D., 1783, Trustee, 1774-1836; Ord. London, by the Bsp. of London, 25 Apr. 1772; K.B., for Pa., 19 May 1772; sett. as asst. Philadelphia, Pa. (Christ Chh. and St. Peter's Chh.), 13 Sept. 1772-1779; as Rector, United Chhs., 1779-1836; Bishop of Pennsylvania, 4 Feb. 1787-1836; member, Am. Phil. Soc., 1768; Chaplain of Congress, 1777-1785, 1789-1801; Ep.; d. Philadelphia, Pa., 17 July 1836, a. 89.

JOSEPH WHITING, A.M., b. Lynn, Mass., 6 Apr. 1641, son of the Rev. Samuel and Elizabeth (St. John) Whiting; A.B., H.C., 1661, A.M.; Fellow, 1664-1665; Ord. Lynn, Mass., 6 Oct. 1680-1682; sett. Southampton, L.I., N.Y., 1682-1716; Cong.; Presb.; d. Southampton, L.I., N.Y., 7 Apr. 1723, a. 82.

ELEAZER WHITTLESEY, A.B., b. Bethlehem, Conn., A.B., Princeton, 1749; Ord. Nottingham (Cecil) Md.; sett. Lower Chanceford (York) Pa., 1751-1752; Peach Bottom (York) Pa., Slate Ridge Chh., 1751-1752; Presb.; d. Slate Ridge, Pa., 21 Dec. 1752.

GEORGE JOSEPH WICHTERMANN, sett. Schaghticoke (Rensselaer) N.Y., St. John's Chh., 1776-1793; Luth.

JOHN H. WICKEL (or Weikel); appeared before the Coetus, 1774, but was refused; sett. Whitpain (Montgomery) Pa., Boehm's Chh., 1775-1779; Worcester (Montgomery) Pa., Wentz's or Skippack Chh., 1776-1779; was living 14 Jan. 1778; left bef. Apr. 1779; Germ. Ref.

JOHN WICKSELL (or Wiesell) sett. Swedesborough (Gloucester) N.J., Trinity Chh. on Raccoon Creek, 1762-1774; Pennsneck (Salem) N.J., St. George's Chh., 1762-1774; Salem (Cumberland) N.J., St. John's Chh., 1762-1774; Sw. Luth.

JOHN GEORGE WIESSNER (or Weisner) sett. Williams (Northampton) Pa., at Cedarville, 1760-1769; Upper Milford (Lehigh) Pa., Zionsville Chh., 1765-1767; Lower Macungie (Lehigh) Pa., Holy Trinity or Zion Chh., Sept. 1765-Dec. 1767; Luth.

CHARLES FREDERICK WILDBAHN, ed. Halle; schoolmaster at Winchester, Va.; lic. 1762; sett. West Manheim (York) Pa., St. David's or Sherman's Chh., 1751-1752; Union (Adams) Pa., St. John's Chh., near Littletown, 1763-1782; Hanover (York) Pa., St. Michael's Chh., 1765-1782; Conewago (Adams) Pa., Zion's Chh., 1765-1782; Frederick, Md., 1768-1770, 1796-1799; Conococheague (Washington) Md., St. Paul's Chh., 1770-1782; Hagerstown (Washington) Md., St. John's Chh., 1770-1771; Taneytown (Carroll) Md., 1770-1782; Reading, Pa., 1782-1796; also at Codorus (York) Pa., St. Jacob's Chh., Owen's Creek, at Monocacy, Md., Thomas Creek, and Point Creek, time unknown; Luth.; d. 1804.

ISAAC WILKINS, D.D., A.B., Columbia, 1760, A.M., D.D., 1811; member of the N.Y. Provincial Assembly, 1772-1775; Presb.; d. 1830.

LEWIS WILLIAMS, sett. Warwick (Chester) Pa., French Creek Chh. at East Nantmeal, time when unknown, but prob. ca. 1750; 7th Day Bapt.

ROBERT WILLIAMS, came from England; arriv. N.Y., N.Y., Oct. 1769: sett. N.Y., N.Y., Wesleyan Chapel, 1769-1769; Va. Conference, 1769-1775; Norfolk (Norfolk) Va., 1774-1775; Meth.; d. near Norfolk, Va., 26 Sept. 1775.

SIMON WILLIAMS, A.M., b. Trim, co. Meath, Ireland, 19 Feb. 1729; A.B., Princeton, 1763, A.M.; sett. Deerfield (Cumberland) N.J., 1764-1766; Ord. Windham, N.H., Dec. 1766-1793; Presb.; d. Windham, N.H., 10 Nov. 1793, a. 64.

WALTER WILMOT, A.M., b. Bridgehampton, L.I., N.Y., ca. 1709/10, son of Alexander and Mary Wilmot; A.B., Y.C., 1735, A.M.; Ord.

Jamaica, L.I., N.Y., 12 Apr. 1738-1744; Presb.; d. Jamaica, L.I., N.Y., 6 Aug. 1744, a. 34.

JOHN CHRISTIAN WILMS, b. abroad, 3 Apr. 1738; Germ. Ref.; service not found; d. 8 Mar. 1802.

HUGH WILSON, ed. in America; Ord. in London, for Mispillion, Del., Christ Chh., 1765; K.B. for Pa., 2 Jan. 1766; drowned at sea on return voyage, 5 Apr. 1766; Ep.

JAMES WILSON (poss. A.B., Princeton, 1770, A.M.), son of Matthew Wilson of Philadelphia, Pa.; sett. Blackwater (Sussex) Del., 1768-1771; New London (Chester) Pa., inst. 15 Oct. 1771-27 Oct. 1778; New Londonderry (Chester) Pa., Fagg's Manor Chh., 1771-1778; Presb.

JOHN WILSON, b. Ireland, 1667; Ord. 1729; came to Pa., 1729; preached at Lower Octoraro, Pa., 1729-1730; Presb.; thought to be the father of the Rev. John Wilson of Chester, N.H.; d. Boston, 6 Jan. 1733, a. 66.

ANDREW WINDRUFA, came from Sweden; asst. minister, Pennsneck (Salem) N.J., St. George's Chh., 1725-1728; Sw. Luth.; d. Pennsneck, N.J., 5 Nov. 1728.

JOHN CONRAD WIRTZ (or Wuertz), b. Zurich, Switzerland, 30 Nov. 1706, son of the Rev. John Conrad and Magdalena (Klinger) Wirtz; practiced law in Zurich; officer in the army of the King of Netherlands; arriv. Philadelphia, 29 May 1735; received by the Presbytery of New Brunswick, 3 Sept. 1751; Ord. (Presbyterian) 5 June 1752; dism. from the Presbytery, 21 Oct. 1761; sett. Whitehall (Lehigh) Pa., Egypt Chh., Sept. 1742-Dec. 1743-1753; Bedminster (Bucks) Pa., Tohickon Chh., June 1745-July 1748; Lower Saucon (Northampton) Pa., 1745-1749; Springfield (Bucks) Pa., Trinity Chh., 1745-1749; also Easton, Pa., Forks of the Delaware Chh., 1745-1749; Salisbury (Lehigh) Pa., Jerusalem Chh., 1745-1749; Lynn (Lehigh) Pa., Allemaengel Chh., 1745-1749; Amwell (Hunterdon) N.J., 1750-1755; German Valley (Morris) N.J., Chh. at Roxbury, 1750-21 Oct. 1761; Lebanon (Hunterdon) N.J., Rockaway Chh. at Clinton, 1750-21 Oct. 1761 (Presb.) and 1755-1756 (Germ. Ref.); Fox Hill, Tewksbury (Hunterdon) Pa., 1752-1762; York (York) Pa., 9 May 1762-1763; Hellam (York) Pa., Kreutz Chh., 1762-1763; Germ. Ref.; Presb.; d. York, Pa., 21 Sept. 1763.

JOHN JACOB WISSLER, b. Dillenburg, Nassau, Germany, 23 Feb. 1727, son of Ernest Wissler; ed. Herborn; Ord. Germany before 1752; arriv. in America, July 1752; sett. Whitehall (Lehigh) Pa., Egypt Chh., 24 Sept. 1752-1754; Heidelberg (Lehigh) Pa., 1752-1754; South Whitehall (Lehigh) Pa., Jordan Chh., 1752-1754; Germ. Ref.; d. Whitehall, Pa., Sept. 1754, a. 28.

President JOHN WITHERSPOON, D.D., LL.D., b. Yester, near Edinburgh, Scotland, 5 Feb. 1722, son of the Rev. James Witherspoon (the President was a descendant through his mother of John Knox who brought the Reformation to Scotland); A.M., Edinburgh, 1743; D.D.,

Aberdeen, 1764; LL.D., Y.C., 1785; sett. Beith, Scotland, 1744-1757; Paisley, Scotland, inst. 16 Jan. 1757-1768; Princeton (Mercer) N.J., 1st Chh., 1768-1794; induct. President of Princeton U., 17 Aug. 1768-1794; lectured on eloquence, composition, taste and criticism, moral philosophy, chronology, history and divinity; 1st Moderator of the General Assembly, Presb. Chh., 1789; Representative for N.J. in Congress, 1776-1782; Signer of the Declaration of Independence, 1776; member, Am. Phil. Soc.; N.J. Senate, 1780; N.J. Assembly, 1783-1790; Presb.; d. Princeton, N.J., 17 Dec. 1794, a. 73 (GS).

JOHN GEORGE WITNER (or Wittner), b. Bellheim, Palatinate, Germany, 13 Aug. 1735, son of the Rev. Abraham Witner; matric. Heidelberg, 12 Dec. 1755; arriv. in America, 1766; sett. Brecknock (Lanc.) Pa., Muddy Creek Chh., 1766-1770; Earl (Lanc.) Pa., Zeltenreich Chh., 1766-1769; Elizabeth (Lanc.) Pa., Zion Chh., 1766-1769; Ephrata (Lanc.) Pa., Bethany Chh., 1766-1770; Maiden Creek (Berks) Pa., 1766-1769; Chestnut Hill (Philadelphia) Pa., 1771-1779; Kestenberg, Pa., 1771-1779; Salisbury (Lehigh) Pa., New Jerusalem Chh., 1771-1779, and Jerusalem Chh., 1771-1779; Upper Milford (Lehigh) Pa., Zionsville Chh., 1771-1779; Germ. Ref.; d. Upper Milford, Pa., 25 Dec. 1779, a. 44.

Dr. CHRISTOPHER WITT (or De Witt), b. Wiltshire, England, 1675; came to America, 1704; joined the Pietist Community at Wissahickon, Pa., as an asst. to Kelpius, 1704-1708; physician and botanist; Germ. Bapt. and Pietist; d. Germantown, Pa., Jan. 1765, a. 90.

MICHAEL WOHLFARTH, b. Memel on the Baltic Sea, 1687; visited North Carolina Germans in 1722; remov. to Mill Creek (Lebanon) Pa., 1724; sett. Tulpehocken (Berks) Pa., 1735-1735 (German Bapt. Community, which during the same year remov. to Ephrata); Ephrata (Lanc.) Pa., Germ. Bapt. Chloister, 1735-1741; was an asst. to Christopher Saur, 1739-1741; Germ. Bapt.; Luth.; d. Ephrata, Pa., 20 May 1741, a. 54.

JOHN AUGUSTUS WOLF, b. Loebejuen, Germany; Ord. Hamburg, Germany, St. Nicholas Chh., 11 May 1734; came to America, 1734; sett. Fairmount (Hunterdon) N.J., Fox Hill Chh. at Tewksbury, 1734-1748; Potterstown (Hunterdon) N.J., Rockaway Chh., 1734-1748; Pluckemin (Somerset) N.J., Chh. at Bedminster, 1734-1748; Mahwah (Bergen) N.J., Ramapo Chh., 1734-1746; German Valley (Morris) N.J., Chh. at Washington, 1734-1748; we infer that his services terminated about 1748 because that was the date his successor appears (except at Ramapo where the date was 1746); Luth.

ELIJAH WOOD, b. 1745; Deacon at Bennington, Vt., 1763-1774; Ord. Amenia (Dutchess) N.Y., 1774-1810; Bapt.; d. Amenia, N.Y., 1810, a. 65.

JOSEPH WOOD, b. near Hull, Yorkshire, England, 1659; came to America, 1684; Ord. 25 Sept. 1708; sett. Lower Dublin, Pa., Pennypack

Bapt. Chh., 1708-1747; sett. Philadelphia, Pa., 1st Bapt. Chh., 1708-1747; Bapt.; d. Cold Spring, Bristol (Bucks) Pa., 15 Sept. 1747 (GS).

Dr. THOMAS WOOD, b. 1708, son of Dr. Thomas Wood, of Hardwick, Buckinghamshire, England; matric. New Coll., Oxford, 5 July 1728, a. 20; A.B., 1732; Ord. London (Bsp. of London) 1749; lic. 29 Sept. 1749; S.P.G. missionary in N.J., 1749-1752; sett. Elizabethtown (Union) N.J., St. John's Chh., 1749-1752; New Brunswick (Middlesex) N.J., Christ Chh., 1749-1 Aug. 1752; sett. Annapolis, Nova Scotia, 1753-1754, 1763-1778; Halifax, N.S., 1754-1763; Granville, N.S., 1762-1763; physician; surgeon, British Army; 1st S.P.G. missionary to visit New Brunswick, Canada; Ep.; d. Annapolis, N.S., 14 Dec. 1778.

JOHN WOODHULL, D.D., b. Suffolk co., L.I., N.Y., 26 Jan. 1744, son of John and Elizabeth (Smith) Woodhull; A.B., Princeton, 1766, Trustee, 1780-1824; V.P., Princeton Seminary, 1821-1824; D.D., Y.C., 1798; Ord. Leacock (Lancaster) Pa., 1 Aug. 1770-1779; sett. Lancaster (Lancaster) Pa., 1770-1779; Freehold, N.J., 1779-1824; Chaplain, Pa. militia, 1777; Moderator of the General Assembly of the Presb. Chh., 1791; Presb.; d. Freehold, N.J., 22 Nov. 1824, a. 80 (GS).

WILLIAM WOODHULL, A.M., b. Brookhaven, L.I., N.Y., son of John and Elizabeth (Smith) Woodhull; A.B., Princeton, 1764, A.M., 1785; sett. Chester (Morris) N.J., at Black River, 1 Sept. 1768-1770; Mount Olive (Morris) N.J., at Schooley's Mountain, 1768-1770; Roxbury (Morris) N.J., Succasunna Chh., 1768-1774; member, N.J. Legislature, 1776-1789, 1790; member, N.J. Constitutional Convention, 1787; Judge, Court of Common Pleas, 1808-1824; Presb.; d. Chester, N.J., 24 Oct. 1824.

BENJAMIN WOODRUFF, A.M., b. Elizabeth, N.J., 1733, son of Alderman Samuel Woodruff; A.B., Princeton, 1753, A.M.; Ord. Westfield (Union) N.J., 14 Mar. 1759-1803; Presb.; d. Westfield, N.J., 3 Apr. 1803.

CHARLES WOOLEY, A.M., U. of Cambridge, A.M., 1677; came to N.Y., 1678; first of the Chaplains in the Fort at N.Y., N.Y., 1678-1680, and the first Ep. minister in N.Y.; he returned to England, 1680, and published a book on New York City in 1701; Ep.

BENJAMIN WOOLSEY, A.M., b. Jamaica, L.I., N.Y., 19 Nov. 1687, son of Captain George and Hannah Woolsey; A.B., Y.C., 1709, A.M., 1723; Ord. Southold, L.I., N.Y., 1st Cong. Chh., July 1720-1736; sett. Hempstead, L.I., N.Y., 1736-1756; Presb.; d. Dosoris, Hempstead, L.I., N.Y., 15 Aug. 1759, a. 71.

WILLIAM WORTH, b. Basking Ridge, N.J., 21 Apr. 1745; Ord. Pittsgrove (Salem) N.J., 15 May 1771-1789; sett. Salem, N.J., 1771-1789; Bapt.

Provost CHARLES MAGNUS WRANGEL, D.D., ed. Vesteras and Upsala Universities; Groningen, Germany; D.D., 1757; Royal Chaplain, 1757-1759; sett. Philadelphia, Pa., Gloria Dei Chh., 1759-1768 and St. James's Chh., Kingsessing, 1765-1768; Upper Merion (Montgomery)

Pa., Christ Chh., 1765-1768; Provost of the Swedish chhs. in New Sweden (America), 1759-1768; returned to Sweden, 1768; minister at Sala, Sweden, 1768-1786; Sw. Luth.; d. Sweden, 1786.

CALEB WRIGHT, a grandson of the Rev. William Rhodes; sett. Oyster Bay, L.I., N.Y., 1752-1752; he died on the day he was to have been ordained; Bapt.; d. Oyster Bay, L.I., N.Y., Nov. 1752.

THOMAS YARREL (or Yarrell) an Englishman, arriv. Bethlehem, Pa., 1742; Ord. deacon, 1755; sett. Mount Joy (Lanc.) Pa., Donegal Chh., 1745-1746; Philadelphia, Pa., 1754-1756; N.Y., N.Y., 1757-1765; Staten Island, N.Y., 1757-1760, 1762-1763; Newport, R.I., 1758-1763; itinerant preacher at the following stations: 1743-1749: Burlington, N.J.; Cranbury (Middlesex) N.J.; Dover (Kent) Del.; Duck Creek, Del.; Durham (Bucks) Pa.; Lewes (Sussex) Del.; Lawrence, N.J., at Maidenhead; Manatawny (Berks) Pa.; Middletown (Monmouth) N.J.; Princeton (Mercer) N.J.; Southampton (Bucks) Pa., Neshaminy Chh.; Trenton, N.J.; Upper Providence (Montgomery) Pa., at the Trappe; itinerant preacher, 1745-1755: Ammasland (Del.) Pa., on Darby Creek; Bridgeton (Cumberland) N.J.; Calkoen's Hook (Del.) Pa., near Chester; Little Egg Harbor, N.J.; Maurice River (Gloucester) N.J.; Pennsneck (Salem) N.J., at Quihawken; Swedish Settlements, N.J.; Swedesborough (Gloucester) N.J., Raccoon Chh.; also Great Egg Harbor, N.J., 1743-1755; and Cape May, N.J., 1745-1749; returned to England, 1766, and was sett. in England and Scotland; preached in English; Moravian.

J. YEARBY, sett. Chester (Del.) Pa., Madison Street Chh., 1774-1774; Chester Circuit, Chester co. Pa., 1774-1774; see Isaac Rollins for Chester co. preaching stations; Meth.

DAVID YOUNGS, A.B., b. Southold, L.I., N.Y., 1719, son of Judge Benjamin Youngs; A.B., Y.C., 1741; Ord. Brookhaven, L.I., N.Y., 12 Oct. 1742; sett. Brookhaven, Setauket Chh., 1742-1751; Presb.; d. Brookhaven, L.I., N.Y., between Sept. 1751 and May 1752, a. ca. 33.

JOHN YOUNGS, b. 1598; was a preacher at Hingham, England; "John: Yonges : of St. Margretts : Suff : minister : aged 35 yeares" tried to leave England in May 1637, but was forbidden to leave; he came to New Haven, Conn., 1640; sett. Southold, L.I., N.Y., 1st minister of the first chh. there, 21 Oct. 1640-24 Feb. 1672; Cong.; d. Southold, L.I, N.Y., 24 Feb. 1672, a. 74.

JOHANN MICHAEL ZAHM (alias Toll), b. Sunzheim, Rheinish-Bavaria; Ord. Dec. 1758; sett. Graceham, Md., 6 Oct. 1758-1762; minister in rural churches; school-teacher; Treas. of the Fund for the Support of the Ministry of the Moravian Chh., 1780-1787; Moravian; d. Bethlehem, Pa., Dec. 1787.

RICHARD ZANCHY, sett. East Hanover (Dauphin) Pa., 1737-1760; Presb.; see Richard Sankey.

JOHN WILLIAM ZANDER, came from Quedlinburg, Prussian Saxony; arriv. Bethlehem, Pa., 26 Oct. 1741; Ord. Bethlehem, Pa., 9 Aug.

1742, as a deacon; sett. Berbice, Guiana, South America, 1742-1745; itinerant preacher, 1745-1761; returned to Europe, 1761; sett. Holland, 1761-1782; Moravian; d. Zeist, Holland, 1782.

DAVID ZEISBERGER, b. Zauchtenthal, Moravia, 11 Apr. 1721, son of David and Rosina Zeisberger; arriv. Savannah, Ga., Aug. 1737; came to Bethlehem, Pa., 1741; Ord. deacon, 1749; studied the Indian languages, 1743-1750; Indian missionary to the Iroquois, 1744-1755; missionary in North Carolina and Connecticut, 1755-1761; wrote an Iroquois Grammar and an Iroquois-German Dictionary; missionary to the Delaware Indians, 1762-1771; missionary to the Indians of Ohio, 1771-1808; founded Gnaddenhuetten, Ohio; sett. Lichtenau, as an Indian missionary, 1776-1781; sett. Goshen (Tuscarawas) Ohio, 1798-1808; Moravian; d. Goshen, Ohio, 17 Nov. 1808, a. 87.

DAVID ZEISBERGER, Jr., cousin of the better known missionary; arriv. N.Y., N.Y., 19 Oct. 1761; sett. Bethlehem, Pa., 1761-1762; Nazareth, Pa.; Moravian.

Bishop ANDREW ZIEGLER, b. ca. 1707, son of the Rev. Michael Ziegler; Ord. Skippack (Montgomery) Pa., 1746; Ord. Bishop, 30 May 1762; sett. Skippack, Pa., 1746-1797; Lower Salford (Montgomery) Pa., 1757-1797; Mennonite; d. 1797 (will made 10 Sept. 1793; prob. 8 May 1797).

MICHAEL ZIEGLER, b. Germany, ca. 1680; came to America, ca. 1717; sett. Perkiomen (Montgomery) Pa., 1722-1763; Skippack (Montgomery) Pa., 1722-1752; treasurer at Skippack, 1739-1741, 1753-1760; Menn.; d. Skippack, Pa., 1763 (will made 7 Feb. 1763; prob. 29 Oct. 1765).

JOHANNES ZIMMERMANN, sett. Conestoga (Lancaster) Pa., 1740-1748; "New Mooner."

Count Bishop NICHOLAS LOUIS von ZINZENDORF, b. Dresden, Germany, 28 May 1700, son of Count Nicholas and Charlotte Justina (von Gersdorf) von Zinzendorf (He was Nicholas Lewis, Count and Lord of Zinzendorf and Pottendorf, Lord of the Baronies of Freydeck, Shoeneck, Thuernstein, and the Vale of Wachovia, Lord of the Manors of Upper, Middle, and Lower Berthelsdorf); matric. Halle, 1710; matric. Wittenberg, 1716, to study law; Stralsund Lutheran U., 1734; Counselor at Dresden, 1721-1727; consecrated Bishop, 1737; joined the Moravian Brethren, 1724, at his estate of Herrnhut; arriv. N.Y., N.Y., 30 Nov. 1741; arriv. Philadelphia, 10 Dec. 1741; minister of St. Michael's Lutheran Chh., Philadelphia, Pa., 24 May 1742-1743; also minister of the Moravian Chh., in Philadelphia, 1742-1743; sett. Warwick (Lanc.) Pa., St. James's Moravian Chh. at Lititz, 1742-1742; Nazareth (Northampton) Pa., Moravian Chh., 21 Dec. 1741-Jan. 1743; departed for Europe, Jan. 1743; he was authorized by the U. of Tuebingen, 19 Dec. 1734, to unite the various Protestant Sects in Pa.; this was not accomplished unfortunately, and he resigned his bishopric, July 1741; Luth.; Morav.; d. Herrnhut, Saxony, 9 May 1760.

JOHN JACOB ZUFALL, b. Obervorschutz, Hessen, Germany, 1730; matric. Marburg, 30 Apr. 1753; arriv. America, 1765; sett. Tulpehocken (Berks) Pa., Host Chh., 13 Sept. 1765-1767; Bethel (Lebanon) Pa., 1765-1767; North Lebanon (Lebanon) Pa., St. Jacob's or Kimmerling Chh., 1765-1767; Mill Creek (Lebanon) Pa., Tulpehocken or Trinity Chh., 1765-1767; Swatara (Lebanon) Pa., 1765-1767; Jackson (Lebanon) Pa., Millbach Chh., 1765-1767; Philadelphia, Pa., Germ. Ref. Chh., 1765-1767; excluded, 1767; Germ. Ref.

CHRISTIAN ZUG, b. 1752; sett. Whiteland (Chester) Pa., Goshen Chh. near Malvern, 1770-1826; Amish; d. East Whiteland, Pa., 1832.

JOHN ZUG, sett. Warwick (Lancaster) Pa., White Oak Chh., 1772 ff.; Tunker or Germ. Bapt.

MICHAEL ZYPERNE (or Zyperius), came from Curacoa, Aug. 1659, to N.Y., N.Y., as a candidate; sett. N.Y., N.Y., Fr. Ref. Chh., 1659-1663; joined the Dutch Ref. Chh. as a student of divinity in Jan. 1660; went to Virginia, 1664; conformed to the Chh. of England; sett. Kingston Parish (Mathews) Va., 1680-1687; French Ref.; Dutch Ref.; Ep.

www.ingramcontent.com/pod-product-compliance
Lightning Source LLC
Chambersburg PA
CBHW070331230426

43663CB00011B/2276